INTRODUCTION TO DETERMINANTS OF FIRST NATIONS, INUIT, AND MÉTIS PEOPLES' HEALTH IN CANADA

INTRODUCTION TO DETERMINANTS OF FIRST NATIONS, INUIT, AND MÉTIS PEOPLES' HEALTH IN CANADA

Edited by
Margo Greenwood
Sarah de Leeuw
Roberta Stout
Roseann Larstone
and Julie Sutherland

Toronto | Vancouver

Introduction to Determinants of First Nations, Inuit, and Métis Peoples' Health in Canada
Edited by Margo Greenwood, Sarah de Leeuw, Roberta Stout, Roseann Larstone, and Julie Sutherland

First published in 2022 by
Canadian Scholars, an imprint of CSP Books Inc.
425 Adelaide Street West, Suite 200
Toronto, Ontario
M5V 3C1

www.canadianscholars.ca

Copyright © 2022 Margo Greenwood, Sarah de Leeuw, Roberta Stout, Roseann Larstone, Julie Sutherland, the contributing authors, and Canadian Scholars.

All rights reserved. No part of this publication may be reproduced, stored in a retrieval system, or transmitted, in any form or by any means, without the prior written permission of Canadian Scholars, under licence or terms from the appropriate reproduction rights organization, or as expressly permitted by law.

Every reasonable effort has been made to identify copyright holders. Canadian Scholars would be pleased to have any errors or omissions brought to its attention.

Library and Archives Canada Cataloguing in Publication

Title: Introduction to determinants of First Nations, Inuit, and Métis peoples' health in Canada / Margo Greenwood, Sarah de Leeuw, Roberta Stout, Roseann Larstone, and Julie Sutherland.
Names: Greenwood, Margo, 1953- author. | De Leeuw, Sarah, author. | Stout, Roberta, author. | Larstone, Roseann, author. | Sutherland, Julie, 1976- author.
Description: Includes bibliographical references and index.
Identifiers: Canadiana (print) 20220233446 | Canadiana (ebook) 20220233675 | ISBN 9781773383194 (softcover) | ISBN 9781773383200 (PDF) | ISBN 9781773383217 (EPUB)
Subjects: LCSH: Indigenous peoples—Health and hygiene—Canada—Textbooks. | LCSH: Indigenous peoples—Health and hygiene—Social aspects—Canada—Textbooks. | LCSH: Health status indicators—Canada—Textbooks. | LCSH: Indigenous peoples—Canada—Social conditions—Textbooks. | LCSH: Health—Social aspects—Canada—Textbooks. | LCSH: Social medicine—Canada—Textbooks. | LCSH: Public health—Social aspects—Canada—Textbooks. | LCGFT: Textbooks.
Classification: LCC RA408.I49 G74 2022 | DDC 362.1089/97071—dc23

Page layout: S4Carlisle Publishing Services
Cover design: Rafael Chimicatti
Cover art: Lisa Boivin

21 22 23 24 25   5 4 3 2 1

Printed and bound in Ontario, Canada

Canada

Dedication

This book is dedicated to a future that is free from anti-Indigenous racism and to all those students who are committed to making such a future possible.

Table of Contents

List of Figures xi
Poetic Foreword: holy, holy, holy Rita Bouvier xiii
Self-Care and Emotional Trigger Warning xv

Introduction: Indigenous Health in Canada and Beyond—A Call for Reflection, Action, and Transformation
Sarah de Leeuw, Roberta Stout, Roseann Larstone, Julie Sutherland, and Margo Greenwood **xvii**

PART I DETERMINANTS OF HEALTH FOR INDIGENOUS PEOPLE

Chapter 1   Reflections on Love and Learning with the *Yintah*
We'es Tes, Sandra Martin Harris and Christine Añonuevo 3

Chapter 2   First Nations, Inuit, and Métis Children's Mental Wellness
Margo Greenwood and Roseann Larstone 15

Chapter 3   Food as Relationship: Indigenous Food Systems and Well-Being
Tabitha Robin 25

Chapter 4   Forced Sterilization: A Malicious Determinant of Health
Yvonne Boyer and Rod Leggett 37

Chapter 5   Matriarchal Wisdom: Indigenous Women's and Perinatal Health
Jennifer Leason and Julie Sutherland 51

Chapter 6   A Reflective Poetic Narrative About a Fine Balance: Indigenous Women's and Gender-Diverse People's Sexual and Reproductive Health
Cassandra Felske-Durksen with Lisa Boivin 68

Part I Creative Contribution: Treaty Letter
Armand Garnet Ruffo 77

PART II GEOGRAPHIES AND ECOLOGIES OF INDIGENOUS LAND, HEALTH, AND PHILOSOPHY

Chapter 7 *Waskitaskamik*: On the Face of the Earth
Madeleine Kétéskwēw Dion Stout and Miyawata Dion Stout 81

Chapter 8 Damaged, Not Broken: An Interview about White Settler Violence and Indigenous Health
Mary Teegee and Sarah de Leeuw 91

Chapter 9 Our Highways, Our Tears: Indigenous Women's and Two Spirit People's Health and Resource Extraction
Ryan O'Toole, Onyx Sloan Morgan, and Laura McNab-Coombs 99

Chapter 10 Legislation, Reconciliation, and Water: Moving Upstream to Implement the UNDRIP in BC and Promote Indigenous Peoples' Health
Danièle Behn Smith and Shannon Waters 114

Chapter 11 Inuktut as a Public Health Issue
Aluki Kotierk 126

Part II Creative Contribution: Cactus and Wild Roses
Garry Gottfriedson 138

PART III SUPPORTING HEALTHY INDIGENOUS COMMUNITIES

Chapter 12 Vaccine Mistrust: A Legacy of Colonialism
Margo Greenwood and Noni MacDonald 145

Chapter 13 Taking Care: Indigenous Peoples' Art, Resurgence, and Wellness
Jaimie Isaac 148

Chapter 14 A Path in the Snow: How Indigenous Medical Trainees Can Inspire Indigenous Youth to Become Medical Doctors
Thomsen D'Hont 166

Chapter 15   Youth Protection, Social Determinants of Health, and Reappropriation of Decision-Making Power: Quebec First Nations Demands
Marjolaine Sioui, Patricia Montambault, Michel Deschênes, Marie-Pier Paul, Leila Ben Messaoud, and Richard Gray (First Nations of Quebec and Labrador Health and Social Services Commission)   180

Part III   Creative Contribution: Angled Windows
Lee Maracle   195

PART IV   PRACTICAL APPLICATIONS

Chapter 16   Transforming Medical Education
Lisa Richardson and Julie Sutherland   199

Chapter 17   Learning from the Elders: Traditional Knowledge and Cultural Safety within Health Science Education
Donna L. M. Kurtz and Elder Jessie Nyberg   212

Chapter 18   Indigenous Food Sovereignty: Realizing its Potential for Indigenous Decolonization, Self-Determination, and Community Health
Charlotte Coté   225

Chapter 19   Walking with Our Most Sacred: Indigenous Birth Workers Clearing the Path for Returning Birthing to Indigenous Communities
Jaime Cidro, Ashley Hayward, Rachel Bach, and Stephanie Sinclair   237

Chapter 20   Systems Innovation through First Nations Self-Determination
Harmony Johnson, Danièle Behn Smith, and Lindsay Beck   250

Part IV   Creative Contribution: ᐃᑦᑎᑐᖅ (to sit down for a long time)
Norma Dunning   264

Glossary   265
Contributor Biographies   271
Index   283

List of Figures

Figure 5.1: *Matriarchal Wisdom*   52

Figure 5.2: *Keesis Sagay Egette: First Shining Rays of Sunlight*   53

Figure 5.3: Christ the King Catholic School Class Photo ca. 1940, Camperville, MB   54

Figure 5.4: Patricia Valerie Marie (Chartrand-Fagnant) Leason Sitting in the Basement of Our Lady of Seven Sorrows Roman Catholic Church, Camperville, MB   54

Figure 5.5: *"I make humans, what's your superpower?"*   57

Figure 5.6: *Slow Down*   58

Figure 5.7: *Teepee Teaching*   63

Figure 5.8: *Ancestors*   63

Figure 6.1: *We Come with Medicine*   68

Figure 6.2: *We Are Medicine*   72

Figure 6.3: *Within and Beyond*   75

Figure 9.1: Sun Low in the Sky along the Highway of Tears, outside of Witset, BC, Unceded and Ancestral Wet'suwet'en Territories   102

Figure 9.2: A Sign Warning Women about the Dangers of Hitchhiking on the Highway of Tears, Listing the Names of Indigenous Sisters Stolen along This Route   105

Figure 9.3: The Fourth Annual REDress Campaign, Held in Lheidli T'enneh Territories, Prince George, BC   109

Figure 13.1: *Breathing Hole*, 2019   150

Figure 13.2: *Breathing Hole*, 2019   151

Figure 13.3: *Kayak is Inuktitut for Seal Hunting Boat*, 2019   152

Figure 13.4: *Buffalo Bone China*, 1997   153

Figure 13.5: *Buffalo Bone China*, 1997   154

Figure 13.6: *Store items I remember in 1950s*, 2014   155

Figure 13.7: *The Gifts*, 2011   156

Figure 13.8: *Last Supper*, 2012   158

Figure 13.9: *Last Supper*, 2012   159

Figure 13.10: *Nativity Scene*, 2017   160

Figure 13.11: *Death of the Virgin (After Caravaggio)*, 2016   162

Figure 13.12: *Resistance Comes from the Four Directions*   163

Figure 14.1: Percentages of Indigenous Peoples, Indigenous Medical Students, and Indigenous Physicians in Canada   169

Figure 15.1: Determinants of Indigenous Peoples' Health   184

Figure 17.1: Cultural Safety as a Life Circle   218

Figure 20.1: BC First Nations Perspective on Health and Wellness   252

Figure 20.2: BC First Nations Health Governance Structure   255

Figure 20.3: First Nations Population Health and Wellness Agenda   260

Poetic Foreword: holy, holy, holy

Rita Bouvier

(dedicated to all who work so hard to remind us that "water is life")

nipi   surrounds our island home.
in my grandfather's hands
it turns into steam
bending the planking for the hull
of the coveted ribbed   canvas wrapped canoe.

it is dew at dawn
on blades of grass   on a spider's web
jewel-like
droplets of condensed water vapor
clinging their way back to the earth.

it is waves crashing against the rocky shoreline
the hand of *the great mystery* (for some   God)
reaching in   and then out again
power to offer life
or death.

it is dark   blueberry clouds
full   ripe and ready to burst
sweeping the residue of humus
into the surrounding ponds and lake—
abundance in a never-ending cycle of life.

on an early autumn day
setting out to check on the nets
it is mist rising off the lake
slowly turning into clouds
to bring rain another day.

in pipon   it is icicles forming
vertically poised on branches of trees
when ice and snow
conspire
with the sun.

it is the sweet water
of birch in spring
in a cauldron over a hot fire
turning into syrupy magic
before your very eyes.

it is a rupturing   a rite of passage
as baptismal ceremony   a cry
when we are born
into this place   this land
this one life.

—from EVENT 50/3, December 2021

Self-Care and Emotional Trigger Warning

Some specific content and/or critical thinking questions in this book may trigger in you a range of thoughts, feelings, and emotions. Be sure to look after yourself. If you feel uncomfortable or triggered, you may want to reach out to a trusted instructor or classmate. For Indigenous readers, some parts of this book may resurface past or current traumas and hurtful memories. Indigenous Peoples who need additional supports can contact the Hope for Wellness Help Line at this toll-free number: 1-855-242-3310. There is also an online chat function available through the Hope for Wellness website (hopeforwellness.ca). (If this link is broken, Google "Hope for Wellness chat" to help you find the site.) If asked, Hope for Wellness counsellors can work with you to find other wellness supports that are accessible near you.

The following distressing subjects appear in this textbook, either in brief passing or in more detail: *residential schools; police brutality; drug dependency or overdose and overdose-related deaths; gender-/sex-based violence, including missing and murdered Indigenous women and girls, forced/coerced sterilization, and homo/transphobic-driven violence; domestic violence; self-harming and suicidal ideation; forced medical experimentation; genocidal policies; child neglect; intergenerational trauma.*

Introduction: Indigenous Health in Canada and Beyond—A Call for Reflection, Action, and Transformation

Sarah de Leeuw, Roberta Stout, Roseann Larstone, Julie Sutherland, and Margo Greenwood

Across every socio-cultural and physical geography in colonial Canada, and for all times after Wednesday, May 26, 2021, no word can be written, no thought can be conceived, no action can be taken without the echo of 215 Indigenous children—some as young as three years old—found buried in a mass grave on the grounds of the Kamloops Indian Residential School.

The introduction to this textbook is no exception. Every paragraph this textbook contains, every image shared in the pages that follow, every action suggested in each chapter, every reflection or experience contributed by every author in this book: everything that follows is haunted by the 215 Indigenous children found in **lands** never ceded (**unceded**) by the Tk'emlúps te Secwépemc First Nation, by the many other First Nations, Inuit, and Métis children who have been found since, and by those who are yet to be found.

The expanse of land commonly known as Canada is a violently colonial country. An ever-present state of **coloniality** (Quijano, 2000), which is linked to racism, patriarchy, ableism, heteronormativity, and ecological destruction, casts its shadow across Indigenous and non-Indigenous people who live (and work and play and love and grieve and pass on) within the confines of this colonial nation state. Coloniality is a key and omnipresent determinant of First Nations, Inuit, and Métis health in so-called Canada (Czyzewski, 2011; Greenwood et al., 2015; Richardson, 2019). It is a driver of economic and gender inequities (for instance, poverty and heteronormativity, both of which are determinants of health) and a driving force of land and water disruption, extractive capitalism, and a refusal of Indigenous **self-determination**: each of these is also a determinant of First Nations, Inuit, and Métis health. Fighting against coloniality is a fight against health inequities and burdens of poor health.

When you pick up this textbook and engage with its stories, we ask that you commit to a fight against coloniality. We ask that you commit, with your full heart, to tackling historical and ongoing colonial violences that persist in every nook and cranny of the Canadian healthcare system. We ask that you commit to understanding coloniality as it determines First Nations, Inuit, and Métis peoples' health and **well-being**. From health policy to clinical practice, from medicine to nursing, from social work to support staff and volunteers, from health governance to healthcare research and writing, from dentistry to physiotherapy, from optometry to homeopathy: coloniality is thriving. This textbook is your guide to combatting it by understanding it.

In February 2021, the Canadian Medical Association (CMA) announced its first-ever incoming Indigenous president. Dr. Alika Lafontaine, of Cree, Anishinaabe, Métis, and Pacific Islander ancestry, is an anesthesiologist working in Grande Prairie, Alberta. From **Treaty** 4 Territory in southern Saskatchewan, Lafontaine responded to announcements about his CMA presidency, stating, "it's time to eliminate racism, sexism, ableism, classism and all other '-isms' that permeate [Canada's] health system culture" (CMA, 2021). Lafontaine's statement followed on the heels of some of Canada's most damning evidence about pervasive and **systemic** anti-Indigenous racism in healthcare: findings reported in *In Plain Sight: Addressing Indigenous-Specific Racism and Discrimination in B.C. Health Care* (Turpel-Lafond, 2020), released by the Province of British Columbia in November 2020. Led by lawyer Mary Ellen Turpel-Lafond from Muskeg Lake Cree Nation, *In Plain Sight* documents negative experiences of thousands of **Indigenous peoples** who have interacted with, and who work within, British Columbia's healthcare system.

In Plain Sight put in writing what First Nations, Inuit, and Métis peoples from coast to coast to coast, in urban and rural geographies, in communities big and small, have known and been saying for decades: they live within a pressing and persistent state of anti-Indigenous racism, structured by coloniality. That state of coloniality rests and thrives on racism, discrimination, marginalization, and inequality (Loppie et al., 2014). It manifests in the horrific deaths of loved ones, such as Brian Sinclair and Joyce Echaquan (Wytenbroek & Peacock, 2020). It allows for Indigenous children to be apprehended at far higher rates than non-Indigenous children (Brown, 2017; de Leeuw, 2014), and it does nothing to stop burdens of poor health being borne disproportionately by First Nations, Inuit, and Métis peoples and communities. Coloniality exercised by Canada consistently refuses and erases the vibrancy and strengths of First Nations, Inuit, and Métis peoples (Alfred & Corntassel, 2005; Lawrence & Dua, 2005). It casts a pall over the survivorship and the potential and wonder of First Nations, Inuit, and Métis communities who have always been here—who are being inherently Indigenous in ways that have always existed (Simpson, 2017).

The persistent state of coloniality is astonishingly visible and acute to those who live it, to those whose very lives are in so many ways determined by it. These are the people, from coast to coast to coast and around the world, fighting against coloniality and refusing its confines. Indigenous peoples are thriving as artists and physicians, as mothers and lawmakers, as Elders and scholars, as brothers and musicians, as activists and land-defenders, as poets and engineers—to name but a few domains claimed by those who are unsettling colonial **hegemonies**. Indigenous peoples are forging allyships with Black settlers and settlers of colour, refusing White-settler supremacy, and actively creating new and better worlds. These are the people who are also the authors of chapters that make up this book.

The never-ending violence of the *Indian Act,* an almost unchanged piece of law from 1876 with the sole purpose of producing a hierarchy of personhood in Canada, is visible to every First Nations person who carries with them a "**Status** Card." The link between health and land/territory theft is deeply felt and experienced by every Métis person in Canada whose lineage includes living on "road allowances" (a fancy term for ditches)—lands that were designated for public use, surveyed, and reserved by the Government of Canada for the purpose of future road development. The diverse groups comprising Inuit communities—Labradormiut (Labrador), Nunavimmiut (Ungava), Nunatsiarmiut (Baffin Island), Iglulingmiut (Iglulik), Kivallirmiut (Caribou), Netsilingmiut (Netsilik), Inuinnait (Copper), and Inuvialuit (Western Arctic)—do not need to read a textbook or report to know their ways of life and communities have been and are continuing to be jeopardized by a state of coloniality that valorizes settler-led extractive capitalist industry, both across their territories and to the south of them.

No Indigenous person in this country needs a textbook to understand, feel, and know the violences of coloniality. The onus is non-Indigenous people—especially those in any field even remotely adjacent to healthcare, but also to all non-Indigenous people—to tirelessly work to dismantle coloniality. That is the call to action of this book.

For all the attention garnered by reports and calls to action issued by the 2015 **Truth and Reconciliation Commission of Canada** (TRC) (Truth and Reconciliation, 2015), for all the media attention paid to Canada finally signing the **United Nations Declaration on the Rights of Indigenous People (UNDRIP)** in 2016, many of coloniality's violences remain remarkably untouched. This book calls for an end to that. This is a book that acknowledges love and territory for the health and well-being of Indigenous peoples (We'es Tes Harris and Añonuevo), that considers food systems as part of health systems (Robin; Coté), and that examines how Indigenous artists engage in health and wellness narratives (Isaac). It is a book that grapples with **Indigenous women**'s and gender-diverse people's reproductive and sexual health, along with other aspects of women's health and well-being (Boyer and Legett; Felske-Durksen and Boivin; Teegee and de Leeuw; Leason and Sutherland), and that promotes the health and welfare of children (Greenwood and Larstone; First Nations of Quebec and Labrador Health and Social Services Commission).

This is also a book that offers deep insights into land, water, ecologies, and geographies as integral to the health of Indigenous families and communities, and that demands that **resource extraction** and other practices informed by racist narratives and histories (e.g., vaccinations) be interrogated as fundamentally colonial (Dion Stout and Dion Stout; O'Toole, Sloan Morgan, and McNab-Coombs; Kotierk; Greenwood and MacDonald; Behn Smith and Waters). Finally, this is a book brimming with chapters that offer practical insights into and applied knowledge about how to transform health systems and how to unsettle the settler-coloniality that runs so deep in healthcare (D'Hont; Richardson and Sutherland; Kurtz and Nyberg; Cidro, Hayward, Bach, and Sinclair; Johnson, Behn Smith, and Beck). This is also a book bracketed by and celebrating creative voice (Bouvier; Ruffo; Gottfriedson; Maracle; Dunning).

With this in mind, and while you read and use this book in your efforts to understand coloniality as a determinant of health, we encourage you to think about a few more things. First, throughout this textbook, we use what has come to be known as **distinctions-based** terminology. Distinctions-based terminology, used when speaking or writing against constraints of **colonialism**, focuses on the specificity of collective or individual First Nations, Inuit, and Métis communities. Rather than using terms such as "Indigenous" or "**Aboriginal**" to characterize what are distinct peoples and communities, a distinctions-based approach clarifies and specifies if you are referring to First Nations, Inuit, or Métis communities (for an example and discussion, see Employment and Social Development Canada [ESDC], 2018).

Even better than using the terms First Nations, Inuit, and Métis is making a determined effort to be even more specific in your language and writings. Wherever possible, name the precise community you are referring to. The Nisga'a, for instance, are deeply different from the Haida. These two First Nations in so-called British Columbia are also very different from the Naskapi or the Mushkegowuk or the Anishinaabe. These individual First Nations are, in turn, distinct from—for instance—the Métis of Red River or the Métis Settlement of Fishing Lake. Inuit, as distinct from both First Nations and Métis people, might be from Nunavut or Nunavik. These are important distinctions to make in anti-colonial work.

In 1996, now a quarter of a century ago, and guided by the powerful prayers and words of Kanatiio Kanesatakeronnon (Allen Gabriel) of the Kanesatake Mohawk, Bear **Clan**, the final report of the **Royal Commission on Aboriginal Peoples (RCAP)** asserted that "contemporary Canadians reject the paternalism of yesterday and recognize that [Indigenous] people know best how to define and promote their own interests" (Canada, 1996a, p. 8). The RCAP Commissioners also wrote that

> Canada is a test case for a grand notion—the notion that dissimilar peoples can share lands, resources, power and dreams while respecting and sustaining their differences. The story of Canada is the story of many such peoples, trying and failing and trying again, to live together in peace and harmony. (Canada, 1996b, para. 3)

The early decades of the twenty-first century may well be read as a time of failing. We must not, as all the authors of this textbook make clear, give up trying to combat anti-Indigenous racism and achieve true, deep, lasting, respectful reconciliation. This textbook is an offering to you, an encouragement to you to keep trying. It strives to introduce you to multiple and intersecting topics that require urgent redress. There are many more areas it could have revealed. We wish there were more voices and words written by urban First Nations, Inuit, and Métis people, who are growing in numbers and strength at unprecedented rates (Peters & Andersen, 2013). We also wish we could have offered you more writings and voices considering the links between land claims, Treaty settlements, and health. We wish we could have included voices of more First Nations, Inuit, and Métis youth: they are the health of tomorrow's generations of Indigenous peoples and communities. There is, in other words, still much work to be done when thinking about the complex and changing worlds of determinants of Indigenous peoples' health in so-called Canada. Which is also to say that you have a role to play in dismantling coloniality and bringing about positive changes in the determinants of Indigenous health. Listen openly and humbly to the wisdoms contained in this book, wisdoms generously contributed by First Nations, Inuit, and Métis leaders, knowledge holders, artists, activists, clinicians, young people, and health researchers. Reflect on the roles you can play in addressing health inequities. Commit to taking action against colonial violences. Work toward transforming your worlds and the worlds you play a part in making.

CRITICAL THINKING QUESTIONS AND ACTIVITIES

1. Write down three actions you would like to take in a committed struggle against coloniality. Keep these actions with you at all times—on a piece of paper in your wallet, as a note in your phone, as a text you've sent to yourself. Commit to checking back on these actions every six months. Have you made progress? What's stood in your way? Would you like to revise your actions?
2. Find one non-academic book by an Indigenous author. Acquire the book (you could order it, or you might find it used, or maybe even free!). Commit to reading it in the next year. Commit to giving it away once you've read it and to talking about it with the person you've gifted it to. Think about how engaging the creative work of Indigenous authors and artists is an anti-colonial act. For book suggestions, check out https://www.cbc.ca/books/35-books-to-read-for-national-indigenous-history-month-1.5585489. (If this link is broken, simply Google "35 books to read for national Indigenous history month CBC" to navigate to the site.) Highwater Press also publishes work by established and emerging Indigenous authors. You can read about some of their publications (including graphic novels) here: https://www.portageandmainpress.com/HighWater-Press (or Google "Highwater Press").
3. What do you think about the idea that "Canada is a test case for a grand notion—the notion that dissimilar peoples can share lands, resources, power and dreams while respecting and sustaining their differences"? Do you think people in colonial Canada will ever be able to share lands, resources, power, and dreams while respecting and sustaining their differences? What role do you envision yourself playing in this "grand notion" of sharing and sustaining differences?

REFERENCES

Alfred, T., & Corntassel, J. (2005). Being Indigenous: Resurgences against contemporary colonialism. *Government and opposition, 40*(4), 597–614.

Brown, H. (2017). The *Child and Family Services Act* in relation to Indigenous Children: Does it measure up to the truth and Reconciliation Commission Report? *Canadian Family Law Quarterly, 36*(2), 171–191.

Canada. (1996a). Royal Commission on Aboriginal Peoples. *Report of the Royal Commission on Aboriginal Peoples.* Vol. 1: *Looking forward, looking back.* Canada Communication Group. https://data2.archives.ca/e/e448/e011188230-01.pdf

Canada. (1996b). *Highlights from the Report of the Royal Commission on Aboriginal Peoples.* https://static1.squarespace.com/static/562e7f2ae4b018ac41a6e050/t/59d0024a9f74567b7ee58b43/1506804313123/RCAP_reading.pdf

Canadian Medical Association (CMA). (2021, Feb. 26). *Dr. Alika Lafontaine elected as 2021 CMA president-elect nominee.* https://www.cma.ca/news/dr-alika-lafontaine-elected-2021-cma-president-elect-nominee

Czyzewski, K. (2011). Colonialism as a broader social determinant of health. *International Indigenous Policy Journal, 2*(1). https://doi.org/10.18584/iipj.2011.2.1.5

de Leeuw, S. (2014). State of care: The ontologies of child welfare in British Columbia. *Cultural Geographies, 21*(1), 59–78.

Employment and Social Development Canada. (2018). *Indigenous early learning and child care framework.* Government of Canada. Retrieved November 23, 2021, from https://www.canada.ca/en/employment-social-development/programs/indigenous-early-learning/2018-framework.html#h2.5

Greenwood, M., de Leeuw, S., Lindsay, N. M., & Reading, C. (Eds.). (2015). *Determinants of Indigenous Peoples' Health.* Canadian Scholars' Press.

Lawrence, B., & Dua, E. (2005). Decolonizing antiracism. *Social Justice, 34*(102), 120–143.

Peters, E. J., & Andersen, C. (Eds.). (2013). *Indigenous in the city: Contemporary identities and cultural innovation.* UBC Press.

Quijano, A. (2000). Coloniality of power and Eurocentrism in Latin America. *International Sociology, 15*(2), 215–232.

Loppie, S., Reading, C., & de Leeuw, S. (2014). *Indigenous experiences with racism and its impacts.* National Collaborating Centre for Aboriginal Health. https://www.nccih.ca/docs/determinants/FS-Racism2-Racism-Impacts-EN.pdf

Richardson, E. T. (2019). On the coloniality of global public health. *Medicine Anthropology Theory, 6*(4), 101–118. https://doi.org/10.17157/mat.6.4.761

Simpson, L. B. (2017). *As we have always done: Indigenous freedom through radical resistance.* University of Minnesota Press.

Truth and Reconciliation Commission of Canada. (2015). *Honouring the truth, reconciling for the future: Summary of the Final Report of the Truth and Reconciliation Commission of Canada.* https://irsi.ubc.ca/sites/default/files/inline-files/Executive_Summary_English_Web.pdf

Turpel-Lafond, M. E. (2020). *In plain sight: Addressing Indigenous-specific racism and discrimination in B.C. health care.* https://engage.gov.bc.ca/app/uploads/sites/613/2020/11/In-Plain-Sight-Summary-Report.pdf

Wytenbroek, L., & Peacock, E. (2020). *The ongoing impact of colonialism and racism on Canada's health care system* [Blog]. Consortium for Nursing History Inquiry at the University of British Columbia School of Nursing. Retrieved June 18, 2021, from https://blogs.ubc.ca/nursinghistory/2020/11/

PART I

DETERMINANTS OF HEALTH FOR INDIGENOUS PEOPLE

Part I examines the varying and intersecting factors that determine **Indigenous Peoples**' health, such as education, income, biology, personal health practices, and culture. Anti-Indigenous racism and systemic discrimination continue to be fundamental drivers of health inequities faced by First Nations, Inuit, and Métis Peoples. However, these inequities are not insurmountable. The chapters in this section reveal pathways to health and wellness that are informed, stimulated, and realized by Indigenous ways of knowing and being.

Chapter 1, "Reflections on Love and Learning with the *Yintah*" (We'es Tes Harris, Añonuevo), considers **self-determination** in the context of the traditional territory of the Wet'suwet'en. The chapter highlights the Wet'suwet'en Nation's **resilience** in the face of a controversial pipeline project. The Wet'suwet'en assert their right to enact holistic laws in a governance system which has survived **colonialism**. They safeguard their cultural, spiritual, and environmental health through relationship with the **Land**, and through languages, stories, ceremonies, and songs.

Chapter 2, "First Nations, Inuit, and Métis Children's Mental Wellness" (Greenwood, Larstone), advances a holistic, upstream approach to children's mental wellness, grounded in Indigenous ways of knowing and being. Such an approach focuses on improving supports that foster children's personal **well-being**. Colonial systems must be dismantled or restructured to make way for traditional, strengths-based, Indigenous-led approaches to Indigenous children's mental health that centre and uphold the critical role of First Nations, Inuit, and Métis families and communities.

Chapter 3, "Food as Relationship" (Robin), demonstrates colonialism's role in **food insecurity**. The chapter introduces the concept of Indigenous food sovereignty (IFS), i.e., the right of Indigenous Peoples to define and govern their own food systems. Because food is inextricably connected with a relationship to land for Indigenous Peoples, their inherent right to govern and protect their land is vital to their food security.

Chapter 4, "Forced Sterilization" (Boyer, Leggett), provides a brief history of **eugenics** and reveals that forced and coerced sterilization of Indigenous women continues today. The authors outline legal and constitutional points that are evidence of Canada's obligation to restore the health of Indigenous Peoples living in Canada. The chapter offers a way forward so that standards in Canada for free, prior, and informed consent to sterilization will be aligned with the **United Nations Declaration on the Rights of Indigenous Peoples** (UNDRIP).

Chapter 5, "Matriarchal Wisdom" (Leason, Sutherland), explains how colonialism has led to Indigenous women disproportionately experiencing adverse wellness and **perinatal** health outcomes. By privileging the voices of Indigenous women, the chapter shows how social determinants of Indigenous Peoples' health (e.g., education, poverty, food security, housing, racism) directly relate to Indigenous women's health and the health of their babies. The chapter celebrates Indigenous women's growing determination to renounce their disproportionate burden of health disparities.

Chapter 6, "A Reflective Poetic Narrative about a Fine Balance" (Felske-Durksen, Boivin), contemplates Indigenous women's and gender-diverse people's sexual and reproductive health. It affirms that Indigenous Peoples are empowered with their own medicine to heal in body, mind, heart, and spirit. It reveals that colonizers subvert Indigenous women's biological agency and control. Finally, it calls on Indigenous women and gender-diverse people to reclaim their sexual and reproductive rights.

Part I closes with a prose poem, "Treaty Letter," by Armand Garnet Ruffo—a contemplation on the ongoing adverse effects of the **treaty** system on Indigenous Peoples living in Canada: hunger, neglect, poverty. It calls out the government bureaucrats, "profiteers," and other opportunists before ending with a call to action and reflection.

CHAPTER 1

Reflections on Love and Learning with the *Yintah*

We'es Tes, Sandra Martin Harris and Christine Añonuevo

Udaggi, yintah tla c'ide'ni, nedilhkat habilh endzin, niwh Dini'ze yu, Tsakë'ze yu, skiy'ze yu tabi habike zentsiy. Negekh niwh zil lhtis kin akh niwh ba inlegh.

Creator God, territory, and ancestors. We ask you to be with the men and women Chiefs and children (of our Clans). We love them, we ask for healing, strength, and comfort.

LEARNING OBJECTIVES

1. To define the term *yintah* and demonstrate its importance to Wet'suwet'en **well-being**.
2. To understand the holistic relationships between **Land**, governance, language, and stories as indicators of health, within a Wet'suwet'en context of **self-determination**.
3. To encourage critical thinking about how industrial extraction projects impact the health and well-being of the Land.

The authors dedicate this chapter to the Unistot'en, *Howilkat*-Freda Huson, Brenda Mitchell, Dr. Karla Tait, the Gitdimt'en, *Sleydo'*-Molly Wickham, *Woos*-Frank Alec, *Madeek*-Jeff Brown and *Gisdaywa*-Fred Tom.

INTRODUCTION

Through a series of reflections, this chapter illustrates the beauty and ongoing struggle of self-determination in a specific context: the Wet'suwet'en Nation, in so-called northwestern British Columbia—a region that has never been ceded and is not subject to treaty. The authors are Sandra—a grandmother, *Tsakë'ze* (hereditary female Chief), mother, daughter, and sister of the Likhsilyu **Clan**—who works at the intersection of Indigenous-focused trauma-informed practice and Indigenous community planning across **Turtle Island**; and Christine—a settler of colour and the spouse of a Wet'suwet'en, Gitxsan, and Tsimshian man—who shares transformative learning moments of witnessing and participating in Wet'suwet'en and Gitxsan ceremony.

On September 13, 2007, the United Nations General Assembly adopted the **United Nations Declaration on the Rights of Indigenous Peoples** (UNDRIP), which recognizes the inherent right to self-determination of **Indigenous Peoples** around the world: "By virtue of that right [Indigenous Peoples] freely determine their political status and freely pursue their economic, social and cultural development" (UN General Assembly, 2007, p. 4). Self-determination is one of the most significant determinants of health for Indigenous populations (Reading & Wien, 2009) and profoundly influences other health-related determinants, such as safety, education, and housing. Yet, federal, provincial/territorial, and municipal policies perpetuate and enforce colonial attitudes, limiting Indigenous Peoples' control over Land, resources, and health services and restricting social, political, economic, and cultural power and decision making.

BACKGROUND

Wet'suwet'en House territories encompass approximately 22,000 square kilometres of land. The Wet'suwet'en Nation is a matrilineal society (family affiliation is passed from mother to child) and has 13 Houses (hereditary groups that collectively engage in political and socio-cultural decision making) within five Clans: Gitimt'en (Bear/Wolf); C'ilhts'ëkhyu (Big Frog); Likhsilyu (Small Frog); Tsayu (Beaver); and Likhts'amisyu (Fireweed). Hereditary House Chiefs[1] (hereafter Chiefs), supported by wing Chiefs and their respective Clan members, govern all aspects of the territory to ensure the health and well-being of the House members and the territory. Wet'suwet'en law establishes that they have the right to control who is allowed to enter and stay on their Lands. It is their duty to protect the land for future generations. According to Wet'suwet'en law, authority for Wet'suwet'en self-determination traditional practices and governance resides with *Dini'ze'*, *Tsakë'ze'*, *Skiy' ze*—the Chiefs, female Chiefs, and children of Chiefs—and their Clans and House groups. Houses and Clans respect all forms of life and ecology, present and future, on their *yintah*, or territory.

YINTAH, KUNGAX, AND THE WISDOM OF ELDERS

Sandra: According to the *kungax* (oral histories), our people are from the *yintah*—the territory. Generations of Wet'suwet'en have been born, lived, and died in our homelands. They have bathed and cleansed in the lakes, rivers, springs, and waterfalls.

The Wet'suwet'en believe the *yintah* has a living memory of, and connection to, the Wet'suwet'en. *Niwhtsi'de'nī'*, our ancestors, are with us: we can feel them on the winds, watching and ever-present.

The *yintah* is a spirit-filled being and a lifegiving force: The phrase *yintah habkits* means "all things come from the Land." This means that all People and all Beings on the Land are interconnected and interdependent. *Sistiy* (my body), *siy seni* (my mind), and *siyzil* (my spirit) are nourished from the life-giving forces of the *yintah*—from the air, *t'oh*—water—plant medicines, *niwhkinic*—our language—and seasonal foods. *Es'des* (Trickster) shares meaningful stories about the absurd and mystical linkages between *yintah*, *t'oh*, food, and a good long life.

Respect and understanding create harmonious relationships between the Wet'suwet'en and the natural world. Wet'suwet'en belong to the Land and are sustained by the Land, and we have a duty to protect and sustain it. Our health and well-being as *denii* (people), Clans, and communities are deeply connected to the *yintah*.

Wet'suwet'en *kungax* play a pivotal role in self-determination. The *kungax* speak to the spiritual, non-linear journeys of the Wet'suwet'en. They also speak to a moral code. The late *Gisdaywa*, also known as Alfred Joseph, said:

> [The *kungax*] are about the people and how we became who we are, about our history, our relationships with one another and our responsibilities and obligations as citizens of our nation. The *kungax* are all about the songs about laws; the laws that govern our relationships and the way we use the lands and resources. The laws are realized in the feast and how we exercise our government in the feast hall. (As cited in Hoffman & Joseph, 2019, p. vi)

Sandra: I remember the booming voice of my maternal grandfather. He was a big man, and when Grandpa Louie was close by, you could feel his big, gentle presence. I remember there being a deep sadness that I could feel too. Grandpa wasn't that old, but something about him felt really old—the sadness, the powerful hands, and the deep-set, sad eyes, surrounded by many wrinkles. I could sense that there was some kind of struggle going on in him; however, at eight years old, I had no understanding of how many hardships he had lived through and witnessed. Many years later, I have a better understanding of **intergenerational trauma**, of how our body carries the stress we experienced in our early years, and of the impacts of that stress and trauma on our body, mind, and spirit (Turcotte & Schiffer, 2014). The stress experienced in our young lives links to serious health outcomes later in life, such as heart disease, autoimmune breakdown, and diabetes (Amos, 2011). I see these health inequities in my own family and in many First Nations communities. When there is much trauma in our lives, we often feel disconnected, alone, helpless, and hopeless. This disconnection can lead to disharmony, and our whole being can suffer as a result.

Grandpa was a quiet man. It felt good and secure to be beside a mountain of strength. I remember one time when he gently said to me, "You have two ears and one mouth." So much shared in a few brief words. Being a little chatterbox, I was like, "Hmmm mmm," not fully understanding the importance of that teaching until much later: the importance of listening; helping someone through something; listening to the wind; just being (Redvers, 2019). The more I listen and learn how to be present and self-aware, the greater connection I feel to the oneness of Life and Land, to the interconnection of the *yintah*. I feel calmer, and I can get myself through upsetting times. I learn how to get out of my head by asking sister *Tsalik* (squirrel) to take a rest. She is so busy in my mind, keeping track of many things and worrying. When she rests, I can sink into my whole body and connect with the life-giving forces, the sacredness of life, the *yintah*. When I do this, I find my strengths, and I can transform the worry, hurt, or anxiety. I shift those energies, literally set them down, lean into the Land, take a full breath, and notice the restoring power of fresh air, the sunshine on my face. These modes of body-centred and **Land-based healing** take practice. But when I practise them, I am more **resilient**, my overall health improves, and I can heal.

Grandpa was checking out the log house mom and dad were building. He told us to pay attention to the trees—to the stumps all around us. He said that the trees are always watching us. At first, this terrified me. Yet, I didn't question that they could watch or see. After sitting with this, it was comforting to know that the trees were there. It helped me behave better and know that I was not alone. I believe that was the teaching. The trees are like grandparents—they keep an eye out for us, nurture us, and take care of us. In Land-based teaching, the trees are like family. The oldest are Hub trees, which nurture and connect with each new generation of growth. All the trees are connected and nurturing. They grow together as a family. In this way, they are intergenerational—like human families. Greater connections with family and community, which are the primary life-giving forces, can improve health and well-being.

According to Wet'suwet'en kinship laws, because my father is Euro-Canadian, the responsibilities of the father Clan are with my maternal grandfather. As I learn more about the importance of my father Clan in guiding, disciplining, and supporting me, I see how grandpa was sharing his ways with me. The father Clan acts like the sinew or connective tissue that connects, protects, and supports me throughout my life. "Listen to that bird," he'd say. "When it whistles you know the ancestors are close by, you are not alone." Throughout my life, the bird's song has shown up when needed most. We are the Land, and the Land is us. It listens and supports my body, mind, and spirit. We must have a good relationship. This beautiful connection restores and replenishes my well-being, my health. If I listen well, I might notice the connection between the Land and me that comes on the wind in the trees, or in the bird's song. Me, my family, my mother, and my father Clan are a collective, and together, we live in this place, this community, in this beautiful **watershed**, along the *Widzin Kwah* and Skeena rivers.

Since my grandfather's and uncle's tragic passing, their voices, their support, are deeply missed. Since their passing, the father Clan is nearly silent. In my community development work, I can see how the role of the father Clan has been greatly affected by paternalism—by the interference of the church and state. The patriarchal policies of the federal government have diminished the strength of our father Clans. They have changed our culture from one of self-reliance and interdependence to one of dependency.

ROLE OF THE FEAST HALL

The feast hall is where social, political, and economic decisions are made, and where important ceremonies (e.g., weddings, funerals) take place. The Wet'suwet'en word for feast is *denii ne'aas*, which translates into "people coming together," although the Chinook word ***potlatch*** is also used. In 1884, the federal government banned the potlach. This was part of a larger racist project banishing cultural practices that impeded the government's policy of assimilation—a policy that has traumatically impacted many generations. The Anti-Potlatch Law was lifted in 1951 but has created lingering, intergenerational health inequities.

Christine: The first time I went for a walk in the Hazeltons, near Hagwilget, my spouse shared stories about where his ancestors once held feasts. Because feasts were banned by the Canadian government, Chiefs in the area had to go underground with their ceremonies. The strength of the feast system continues today because Chiefs refused to relinquish their foundational forms of governing despite threats and incarceration. I have great appreciation for those who struggled and continue to struggle to keep their ancestral knowledge alive in the minds and hearts of their people.

When my spouse received a traditional name, I was a witness in the feast hall. His Clan and House group hosted. I participated in the *indeminik*—the spouse's dance—which affirmed my relationship to my spouse and his hosting Clan. During this ceremony, all the spouses of the hosting Clan, dressed in blankets and with money pinned to their clothes, performed a dance. The father Clan also sang some traditional songs.

BEING ON THE LAND

C'idede (teaching stories) centre on respectful relationships with animals and the spirit world. The Wet'suwet'en Nation's pursuit of balanced relationships with all creation precedes language and is considered part of *Anuk Niwh'it'ën*—our laws. *Anuk Niwh'it'ën* help everyone work together to protect the health of the people and the Land. They are foundational to sovereignty and self-determination. They include the boundaries of collective responsibilities kept by Chiefs, Clans, and House systems. They are reflected in the Wet'suwet'en harvesting practices: something is always left behind for growth to ensure all Clan/House members share in the bounty of seasonal wealth. *Anuk Niwh'it'ën* are even reflected in how the Wet'suwet'en people speak about and treat creatures (Morin, 2016).

Christine: Each summer, we go to a fishing spot that has been in the family for generations. We help my spouse's uncle, who's in his 70s, with his fishing net. Pulling the net to check for salmon is physically demanding. We count the fish, observe them, and then identify which type of salmon we caught. We leave something behind for the eagles. Uncle notices the changes in the weather, in how many fish return or not. He is usually the first to pack the fish on his back and start up the steep hill to return to our vehicles. We clean and wash the fish; sometimes we smoke it in the smokehouse, burning cottonwood at all hours for several days. We thank the river for its life-giving nature.

I was invited to a Wet'suwet'en women's wellness camp a few summers ago. It was my youngest son's first camping trip. We drove past Houston to a campsite on the traditional territory of the Unistot'en. Elders shared stories at the camp, chatting about what had changed since the last time they had gathered there, and noticing what berry patches had been casualties of logging. I have learned the importance of observation out on the Land from Elders. By observing carefully, you become more in tune with the surrounding landscape.

I see a connection between the Elders observing everything on the Land and them observing activity in the feast hall. Hereditary Chiefs sit at the back of the feast hall, where they have the best view and can watch everything. As a non-Indigenous person, learning through observation is a value I learned from being in the feast hall and being on the Land with Wet'suwet'en Elders. Just as observation takes time, so too must one await understanding (Davidson & Davidson, 2018). I see another connection: Wet'suwet'en people have a timeless relationship with the Land; the Land is what sustains their communities and their identities. This sustenance and wisdom has been gathered over thousands of years of observation and experience.

For settlers in Canada, Land is central to economic security and therefore has become a resource that industry and government commodify and profit from. Settlers used violence to take Land from Indigenous communities. Residential Schools, the sterilization of Indigenous Peoples, and the **Sixties Scoop** are examples of Canadian policies and practices by which settlers sought to assimilate and dehumanize Indigenous Peoples and to erase their relationship with the Land. Being on the Land is integral for self-determination and sovereignty for the Wet'suwet'en. Large-scale industrial pipelines and harmful drilling beneath sacred rivers such as the *Wedzin Kwah* are in direct conflict with Wet'suwet'en practices and forms of governance.

ALLIANCES BETWEEN NEIGHBOURING NATIONS

In 1984, the Wet'suwet'en and Gitxsan Nations came together to affirm their oral histories, culture, and laws in a landmark court case for Indigenous title (ownership of traditional Land) and territorial management. The plaintiffs—39 Gitxsan and 12 Wet'suwet'en Chiefs—filed a land title action with the Supreme Court of British Columbia, collectively claiming jurisdiction over 58,000 square kilometres of territory. *Delgamuukw*, the Gitxsan Hereditary Chief, and *Gisdaywa*, the Wet'suwet'en Hereditary Chief, were the main plaintiffs.[2] At the time of the case, Alfred Joseph held the name *Gisdaywa*, and three different people held the name *Delgamuukw*: Albert Tait, who filed the statement of claim, Ken Muldoe, who began the court proceedings, and Earl Muldoe, who heard the final statements.

In 1991, Chief Justice Allan McEachern ruled against the plaintiffs, dismissing their land claim and citing their oral testimony about their historical right to the land as hearsay evidence. The two Nations appealed to the British Columbia Court of Appeal, which ultimately backed McEachern's decision. The two Nations took their case to the Supreme Court of Canada in 1997, which affirmed Wet'suwet'en land rights and the roles of Chiefs as title holders. This set a precedent for confirming the validity of Indigenous oral history as evidence in establishing proof of Indigenous title (McCreary, 2018). The case did not affirm where land title applied (and the Nations did not have the resources to continue the case), but other court decisions, including *Tsilhqot'in Nation v. British Columbia*, have further clarified and strengthened the question of title for the Wet'suwet'en.

British Columbia no longer uses the court system for treaty negotiations. Instead, they negotiate with Chiefs. Many Indigenous Nations have settled for very little territory in exchange for limited self-governance and financial agreements in these modern treaties; however, since the landmark case, Wet'suwet'en Hereditary Chiefs have demanded respect and the recognition of their rights and title to their House territories from successive federal and provincial governments.

Sandra: I was part of a team negotiating a treaty agreement following the *Delgamuukw* decision. We did not succeed. Now our people have assembled to support the Unistot'en (see below) and Gitdimt'en Clans, asserting our title and rights to the territory in the face of large-scale industrial, extractive projects.

UNISTOT'EN

The Unistot'en, along with other Wet'suwet'en Houses and Clans, view hunting, fishing, berry and medicine picking, and having access to clean water as vital to the peoples' health and healing. Several pipeline companies have tried to gain access to their territory. In response to these efforts, Freda Huson, a Wet'suwet'en Nation Chief, set up an Access Protocol agreement aligning with Wet'suwet'en law and including a 44-km checkpoint barricade at the Morice River Bridge. This bridge spans the *Wedzin Kwah* (Morice and Bulkley) rivers, which are part of the waterway system providing the territory with its primary source of clean water and salmon, which it depends on for survival.

Coastal GasLink contested this restricted access and on December 31, 2019, the Supreme Court of British Columbia issued an injunction (an authoritative order) stating that the defendants (the Unistot'en) were prohibited from "physically preventing, impeding, restricting or in any other way physically interfering with . . . any person or vehicle travelling to or accessing the vicinity in and around the Morice River Bridge" (Coastal GasLink Pipeline Ltd. v. Huson, 2019). Once an injunction is in place, the RCMP have the right to arrest anyone who disobeys the order. In January 2019, militarized tactical units and the RCMP dismantled the barricade and made 14 arrests, including the arrest of *Sleydo'* (also called Molly Wickham), who rebuked the RCMP in a statement following her arrest as being "mercenaries for industry" (Smith, 2019, para. 4). Chiefs, fearing further police violence, agreed to allow the removal of the barricade at Morice River Bridge. In October 2019, the province of British Columbia passed legislation to implement the Declaration on the Rights of Indigenous Peoples Act (DRIPA), which explicitly stipulates that free, prior, and informed consent must be obtained in decisions that will have major impacts on the lives of Indigenous Peoples.

Despite this legislation, in February 2020, the RCMP mobilized a militarized tactical team, K9 units, and aerial surveillance (planes, helicopters, and drones) and, along with Coastal GasLink workers, bulldozed their way through Unistot'en territory, dismantled three small tent camps and the multi-building Unistot'en Healing Centre where unarmed, peaceful Land defenders were camping out, and made multiple arrests (over 20 people in the first three days). Arrests included those of Freda Huson (Chief Howihkat), her sister, Brenda Michell (Chief Geltiy), and Dr. Karla Tait, Director of Clinical Programming at the Unist'ot'en Healing Centre, who were detained while holding a ceremony honouring missing and murdered **Indigenous women** and girls.

In other words, despite the DRIPA, provincial and federal governments continue to re-enact colonial patterns of denying Indigenous Peoples their inherent, constitutional right to live as Indigenous Peoples. Instead, they are met with state surveillance and arrests, labelled as economic terrorists, and criminalized for pursuing their right to be on, and live in relationship with, their Land. If the Land is destroyed via extractive projects, Wet'suwet'en self-determination, culture, language, interconnectedness, stories, and health are also effectively destroyed.

The RCMP have been criticized for creating an "exclusion zone"—an access control checkpoint—which was not part of the injunction order, and which has been used to deny Wet'suwet'en peoples' access to their own territories and harass Indigenous individuals and supporters in the vicinity. They have also been criticized for removing, detaining, and threatening to arrest journalists attempting to cover the events. Numerous highly credible bodies have condemned the RCMP's violation of Indigenous and human rights, including the Canadian Civil Liberties Association, the (BC)

First Nations Leadership Council, the Canadian Association of Journalists, Amnesty International, and the United Nations Committee to End Racial Discrimination.

> For further reading about the Wet'suwet'en's ongoing efforts to exercise their **unceded** right to govern and live freely in their Lands, please see unistoten.camp and yintahaccess.com. If these links are broken, Google "Unist'ot'en heal the people" for the first and "Gidimt'en yintah access" for the second to help you locate the websites.

CONNECTION AS MEDICINE

Sandra: *Udaggi* (Creator) has blessed our people with ceremony, with a deep, implicit knowing in our body that connects us to ancestors, to the sacredness of life and Land—that helps us find balance, that helps us see how language and the knowledge of plant medicines keep us moving forward. This Land-based way helps me work through the grief and loss in whatever way they show up. I don't stay in one place too long, with the overwhelming familial grief and loss, as I dip into the big sadness. For, this could easily turn into depression. I take small steps and pay attention to my body. I notice when the overwhelm or the sadness shows up, and I take the time to check in and reach out for support. I have worked in many First Nations communities in BC, and so I have seen how much tragic loss we have in our families, how it spans so many generations. And often the tragedy shows up when an unexpected loss hits our families. The depression and anger we experience is often connected to the collective and intergenerational losses and grief that we hold.

An Indigenous trauma tool called Indigenous-Focused Oriented complex therapy has transformed my life. It is a person-centred approach to healing that honours my family's and my community's values and traditions (Turcotte & Schiffer, 2014). It has taught me that our history matters, that the wounds of tragic losses and injustices are still being carried in our body, mind, and spirit. It's important that I learn to notice when I am carrying so much hurt. The hurt and pain are at times loud, violent, or silent. They can take over the goodness that we carry (Oré et al., 2016). Our health outcomes share that story. Sometimes one person carries the hurt for the whole family. We often see this reflected in the compromised health of our children and young people. We are a collective. We share. It is a blessing that we can hold each other up, and so we need to pay attention when we hold or carry too much. If we don't learn how to make time in our daily lives for rest, we get sick, we can't sleep, or we get cranky. Our body tells us when we need to rest, when we are out of balance and need to help ourselves get centred again, to be whole, healthy, and *Ihtis* (strong). And so, our strengths—our songs and medicines, our connections to territory and ceremony—help us heal, find balance, and make room for love and care, for joy and laughter. The social determinants of health are good at framing the illness in our lives. We need to make space for the strengths and **resilience** embedded in our cultural governance and self-determination.

Christine: I work for a place-based organization that oversees Land-based programs for youth on Gitxsan territory. One of the most important things that I have learned is about **reciprocal** relationships, of sharing our skills, time, and energy. Our youth program begins with the introductions of the youth and staff to the Chief. She often gifts us with stories. We try to take a holistic approach to our programming, focusing on physical, cultural, spiritual, and environmental wellness, while honouring Elders. The youth explore various territories, harvesting medicinal plants and berries, such as stinging nettle, wild rose, and devil's club. They travel the highways of their ancestors on rafts. There are many transformative moments for the youth: connecting with their House group, being on the Land, leaning into the Land, and digging deeper into their *ootsin* (spirit). One of the most important lessons the youth learn is that you do not go into someone else's territory without permission (Mills, 1994).

CONCLUSION

The Wet'suwet'en Nation's holistic laws are reflected and enacted in their governance system, which has survived for millennia. Wet'suwet'en continue to live on and be with the Land. It is their inherent right to govern it—to "freely determine their political status and freely pursue their economic, social and cultural development," to return to the UNDRIP statement above. Moreover, their cultural, spiritual, and environmental health depends on it. Fostering a relationship with the Land and ensuring its health, celebrating the shared language, stories, ceremonies, and songs in the feast hall and on the Land, and honouring the traditional knowledge kept by Elders are cultural practices that reflect an interconnectedness with the *yintah* and that restore us and help us with our personal, familial, and collective health and well-being.

Sandra: We grow up and work alongside many settlers, colleagues, and co-workers who understand the injustices the Wet'suwet'en face and appreciate the importance of learning about our shared history of this region and getting involved. These individuals understand that we cannot be bystanders—that we must stand up and speak out for social justice, sustainable development, Indigenous rights, and health promotion (Ratima, 2019). We, as Wet'suwet'en, and many other Indigenous Peoples and settlers live together in various settlements in the *yintah*; this is our home. Collectively, we need to find a way for respectful relations between everyone and everything, which will lead to better health equity and improved **population health** outcomes for our children, grandchildren, men, women, seniors, and Elders, all genders, and all Beings, including the *yintah* itself.

CRITICAL THINKING QUESTIONS

1. What role does the *yintah* play in the health of the Wet'suwet'en Nation?
2. What are the impacts of government policies and large-scale industrial projects on the *yintah*?
3. Why is self-determination fundamental to the socio-cultural, linguistic, spiritual, and environmental health of the Wet'suwet'en Nation?

NOTES

1. Each House group is led by a Chief, which refers to someone who has a leadership and caretaking position that has been inherited or earned by merit. Chief names are timeless, as each Chief's history is added to the history of the name. Collectively, Hereditary House Chiefs make decisions that are ratified in the feast hall.
2. Hereditary Chief names are passed from generation to generation.

REFERENCES

Amos, H. (2011, July 7). At the root of the problem. *UBC News*. University of British Columbia. Retrieved April 1, 2020, from https://news.ubc.ca/2011/07/07/at-the-root-of-the-problem/

Coastal GasLink Pipeline Ltd. v. Huson. (2019). Supreme Court of British Columbia. https://www.coastalgaslink.com/siteassets/pdfs/about/regulatory/2020-01-07-order-re-interlocutory-injunction.pdf

Davidson, S. F., & Davidson, R. (2018). *Potlatch as pedagogy: Learning through ceremony*. Portage & Main Press.

Hoffman, R., & Joseph, A. (2019). *Song of the earth: The life of Alfred Joseph*. Creekstone Press.

McCreary, T. (2018). *Shared histories: Witsuwit'en-Settler relations in Smithers, British Columbia, 1913–1973*. Creekstone Press.

Mills, A. (Ed.). (1994). *Eagle Down is our law: Witsuwit'en law, feasts and land claims*. UBC Press.

Morin, M. H. (2016). *Niwhtsi'de'nï 'ni Hibii: The ways of our ancestors* (2nd ed.). Witsuwit'en History & Culture, Throughout the Millennia. School District #54.

Oré, C. E., Teufel-Shone, N. I., & Chico-Jarillo, T. (2016). American Indian and Alaska Native resilience along the life course and across generations: A literature review. *Center for American Indian and Alaska Native Mental Health Research*, *23*(3), 134–157. Colorado School of Public Health. https://dx.doi.org/10.5820/aian.2303.2016.134

Ratima, M. (2019). Leadership for planetary health and sustainable development: Health promotion community capacities for working with Indigenous Peoples in the application of Indigenous knowledge. *Global Health Promotion*, *26*(4). https://doi.org/10.1177/1757975919889250

Reading, C., & Wien, F. (2009). *Health inequalities and social determinants of Aboriginal Peoples' health*. National Collaborating Centre for Aboriginal Health.

Redvers, N. (2019). The science of the sacred: Bridging global Indigenous medicine systems and modern scientific principles. North Atlantic Books.

Smith, C. (2019, December 21). Gidimt'en spokesperson Sleydo', a.k.a. Molly Wickham, accuses RCMP of acting as mercenaries for industry. *The Georgia Straight*. Retrieved September 10, 2020, from https://www.straight.com/news/1339641/gidimten-spokesperson-sleydo-aka-molly-wickham-accuses-rcmp-acting-mercenaries-industry

Turcotte, S., & Schiffer, J. (2014). Aboriginal Focusing-Oriented Therapy. In G. Madison (Ed.), *Emerging practice in Focusing-Oriented Psychotherapy. Innovative theory and applications* (pp. 48–64). Jessica Kingsley Publishers.

UN General Assembly. (2007). *United Nations Declaration on the Rights of Indigenous Peoples: Resolution / adopted by the General Assembly*, 2 October 2007, A/RES/61/295. Retrieved September 9, 2020, from https://www.refworld.org/docid/471355a82.html

CHAPTER 2

First Nations, Inuit, and Métis Children's Mental Wellness

Margo Greenwood and Roseann Larstone

LEARNING OBJECTIVES

1. To describe historical and current impacts of colonial structures and policies, as well as determinants of Indigenous health that have disrupted Indigeneity and Indigenous knowledge systems.
2. To illustrate Indigenous conceptualizations of mental wellness.
3. To consider how Indigenous knowledge systems and conceptualizations of mental health can ensure greater mental well-being for Indigenous children.

INTRODUCTION

Mental wellness is fundamental to overall health and quality of life. More than the absence of mental illness, mental wellness is a state of well-being in which, among other things, individuals can effectively cope with everyday challenges and contribute meaningfully to their communities (Atkinson, 2017; Mental Health Commission of Canada [MHCC], 2012). Although Indigenous children disproportionately experience mental ill health as compared to non-Indigenous children (Atkinson, 2017; Malla et al., 2018; Nelson & Wilson, 2017), prevalence rates of common mental disorders (e.g., depression, anxiety) vary considerably among First Nations, Inuit, and Métis individuals and communities (Canada, 2006).

Discussions of the incidence and prevalence of optimal mental wellness (and its inverse) among First Nations, Inuit, and Métis must consider historical and current impacts of colonial structures and policies, as well as determinants of Indigenous health, such as marginalization, **intergenerational trauma**, racism, and **self-determination** (Nelson & Wilson, 2017). **Western** approaches to mental health are biomedical and deficit based. They consider health in isolation from other factors (e.g., social, emotional) and focus on deficits rather than strengths. The emphasis in the literature on the prevalence of mental illness in different Indigenous populations and communities has reflected these Western approaches. A dominant focus has been on indicators of mental illness, including suicide, substance use, and addiction. In this literature, these indicators are most often linked to intergenerational trauma and the ongoing impacts of **colonialism** (MHCC, 2012; Nelson & Wilson, 2017). Such a deficit approach to understanding mental illness fails to consider mental wellness, **resilience**, and "upstream prevention approaches"[1] among First Nations, Inuit, and Métis individuals, families, and communities. Evidence of outcomes from recent, relevant, community-developed, and culturally appropriate interventions is also limited (Nelson & Wilson, 2017).

Indigenous understandings of and approaches to mental wellness starkly contrast these approaches. First Nations, Inuit, and Métis, in diverse ways, consider the critical roles of families and communities, values, worldviews, and knowledges as being central to mental wellness (Tourand et al., 2016; Vukic et al., 2011). Taking these into account, self-determined, community-developed, culturally safe, and strengths-based mental wellness services are vital for young Indigenous children's optimal mental wellness (Atkinson, 2017).

DETERMINANTS OF INDIGENOUS HEALTH AND CHILDREN'S MENTAL WELLNESS

In 2008, the global report on social determinants of health illuminated health inequities in the lives of **Indigenous peoples** (World Health Organization [WHO], 2008). With respect to these inequities, the phrase "the causes of the causes" (Rose, 1992, as cited in Marmot, 2005, p. 1102) has been used to explain the need to examine "the social conditions that give rise to high risk of non-communicable disease whether acting through unhealthy behaviors or through the effects of impossibly stressful lives" (Marmot, 2005, p. 1102). For Indigenous peoples, the "causes of the causes of the causes" is more accurate because it points directly to the colonial experience underlying the "causes of the causes."

Colonization is the single-most profound determinant of Indigenous peoples' health and well-being. It presented, and continues to present, a calculated attack on children's identity and the Indigeneity of the community and Nation. Indigeneity has several characteristics, the most paramount being a close relationship with the **land**, territory, and natural world. Other characteristics include dimensions of time, distinct Indigenous knowledge systems, unique languages, and a vision for a sustainable future. These attributes of Indigeneity, understood both individually and collectively, were points of contestation with colonial governments who strove to alienate Indigenous peoples from their physical, cultural, and intellectual identities (e.g., language, values, families). The intergenerational effects of this assault on their personhood and **Nationhood** (e.g., prolonged grief and loss), along with ongoing **systemic racism** (e.g., discriminatory access to health services), have led to profound mental and physical health challenges among First Nations, Inuit, and Métis children, adults, and communities (Durie, 2008).

The process of colonization disrupted Indigenous children's connections to land, family, knowledge systems, language, and much more. It included developing a residential school system, which operated in Canada between 1831 and 1996. Instead of growing up in caring home and family environments, children were sent to schools that were designed to "civilize Indians," as Davin reported in 1879: "If anything is to be done with the Indian, we must catch him very young. The children must be kept constantly within the circle of civilized conditions" (as cited in Hanson, 2009, para. 6). When the residential schools began shutting down, children were still removed from their families, but now they were placed into foster families (mostly non-Indigenous) in an ongoing practice beginning with the **Sixties Scoop** and extending to the **Millennium Scoop**.

It is no surprise, then, that the mental wellness of adults and children is deeply impacted across generations: the residential school system and child welfare system continues to erode Indigeneity on multiple fronts. A research study undertaken between 1995 and 1997 found that the effects of traumatic events in childhood can be linked to mental illness, substance use, and other health problems in adulthood, as well as having negative impacts on education, job opportunities, and earning potential (National Center for Injury Prevention and Control, 2021). This study, although not specific to Indigenous peoples, underscores the importance of the early years in human growth and development and becomes even more meaningful when considered alongside of the histories of First Nations, Inuit, and Métis peoples. While addressing mental health is crucial for the well-being of all populations in Canada, a focus on strong mental health among Indigenous children is particularly important, given the Indigenous population is younger and growing faster in this country than the non-Indigenous population.[2]

The impact of intergenerational trauma on Indigenous peoples, when compared with non-Indigenous people, is evidenced today in many ways: lower levels of education, employment, and income, resulting in greater risk of **food insecurity**, especially in Northern and remote communities (Leblanc-Laurendau, 2020); higher rates of suicide (Statistics Canada, 2019); higher drug overdose rates and overdose-related deaths (First Nations Health Authority, 2020); higher over-representation in the child welfare system (Canada, 2018); vast over-representation in the Canadian correctional system (Canada, 2019); higher rates of communicable diseases (e.g., COVID-19, HIV/AIDS) (Andermann, 2016); and disproportionate numbers of significant chronic diseases (e.g., diabetes, cancer) (Earle, 2011).

The health outcomes described as a result of the colonial experience do not similarly affect all Indigenous children, families, and communities since each individual child and family is unique. Nevertheless, the devastating impacts of colonialism continue to profoundly shape Indigenous peoples' lived realities and affect the mental well-being of children and families, both individually and as collectives across Indigenous populations. One must consider these impacts, therefore, in the context of the child in family, community, and Nation when developing mental wellness interventions for young Indigenous children.

The impact of colonization on First Nations, Inuit, and Métis lives creates a unique social political reality in which Indigenous peoples must strive to ensure the continuity of their cultures and Nations. Children are highly valued for their centrality to this survival. In many Indigenous societies, children are viewed as gifts from the Creator. Some believe that children bring with them a special gift that will benefit the collective while others believe children are the ancestors reborn. Still others understand that "each person has a unique spirit that is predetermined before [their] body grows into it" (Battiste & Henderson, 2000, p. 52). Each child also brings unique assets with which to support their physical and mental development and strengthen the wellness of the whole community. From these perspectives, care and education of children is a sacred and valued responsibility, and learning is coming to know oneself and one's connection to the land and the spirit.

INDIGENOUS CONCEPTUALIZATIONS OF MENTAL WELLNESS: STRENGTHS-BASED PERSPECTIVES

How can First Nations, Inuit, and Métis communities' conceptualizations of mental wellness drive us toward what we need to do to better support Indigenous children's mental health? One important aspect is to understand ways in which First Nations, Inuit, and Métis perceptions of mental wellness extend beyond mainstream definitions.

The World Health Organization (WHO) defines mental wellness as a "state of well-being in which an individual realizes his or her own abilities, can cope with the normal stresses of life, can work productively, and is able to make a contribution to his or her community" (WHO, 2018, n.p.). First Nations, Inuit, and Métis conceptualizations of mental wellness reflect a range of constructs that align with this definition, such as personal well-being, resilience, and adaptability (Bartlett, 2005; Vukic et al., 2011). However, Western worldviews pathologize Indigenous overall health (Allan & Smylie, 2015). What is more, mainstream frameworks typically do not consider the challenges inherent in structures (e.g., policy, legislation) and systems (e.g., education, justice, health) that drive health inequities experienced by First Nations, Inuit, and Métis. A recent review of data and information sources focusing on the health and well-being of young First Nations, Inuit, and Métis children also revealed that national, provincial, and Indigenous-specific data and information are out-of-date, and none of the available sources are distinctions-based (Greenwood et al., 2020).

The lack of current and disaggregated data[3] is particularly acute relative to Métis and Inuit populations, resulting in an uneven patchwork of information about young Indigenous children's mental wellness.

In short, colonial practices, anchored in Western worldviews and anti-Indigenous racism, have disrupted traditional approaches to mental wellness, which are situated in Indigenous knowledge systems, and which can be drawn upon to ensure greater mental well-being for Indigenous children. The following paragraphs will focus on Indigenous conceptualizations of mental wellness to show the strengths-based approaches First Nations, Inuit, and Métis communities take to improving individual and collective mental health.

First Nations view health and well-being holistically: they are based on a balance between a person's spiritual, emotional, mental, and physical aspects (Carriere & Richardson, 2013). The *First Nations Mental Wellness Continuum Framework* (Health Canada, 2015) noted that mental wellness for First Nations peoples is supported by a sense of belonging and purpose, as well as by a hope for a future "that is grounded in a sense of identity ... [and] unique Indigenous values" (Health Canada, 2015, p. 1). It added that, to ensure the health of "individual, community, and family life, mental wellness needs to be contextualized to a First Nations environment so that it is supported by culture, language, Elders, families, and creation" (p. 6). To these protective factors must be added culturally safe and culturally grounded mental wellness programs, which are vital to the support of individual, family, and community wellness (Health Canada, 2015).

For Inuit, mental wellness is "an all-inclusive term encompassing mental health, mental illness, suicide prevention, violence reduction, and reduction of substance abuse and addictions" (Alianait Inuit-Specific Mental Wellness Task Group [Alianait], 2007, p. 5). The *Alianait Inuit Mental Wellness Action Plan* defined mental wellness as "self-esteem and personal dignity flowing from the presence of harmonious physical, emotional, mental, spiritual wellness and cultural identity" (p. 9). The importance of physical, mental, emotional, and spiritual balance is reflected within *inuuqatigiittiarniq*, a holistic worldview of Inuit health (Little Bear, 2000, as cited in Richmond et al., 2007) that focuses on respect and care for the entire community in a way that strengthens individuals and the collective. The concept of *inuuqatigiittiarniq* also emphasizes relationship building. Indeed, mental wellness is located in "positive thinking that comes with an environment of love, support and active encouragement, grounded in meaningful relationships and supported with high expectations" (Tagalik, 2012, p. 6).

Traditional cultural approaches to mental wellness promotion are vital for Inuit. These include eating country foods and spending time on the land, which support maintaining strong cultural identity and nurturing the relationship between Inuit and Inuit Nunangat[4] (Alianait, 2007). Equally important in supporting Inuit mental wellness are protective factors, including resilience, food security, and the role of Elders as traditional healers (Alianait, 2007).

For Métis, mental wellness means maintaining connections to history, culture and traditions, way of life, and a sense of Nationhood and rights:

> Métis traditional environmental knowledge was developed from community practices and has evolved into a unique Métis holistic worldview with distinct values and spiritual beliefs. Métis understand the environment in terms of sacred relationships that link language, tradition, and land to community spiritual, physical, intellectual, and emotional health. (Métis National Environment Committee, 2011, as cited in MHCC, 2012, p. 102)

One study found Métis adults understand mental wellness as being interconnected with emotional, spiritual, and physical health (Auger, 2017). In this study, participants also referenced finding balance and nurturing a sense of identity and self-awareness as important aspects of mental wellness and physical wellness. Métis culture, language, and connection to land are important components for mental wellness (Auger, 2017). Similarly, in a province-wide study from British Columbia, Métis youth cited cultural connectedness as an important factor in supporting positive mental wellness (Tourand et al., 2016).

Taken together, optimal health for Indigenous peoples, including mental wellness, is experienced across physical, mental, emotional, and spiritual domains. Wellness is defined as living in harmony with family, community, nature, and environment (First Nations Health Authority et al., 2013; Health Canada, 2015; King et al., 2009; Vukic et al., 2011). To support positive mental wellness outcomes for Indigenous children and youth, mental wellness approaches must be culturally grounded, and they must work across multiple levels, including home, school, and community. They must integrate evidence-based protective factors and reinforce these by understanding wellness from a whole-person perspective (Health Canada, 2015).

CONCLUSION: WHERE TO FROM HERE?

As the previous section showed, First Nations, Inuit, and Métis each have distinct ways of understanding and describing mental wellness, which are underpinned by Indigenous values and worldviews. Young Indigenous children's mental wellness will be optimized by building on **distinctions-based approaches** to developing strengths and assets, "including reinforcing a strong sense of cultural identity and relationships with family, community, and cultural and spiritual practices" (Greenwood et al., 2020, p. 32). In the context of direct service provision, this will mean supporting and enhancing Indigeneity, Indigenous knowledge systems, and ways of being—as evidenced in values, traditions, and protocols—to foster continuity of communities and Nations.

Promising upstream mental wellness interventions include "Indigenous concepts such as holism, **reciprocity** and plurality; Indigenous contexts including acknowledgement of inequalities and colonialism; and Indigenous processes such as community control, community engagement, and cultural responsiveness" (Reading & Reading, 2012, as cited in Atkinson, 2017, p. 6). Local Indigenous knowledge must underpin mental wellness programs and services for young Indigenous children if they are to be responsive and effective (Boska et al., 2015, and Kirmayer et al., 2016, as cited in Atkinson, 2017). It is also essential that strategies to support young Indigenous children's mental wellness emphasize connection to culture, language, and land. This will build resilience as it will foster a strong sense of self that is situated in, and connected to, family and community (Atkinson, 2017).

Above all, colonial systems such as education, justice, health, and welfare must be dismantled or restructured. These systems uphold practices and policies that not only contribute to mental illness among First Nations, Inuit, and Métis youth, but also prolong intergenerational trauma. Instead of reinforcing and upholding anti-Indigenous racism, these structures must partner with Indigenous communities, draw on Indigenous ways of knowing and being, and recognize the importance of strengths-based approaches to mental health so that future generations of Indigenous children have their best chance at a healthy life.

CRITICAL THINKING QUESTIONS

1. What determinants of health (at individual, systems, and structural levels) other than colonialism may disrupt or ease access to culturally safe mental wellness programs and services for Indigenous children?
2. What can you do to contradict the colonial systems that contribute to Indigenous children's trauma?
3. You are explaining the impact of intergenerational trauma on First Nations, Inuit, and Métis peoples to your friend. What would you say?
4. Why is self-determination critical to optimal mental wellness for Indigenous children, families, communities, and Nations?

NOTES

1. "Upstream interventions and strategies focus on improving fundamental social and economic structures in order to decrease barriers and improve supports that allow people to achieve their full health potential" (National Collaborating Centre for Determinants of Health, 2021, para. 1).
2. "From 2006 to 2016, the number of First Nations, Métis and Inuit youth aged 15 to 34 increased by 39%, compared to just over 6% for . . . non-Indigenous youth" (Statistics Canada, 2018, n.p.). Additionally, "The Indigenous population is on average, nearly a decade younger than the rest of the population in Canada: The Inuit are the youngest of the three groups, with an average age of 27.7 years, followed by First Nations people (30.6 years) and Métis (34.7 years)" (Statistics Canada, 2018, n.p.).

3. Data that have been subdivided into categories.
4. An **Inuktitut** term describing Inuit lands (Inuit homeland) that takes into account the centrality of land, water, and ice to Inuit ways of life and culture. Inuit Nunangat includes the land claims regions of Nunavut, Nunavik (in Northern Quebec), and Nunatsiavut (in Northern Labrador). It also encompasses the Inuvialuit Settlement Region of the Northwest Territories.

REFERENCES

Alianait Inuit-Specific Mental Wellness Task Group (Alianait). (2007). *Alianait Mental Wellness Action Plan*. Inuit Tapiriit Kanatami. https://www.itk.ca/wp-content/uploads/2009/12/Alianait-Inuit-Mental-Wellness-Action-Plan-2009.pdf

Allan, B., & Smylie, J. (2015). *First Peoples, second class treatment: The role of racism in the health and well-being of Indigenous peoples in Canada*. The Wellesley Institute. https://www.wellesleyinstitute.com/wp-content/uploads/2015/02/Report-First-Peoples-Second-Class-Treatment-Feb-2015.pdf

Andermann, A. (2016). Taking action on the social determinants of health in clinical practice: A framework for health professionals. *Canadian Medical Association Journal, 188*(17–18), E474–E483. https://doi.org/10.1503/cmaj.160177

Atkinson, D. (2017). Considerations for Indigenous child and youth population mental health promotion in Canada. National Collaborating Centre for Indigenous Health. http://nccph.ca/images/uploads/general/07_Indigenous_MentalHealth_NCCPH_2017_EN.pdf

Auger, M. D. (2017). *Understanding our past, reclaiming our culture: Conceptualizing Métis culture and mental health in British Columbia* [Unpublished master's thesis]. Simon Fraser University.

Bartlett, J. G. (2005). Health and well-being for Métis women in Manitoba. *Canadian Journal of Public Health, 96*(S1), S22–S27.

Battiste, M., & Henderson, J. Y. (2000). *Protecting Indigenous knowledge and heritage: A global challenge*. UBC Press.

Canada. (2006). *The human face of mental health and mental illness in Canada*. Minister of Public Works and Government Services Canada. https://www.phac-aspc.gc.ca/publicat/human-humain06/pdf/human_face_e.pdf

Canada. (2018). *Media Brief | Backgrounder – Child & Family Services*. Indigenous Services Canada. https://www.canada.ca/en/indigenous-services-canada/news/2018/01/media_brief_backgrounder childfamilyservices.html

Canada. (2019). *Spotlight on* Gladue*: Challenges, experiences, and possibilities in Canada's criminal justice system*. Department of Justice. https://www.justice.gc.ca/eng/rp-pr/jr/gladue/index.html

Carriere, J., & Richardson, C. (2013). Relationship is everything: Holistic approaches to Aboriginal child and youth mental health. *First Peoples Child & Family Review, 7*(2), 8–26.

Durie, M. (2008, April). *Mental health at the interface: Indigeneity and science* [Conference session]. Vancouver, BC, Canada.

Earle, L. (2011). *Understanding chronic disease and the role for traditional approaches in Aboriginal communities*. National Collaborating Centre for Aboriginal Health. https://www.nccih.ca/docs/emerging/FS-UnderstandingChronicDisease-Earle-EN.pdf

First Nations Health Authority. (2020). *COVID-19 pandemic sparks surge in overdose deaths this year.* https://www.fnha.ca/about/news-and-events/news/covid-19-pandemic-sparks-surge-in-overdose-deaths-this-year

First Nations Health Authority, BC Ministry of Health, & Health Canada. (2013). *A path forward: BC First Nations and Aboriginal People's Mental Wellness and Substance Use 10-Year Plan.* https://www.fnha.ca/Documents/FNHA_MWSU.pdf

Greenwood, M., Larstone, R., & Lindsay, N. (2020). *Exploring the data landscapes of First Nations, Inuit and Métis children's early learning and child care (ELCC).* National Collaborating Centre for Indigenous Health. https://www.ccnsa.ca/Publications/Lists/Publications/Attachments/316/NCCIH%20_RPT-FNIM-%20ELCC-MAIN.pdf

Hanson, E. (2009). *The residential school system.* First Nations and Indigenous Studies. University of British Columbia. Retrieved June 23, 2021, from https://indigenousfoundations.arts.ubc.ca/the_residential_school_system/

Health Canada. (2015). *First Nations mental wellness continuum framework.* https://thunderbirdpf.org/first-nations-mental-wellness-continuum-framework/

King, M., Smith, A., & Gracey, M. (2009). Indigenous health part 2: The underlying causes of the health gap. *The Lancet, 374*(9683), 76–85.

Leblanc-Laurendau, O. (2020). *Food insecurity in Northern Canada: An overview.* Library of Parliament. https://lop.parl.ca/staticfiles/PublicWebsite/Home/ResearchPublications/BackgroundPapers/PDF/2020-47-E.pdf

Malla, A., Shah, J., Iyer, S., Boksa, P., Joober, R., Andersson, N., Lal, S., & Fuhrer, R. (2018). Youth mental health should be a top priority for health care in Canada. *Canadian Journal of Psychiatry, 63*(4), 216–222.

Marmot, M. (2005). Social determinants of health inequalities. *The Lancet, 365,* 1099–1104. https://doi.org/10.1016/s0140-6736(05)71146-6

Mental Health Commission of Canada (MHCC). (2012). *Changing directions, changing lives: The mental health strategy for Canada.* https://www.mentalhealthcommission.ca/sites/default/files/MHStrategy_Strategy_ENG_0_1.pdf

National Center for Injury Prevention and Control, Division of Violence Prevention. (2021). *Preventing Adverse Childhood Experiences.* U.S. Department of Health & Human Services. https://www.cdc.gov/violenceprevention/aces/fastfact.html

National Collaborating Centre for Determinants of Health. (2021). *Glossary.* Retrieved June 23, 2021, from https://nccdh.ca/glossary/entry/upstream-downstream

Nelson, S. E., & Wilson, K. (2017). The mental health of Indigenous peoples in Canada: A critical review of research. *Social Science and Medicine, 176,* 93–112. http://dx.doi.org/10.1016/j.socscimed.2017.01.021

Richmond, C. A. M., Ross, N. A., & Bernier, J. (2007). Exploring Indigenous concepts of health: The dimensions of Métis and Inuit health. *Aboriginal Policy Research Consortium International (APRCi).* Paper 115. http://ir.lib.uwo.ca/aprci/115

Statistics Canada. (2018). *First Nations People, Métis and Inuit in Canada: Diverse and growing populations.* Retrieved June 24, 2021, from https://www150.statcan.gc.ca/n1/pub/89-659-x/89-659-x2018001-eng.htm

Statistics Canada. (2019). *National Household Survey: Aboriginal Peoples—Suicide among First Nations people, Métis and Inuit (2011-2016): Findings from the 2011 Canadian Census Health and Environment Cohort (CanCHEC)*. Retrieved June 24, 2021, from https://www150.statcan.gc.ca/n1/pub/99-011-x/99-011-x2019001-eng.htm

Tagalik, S. (2012). *Inunnguiniq: Caring for children the Inuit way*. National Collaborating Centre for Indigenous Health. http://www.nccah-ccnsa.ca/docs/fact%20sheets/child%20and%20youth/Inuit%20caring%20EN%20web.pdf

Tourand, J., Smith, A., Poon, C., Stewart, D., & McCreary Centre Society. (2016). *Ta Saantii: A profile of Métis youth health in BC*. McCreary Centre Society. http://www.mcs.bc.ca/pdf/ta_saantii.pdf

Vukic, A., Gregory, D., Martin-Misener, R., & Etowa, J. (2011). Aboriginal and Western conceptions of mental health and illness. *Pimatisiwin: A Journal of Aboriginal and Indigenous Community Health, 9*(1), 65–86.

World Health Organization. (2008). *Closing the gap in a generation: Health equity through action on the social determinants of health. Final Report of the Commission on Social Determinants of Health*. https://www.who.int/publications/i/item/WHO-IER-CSDH-08.1

World Health Organization. (2018). *Mental health: Strengthening our response* [Fact sheet]. https://www.who.int/news-room/fact-sheets/detail/mental-health-strengthening-our-response

CHAPTER 3

Food as Relationship: Indigenous Food Systems and Well-Being

Tabitha Robin

LEARNING OBJECTIVES

1. To conceptualize what food means for **Indigenous Peoples** in Canada.
2. To examine the relationships between food, **land**, and **well-being**.
3. To encourage students to consider their own relationships with land.

INTRODUCTION

Connections between food and health are plentiful (Kuhnlein et al., 2006). However, they largely favour food as a source of nutrients. For Indigenous Peoples, food is more than sustenance. Food is an opportunity to honour ancestors, nations, and lands. Food is an act of belonging and communion (Nabigon, 2006; Robin, 2019). While many studies have examined food security for Indigenous Peoples, less attention has been paid to the role of food as a contributor to a larger sense of well-being (see Ray et al., 2019 as an outlier). Food security studies have become standard, but studies detailing **food insecurity** for Indigenous Peoples fail to consider the intricate, holistic relationships Indigenous Peoples have with their food systems. Food is a powerful relationship builder, a vehicle for connecting Indigenous Peoples with their cultures, lands, and histories. Being actively involved in one's food system is foundational to well-being. Indigenous food sovereignty (IFS), a timeless practice that has gained scholarly attention in the last decade, emphasizes relationships between people, food, and land over food as something to be eaten. It helps better describe the Indigenous Peoples' understanding of food and well-being. As a movement, IFS advocates for connections between and across disciplines, particularly with respect to holistic health.

This chapter will outline food studies for Indigenous Peoples. It will first summarize the implications and limitations of food security. It will then delineate a more robust understanding of Indigenous relationships to food systems. The chapter will conclude by explaining how IFS is being enacted in community. While practices of Indigenous food sovereignty exist around the globe, this chapter's focus will be on North America, with a particular emphasis on Canada.

FOOD SECURITY

The term "food security" was first proposed in 1974 to describe a global crisis marked by discrepancies in the global food supply and the growing experiences of hunger worldwide. The term has evolved considerably. Early definitions include the United Nations Food and Agriculture Organization's (UNFAO) (1996): food security exists "when all people at all times have access to sufficient, safe, nutritious food to maintain a healthy and active life" (para. 1, 1n.). Today, Indigenous Peoples across Canada face higher levels of food insecurity than non-Indigenous people (Tarasuk et al., 2013). Their conditions of hunger are marked by an inability to access fresh, nutritious, and culturally appropriate foods. Indeed, being of Indigenous heritage is a characteristic associated with a higher likelihood of food insecurity (Tarasuk, et al., 2013). As poverty levels grow, food insecurity intensifies (Power, 2008). Loss of land, culture, and identity as well as a lack of control over food, resources, and livelihoods have prevented Indigenous Peoples from experiencing food security (Willows et al., 2009). Ultimately, these losses are consequences of **colonialism** and are connected to early attempts to starve and experiment on Indigenous bodies and lands in order to rid Canada of its "Indian Problem."

Food insecurity creates significant socio-economic and health barriers for Indigenous Peoples. It is linked to "high levels of poverty, multi-child households, low levels of educational achievement and labour force participation, reliance on social assistance and welfare, and female lone-parent families" (Willows et al., 2009, p. 1150). Malnutrition resulting from food insecurity has been connected to decreased academic performance and increased troubles in learning environments (e.g., diminished comprehension, intensified behavioural problems) (Cook et al., 2004). Food insecurity also contributes to higher levels of stress, life dissatisfaction, and a poor sense of community belonging (Willows et al., 2009). Lowered health indicators are also common for individuals experiencing food insecurity. Moreover, food insecurity presents an obstacle to caring for oneself. Mikkonen and Raphael (2010) reported that households facing food insecurity are 80% more likely to have diabetes, with 60% of households reporting high blood pressure. Fresh foods, particularly fruits and vegetables, are necessary to support health and control diabetes. Yet, access to fresh foods is a major challenge for Indigenous Peoples. On reserve, fresh foods are prohibitively expensive, and consumers may suffer from an inconsistent supply chain because of many reserves' remote, inaccessible locations.

In Canada, hunger and malnutrition are largely addressed through charitable organizations and food banks. However, these interventions are not designed for Indigenous Peoples and do not address the power dimension of food. While food banks and other in-kind food programs provide food directly to clients, they have been criticized for being dumping grounds for less healthy, leftover food (Wittman et al., 2010); moreover, they work only to alleviate hunger, thus taking a one-dimensional approach to combatting hunger. In the context of food security for First Nations, Inuit, and Métis Peoples, such benevolence does little to confront the systemic poverty they experience in Canada. Poverty is clearly related to health: what people eat is determined by what they can afford (Richmond & Ross, 2009).

Power (2008) noted that food security studies lack attention to the cultural aspects of food for Indigenous Peoples. Surveys used to determine rates of food insecurity, for example, are often, if not always, conducted in English and do not include questions about accessing or sharing traditional foods. Importantly, a 2012 study by the First Nations Information Governance Centre (FNIGC) revealed that over 85.5% of First Nations households had received traditional food through mechanisms of sharing (FNIGC, 2012). Sharing is a key value in Indigenous cultures; however, food security studies aiming to support the enhancement of Indigenous diets pay scant attention to the values and perspectives of Indigenous Peoples. By focusing on the supply side of food through treating food as a commodity, these studies and the resulting interventions miss the mark.

UNDERSTANDING INDIGENOUS FOOD SYSTEMS

Defining an Indigenous food system is necessary for understanding the role Indigenous food plays in health outcomes. Indigenous food systems are intimately and intricately connected to the land: Indigenous cultures view foods as gifts, and they understand the land—itself a gift from Creator—to be the source of these gifts. **Reciprocity**, as part of Indigenous ways of knowing, being, seeing, and doing, ensures that Indigenous Peoples uphold their commitment to the safety, security, and continuation of the land for future generations. For most Indigenous cultures in Canada, land is part of a collective. It belongs to no one person or group. Too often, food systems are examined solely as mechanistic parts: the soil, the carrot, the market, and (later) the consumption. But this perpetuates a narrow view of a food system that does not align with Indigenous worldviews.

The many existing Indigenous worldviews each privilege Indigenous knowledges as sources for understanding the natural world, which itself provides instructions, insight, and learning opportunities. Hart (2007) explained that Indigenous knowledges do not "separate realities into disciplines such as religion, philosophy, art, physical sciences, and social sciences" (p. 84); rather, "understandings stemming from these various sources are seen as being mutually dependent on one another, thus making it irrational to divide them" (p. 84). The strength of Indigenous food systems lies not in the sum of their disparate parts but in the relationships between all the parts: the soil and plants, the water, sky, sun, moon and stars, and the animals all play distinct, yet interdependent roles in an Indigenous food system. In fact, this interdependency is a powerful source of energy for all living things. The sun, for example, provides plants with energy; plants make nutrients that can be eaten or returned to the land to fertilize the soil to grow more plants.

The term "all my relations" is a valuable framework for understanding Indigenous food systems:

> "All my relations" is at first a reminder of who we are and of our relationship with both our family and our relatives. It also reminds us of the extended relationship we share with all human beings. But the relationships that Native people see go further, the web of kinship extending to the animals, to the birds, to the fish, to the plants, to all the animate and inanimate forms that can be seen or imagined. More than that, "all my relations" is an encouragement for us to accept the responsibilities we have within this universal family by living our lives in a harmonious and moral manner (a common admonishment is to say of someone that they act as if they have no relations). (King, 1990, p. ix)

Indigenous food systems are based on principles of respect, reciprocity, and responsibility. Morrison (2011) explained: "Consisting of a multitude of natural communities, Indigenous food systems include all land, soil, water, air, plants and animals, as well as Indigenous knowledge, wisdom, and values" (p. 98).

The values of caring, sharing, and kindness underscore Indigenous relationships in food systems. Through relationships with the land and guided by local values and knowledges, Indigenous food systems also include cultural practices, such as ceremony. Indeed, Indigenous Peoples have a responsibility to practise their food cultures, to carry on the work of their ancestors (Coté, 2016; Morrison, 2011; Robin, 2019). Responsibility comes through an understanding of Natural Laws, a recognition of Indigenous roles and responsibilities, and the act of naming, Nation, territory, and **clan** systems. Indigenous food systems thus extend to ceremony, language, songs, and art, along with family, clan systems, and the continued enhancement of Indigenous nations. This means that land is the source of knowledge, nourishment, and, ultimately, well-being. Nature is not something that exists outside of people; it is the basis of Indigenous languages, ceremonies, songs, celebrations, ways of knowing, being, seeing, and doing.

FOOD SOVEREIGNTY

In 1996, the term "food sovereignty" was proposed by La Vía Campesina, an international movement of peasants, small-farm workers, and Indigenous Peoples in the Global South to capture the political and economic powers inherent in food production (Wittman et al., 2010). Repudiating the dominant discourse in food politics, La Vía Campesina highlighted the inequities and injustices of short-sighted food security initiatives that did not encourage local production. Thus, the language of food sovereignty is deliberate and political. Masioli and Nicholson (2010) described food sovereignty as "a political right to organize ourselves, to decide what to plant, to have control of seeds . . . a very broad concept that includes the right of access to seeds, the right to produce, to trade, to consume one's own foods . . . it is a concept that is linked to the autonomy and sovereignty of peoples" (p. 34).

A food sovereignty framework prioritizes care for inherent parts of food systems: people and land. Protection and redistribution of lands are critical, with the idea that people of the land should have the right to produce food and control land-based resources, water, and seeds (Wittman et al., 2010). A new land-based ethic that considers justice, respect for life, and democracy guides this movement. Through food sovereignty, food must be produced in ecologically sound ways, with special attention to economic, environmental, and social sustainability.

Food sovereigntists advocate the health and strength of relationships for communities and individuals within a food system. Importantly, La Vía Campesina's food sovereignty campaigns have included ending violence against women, a common occurrence that women face as food providers (Wittman et al., 2010). Food sovereignty has become the new framework for examining tensions, injustices, and inequalities within food systems and the larger food complex. However, Indigenous food sovereignty, though grounded in the work of food sovereigntists, has taken its own evolutionary route. It carries special resonance for people whose histories and futures have been altered through colonial processes.

INDIGENOUS FOOD SOVEREIGNTY

The *Healthy Food Guidelines for First Nations Communities* defines Indigenous food sovereignty (IFS) as "the Right of peoples, communities, and countries to define their own agricultural, labour, fishing, food and land policies, which are ecologically, socially, spiritually, economically and culturally appropriate to their unique circumstances" (First Nations Health Council, 2009, p. iii). IFS has gained recent attention in the literature, but it has been in practice since time immemorial (Morrison, 2011).

While fluctuating weather and animals' changing migration patterns interfered with land-based food practices prior to European contact, ample evidence shows that pre-contact food systems were plentiful. Historically, food shortages were seen not as a consequence of animal and land exploitation, but rather as part of a larger spiritual imbalance (Stonechild, 2016). In the face of these shortages, communities would modify their behaviours to reaffirm spiritual connections with the land.

Indigenous food systems have changed dramatically since European contact (Coté, 2016; Daigle, 2019). Important species such as the bison, beaver, otter, cedar, and salmon have faced near-extinction from regions in attempts to clear the land for development and colonial settlement (Kimmerer, 2013; Lux, 2001). Moreover, the introduction of reserves resulted in forced migration, land dispossession, and the resultant loss and grief. In many cases, reserve lands were chosen for their inactivity and unprofitability: their poor soil and climatic conditions and their lack of access to potable water made them undesirable for settlers in the expansion of **Western** agriculture (Monchalin, 2016). Moreover, even though Western agricultural practices were offered to Indigenous Peoples as a tool to assimilate them into Canadian society, non-Indigenous farmers saw this as a threat to their own livelihoods. A series of policy and regulation changes starting in the 1870s and continuing to today eliminated agriculture for Indigenous farmers (Monchalin, 2016), despite Indigenous Peoples' long history of living harmoniously with the land. These policies altered Indigenous lands dramatically in a short time.

The increased interest in IFS comes at a critical time. Climate change, land extraction, and resource development, coupled with rampant food insecurity, have accelerated the need for stronger relationships to food and land. This is a time for resurgence, (re)connections to the land and to each other, and a revitalization of Indigenous food systems. In Canada, conversations about IFS are largely attributed to the Working Group on Indigenous Food Sovereignty (WGIFS), a grassroots organization whose advocacy work for land reform and revitalization of holistic, traditional food systems through a responsibility-based paradigm has been foundational to understanding IFS (Robin, 2019). Indeed, Morrison (2011) posited that denying a responsibility-based paradigm perpetuates a production-based paradigm where Indigenous roles are pigeon-holed into food production: "Indigenous food sovereignty is ultimately achieved by upholding our long-standing sacred responsibilities to nurture healthy, interdependent relationships with the land, plants, and animals that provide us with our food" (Morrison, 2011, p. 100). According to Morrison (2011), key principles of IFS include: a recognition of the sacredness of food; action through continued participation in traditional food systems; **self-determination**; and policy reform.

The theoretical underpinnings of IFS are values-based, holistic, local, contextual, and **decolonizing** (Coté, 2016; Daigle, 2019; Morrison, 2011; Robin, 2019). Because IFS belongs to communities, nations, and clans, Indigenous communities—which are varied and unique, with their own languages, ceremonies, protocols, and cultural practices—have myriad expressions for their food systems and sovereignty. Indeed, Daigle (2019) referred to these expressions as food *sovereignties*. There is no one food sovereignty, nor can food exist in isolation from issues of power, control, and sovereignty. Thus, the word "sovereignties" is an important consideration for the movement: with countless factors affecting the vision and practice of IFS, "sovereignties" acknowledges that communities are not uniform and that culture is not static.

In moving away from reliance on a global, industrialized food system, IFS is inherently decolonizing (Coté, 2016). For those living in Northern Canada, food sovereignty can reduce reliance on grocery stores, where food prices are exorbitantly high, and complaints about food cost, availability, and quality are standard. With a focus on the revitalization of Indigenous food systems and food practices, IFS supports local production and relationships with local lands based on (re)claiming traditional food practices. Decolonization also occurs through the critical examination of Indigenous Peoples' rights and responsibilities toward the land, community, and nation. This includes policies related to food production, land health, and access to traditional hunting, fishing, and trapping grounds. Take, for example, the *Safe Food for Canadians Act*, which governs Indigenous Peoples' ability to share and sell traditional food obtained through **subsistence** and recreational practices (Minister of Justice, 2012). Under the Act, hunters with hunting licenses (outside of Nunavut) may share food with their family but not with their community; even making an offer to sell the food is illegal. This means that land-based food harvested by Indigenous Peoples cannot be legally shared at public events. An IFS framework decolonizes these food policies so that Indigenous communities can self-determine their protocols for food safety. Indeed, Coté (2016) explained how "Indigenizing" the food sovereignty movement occurs through privileging a responsibilities-based discourse over a rights-based discourse. She described how, for the Nuu-chah-nulth in British Columbia, this Indigenization has been enacted through the (re)development of "environmental and food policies grounded in traditional principles" (p. 2). Despite challenges, Indigenous Peoples across the country are innovatively (re)enacting their food sovereignties. IFS is a reminder that Indigenous Peoples and their ways of knowing, seeing, being, and doing have survived.

What Does Indigenous Food Sovereignty Look Like?

Indigenous food sovereignty varies from nation to nation, depending on the nation's geography, history, local needs, desires, and challenges. Additionally, the presence and impacts of **resource extraction**, mining, pipelines, and hydro development and histories affect the extent to which each Indigenous community addresses food sovereignty (LaDuke, 2016). In some cases, these threats have propelled the work of Indigenous food sovereigntists. For example, Winona LaDuke has gained attention for her efforts to protect wild rice from genetically modified seeds and to establish legal rights for *manoomin* (Ojibwe for wild rice) (LaDuke, 2019). This Right of Nature (re)affirms the Indigenous Peoples' responsibility for and relationship to land

and society. Relationship to land is also shown through the emergence of culture, language, and land-based camps that are part educational endeavour, part communion. Indeed, the strength of educational programming within an IFS framework is in how a community comes together to learn, teach, and share. For example, the Ladybug Garden and Greenhouse Program in T'Sou-ke, British Columbia incorporates language into their food, culture, and education programming. As one staff member explained, "We also take our members and youth out onto our traditional territories for hikes to practice our culture by way of prayers and blessings, exercise, plant identification, and language practices. . . . That's like a classroom out on the beach" (George, as cited in Robin, 2019, p. 93). Other examples of IFS education and growth abound. Kamal et al. (2015) described land-based programming for youth in O-Pipon-Na-Piwin Cree Nation in Manitoba not only as decolonizing but also as part of a larger system of caring for one another. Through their food sovereignty initiatives, O-Pipon-Na-Piwin Cree youth learn to hunt, fish, berry-pick, harvest, garden, and prepare wild foods. Youth also learn the health benefits of foods through a framework that focuses on the Cree concept of *Wechihituwin*, or "any means of livelihood that is shared and used to help another person, family or community" (Kamal et al., 2015, pp. 565–66).

Community initiatives such as hunts, freezers, and kitchens offer further insight into how IFS helps to mobilize community. In Manitoba, the Nelson House Country Foods Program compensates hunters, fishers, trappers, gatherers, and growers. Harvesters bring their food to be processed, butchered, and stored before it is distributed to the community, particularly to those who can't access the land. Community freezers and hunts help to ensure that community members are not hungry (Robin, 2019). In Ontario, the Shkagamik-Kwe Health Centre operates a wild-foods bank to access traditional foods such as moose meat (Ray et al., 2019). In operation for over seven years, it has served over five thousand clients. Another IFS practice is whaling, a tradition undertaken in coastal and Northern communities (Coté, 2016). Whale meat is considered a healthy food source, and "the tradition of whaling maintains community solidarity and collective security through the communal hunts and the processing, distributing, and consuming of whale products by community members" (Coté, 2016, p. 10).

Reclaiming Home

Delormier et al. (2017) argued that "Indigenous Peoples' health inequities are embedded in histories of dispossession from their homelands and the destruction of their social systems" (p. 1). Human-based interventions on nature have resulted in environmental dispossession, marked by a lack of access to traditional environments (Richmond & Ross, 2009).

> Environmental dispossession refers to loss of land—as well as loss of access to land and cultural resources—through processes of, for example, resource extraction, contamination, and disputes over land rights. Indigenous communities experience these changes first-hand through hydro development, mining, pipelines, flooding, and contamination of land and food (Richmond & Ross, 2009). Indigenous Peoples who are removed from their homelands experience a sharp separation from the lands that birthed their family and ancestors—lands that hold their stories, songs, and ceremonies. This loss results in grief and trauma.

For Indigenous Peoples to have a strong relationship with their food systems, a safe and secure land base is necessary. But what happens when the land that birthed you, the land that holds your family, ancestors, languages, stories, and songs is under threat? What happens when you have lost that land or been removed from it? For Indigenous Peoples, home is the land and all that is contained within it. Home is territory and community. Being part of community is an act of communion. Thus, to be in communion at home means to be in communion with the land. Notions of community extend outwards to include the connections between living and non-living things. When one considers the land, water, sun, moon, skies, plants, and animals to be part of their community, the level of responsibility for their community grows. Councillor Frank Meuse, from Mi'kmaq territory (much of what is now Eastern Canada), shared the following about Indigenous Peoples' connection with all these elements: "If we don't have natural resources, then we don't exist as Mi'kmaq. I really feel that culture is bound with all other living things. . . . we are affected by everything around us" (as cited in Pictou, 2017, p. 103).

CONCLUSION

The health and well-being of Indigenous Peoples is mirrored in the health of the land. Food is medicine; it is needed to heal. An ancestral and generational approach is necessary to considering the future of the land and food systems, as Nabigon (2006) observed: "we are responsible for the quality of sustenance for the next **seven generations**" (p. 61). To talk about food is to talk about land. And to talk about land is to talk about home. Without a safe land base, Indigenous Peoples' relationships to their food systems will continue to be challenged. As all life is interrelated, the energy spent on relationships results in harmony and balance; conversely, disconnections result in dis-ease. In describing her experiences collecting maple syrup, Potawatomi scholar Robin Wall Kimmerer (2013) articulated the responsibilities that Indigenous Peoples have to *participate* in their food systems: "**Nanabozho** made certain that the work will never be too easy. His teachings remind us that one half of the truth is that the earth endows us with great gifts, the other half is the gift is not enough. The responsibility does not lie with the maples alone. The other half belongs to us; we participate in its transformation" (p. 69).

Traditional food practices facilitate a connection to culture, land, and community; this view respects that Indigenous health arises from positive interactions with one's surroundings. For the Cree (Iyiyuu) of Whapmagoostui, Quebec, the term *Miyupimaatisiiun* translates into English as "being alive well." It describes a state where Cree foods are eaten and where hunting and traditional lifestyles are practised to sustain oneself, to keep warm and meet one's goals for self-care (Adelson, 1998). Thus, to practise one's culture, including engaging in traditional food practices, is to work toward being well. Wellness is a community endeavour, however, and Indigenous food sovereignty uncovers a powerful path. It provides a living, breathing example of resurgence. Protecting the land through policy change and land reform, with a particular emphasis on climate change, is critical to maintaining Indigenous food systems and well-being.

CRITICAL THINKING QUESTIONS

1. How would you describe your relationship to the land?
2. How can you show gratitude for all of the gifts that the land provides?
3. What changes are happening in your own community that threaten the land? How can you get involved?

REFERENCES

Adelson, N. (1998). Health beliefs and the politics of Cree well-being. *Health, 2*(1), 5–22.

Cook, J., Frank, D., Berkowitz, C., Black, M., Casey, P., Cutts, D., Meyers, A. F., Zaldivar, N., Skalicky, A., Levenson, S., Heeren, T., & Nord, M. (2004). Food insecurity is associated with adverse health outcomes among human infants and toddlers. *The Journal of Nutrition, 134*(6), 1432–1438.

Coté, C. (2016). "Indigenizing" food sovereignty: Revitalizing Indigenous food practices and ecological knowledges in Canada and the United States. *Humanities, 5*(3), 57.

Daigle, M. (2019). Tracing the terrain of Indigenous food sovereignties. *The Journal of Peasant Studies, 46*(2), 297–315.

Delormier, T., Horn-Miller, K., McComber, A., & Marquis, K. (2017). Reclaiming food security in the Mohawk community of Kahnawà:ke through Haudenosaunee responsibilities. *Maternal & Child Nutrition, 13*, e12556.

First Nations Health Council. (2009). *Healthy food guidelines for First Nations communities*. https://www.fnha.ca/Documents/Healthy_Food_Guidelines_for_First_Nations_Communities.pdf

First Nations Information Governance Centre. (2012). *First Nations regional health survey (RHS) 2008/10: National report on adults, youth and children living in First Nations communities*. https://fnigc.ca/wp-content/uploads/2020/09/5eedd1ce8f5784a69126edda537dccfc_first_nations_regional_health_survey_rhs_2008-10_-_national_report_adult_2.pdf

Hart, M. (2007). Indigenous knowledge and research: The Míkiwáhp as a symbol for reclaiming our knowledge and ways of knowing. *First Peoples Child & Family Review, 3*(1), 83–90.

Kamal, A., Linklater, R., Thompson, S., Dipple, J., & Ithinto Mechisowin Committee. (2015). A recipe for change: Reclamation of Indigenous food sovereignty in O-Pipon-Na-Piwin Cree Nation for decolonization, resource sharing, and cultural restoration. *Globalizations, 12*(4), 559–575.

Kimmerer, R. (2013). *Braiding sweetgrass: Indigenous wisdom, scientific knowledge and the teachings of plants*. Milkweed Editions.

King, T. (Ed.). (1990). *All my relations: An anthology of contemporary Canadian Native fiction*. McClelland & Stewart.

Kuhnlein, H., Erasmus, B., Creed-Kanashiro, H., Englberger, L., Okeke, C., Turner, N., Allen, L., & Bhattacharjee, L. (2006). Indigenous Peoples' food systems for health: Finding interventions that work. *Public Health Nutrition, 9*(8), 1013–1019.

LaDuke, W. (2016). *The Winona LaDuke chronicles: Stories from the front lines in the battle for environmental justice* (S. Cruz, Ed.). Spotted Horse Press.

LaDuke, W. (2019). The White Earth Band of Ojibwe legally recognized the rights of wild rice. Here's why. *Yes! Solutions to Journalism*. Retrieved December 21, 2019, from https://www.yesmagazine.org/environment/2019/02/01/the-white-earth-band-of-ojibwe-legally-recognized-the-rights-of-wild-rice-heres-why/

Lux, M. (2001). *Medicine that walks: Disease, medicine and Canadian Plains Native people, 1880–1940*. University of Toronto Press.

Masioli, I., & Nicholson, P. (2010). Seeing like a peasant: Voices from La Via Campesina. In H. Wittman, A. Desmarais, & N. Wiebe (Eds.), *Food sovereignty: Reconnecting food, nature, and community* (pp. 33–44). Fernwood Publishing.

Mikkonen, J., & Raphael, D. (2010). *Social determinants of health: The Canadian facts*. York University School of Health Policy and Management. https://thecanadianfacts.org/the_canadian_facts.pdf

Minister of Justice. (2012). *Safe Food for Canadians Act*. Retrieved January 10, 2020, from https://laws-lois.justice.gc.ca/eng/acts/S-1.1/index.html

Monchalin, L. (2016). *The colonial problem: An Indigenous perspective on crime and injustice in Canada*. University of Toronto Press.

Morrison, D. (2011). Indigenous food sovereignty: A model for social learning. In H. Wittman, A. Desmarais, & N. Wiebe, (Eds.), *Food sovereignty in Canada: Creating just and sustainable food systems* (pp. 97–113). Fernwood Publishing.

Nabigon, H. (2006). *Hollow tree: Fighting addiction with traditional Native healing* (No. 49). McGill-Queen's University Press.

Pictou, S. (2017). *Decolonizing Mi'kmaq memory of treaty: L'sitkuk's learning with allies in struggle for food and lifeways* [Doctoral dissertation, Dalhousie University]. https://dalspace.library.dal.ca/xmlui/bitstream/handle/10222/72811/PICTOU-SHERRY-IDPHD-APRIL_2017.pdf_.pdf?sequence=1&isAllowed=y

Power, E. (2008). Conceptualizing food security for Aboriginal people in Canada. *Canadian Journal of Public Health, 99*(2), 95–97.

Ray, L., Burnett, K., Cameron, A., Joseph, S., LeBlanc, J., Parker, B., Recollet, A., & Sergerie, C. (2019). Examining Indigenous food sovereignty as a conceptual framework for health in two urban communities in northern Ontario, Canada. *Global Health Promotion, 26*(3_suppl), 54–63.

Richmond, C., & Ross, N. (2009). The determinants of First Nation and Inuit health: A critical population health approach. *Health & Place, 15*(2), 403–411.

Robin, T. (2019). Our hands at work: Indigenous food sovereignty in Western Canada. *Journal of Agriculture, Food Systems, and Community Development, 9*(B), 1–15.

Stonechild, B. (2016). *The knowledge seeker: Embracing Indigenous spirituality*. University of Regina Press.

Tarasuk, V., Mitchell, A., & Dachner, N. (2013). *Household food insecurity in Canada 2011. Research to identify policy options to reduce food insecurity* [PROOF]. https://proof.utoronto.ca/wp-content/uploads/2016/04/Household-Food-Insecurity-in-Canada-2014.pdf

United Nations Food and Agriculture Organization. (1996). *Rome declaration on world food security and world food summit plan of action*. World Food Summit 13–17 November 1996 Rome Italy. Retrieved January 10, 2020, from http://www.fao.org/docrep/003/w3613e/w3613e00.HTM

Willows, N., Veugelers, P., Raine, K., & Kuhle, S. (2009). Prevalence and sociodemographic risk factors related to household food security in Aboriginal peoples in Canada. *Public Health Nutrition, 12*(8), 1150–1156.

Wittman, H., Desmarais, A., & Wiebe, N. (2010). The origins and potential of food sovereignty. In H. Wittman, A. Desmarais, & N. Wiebe (Eds.), *Food sovereignty: Reconnecting food, nature, and community* (pp. 1–12). Fernwood Publishing.

CHAPTER 4

Forced Sterilization: A Malicious Determinant of Health

Yvonne Boyer and Rod Leggett

LEARNING OBJECTIVES

1. To introduce the role of **Indigenous women** in early societies and how **colonialism** disrupted it.
2. To outline the development of the historical injustices First Nations, Métis, and Inuit women have faced in Canada and describe its effects on the health and **well-being** of **Indigenous Peoples** today.
3. To introduce the issue of the forced and/or coerced sterilization of First Nations, Métis, and Inuit women in Canada.

INTRODUCTION

Through efforts such as the **Truth and Reconciliation Commission** (2015), Canadians are slowly beginning to understand how the Canadian colonial state disrupted and attempted to eradicate the cultures of the Métis, Inuit, and First Nations Peoples. Harnessing a malignant belief in their superiority, French and British colonial policy severely damaged existing Indigenous institutions, values, and languages. British policy ridiculed Indigenous Peoples' "respect for the wisdom of elders, their concept of family responsibilities, their willingness to share, their special relationship with the land," and their traditions of healing and medicines (Berger 1977, p. xviii). Less well known is the unique and critical role Indigenous women played in early society; the ways they were targeted by colonial policies following contact; and how they continue to pay the biggest price of a centuries-long systemic assault that has compounded into catastrophic impacts on their health and well-being.

This chapter traces Canada's history of systemic gender-based violence perpetuated by the Canadian state, with a specific focus on recent findings revealing a legacy of forced and/or coerced sterilization, one that appallingly continues to be practised today (Boyer & Bartlett, 2017). First, the chapter contrasts the revered place women held in early societies with the condition and status of women in European societies. Next, it examines how Canada's early colonial laws and legislation were marshalled to subjugate Indigenous women and explains how the legacy of colonialism continues to underpin contemporary health policies. It then details the practice of forced and coerced sterilization as well as the legal and constitutional questions the practice raises before offering a reconciliation framework in which healthcare policies and regulations can address forced and coerced sterilization. It concludes by considering how the healthcare system should be rewritten to reflect the sacred relationship and role women have with the family, the land, and the Creator.

THE REVERED PLACE OF WOMEN IN EARLY SOCIETY

Women played diverse roles in early Indigenous societies, but there is a common thread that becomes especially apparent when juxtaposed against the gender roles of European-rooted cultures and their Graeco-Judeo-Christian inheritance (Fox, 2002). European patriarchy developed power relations which privileged men over women. Men were "considered rational, aggressive, competitive, political, dominating leaders," traits that continue to dominate the political sphere today, while women were seen as "emotional, passive, nurturing, domestic, subordinate followers" (Francis & Smith, 2017, para. 7). When more gender equality penetrated European political culture, its basis was rooted in an equality of individualism and separateness, one that recognized with difficulty a relationship with community and difference. In Europe, women were in positions of subordination and domesticity; in fact, the common law view of women when Europeans arrived in Canada was that they were chattel—property that was dependent first on their fathers and then their husbands (Boyer, 2006). Conversely, Indigenous women controlled the societal power and directed daily affairs.

As Sugar and Fox (1990) explained, "Aboriginal[1] culture teaches connection and not separation. Our nations do not separate men from women, although we do recognize that each has its own unique roles and responsibilities. The teachings of creation require that only together will the two sexes provide a complete philosophical and spiritual balance. We are nations and that requires the equality of both sexes" (p. 19).

Indigenous women's influence would have been alien to a contemporary European woman. They controlled "the economy through the distribution of bounty and ruled the social sphere" (Boyer, 2006, p. 9). They held power in their own way, in "social practices such as inheritance through the female line; female-headed households; pre- and extra-marital sexual relations for women; female-controlled fertility; permissive child rearing; adoptions; trial marriages; mother-dictated marriages; divorce on demand; maternal custody of children on divorce and polyandry" (Mann, 2000, p. 60).

In religious, political, and economic spheres, the place of Indigenous women was complementary, not dependent. Compared to the subordinate condition of women in European societies at the time of European arrival to North America, an Indigenous woman enjoyed a higher standing, more honour, greater equality, and political power among her people (LaRocque, 1994). Additionally, prior to **colonization**, many North American Indigenous cultures were matriarchal. When these matriarchal cultures were forcibly dislodged, the health of Indigenous women and their communities began to deteriorate.

COLONIALISM: THE ARRIVAL OF PATRIARCHAL LAW AND MORES

Canada's institutions claim to be value-free; yet, as we have seen, they reflect, and are rooted in, a Eurocentric worldview and a dominantly male construction of reality. What constitutes "normal" is permeated with patriarchal assumptions that are often alien to Indigenous cultures and the experience of women within these cultures.

From the beginning, colonial statecraft and Britain's economic imperialism targeted Indigenous women's inherent power. The early fur trade, during which fur traders refused to deal with First Nations women, signalled the vicious and damaging transformation to come. An early assault on Indigenous women was legislation passed in 1857, commonly known as the *Gradual Civilization Act*, which framed the inclusion of Indigenous Peoples under British control, i.e., their assimilation, as a form of "honour" and one tied "to the acquisition of private property" (Boyer, 2014). Less than 20 years later, the Canadian Parliament passed the *Indian Act* of 1876, when Indigenous women became locked in a patriarchal system. Their lives became, from cradle to grave, dictated by the Minister of Indian Affairs and the Government of Canada through guardianship by their fathers and brothers (Boyer, 2006).

Section 3 of the *Indian Act* defined an "Indian" as "any male person of Indian blood reputed to belong to a particular **band**; . . . any child of such person; . . . any woman who is or was lawfully married to such person" (Government of Canada, 1876). Not only did the *Indian Act* impose an alien and regressive conception of gender relations onto Indigenous women but it also denied their access to institutions where they could be empowered. For example, entry into medical schools or law schools was prohibited and, later, **Status Indians** would be denied the right to vote or sit on a jury (Henderson, 2020).

Arguably the assimilation powers of the *Indian Act* had its most devastating effects in the creation of the residential school system. Under section 114, the Minister of Indian Affairs was mandated to educate, "civilize," and eventually eradicate the Indian Problem, a process that Justice Murray Sinclair, now a Canadian Senator, termed "cultural genocide" (Truth and Reconciliation, 2015, p. 5). Residential schools separated children from their families. Parents were forbidden to visit their children. The separation facilitated the abuses experienced in the schools, the indoctrination of **Western** norms of living and thinking, and the disintegration of the family unit. With this disintegration came sickness, disease, trauma, and a disastrous cycle of violence that continues today, with Indigenous women bearing the brunt of it (Henderson, 2000; Boyer 2014).

THE DETERMINANTS OF HEALTH AND VIOLENCE

A human is not isolated, but rather is interconnected with family, community, and ecology. Colonization severed this interconnectedness at almost every branch for Indigenous Peoples, resulting in numerous harms affecting Indigenous women. The following offers a glimpse into the results of generations of colonial policies:

- Life expectancy for Aboriginal women is 76.2 years vs. 81.0 for non-Aboriginal women (Government of Canada, 2016).
- Indigenous women are often the victims of family dysfunction resulting from alcohol or substance abuse (National Collaborating Centre for Aboriginal Health [NCCAH], 2012).
- Hospital admissions for alcohol-related accidents are three times higher among Indigenous females than they are for the general Canadian population (Scott, 2007).
- Over 50% of **Aboriginal people** view alcohol abuse as a social problem in their communities. Fetal Alcohol Syndrome (FAS) and Fetal Alcohol Effects (FAE) have emerged as a health and social concern in some First Nations, Métis, and Inuit communities (Public Health, 2016).
- Suicide rates remain consistently higher for the Indigenous population than for the general Canadian population in almost every age category (Kumar & Tjepkema, 2019).

Adding to the above statistics, the burden of poverty of Indigenous women is double that of non-Indigenous women (Townson, 2005). The National Inquiry into Missing and Murdered Indigenous Women and Girls (MMIWG) found that First Nations, Inuit, and Métis women, girls, and **Two Spirit**, lesbian, gay, bisexual, transgender, queer, questioning, intersex, and asexual people (now referred to as MMIWG2S+) have been the targets of violence amounting to a form of genocide (National Inquiry, 2019a, 2019b). Closely linked to the MMIWG's findings is the issue of human trafficking: Indigenous women and girls are disproportionately present in the sex trade, even at times experiencing violence and racism at the hands of those mandated to protect them: the police (Boyer & Kampouris, 2014).

BRIEF HISTORY OF STERILIZATION

The extent of Canada's **eugenics** movement in Canadian law has been known to scholars for some time, but before Drs. Boyer and Bartlett published their 2017 *External*

Review: Tubal Ligation in the Saskatoon Health Region, Canadians generally believed that forced sterilizations no longer occurred. However, Indigenous women continue to be forced or coerced into sterilization, with reports as recently as December 2018 of two separate incidents of coerced sterilization of Nêhiyaw (Cree) women in Saskatchewan and Manitoba. There are between one hundred and two hundred recorded cases of forced sterilization of Indigenous women in Canada today. We believe this is simply an extension and carry-over of the genocidal policies predating confederation.

Canada typically ranks high in its human rights record, but historically has committed gross human rights violations. Eugenics is most typically associated with the Soviet and Nazi regimes. However, long before these terroristic regimes ravaged populations, national eugenic societies—which had created the International Congress for Eugenics in 1912 and which regularly lobbied their national governments—were present in the USA, Great Britain, France, and Canada, and between 1929 and 1938, the Nordic countries introduced sterilization legislation.

As the modern administrative state expanded in the Western world, it was often accompanied by a belief in "meritocracy," a consequence of eugenics thinking. Meritocracy is the belief that humankind can be fixed and readied for modern industrial society through the application of scientific technique. It was a view that especially appealed to health and welfare professionals (e.g., social workers, public servants, doctors, nurses). Individuals identified as in need of reform ranged from those with sexually transmitted diseases or epilepsy to those who were alcoholics or homosexuals; however, across Europe and North America, those identified as having mental disabilities suffered the most from social engineering. Many Indigenous citizens fell into this category. Because of their lower social strata placement, Indigenous women were greatly affected and sterilized in great numbers.

In Canada, this "meritocratic" logic found concrete expression at the provincial level; eugenics legislation was enacted in Alberta (1928) and British Columbia (1933). Though legislation was never enacted in Ontario, sterilizations also took place there. Scholars estimate that over one thousand Indigenous women were sterilized in Ontario alone until the early 1970s (Stote as cited in Senate of Canada, 2019). Though the laws did not directly target Indigenous Peoples and women, sterilization laws nonetheless proved especially dangerous for them. Since Indigenous women did not conform to the social mores established by the colonizers, white-collar professionals of European descent derided their attitudes toward sexuality. As these professionals held the women's declined social standing in equal disdain, a large percentage of Indigenous women were deemed "feebleminded" and thus subject to sterilization (Stote, 2015). For example, while the Indigenous population of Alberta was just over 3%, it represented over 25% of the total people sterilized (Boyer, 2014). We find similar numbers among the Inuit, where the Canadian government had sterilized "26% of women of Igloolik between 30 and 50" (as cited in Boyer, 2014, p. 85). These acts have been qualified as ones of genocide (LeChat, 1976, as cited in Stote, 2015).

The Sterilization of Indigenous Women: A Global Problem

The sterilization of Indigenous women has impacted communities around the world. For example, during the 1990s, approximately 200,000 Peruvian women were sterilized in a family planning program, a crime perpetrated by the Fujimori regime. Most were poor, rural Indigenous and Amazonian women. Maria Ysabel Cedano, Director of Estudio para la Defensa de los Derechos de la Mujer (DEMUS), a Peruvian feminist organization that defends human rights, explained that the women are not only sterilized but are also the targets of sexual violence by **resource extraction** companies and armed soldiers who are bent on profiting from the wealth of the minerals and forests (Cedano, 2019). These atrocities have occurred and are occurring in other countries, such as Australia, Bolivia, Chile, the United States, and Vietnam.

STERILIZATION AND REPRODUCTIVE HEALTH TODAY

In 2015, the Saskatoon Health Authority commissioned an independent external review to uncover why several Indigenous women reported having been coerced into undergoing a tubal ligation procedure in Saskatoon. In response to the external reviewers' call for more information, 16 women called in; how many Indigenous women called but did not leave a message is unknown. Six women were then interviewed face-to-face, and one was interviewed by telephone. Seven more women made appointments but did not attend the scheduled interview. Eight interviews were completed with Saskatoon Health Region healthcare providers. Two additional individuals from the Government of Saskatchewan's Child and Family Services were interviewed together. Importantly, Elders were present to help the women tell their stories and ensure the presence of someone that could, as the authors put it, "hug them back together."

Boyer and Bartlett completed *External Review: Tubal Ligation in the Saskatoon Health Region: The Lived Experience of Aboriginal Women* in 2017. The report illuminated not only one of the countless human rights violations perpetuated against Indigenous women in the past but also one that continues well into the twenty-first century. In their interviews with the women, Boyer and Bartlett discovered abuses of power on the part of healthcare professionals and a general sense of powerlessness on the part of Indigenous women. These abuses of power are rooted in the perverse effects of the Guardian and Ward Theory[2] (Boyer, 2011), which continues to shape the healthcare services for Indigenous women in Canada.

In the interviews, the women reported that, while in hospital and many in active labour, they were:

- given little to no information about what a tubal ligation was or about its consequences for reproductive health;
- intimidated by scare tactics and pressured into signing consent forms;

- discriminated against because of their race;
- threatened that their children could be taken away;
- alienated by the healthcare providers and healthcare system, often feeling invisible;
- forcibly sterilized despite saying "no, the consent form for tubal ligation was just given to me; not explained," or "I refused right up to the very end. Like in the morning. 'You need to sign.' I didn't want to, even on the table" (Boyer & Bartlett, 2017).

In most circumstances, upon seeking advice from a doctor, a woman may choose to have a tubal ligation or select a method of birth control to regulate her reproductive capacity. However, according to Canadian law and basic principles of human rights, a woman's choice must be given with "free, prior and informed consent" (UN General Assembly, 2007, Article 19, p. 6).

In December 2018, the United Nations Committee on Torture (UNCT) called on the federal government to investigate all allegations of forced and coerced sterilization. In March 2021, the Canadian government has yet to fully comply. However, in its reply to the UNCT, the government stated its concern over the reports, expressing it had sent letters of inquiry to provincial and territorial ministers, as well as medical associates and professional regulatory bodies (Amnesty International, 2020). At the Senate of Canada, in spring 2019, the Standing Committee on Human Rights conducted a short study in the 42nd Parliament which had not been tabled yet as of 2021 and heard from several subject matter experts and Indigenous women's organizations. The Senate hearings revealed that the magnitude of the forced and coerced sterilizations was bigger than previously imagined and that other vulnerable communities (e.g., African Nova Scotian women) have been subject to unwanted hysterectomies. Further, peoples with disabilities, intersex children, and racialized persons have also been sterilized. The Standing Committee on Health at the House of Commons also heard witnesses on the issue of forced and coerced sterilization, which they followed up with a series of recommendations to a Government that remains unresponsive.

The class action lawsuits against the provinces of Saskatchewan, Manitoba, and Nova Scotia, led by advocate Alisa Lombard, has cast further light on the extent of the issue. We now know of a minimum of one hundred Indigenous women from across Canada who have reported being forcibly sterilized. Their stories are horrific and tragic, mirroring similar experiences the participants recounted to Boyer and Bartlett that appear in the *External Review*. Along with the human rights violation of having had their reproductive capacity forcibly removed, the women also report high instances of mental health issues and familial and socio-economic marginalization—not to mention the increased likelihood of their being subject to disease because they have been so traumatized that they refuse to seek medical care for themselves or their families. Some stated that as a result, they had never even had a potentially life-saving procedure (e.g., Pap test) performed (Boyer & Bartlett, 2017, p. 22)

LEGAL AND CONSTITUTIONAL QUESTIONS[3]

Indigenous Peoples in Canada have unique constitutionally entrenched rights to health and healthcare. The entrenchment of Indigenous and **treaty** rights in the Constitution means that every Indigenous person carries a set of rights found in section 35 of the *Constitution Act, 1982*. Constitutional rights authorize the fair distribution of power. They determine and limit federal and provincial authority over healthcare and research into traditional health practices. While the *Canada Health Act* is designed to distribute healthcare to all Canadians equally, Indigenous Peoples argue that constitutional difference is a relevant consideration in the just distribution of health rights and entitlements. Treatment of Indigenous Peoples as merely "other peoples" ignores the legacy of colonial violence and their constitutional rights, resulting in the unequal distribution of services and substandard care.

In 1985, when the *Charter of Rights and Freedoms* came into effect, the conception of equality articulated through the provisions in section 15 was that the effect of the law would be to give substantive equality (equality of result) to all Canadians. But equality should not be understood as "sameness," especially where Indigenous cultures and traditions are concerned. The Charter requires an approach that is interpreted by an important distinction: formal equality (equality of treatment), which is the way equality is typically understood, must not be the only consideration; the principle of substantive equality must also be applied. This distinction is important because it affirms that equality should not be construed in the Eurocentric, feminist, or Western legal tradition understandings of "balance" as equating "equality." Indigenous law is not ordered around Eurocentric values or perceptions of what is "balance" or "equality." Rather, for Indigenous women, balance is understood as respecting the laws and relationships that Indigenous women have in their relations to their society (and laws) and the ecological order of the universe.

A complementary understanding of the law is required. Indigenous Peoples in Canada not only possess section 35 rights individually and collectively, but they also possess the individual-based rights identified in the Charter. Moreover, the equality provisions in section 15 of the Charter do not invalidate Aboriginal or treaty rights. The final report of the **Royal Commission on Aboriginal Peoples** explained how the Charter should be approached:

> The Canadian Charter of Rights and Freedoms applies to Aboriginal governments and regulates relations with individuals falling within their jurisdiction. However . . . the Charter must be given a flexible interpretation that takes account of the distinctive philosophies, traditions and cultural practices of Aboriginal peoples. Moreover . . . Aboriginal nations can pass notwithstanding clauses that suspend the operation of certain Charter sections for a period. Nevertheless, by virtue of sections 28 and 35(4) of the

Constitution Act, 1982, Aboriginal women and men are in all cases guaranteed equal access to the inherent right of self-government and are entitled to equal treatment by their governments. (Canada, 1996)

Section 35(4) has rarely been used to advance the equality rights of Indigenous women. Often the gender equality/balance rights that Indigenous Peoples collectively possess are viewed as non-existent, created by statute or "given" to Aboriginal women post-European contact. This understanding is rooted in an erroneous view of history. As discussed above, gender relations in pre-contact Indigenous societies were more progressive than European ones. To suggest Indigenous women were only given rights post-contact perpetuates a colonial view that continues to marginalize and discriminate against Indigenous women.

When a holistic interpretation of the Charter and Constitution is considered, we see not only how the reproductive rights of Indigenous women are protected as individual rights (section 7 and section 15) but also how Indigenous women are equally protected by the principle of substantive equality (section 35). Canadian state, lawmakers, and regulators are obliged to see to the restoration of the health of Indigenous Peoples in this country, especially that of Indigenous women. Their forced and coerced sterilization suggests that Canada is moving in the opposite direction of its obligation—one the country sometimes speaks of in terms of reconciliation. In this spirit, we want to conclude with a possible way forward.

CALLS TO ACTION AND FURTHER RECOMMENDATIONS ON WHERE WE GO FROM HERE[4]

As the twentieth century came to a close, Canada had taken some preliminary steps in addressing the apartheid-like condition for Indigenous Peoples in Canada. In January 1998, the federal government responded to the Royal Commission on Aboriginal Peoples (RCAP). One of the recommendations in the final report was to design and administer programs that could help the healing process and rebuild community life. A related recommendation was to provide funding for treatment of affected individuals and their families. The Aboriginal Healing Foundation (AHF) was created, and we think a similar approach can be taken to address the women who have been forced or coerced into sterilization.

The AHF was designed and run by and for Métis, Inuit, and First Nations. The Board of Directors held a gathering with the survivors of residential schools and their families, from whom the Board received their marching orders. Such gatherings became quite commonplace as the AHF continually sought guidance from those affected. It understood that residential school survivors were the experts on what they had been through, what they had lost, and what they needed. The same should be the case for the women who have been forcibly sterilized and their families and communities.

By making strategic investments, and by contributing to a climate of care, safety, good will, and understanding, the AHF funded effective healing processes relevant to the diverse needs and circumstances of Métis, Inuit, and First Nations, whether on or off reserves, whether status or non-status, based on what they said they needed.

The AHF supported: healing circles, day treatment services, sex offender programs, and sexual abuse awareness initiatives; wilderness and on-the-land retreats; Elder support networks; education and training materials; and memorials and commemorations. Their vision statement addressed the unresolved trauma and intergenerational cycles of abuse.

The AHF is the type of organization which can not only offer reparations but also provide a way to empower Indigenous women who have been sterilized. Most importantly, the AHF model demonstrates that Indigenous Peoples can, and must, take control of their healing.

The principles which informed the AHF model were as follows:

- an independent, Indigenous governance and operating structure
- mandatory and meaningful participation of survivors
- survivor control over how needs are defined
- accountability to government, the public, and Indigenous Peoples

In 2010, the federal government decided to cut the AHF's funding, despite numerous endorsements of its work, including a recommendation from Indian Affairs to renew its funding. There was broad support for the AHF in the media, the Aboriginal Affairs and Northern Development Standing Committee, Parliament, and elsewhere. There was even a rare emergency debate on AHF funding, but in the end, this would not save the organization. We highlight this to show the important role government must play in the reconciliation process and the enormous role it plays in righting the wrongs of colonialism.

One way forward is to have one province take the initiative by passing legislation, drafted by a team of experts, that creates and focuses on a common and high standard for free, prior, and informed consent to sterilization that is consistent with the principles in the **United Nations Declaration on the Rights of Indigenous Peoples** (UNDRIP). If Canadian law can harmonize with the principles that are embedded in the UNDRIP, it will recognize how mental, spiritual, and social well-being is integral to the individual and collective health of Indigenous Peoples. For instance, article 24 recognizes the right of Indigenous Peoples to their traditional medicines and health practices, as well as access to established social and health services without discrimination; article 25 acknowledges the right of Indigenous Peoples to maintain and strengthen their unique spiritual relationship with territories that they have traditionally occupied or used, including bodies of water and other resources. The regulations and policies ensuing from the legislation can be implemented in mandatory province-wide hospital policies. This can serve as a model for other provinces and territories. Work building toward this legislation should include an in-depth consultation and co-partnership with the women who have been sterilized.

CONCLUSION

This chapter began by describing the sacred role Indigenous women played in early societies. Indigenous women were revered as givers of life and honoured for their unique relationships with the family, the land, and the Creator. They also had considerable social power, and Indigenous societies benefitted from their wisdom and unique gifts. With the arrival of the Europeans and their patriarchal mores and legal systems, Indigenous communities, especially the women, suffered an incredible loss. Their ways of life were rejected, and the displacement of their role in society engendered an imbalance that continues to haunt Indigenous communities. Without the presence of Indigenous women who were empowered by their traditional roles, Indigenous societies lost centres of gravity which they are only now slowly rediscovering.

Though awareness of the disastrous consequences of colonialism on First Nations, Métis, and Inuit has increased, the precariousness and plight of Indigenous women is not understood, and policy responses are inadequate. The National Inquiry into Missing and Murdered Indigenous Women and Girls has some shed light on the systemic injustices Indigenous women continue to face. As lawyers and researchers uncover the issue of the forced and coerced sterilizations of Indigenous women, we can even better appreciate the systemic nature of racism and genocide in Canada. Indigenous women are marginalized in poverty, in the highest incarceration rates in the country, in being trafficked, and in vanishing. Removing their capacity to give birth is an affront against their dignity and a way to rob them of a future. Further research into the issue of forced and/or coerced sterilization of Indigenous women—and of other groups of peoples, such as those with disabilities, intersex people, and racialized Canadians, who we know have also been subject to sterilization—is necessary if we are to fully understand its scope and how it continues to happen today.

CRITICAL THINKING QUESTIONS

1. Explain the constitutional rights that could help Indigenous Peoples gain greater access to healthcare services.
2. What do you see as the best way to reform the system based on the sterilization cases?
3. Can you identify the jurisdictional clash between the powers of the federal government and provincial government? Give examples, particularly in healthcare.
4. How can the UNDRIP be used to improve Indigenous Peoples' health in Canada?
5. Do you think the law can be a determinant of health? Why or why not? Give examples.

NOTES

1. In the *Constitution Act, 1982*, "aboriginal people of Canada," includes "Indian, Inuit, and Métis." There is ongoing debate among lawyers, scholars, and academics on the correctness of "Aboriginal," with some preferring to use the terms First Peoples, North American Indian, or Indigenous. The term Aboriginal people is used here as a collective name for the original people living in Canada. The terms First Nation, Indian, Métis, Inuit, Indigenous, and Aboriginal are employed interchangeably depending upon the documentation of the historical and legal language used. It is also recognized that some Nations do not consider themselves citizens of Canada.
2. Prior to 1984, the Crown–Aboriginal relationship was understood to be that of "guardian and ward." This dates back to a trilogy of American case law, particularly the 1831 case of Cherokee Nation v. State of Georgia, where the United States Supreme Court stated that the Cherokee Nation's relationship to the United States "resembles that of a ward to his guardian."
3. Portions of the following section derive from Boyer, 2006.
4. Portions of the following section derive from remarks co-authored by Wayne K. Spear that Senator Boyer delivered in January 2020 at the Informed Choice and Consent conference, organized by the National Collaborating Centre for Indigenous Health, that addressed the forced and coerced sterilization of Indigenous women.

REFERENCES

Amnesty International. (2020). *Canada: Submission to the United Nations Committee Against Torture, follow-up, April 2020.* https://www.amnesty.org/download/Documents/AMR2020992020ENGLISH.pdf

Berger, T. (1977). *Northern frontier, Northern homeland: The report of the Mackenzie Valley Pipeline Inquiry. Volume 1.* Minister of Supply and Services Canada.

Boyer, Y. (2006). First Nations, Métis and Inuit Women's Health. NAHO Discussion Paper.

Boyer, Y. (2011). *First Nations, Métis and Inuit health and the law: A Framework for the future* [Doctoral dissertation, University of Ottawa]. uO Research.

Boyer, Y. (2014). *Moving Aboriginal health forward: Discarding Canada's legal barriers.* Purich Publishing Limited.

Boyer, Y., & Bartlett, J. (2017). *External review: Tubal ligation in the Saskatoon health region.* https://www.saskatoonhealthregion.ca/DocumentsInternal/Tubal_Ligation_intheSaskatoonHealthRegion_the_Lived_Experience_of_Aboriginal_Women_BoyerandBartlett_July_22_2017.pdf

Boyer, Y., & Kampouris, P. (2014). *Trafficking of Aboriginal Women and Girls.* Public Safety Canada Report 2014. Public Safety Canada. https://www.publicsafety.gc.ca/lbrr/archives/cn38634-eng.pdf

Canada. (1996). Royal Commission on Aboriginal Peoples. *Report of the Royal Commission on Aboriginal Peoples.* Vol. 4: *Perspectives and Realities.* Canada Communication Group. http://data2.archives.ca/e/e448/e011188230-04.pdf

Cedano, M. (2019). *Report to the Senate of Canada Standing Committee on Human Rights so that victims of forced sterilization can seek the truth, justice and comprehensive reparation, taking into account the experience in Peru.* DEMUS. https://sencanada.ca/en/committees/RIDR/Briefs/42-1?oor_id=499101

Fox, V. (2002). Historical perspectives on violence against women. *Journal of International Women's Studies, 4*(1), 15–34.

Francis, L., & Smith, P. (2017). Feminist philosophy of law. *The Stanford encyclopedia of philosophy*. The Metaphysics Research Lab, Center for the Study of Language and Information (CSLI), Stanford University. Retrieved March 14, 2020, from https://plato.stanford.edu/entries/feminism-law/

Government of Canada. (1876). *Excerpt from the Indian Act, CHAP. 18. An Act to amend and consolidate the laws respecting Indians. [Assented to 12th April 1876]*. Retrieved February 27, 2022, from https://nctr.ca/wp-content/uploads/2021/04/1876_Indian_Act_Reduced_Size.pdf

Government of Canada. (2016). *Health Status of Canadians 2016: Report of the Chief Public Health Officer—How healthy are we?—Life expectancy at birth*. Retrieved January 10, 2020, from https://www.canada.ca/en/public-health/corporate/publications/chief-public-health-officer-reports-state-public-health-canada/2016-health-status-canadians/page-4-how-healthy-are-we-life-expectancy-birth.html

Henderson, B. (2020). *Notes on the Indian Act*. bloorstreet.com. Retrieved January 10, 2020, from http://www.bloorstreet.com/200block/sindact.htm

Henderson, J. (2000). Postcolonial ghost dancing: Diagnosing European colonialism. In M. Battiste (Ed.), *Reclaiming Indigenous voice and vision* (pp. 57–77). UBC Press.

Kumar, M. B., & Tjepkema, M. (2019). *Suicide among First Nations people, Métis and Inuit (2011-2016): Findings from the 2011 Canadian Census Health and Environment Cohort*. National Household Survey: Aboriginal Peoples. Retrieved January 10, 2020, from https://www150.statcan.gc.ca/n1/pub/99-011-x/99-011-x2019001-eng.htm

LaRocque, E. (1994). *Violence in Aboriginal communities*. Health Canada. http://publications.gc.ca/collections/Collection/H72-21-100-1994E.pdf

Mann, B. (2000). *Iroquoian women: The Gantowisas*. Peter Lang.

National Collaborating Centre for Aboriginal Health (NCCAH). (2012). *The State of Knowledge of Aboriginal Health: A Review of Aboriginal Public Health in Canada*. https://www.ccnsa-nccah.ca/docs/context/RPT-StateKnowledgeReview-EN.pdf

National Inquiry into Missing and Murdered Indigenous Women and Girls. (2019a). *Reclaiming power and place: The final report of the National Inquiry into Missing and Murdered Indigenous Women and Girls (Volume 1a)*. https://www.mmiwg-ffada.ca/wp-content/uploads/2019/06/Final_Report_Vol_1a-1.pdf

National Inquiry into Missing and Murdered Indigenous Women and Girls. (2019b). *Reclaiming power and place: The final report of the National Inquiry into Missing and Murdered Indigenous Women and Girls (Volume 1b)*. https://www.mmiwg-ffada.ca/wp-content/uploads/2019/06/Final_Report_Vol_1b.pdf

Public Health Agency of Canada. (2016). *The Chief Public Health Officer's Report on the state of public health in Canada 2015: Alcohol consumption in Canada*. https://healthycanadians.gc.ca/publications/department-ministere/state-public-health-alcohol-2015-etat-sante-publique-alcool/alt/state-phac-alcohol-2015-etat-aspc-alcool-eng.pdf

Scott, Susan. (2007). *All our sisters: Stories of homeless women in Canada*. University of Toronto Press.

Senate of Canada. (2019, April 3). Standing Senate Committee on Human Rights: Evidence. Senate of Canada. Retrieved April 3, 2019, from https://sencanada.ca/en/Content/Sen/Committee/421/RIDR/54643-e

Stote, K. (2015). *An act of genocide: Colonialism and the sterilization of Aboriginal women*. Fernwood Publishing.

Sugar, F., & Fox, L. (1990, January 15). *Creating choices: The report of the Task Force on Federally Sentenced Women*. Correctional Service Canada. https://www.csc-scc.gc.ca/women/092/002002-0001-en.pdf

Townson, M. (2005). *Poverty issues for Canadian women: Background paper*. Status of Women Canada. http://citeseerx.ist.psu.edu/viewdoc/download?doi=10.1.1.507.3424&rep=rep1&type=pdf

Truth and Reconciliation of Canada. (2015). *What we have learned: Principles of Truth and Reconciliation*. https://publications.gc.ca/site/eng/9.800280/publication.html

UN General Assembly. (2007). *United Nations Declaration on the Rights of Indigenous Peoples: Resolution / adopted by the General Assembly*, 2 October 2007, A/RES/61/295. Retrieved March 14, 2020, from: https://www.refworld.org/docid/471355a82.html

CHAPTER 5

Matriarchal Wisdom: Indigenous Women's and Perinatal Health

Jennifer Leason and Julie Sutherland

LEARNING OBJECTIVES

1. To engage with storytelling (personal experiences) as an Indigenous pedagogy for understanding **Indigenous women's** perspectives on social determinants of health.
2. To outline how social determinants of health impact Indigenous women's health outcomes and **perinatal** health outcomes in Indigenous populations.

STORIES ARE MEDICINE

Stories are medicine. Stories are powerful. Storytelling as an Indigenous methodology allows readers to learn about Indigenous experiences and perspectives. This chapter begins with a story demonstrating how internalized **colonialism**, racism, and sexism have impacted Indigenous women, which in turn can impact perinatal health.

In July 2013, my mother Patricia, my partner, my two children, and I (Jennifer Leason) returned to my mother's birthplace in Camperville, Manitoba. I intended to research my family genealogy and learn as much Anishinaabemowiin[1] as I could from my great aunts and uncles. During our visit, I learned that my grandmother, Eva Cecile Chartrand, attended Christ the King Catholic School, run by Our Lady of Seven Sorrows Roman Catholic Church (Figure 5.3). My mother and I visited the church, where the priest showed us leather-bound books accounting for every birth, marriage, and death that occurred in and around Camperville from the mid-1800s to the present day

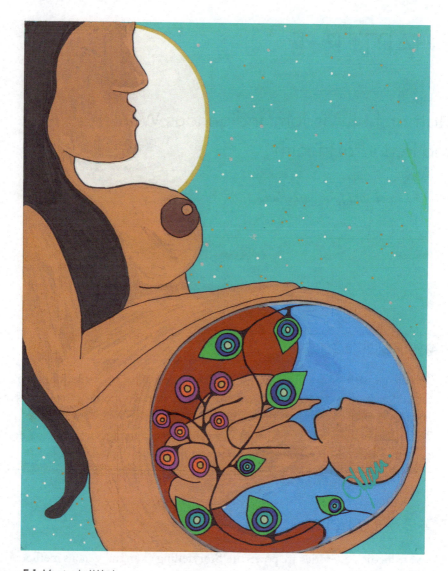

Figure 5.1: *Matriarchal Wisdom*
© Jennifer Leason, 2019.

(Figure 5.4). I was told that I could not copy my family's documents because they "were sacred, confidential and property of the church." Later, I recalled how angry I felt:

> I'll never forget that day, sitting in the church basement while the names of the people we loved were displayed upon the pages. People I had never met or briefly knew; but who you [my mother] knew well. You sat there, shoulders shrunken with tears rolling down your cheeks. I was angry at how upset you were. I was angry while you sat there and did nothing. I was angry that you said nothing. I was angry at you and more so at the priest—you can't tell

Figure 5.2: *Keesis Sagay Egette: First Shining Rays of Sunlight*
© Jennifer Leason, 2020.

me no! You don't own our history! As we headed up the stairs, I held your hand and said, "don't worry mom, we'll get a copy." I'll never forget what you said to me. You said: "who's gonna listen to us? We're just a bunch of Indians." (Personal Journal, July 18, 2012)

A year later, when I revisited the photos of our trip, I was deeply impacted when I put two photos side by side.

- How are the children in the 1940 photo (Figure 5.3) sitting?
- How is my mother in the 2013 photo (Figure 5.4) sitting?

The residential school students circa 1940 (Figure 5.3) are sitting on their hands, with the nun standing in the background. Look at the 2013 photo of my mother (Figure 5.4), nearly 75 years later: she is also sitting on her hands, with the priest in the background. The impacts of **colonization**, including the residential schools' damaging effects, have resulted in generations of **Indigenous Peoples** who feel they must sit on their hands, be quiet, obey authority, and accept what they are given, even if is it unfair and unjust.

Figure 5.3: Christ the King Catholic School Class Photo ca. 1940, Camperville, MB.

Photo credit: Jennifer Leason, personal archives.

Figure 5.4: Patricia Valerie Marie (Chartrand-Fagnant) Leason Sitting in the Basement of Our Lady of Seven Sorrows Roman Catholic Church, Camperville, MB.

Photo credit: Jennifer Leason, August 2013.

My mother's feelings of powerlessness are cruelly ironic. Traditionally, Indigenous women and mothers commanded the highest respect as water carriers and the givers of life. They were sacred (Anderson, 2000) and powerful because they "birth[ed] the whole world" (Bear, 1990, p. 136). Despite their vital role in the preservation of the First Peoples in Canada, Indigenous women disproportionately experience adverse maternal wellness and perinatal health outcomes. This chapter weaves together Indigenous women's narratives and health-related statistics to show how social determinants of health have affected Indigenous women and their babies.

Residential Schools and Intergenerational Trauma

"Historical trauma occurs when trauma caused by historical oppression is passed down through generations. For more than one hundred years, the Canadian government supported residential school programs that isolated Indigenous children from their families and communities.... Under the guise of educating and preparing Indigenous children for their participation in Canadian society, the federal government and other administrators of the residential school system committed what has since been described as an act of cultural genocide. As generations of students left these institutions, they returned to their home communities without the knowledge, skills or tools to cope in either world. The impacts of their institutionalization in residential school continue to be felt by subsequent generations. This is called intergenerational trauma." (Intergenerational Trauma, 2020, para. 1)

As I reflect on my mother's words—"who's gonna listen to us? We're just a bunch of Indians"—I am reminded that no one listened to, believed, or stood up for injustices against "Indians"—especially an "Indian" woman. Indigenous women's voices were silenced by historical, social, political, and economic inequities and power imbalances that have been reinforced through institutions, structures, and policies that continue to suppress, marginalize, and exclude them. They have impeded access to resources and supports, thus impacting the health and **well-being** of Indigenous women and their children.

As we keep telling our stories so that our children understand our traditional ways of being and the ways they were disrupted, we must also continue to speak out about how colonial practices have resulted in inequalities in education, income, food security, safe housing, and access to/confidence in healthcare, among other social determinants of health. These have affected Indigenous Peoples and other racialized and marginalized groups, who have poorer health outcomes than White/non-Indigenous people living in socio-economically advantaged environments (Government of Canada, 2018). Social conditions determine health trajectories and outcomes. The stress these social conditions create widens the gap in health outcomes (Prather, 2020). Because women carry the next generations, their health is vital to the continuance of humankind, and yet the stressful reality of many Indigenous women's lives means they and the children they carry are at risk.

THE PHYSICAL AND MENTAL IMPACTS OF MATERNAL STRESS ON WOMEN AND THEIR BABIES

Many women who live in disadvantaged environments experience chronic stress that can affect their pregnancies and result in poor birth outcomes. Prenatal stress can trigger preterm birth and/or result in a newborn who is small-for-gestational age (Borders et al., 2007). Prenatal stress is also related to infection or inflammation during pregnancy (Alder et al., 2007; Ruiz & Avant, 2005). The number, frequency, and duration of stressful life events impact social health and well-being, including increased maternal psychological morbidity and postnatal depression (Clout & Brown, 2015).

In a recent study (Leason, 2017), Indigenous women shared the importance of social support, talking about emotions and experiences, using humour, exercising, and connecting to nature and culture to help cope with stress:

> *Susan:* I pray a lot and **smudge**. I believe in my surroundings, and I believe in nature. I believe in the drum. I learned about the drum and it's still very healing to me when I hear that drum. I ache to hear it sometimes. (p. 129)
>
> *Lisa:* I pray a lot. Pray and smudge. And I feel instantly better after that. Clear my head. (p. 129)
>
> *Donna:* I started going to sweats [i.e., **sweat lodge ceremonies**] and seeking medicine healers. That's when I started seeking out our culture and understanding it more. Accepting it. And it really did help. It helped a lot because I don't think I've had postpartum depression with this baby because of my reconnecting with culture. (pp. 129–30)
>
> *Mary:* I think that culture has a lot to do with my strength. When I pray, I pray to Creator. I take everything out of my body, and I need to clean my body. Putting it in his hands now. Dancing, smudging, beating the drum . . . all of that helps. (p. 130)
>
> *Linda:* I connect with nature. I get my head in the water. I go for a swim or grab some soil in my hands and feel the earth. Touch a tree. We're part of the earth and people don't realize that, if you let it happen and you give yourself to nature it will take all your worry and stress away. (p. 132)

CONTRIBUTORS TO POOR PERINATAL HEALTH

Despite Canada having among the lowest infant mortality rates (IMR) in the world (5.1 infant deaths/1,000 live births) (Canadian Public Health Association, n.d.a), the IMR among Indigenous Peoples is nearly twice as high as among non-Indigenous people in Canada (Sheppard et al., 2017).

Chapter 5   Matriarchal Wisdom: Indigenous Women's and Perinatal Health   57

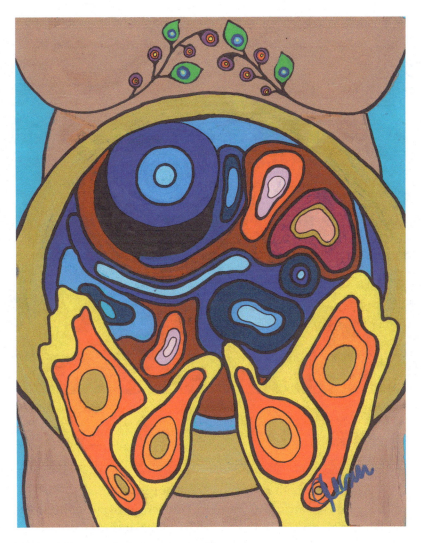

Figure 5.5: *"I make humans, what's your superpower?"*
© Jennifer Leason, August 2018.

The underlying causes of poor perinatal health outcomes are complex, interconnected, and multifaceted. Heaman et al. (2005) found that maternal risk factors, such as previous preterm birth, low weight gain during pregnancy due to nutritional limitations, smoking while pregnant, inadequate prenatal care, and high stress levels contributed to poor perinatal health. Gilbert et al. (2015) discovered a link between poor perinatal health and inadequate fetal growth, placental disorders, and congenital anomalies (i.e., birth defects). Yee et al. (2011) noted that maternal risk factors such as lower participation in health screening and structural barriers related to remote community access contributed to poor perinatal health outcomes. Finally, Varcoe et al. (2013) and Leason (2018) noted that lack of public information and discomfort with

Figure 5.6: *Slow Down*
© Jennifer Leason, 2019.

---

healthcare providers were both risk factors for poor perinatal health. There is a need to support Indigenous women, birth partners, families, and communities by addressing perinatal health disparities and associated inequities, including neonatal or infant death, intellectual disabilities, and behavioural challenges among young children and adolescents (Larson, 2007).

STONES THROWN IN WATER

Indigenous Peoples traditionally understand health holistically, with connections between its spiritual, emotional, mental, and physical aspects. In the same way, Indigenous women's health and perinatal health are not separate from Indigenous Peoples' health more generally. Like a stone thrown in water, the ripples that emanate from the centre represent multiple interrelated determinants that contribute to Indigenous women's and perinatal health. The rest of this chapter will consider a variety of determinants of health (e.g., education, food security, housing) that have either directly or indirectly affected Indigenous Peoples across Canada, and in particular Indigenous women and children.

EDUCATION

Indigenous women experience lower rates of secondary school graduation and lower rates of college/university degree completion than non-Indigenous women in Canada (Aboriginal Affairs, 2006). That said, Indigenous women prioritize education as a pathway to increased income and for its role in improving their self-confidence and opening doors for themselves and their children:

> *Susan*: Education is key to a good income. You can't make money without an education; you can't even get a job without a grade twelve now. So education is key. I'm doing this [getting an education] for a reason. My reasons are my babies. (Leason, 2017, p. 117)
>
> *Mary*: I love my job. I love what I do. I can't wait to go back [after maternity leave]. School gave me confidence. I was so proud the day I got my degree. My whole family is proud of me. And I want that for my kids. I want them to go to school and have a good life. (p. 114)

Despite their desire to receive education, many barriers exist for Indigenous women with children: poor access to safe and affordable childcare, poor access to student loans, and higher costs of raising children related to living in remote and rural regions. Education is vital, however, to improved perinatal health, in part because it "helps build the kind of behaviours and habits that have a positive impact on an individual's health" (Veneman, n.d., para. 5). Women (Indigenous and non-Indigenous) with less than high school education, for example, reported higher rates of smoking during pregnancy; they were also more likely to experience physical abuse and to have experienced three or more stressful life events in the 12 months leading up to the birth of their baby (Public Health Agency of Canada [PHAC], 2009). Higher proportions of post-partum depression were also reported in women with less than a high school education, and women with lower educational levels "were also more likely to report not having enough information about maternity-related topics" (PHAC, 2009, p. 19).

POVERTY

Canada's family poverty rates are among the highest in the minority world (i.e., nations commonly considered "developed") (Canadian Public Health Association, n.d.b), with Indigenous Peoples being among those experiencing the highest rates of poverty (National Collaborating Centre for Indigenous Health, 2020). One study from Manitoba found that women who identified as both Indigenous and living in poverty were less likely to receive adequate prenatal care—especially when they also lived high-stress lives and had low self-esteem

(PHAC, 2009). Two participants in a recent study (Leason, 2017) spoke about their income-related stress:

> *Donna:* I worry about money all the time. I worry about how I'm gonna pay the bills and if I have enough for rent. It's the third time I've been late with rent and I'm scared they'll ask me to leave. Then where are we gonna go? (p. 116)
>
> *Lisa:* I'm doing the best I can [tears rolling down her face, she hugs her two-year old son and kisses him on top of his head]. There are some days I just don't want to get out of bed, but I know I have to for my kids. I gotta be strong for them. But honestly, some days it's tough and I honestly don't know how I'm gonna pay for everything. (p. 116)

Education affects employment levels, employment impacts income, and income influences access to food, clothing, and shelter. In turn, these determinants of health affect access to prenatal care. Lower-income individuals more often have less reliable transportation and are less likely to have employment in which they feel comfortable to request time off. In fact, their lack of access to transportation might be one reason they struggle to find or keep work, which perpetuates the cycle (Allen & Farber, 2019).

FOOD SECURITY AND FOOD HEALTH

Income also determines food access, food availability, nutrition, and food security. A 10-year study examining diet and nutrition patterns among First Nations populations in Canada found that nearly 50% of First Nations experienced **food insecurity** (Assembly of First Nations et al., 2019)—a challenge that is generally more severe for Indigenous women than Indigenous men (Smylie, 2014). Exorbitant food costs in remote communities and barriers to traditional modes of retrieving food have resulted in alarmingly high rates of food insecurity amongst First Nations, Inuit, and Métis populations, both on and off reserve.

Food insecurity is also a result of the expenses incurred when expectant mothers need to travel long distances to give birth—a common occurrence for Indigenous women living in remote and rural communities (see more on this below). The increased expenses related to travel (including the father's loss of income if he must stay home to care for other children or accompany the expectant mother) make it challenging to afford healthy food, therefore affecting prenatal nutrition (Kolahdooz et al., 2016). Studies have noted the need for further inquiry into the unique challenges that result in food insecurity for Indigenous Peoples and have advocated supporting Indigenous Peoples' traditional food acquisition methods and food sharing practices (Skinner et al., 2013).

SAFE, ADEQUATE, AND AFFORDABLE HOUSING

Access to safe, adequate, and affordable housing is an important social determinant of health. Significantly, 17.5% of Indigenous women, compared to 5.2% of non-Indigenous women, live in households with six or more people (PHAC, 2009). Overcrowding is associated with asthma and allergies (Berghout et al., 2005), increased risk of transmitting infectious disease, respiratory tract infections, and higher rates of injury and family tension.

In addition to overcrowded housing, Indigenous women in one study expressed that they experienced barriers to safe, affordable, and stable housing (Leason, 2017). Some Indigenous women on reserve, including pregnant women, also articulated concerns about safety in their current housing, about homelessness or about the safety of migration from on reserve to urban areas. For example:

> *Susan:* I lived out on the reserve and I felt like I had to get out of there. It [the violence] just got to be too much. I left. I was scared, pregnant, and had nowhere to go. I went into a women's shelter in the city and I thought I needed a new start from there. That's what I needed to do, so I went to the shelter and I applied for low-income housing and I stayed with family members for six months because I couldn't get into low-income housing while I was at the shelter. I eventually got into low-income housing and finally things were starting to come together. (Leason, 2017, p. 119)

RACISM, DISCRIMINATION, AND BARRIERS TO HEALTHCARE

In 2019, a survey carried out by Environics Institute for Survey Research and the Canadian Race Relations Foundation found that 53% of Indigenous Canadians have experienced discrimination because of race or ethnicity "from time to time if not regularly" and that "Indigenous Peoples (especially First Nations) are noticeably less likely than others to see race relations as good or having improved over time" (as cited in Johal, 2019, paras. 5, 11). Indigenous mothers face unique barriers when accessing mainstream healthcare, including healthcare providers' perceptions of Indigenous women (Van Herk et al., 2011), discrimination when accessing mainstream healthcare (Browne & Fiske, 2001), and fear of accessing healthcare when child apprehension by government officials is being threatened (Denison et al., 2014; Leason, 2017).

Indigenous women's birth outcomes are inextricably connected with the extent to which they have power, choice, and control over their maternal health and maternity experiences (Varcoe et al., 2013). These women's experiences could improve significantly if the healthcare system were **decolonized** (Varcoe et al., 2013). This means a change to colonial practices and policies, such as Canada's Birth Evacuation Policy, which represents a number of federal and provincial policies affecting women living outside urban centres. These have especially negatively impacted Indigenous women, who are removed not only from their families and communities but also from their traditional birth-giving practices (Cidro et al., 2019). A few weeks before they are due to give birth, expectant Indigenous mothers must be transferred to hospitals that are sometimes hundreds of kilometres from their homes and families to await delivery. Indigenous women must be supported in regaining control over their birthing experiences. This includes modifying policies so that women can deliver their babies closer to home.

REPRODUCTIVE AND OBSTETRIC VIOLENCE AGAINST INDIGENOUS WOMEN AND GIRLS

Ongoing racism and colonial structures have directly resulted in increased violence toward Indigenous Peoples, and particular targets have been Indigenous women and girls and 2SLGBTQQIA people (National Inquiry, 2019). Acts of violence against Indigenous women have included such biopolitical strategies as forced and coerced sterilization (Boyer, 2020; Stote, 2015). Over a five-year period (1970–1975), an estimated 1,600+ individuals were sterilized in "Indian hospitals" throughout Northern Ontario, where certain communities were also targeted for birth control initiatives and abusive abortions for "unfit mothers" (Stote, 2015). Forced and coerced sterilization continues to impact Indigenous women and girls in Canada. There is currently a class action lawsuit by over one hundred Indigenous women nationwide who disclosed that they were sterilized without their consent. The lawyer representing the women, Alisa Lombard, explained:

> Indigenous women . . . reported to us that they had gone into publicly funded administered hospitals in Saskatchewan to have their babies. And while they were in the throes of labour, they would be approached, pressured, harassed to sign consent forms in some cases. In other cases, there was no such signing of a consent form. And in yet other cases, they would revoke consent either on the operating table or shortly after they had actually signed. And so, they would leave essentially, after having given birth, incapable of giving birth ever again. (NPR, 2018)

These acts demonstrate contemporary reproductive and obstetric violence against Indigenous women and the ongoing colonization of women's bodies by the healthcare system.

[handwritten annotation: Why?]

Figure 5.7: *Teepee Teaching*
© Jennifer Leason, 2019.

Figure 5.8: *Ancestors*
© Jennifer Leason, 2019.

CONCLUSION: INTERGENERATIONAL RESILIENCE

While reflecting on my grandmother and mother sitting on their hands, accepting and internalizing the colonial power imbalances that give rise to anti-Indigenous racism and sexism, I (Jennifer Leason) am also reminded of their strength, beauty, and **resilience**. Despite violence, injustice, adversity, and inequities, Indigenous women are surviving, thriving, and resurging. They are asserting their matriarchal power and wisdom. I am reminded of my mother's inspirational words, "Just keep going." I come from a generation of Indigenous women who refuse to sit on our hands—who refuse to accept the unfair and disproportionate burden of women's and perinatal health disparities. I urge you to question and challenge Indigenous health disparities for all women and their children and work to ensure the health and well-being for all, in this generation and for generations to come.

CRITICAL THINKING QUESTIONS

1. What determinants of health discussed above do you think directly affect Indigenous women's health? Which ones are indirect? How do the indirect determinants of health play a role in health inequities experienced by Indigenous mothers and mothers-to-be?
2. What actions can you, as students, take to address perinatal health disparities between Indigenous and non-Indigenous women?

NOTE

1. An Ojibwe language spoken across the territory spanning from Manitoba to Quebec. The greatest concentration is around the Great Lakes.

REFERENCES

Aboriginal Affairs and Northern Development Canada. (2006). *Strategic research: Aboriginal women: Education and major fields of study.* https://www.sac-isc.gc.ca/DAM/dam-inter-hq/staging/texte-text/ai_res_aborig_edu_pdf_edu_1331068496387_eng.pdf

Alder, J., Fink, N., Bitzer, J., Hösli, I., & Holzgreve, W. (2007). Depression and anxiety during pregnancy: A risk factor for obstetric, fetal and neonatal outcome? A critical review of the literature. *Journal of Maternal-Fetal and Neonatal Medicine 20*(3),189–209. https://doi.org/10.1080/14767050701209560

Allen, J., & Farber, S. (2019). Sizing up transport poverty: A national scale accounting of low-income households suffering from inaccessibility in Canada, and what to do about it. *Transport Policy, 74,* 214–223. https://doi.org/10.1016/j.tranpol.2018.11.018

Anderson, K. (2000). *A recognition of being: Reconstructing Native womanhood*. Canadian Scholars' Press.

Assembly of First Nations, University of Ottawa, & University of Montreal. (2019). *FNFNES final report for eight Assembly of First Nations regions: Draft comprehensive technical report*. http://www.fnfnes.ca/docs/FNFNES_draft_technical_report_Nov_2__2019.pdf

Bear, S. (1990). Equality among women. *Canadian Literature, 124–125*, 133–136.

Berghout, J., Miller, J. D., Mazerolle, R., O'Neill, L., Wakelin, C., Mackinnon, B., Maybee, K., Augustine, D., Levi, C-A., Levi, C., Levi, T., & Milliea, B. (2005). Indoor environmental quality in homes of asthmatic children on the Elsipogtog Reserve (NB), Canada. *International Journal of Circumpolar Health, 64*(1), 77–85. https://doi.org/10.3402/ijch.v64i1.17956

Borders, A. E. B., Grobman, W. A., Amsden, L. B., & Holl, J. L. (2007). Chronic stress and low birth weight neonates in a low-income population of women. *Obstetrics & Gynecology 109*(2), 331–338. https://doi.org/10.1097/01.AOG.0000250535.97920.b5

Boyer, Y. (2020). *Our fight against coerced and forced sterilization*. https://senatorboyer.ca/wp-content/uploads/2020/06/Sterilization-Newsletter.pdf

Browne, A. J., & Fiske, J. A. (2001). First Nations women's encounters with mainstream health care services. *Western Journal of Nursing Research, 23*(2), 126–147. https://doi-org.prxy.lib.unbc.ca/10.1177%2F019394590102300203

Canadian Public Health Association. (n.d.a). *Overview: Healthier mothers and babies*. https://www.cpha.ca/overview-healthier-mothers-and-babies

Canadian Public Health Association. (n.d.b). *What are the social determinants of health?* https://www.cpha.ca/what-are-social-determinants-health

Cidro, J., Bach, R., & Frohlick, S. (2019). Canada's forced birth travel: Towards feminist Indigenous reproductive mobilities. *Mobilities 15*(2), 173–187.

Clout, D., & Brown, R. (2015). Sociodemographic, pregnancy, obstetric, and postnatal predictors of postpartum stress, anxiety and depression in new mothers. *Journal of Affective Disorders, 188*, 60–67. https://doi.org/10.1016/j.jad.2015.08.054

Denison, J., Varcoe, C., & Browne, A. J. (2014). Aboriginal women's experiences of accessing health care when state apprehension of children is being threatened. *Journal of Advanced Nursing, 70*(5), 1105–1116. https://doi-org.prxy.lib.unbc.ca/10.1111/jan.12271

Gilbert, N. L., Auger, N., & Tjepkema, M. (2015). Stillbirth and infant mortality in Aboriginal communities in Quebec. *Health Rep, 26*(2), 38. PMID: 25692938.

Government of Canada. (2018). *Key health inequalities in Canada: A national portrait: Executive summary*. https://www.canada.ca/en/public-health/services/publications/science-research-data/key-health-inequalities-canada-national-portrait-executive-summary.html

Heaman, M. I., Gupton, A. L., & Moffatt, M. E. K. (2005). Prevalence and predictors of inadequate prenatal care: A comparison of Aboriginal and non-Aboriginal women in Manitoba. *Journal of Obstetrics and Gynaecology Canada, 27*(3), 237–248. https://doi.org/10.1016/S1701-2163(16)30516-3

Intergenerational Trauma and Residential Schools. (2020). *The Canadian Encyclopedia.* https://www.thecanadianencyclopedia.ca/en/article/intergenerational-trauma-and-residential-schools

Johal, R. (2019, December 11). Majority of Canadians who are Black or Indigenous have experienced racism: Survey. *DH News—Vancouver.* Retrieved October 7, 2020, from https://dailyhive.com/vancouver/black-indigenous-canadian-racism-survey

Kolahdooz, F., Launier, K., Nader, F., Kyoung, J. Y., Baker, P., McHugh, T-L., Vallianatos, H., & Sharma, S. (2016). Canadian Indigenous women's perspectives of maternal health and health care services: A systematic review. *Diversity and Equality in Health and Care 13*(5), 334–348.

Larson, C. P. (2007). Poverty during pregnancy: Its effects on child health outcomes. *Paediatrics & Child Health, 12*(8), 673–677. https://doi.org/10.1093/pch/12.8.673

Leason, J. (2017). *Exploring the complex context of Indigenous women's maternity experiences in the Okanagan Valley, British Columbia by expanding on Aboriginal women's responses to the Canadian maternity experiences survey* [Unpublished doctoral dissertation]. University of British Columbia.

Leason, J. (2018). Exploring the complex context of Canadian Indigenous maternal child-health through maternity experiences: The role of social determinants of health. *Social Determinants of Health 4*(2), 54–67. https://doi.org/10.22037/sdh.v4i2.19504

National Collaborating Centre for Indigenous Health. (2020). *Poverty as social determinant of First Nations, Inuit, and Métis health.* https://www.nccih.ca/495/Poverty_as_a_social_determinant_of_First_Nations,_Inuit,_and_M%C3%A9tis_health.nccih?id=289

National Inquiry into Missing and Murdered Indigenous Women and Girls. (2019). *Reclaiming Power and Place: The Final Report of the National Inquiry into Missing and Murdered Indigenous Women and Girls, Volume 1a.* https://www.mmiwg-ffada.ca/wp-content/uploads/2019/06/Final_Report_Vol_1a-1.pdf

NPR. (2018). *Indigenous women in Canada file class-action suit over forced sterilization* [Podcast transcript]. Retrieved October 9, 2020, from https://www.npr.org/2018/11/19/669145197/indigenous-women-in-canada-file-class-action-suit-over-forced-sterilization

Prather, A. A. (2020, February 24). Stress is a key to understanding many social determinants of health. *Health Affairs.* Retrieved October 7, 2020, from https://www.healthaffairs.org/do/10.1377/hblog20200220.839562/full/#:~:text=Stress%20is%20an%20important%20pathway,risk%20for%20poor%20health%20outcomes

Public Health Agency of Canada (PHAC). (2009). *What mothers say: The Canadian maternity experiences survey.* https://www.canada.ca/content/dam/phac-aspc/migration/phac-aspc/rhs-ssg/pdf/survey-eng.pdf

Ruiz, R. J., & Avant, K. C. (2005). Effects of maternal prenatal stress on infant outcomes: A synthesis of the literature. *Advances in Nursing Science, 28*(4), 344–355. https://doi.org/10.1097/00012272-200510000-00006

Sheppard, A. J., Shapiro, G. D., Bushnik, T., Wilkins, R., Perry, S., Kaufman, J. S., Kramer, M. S., & Yang, S. (2017). *Health reports: Birth outcomes among First Nations, Inuit and Métis populations.* Statistics Canada. Retrieved September 30, 2020, from https://www150.statcan.gc.ca/n1/pub/82-003-x/2017011/article/54886-eng.htm

Skinner, K., Hanning, R. M., Desjardins, E., & Tsuji, L. J-S. (2013). Giving voice to food insecurity in a remote Indigenous community in subarctic Ontario, Canada: Traditional ways, ways to cope, ways forward. *BMC Public Health, 13*(427). https://doi.org/10.1186/1471-2458-13-427

Smylie, J. (2014). *Strong women, strong nations: Aboriginal maternal health in British Columbia*. National Collaborating Centre for Indigenous Health. https://www.nccih.ca/docs/health/FS-AboriginalMaternalHealth-Smylie-EN.pdf

Stote, K. (2015). *An act of genocide: Colonialism and the sterilization of Indigenous women*. Fernwood Publishing.

Van Herk, K. A., Smith, D., & Andrew, C. (2011). Examining our privileges and oppressions: Incorporating an intersectionality paradigm into nursing. *Nursing Inquiry, 18*(1), 29–39.

Varcoe, C., Brown, H., Calam, B., Harvey, T., & Tallio, M. (2013). Help bring back the celebration of life: A community-based participatory study of rural Aboriginal women's maternity experiences and outcomes. *BMC Pregnancy and Childbirth, 13*(1), 26.

Veneman, A. M. (n.d.). Education is key to reducing child mortality: The link between maternal health and education. *UN Chronicle*. Retrieved November 9, 2020, from https://www.un.org/en/chronicle/article/education-key-reducing-child-mortality-link-between-maternal-health-and-education

Yee, J., Apale, A., Deleary, M., Wilson, D., de la Ronde, S., Lalonde, A., Lessard, P., Lessard, P., Senikas, V., Baily, G., Ferrante, J., Cauthier, H., & Stevens, V. (2011). Sexual and reproductive health, rights, and realities and access to services for First Nations, Inuit, and Métis in Canada. *Journal of Obstetrics and Gynaecology Canada, 33*(6), 633–637.

CHAPTER 6

A Reflective Poetic Narrative About a Fine Balance: Indigenous Women's and Gender-Diverse People's Sexual and Reproductive Health

Cassandra Felske-Durksen with Lisa Boivin

Figure 6.1: *We Come with Medicine*
© Lisa Boivin. Reprinted with the kind permission of the artist.

Here is the good news: we all come with the medicine. You see in this painting above—you see the prayers of the mother, she is reaching up into the sky and bringing the prayers into the baby. Then we have the prayers that creator sends us with: they are in utero with the baby. There are lots of things in the painting that are meaningful to me—and that have spiritual meaning. We have the flowers which represent the teachings of the ancestors. Then we also have strawberries, which are women's medicine. One Elder told me it's the only berry strong enough to wear her seeds on the outside. (Lisa Boivin)

COMING WITH MEDICINE

Here is the good news.
Every Indigenous birth is an act of radical resistance[1] against the genocide.
Here is the good news: we all come with the medicine.
Here is the good news.
We have prayers of a mother. She is reaching up into the sky and bringing the prayers into the baby. We have the prayers that creator sends us with: they are in utero with the baby.
Here is the good news: we all come with medicine.
Here is the good news.
Teachings of the Medicine Wheel—body, mind, heart, and spirit—offers to us
balance, a fine balance,   Indigenous reproductive and sexual health.
Consider this. Otipemisiwak Medicine Wheel teachings from Elder Marge Friedel.
Elder Marge Friedel has passed on. Elder Marge taught
that the four quadrants of the wheel represent the
interconnectivity.   East represents the development of our body.
                                South represents our mind.
                                West, the woman's direction, represents our heart.
                                North represents spirit.
In order for us to feel whole and balanced, each one of our quadrants
requires care,   love.

FLESH AND BONE

Here is the terrifying news.
Indigenous women's bodies have been demonized.
Objectified.
Pathologized.
Weaponizing against ourselves.
Self-imprisonment.
By flesh and bone.

If I were a White Man, these are the things that I would be doing to control Indigenous women:
> I would be writing Laws and Bibles.
> I would be making it so that they can't move, can't travel.
> I would be making it so that they can't speak, can't write.
> I would be making it so they can't gather.
> Can't vote.
> Can't get an abortion.
> Can't have a baby unless I say so.
> Can't take care of that baby once they do have it.
> If I were a White Man, these are the things that I would do to control that which is more powerful than me and that which I can't understand.

ONE SONG, LAND

Here is the good news.
Our response: *radical resistance and generative refusal.*[2]
Returning to the land.
Remembering what we were taught (even if only through blood memory).
Identifying as we choose.
Living as we have always done or choose to, without corruption.
See, my people say that we are all one song.
We are born of the same spiritual energy. [...]
The heartbeat. The drum of her.[3]

BODY (east)

We are more than ourselves
> as flesh and bones and neurotransmitters.

We are ourselves in this place
> how we connect to the land
> and the heartbeat.

Anatomy and physiology.
> Not disease-defined.

We are overlapping   anatomy and physiology
our reproductive, endocrine, and central nervous systems.
Sexual and reproductive health are   more than our bodies.
They include our mind, heart and spirit.
We are holistic understandings. We are balance as management. Strengths-based. Protective focused. Community centred. Culturally perpetuating. Relational.

We are a positive and respectful approach to sexuality and sexual relationships.
We are *pleasurable and safe sexual experiences, free of coercion, discrimination and violence.*[4]
We are cisgender, transgender, and gender nonbinary.
We are Two Spirit
Flip the lens on White Euro-Canadian disease-defined diagnostic approaches.
Flip the lens.
Never make assumptions or judgements regarding others' relationships or sexual encounters.
Flip the lens.
Indigenous women's biological agency and control.
Flip the lens.
What is the colonizer's interest in controlling Indigenous women's bodies?
Flip the lens.
Indigenous women—creators of life, are a threat to the colonial agenda.
Flip the lens.
Creation extends far past, and encompasses far more, than literal reproduction.
Flip the lens.

MIND (south)

Healing-Centered Engagement.
Revolutionary questions.
      Revolution of love.
Moving beyond
'what happened to you'
to 'what's right with you.'
those exposed to trauma
are agents in the creation
of their own well-being.
Not victims of traumatic events.[5]
For Indigenous peoples
exposed to trauma
the trauma is experienced
on multiple levels.
Family, community, institutions, systems.
All in parallel.
We are not victims of traumatic events.
Facilitate reclamation
and resistance through creation.

HEART (west)

Figure 6.2: *We Are Medicine*
© Lisa Boivin. Reprinted with the kind permission of the artist.

Remember who you are.
Something my dad used to say to me.
When I felt overwhelmed.
He wanted me to know that I am from generations of matriarchs.
We are from generations of strawberry teachings.
Strawberries are little hearts.
We are always loved by our ancestors.
Are cradled by the love of the land.
This is revealed to us through the little hearts.
We are matriarchs.
We have been left with almost nothing.
We are revitalizing our knowledge systems.
As we piece together what is left.

SPIRIT (north)

Sometimes it hurts to be water.
As we form, we form in water.
As we are born, water precedes us.
Water gives life   carries life away
The Earth is said to be female, and water: her lifeblood.
The Earth is a drum, a spiritual being, and the beat of it is the first sound we hear in the darkness.
The drum of her.[6]
    Christian rhetoric of Mary.
    Saintly mother of Jesus
    versus Eve, the sinful mother
    of humankind. Colonizers imposed this
division on Indigenous women.
Indian Princess or Village Squaw.
The Canadian government took
active steps to subvert
Indigenous women's biological
agency and control.
Exposure to colonization
is the risk factor,
The pathology.
Racism and coloniality in medicine
continue to perpetuate
poor health outcomes
for Indigenous peoples.
Europeans arrived in the lands now called Canada,
and forced their view of gender
on Indigenous Peoples.
Women were viewed   surveyed
Women were viewed as inferior.
Indigenous women are surveilled   as inferior.
Indigenous peoples have the right
to self-identification,
self-determination
and self-governance.
We have the right to celebrate
healthy and positive sexuality
and sex in body, mind, heart, and spirit.
We have the right to decide

if and when to reproduce.
We have the right of access to safe pregnancy
services, giving us the best chance
of a healthy infant and family.
Decolonization of healthcare
requires having a reflective practice.
Fostering cultural humility.
Holding an ethical space.
Make space for Indigenous women.
Our right to self-identify.
Our right to reclaim body sovereignty.
Our right to self-determine our health
and healthcare delivery.
Holding an ethical space.

RETURNING, CLOSING, THE CIRCLE

Here is the good news.
Every Indigenous birth is an act
of radical resistance against the genocide.
Here is the good news: we all come with medicine.
Indigenous delivery
the growth of every Indigenous family
is an act of resistance against
the ongoing genocide.
Every act of sexual and reproductive
choice, is an act of resistance
to White cisheteropatriarchy.
I am a self-identified Otipemisiwak
cisgender woman and physician
in the area of Indigenous women's and gender diverse health.
I am not representative of Indigenous physicians
or of Indigenous women.
      The diversity of Indigenous peoples
          on Turtle Island.
The teachings I offer were passed
on to me from others
          Balance born from love.
               Strawberries are little hearts.
                   Sometimes it hurts to be water.
                       The heartbeat. The drum of her.

Here is the good news.
We all come with medicine.

Figure 6.3: *Within and Beyond*
© Quill Violet Christie-Peters. Reprinted with the kind permission of the artist.

NOTES

1. Radical resistance is a term used by Michi Saagiig Nishnaabeg writer Leanne Betasamosake Simpson in *As We Have Always Done* (2017) to describe the kind of political resurgence many Indigenous Peoples engage in as they assert their right to self-identification and self-determination.
2. Simpson (2017) described generative refusal as a strengths-focused approach to resisting colonialism. She provided an example in nature of this kind of resistance:

   > Yesterday, Ellen Gabriel drove me around her community, past the golf course and through those glorious Kanien'kehá:ka Pines—the magnificent trees of peace that used to exist all over her territory and mine and now only barely exist in small stands. I'm not sure I've ever seen trees this size in my territory. The Pines are peace. They are full of quiet beauty. To me, the Pines themselves are generative refusal. They refused the golf course, and within their roots, barks, needles, and spirit, they continue to generate peace as they have always done. The Kanien'kehá:ka people that protected this place in 1990 are also generative refusal. (p. 233)

3. Simpson (2017), p. 199.
4. International Conference on Population and Development, 2002, as cited in World Health Organization (2008), p. 5.
5. Ginwright (2018), para. 10.
6. Wagamese (2019), p. 23.

REFERENCES

Ginwright, S. (2018, May 31). The future of healing: Shifting from trauma informed care to healing centered engagement. Medium.com. Retrieved January 8, 2021, from https://medium.com/@ginwright/the-future-of-healing-shifting-from-trauma-informed-care-to-healing-centered-engagement-634f557ce69c

Simpson, Leanne Betasamosake. (2017). *As we have always done: Indigenous freedom through radical resistance*. University of Minnesota Press.

Wagamese, R. (2019). *One drum: Stories and ceremonies for a planet*. Douglas and McIntyre.

World Health Organization. (2008). *Integrating poverty and gender into health programmes: A sourcebook for health professionals. Module on sexual and reproductive health*. WHO Western Pacific Region. https://apps.who.int/iris/handle/10665/206996

PART I CREATIVE CONTRIBUTION

Treaty Letter

Armand Garnet Ruffo

In this country I turn to writing after all these years. In Canada we are all treaty people.

I had just moved to Ottawa and found an apartment in what is called Centretown, once the heart of the city before urban sprawl. My apartment was on the third floor in the rear of a stately brick house on a quiet, tree-lined street. I thought, perfect. One day I was talking to the landlord (what's the etymology of *landlord* anyway: lord of the land?) and learned that the area dated to the nineteenth century and had housed the city's countless civil servants. I also learned that where I was living had been the servants' quarters. The notion of employing domestics came to me in a small voice telling me to ask to see the grand living room with its stained glass windows overlooking what once had been an elegant garden. Maids. Butlers. Piano recitals. Poetry recitals. Crystal. Chandeliers. The accoutrements of Civilization (capital *C* here).

That is when it hit me. At the risk of sounding overly dramatic, I swear it was as if two polar opposites, two opposing forces, suddenly struck a resounding chord and came crashing down around me (like a setting of china perhaps. Did I forget to mention fine dining?). To say it all started to make sense in the pretext of a feeble explanation is an understatement. I had inadvertently landed in the nation's capital, that self-same town where decisions by ministers and assistant deputy ministers – though I could easily call them sinisters – of Indigenous Affairs (read Indian) are still being made – or not being made – on our behalf. I went to a file folder and retrieved an old letter I had copied from a document about the treaty negotiations in northern Ontario.

I had kept my great-great-grandfather's yellowed letter throughout all my years of moving around.

> All of my old people who used to hunt
> near here are in great need. The white trappers
> have stolen all our beaver, so there is nothing left
> for them to hunt, and they are too old to go anywhere
> else. There are also about twenty old sick women,
> invalids and orphans who are very badly off
> and they all join me in asking you to help us.
>
> Chief Sahquakegick, Lake Pogamasing,
> Ontario, Canada, December 1884

My pencilled scribbling, my marginalia – if I can call it that – was still legible. Dramatic and angry as the colour of youth. (I include it now with veiled anxiety.)

Children die of hunger as their parents look on. Mothers wail and pull their hair out by the handfuls. An old woman digs with her bare hands for a few roots under a snowbank while her family, too weak to move, wait for her. Without recourse Sahquakegick turns to paper and pen and puts his faith in the Government of Canada. But his appeal lands on a bureaucrat's desk and sinks to the bottom of some dark water. (Too busy. Christmas festivities at the Club Royal?) No help comes. The CPR continues to rake in the cash. The speculators continue to wheel and deal. The profiteers continue to fill their pockets. Desperate whites continue to flood the land looking for a better life. When a treaty commission does arrive Sahquakegick's people will sign anything to stop the suffering. They would trade the sky if they could and really the commissioners want nothing less.

And my friend, now with the passage of time I ask simply: What would you do?

"Treaty Letter" from *Treaty #* (Wolsak and Wynn, 2019) by Armand Garnet Ruffo is reprinted with the permission of the author and the publisher.

PART II

GEOGRAPHIES AND ECOLOGIES OF INDIGENOUS LAND, HEALTH, AND PHILOSOPHY

Part II explores geographies and ecologies of Indigenous **land**, health, and philosophy. Geography is the study of both the earth's physical features and people's relationships with their environment. Similarly, ecology is the study of the interconnectedness of nature and the human and more-than-human world. *Ecology* is derived from the Greek word *oikos*, which means *family* or *home*, and so the study of interrelations of the human and more-than-human world becomes a study of living beings and their homeland. Ecology is particularly significant in the context of **Indigenous Peoples'** health as a function of the relationship they have had with the land since time immemorial. In the chapters in this part, Indigenous voices teach us about the land and its ecology.

Chapter 7, "*Waskitaskamik*" (Dion Stout, Dion Stout), demonstrates the power of storytelling to connect young people to their ancestry. Personal stories illustrate the authors' commitment to upholding cultural strengths in the face of colonial structures, practices, and worldviews that strove, unsuccessfully, to destroy their family and community's ways of knowing and being. The chapter highlights the importance of example setting so that young people's strength and goodness can survive the stark realities of the present day.

Chapter 8, "Damaged, Not Broken" (Teegee, de Leeuw), reflects on the daily impact of White settler violence on the health of Indigenous communities, families, and individuals. It depicts how colonial laws and policies were introduced with the aim of destroying Indigenous Peoples' languages, traditional roles, customs, and practices. The chapter pays particular attention to the ways in which colonial violence endangers women and children; but, crucially, the author emphasizes that while Indigenous Peoples are damaged, they are not broken.

Chapter 9, "Our Highways, Our Tears" (O'Toole, Sloan Morgan, McNab-Coombs), traces how **resource extraction** has created unique health disparities among **Indigenous women** and **Two Spirit** people. It underscores how the interconnection between land and living beings relates to Indigenous Peoples' health. The authors introduce the concept of "environmental violence" to show the impact of resource extraction on lands and bodies. They also honour the creativity and strength of Indigenous communities that engage in myriad ways to combat gender-based violence through systemic transformation.

Chapter 10, "Legislation, Reconciliation, and Water" (Behn Smith, Waters), argues for the reconciliation of Indigenous and **Western** perspectives of water to advance Indigenous **self-determination**, health, and **well-being**. The chapter outlines legislation and strategies in British Columbia that regulate and protect drinking water, and it advocates "environmental personhood" legislation as a means for Indigenous Peoples to uphold their reciprocal relationship with nature.

Chapter 11, "Inuktut as a Public Health Issue" (Kotierk), introduces readers to language as a vital determinant of health. It reveals that most Inuit in Nunavut do not have access to adequate health services in their mother tongue, **Inuktut**. It celebrates the **resilience** of Inuit, who keep Inuktut alive despite a lack of federal support. It stresses that an equitable healthcare system—one which offers services in a language patients can understand—plays an important role in reconciliation.

Part II closes with a poem, "Cactus and Wild Roses" (Gottfriedson), which celebrates nature as a lifegiving force. The poem draws attention to "sloppy policies" and "foreign laws" that compromise the health of the people while also illuminating the people's resilience and the **land-based healing** that empowers them to resist "wrongful acts" against both them and the land.

CHAPTER 7

Waskitaskamik: On the Face of the Earth

Madeleine Kétéskwēw Dion Stout and Miyawata Dion Stout

My kohkom—my grandmother—and I were born 60 years apart. When I was small, if I couldn't remember her exact age, I only had to add 60 to my own. As a little girl, I didn't ask too many questions about her life, unless it was bedtime and I wanted an old-time story. But now a youth exploring my Cree identity, I'm asking more questions of her. I see how dramatically the world can change in only 60 years. My name is Miyawata Dion Stout. I am in Grade 8 and a climate activist. Writing is my passion. My family hails from the Kehewin First Nation in Alberta. As a person born in today's world, I was raised in a highly urbanized environment. The city has brought many opportunities for me, but like others around me, I feel a disconnection from the land. In just 60 years, our family has gone from living in log cabins to inhabiting sprawling urban houses. We went from a life of surviving off the land, in relationship with animals, to one dependent on technology and superstores.

I have also always been drawn to my kohkom's stories and the ethereal past they offer a window into. As young people in a rapidly changing world, the importance of storytelling cannot be understated by us. The disconnection we feel vanishes as we immerse ourselves in the gentle words and adventures of the people before us. On a recent winter afternoon, I sat down with my kohkom and asked her to tell me some old-time stories about our family and about what she experienced growing up. I also asked her if she could have ever known of the changes that would descend upon the Cree people.

Miyawata, *nōsisim, mistahi ninanāskomon enaniswapiýa kici kācimostatan kayas ōma kakispaýik.* Miyawata, my grandchild, I'm really grateful we have this time to sit together so I can tell you some old-time stories. I hope you see how these stories captured events that forced us to respond to the futures they foretold for your ancestors, the earth, and earthly beings like you and the people who will be reading the stories I will be sharing with you. We Cree, *nēhiýawak,* have a lot at stake in these changing times—therefore, we have to know and learn from our identity stories. The best way I can explain this urgency to you and other readers is as follows:

Kēhtē-iÿinowâk, the Ancient Ones, were strongly committed to their heritage, *tāhkinowin*, a reality that was most evident on the ground, often at the most ordinary levels. Even though they often struggled to do so, *kēhtē-iÿinowâk* very rarely squandered an opportunity to showcase our ancestors, creation stories, history, lands, and languages. Their connection to spirituality, to *ahcahkowin*, was unmistakable, unapologetic, and exemplary, for they called one's spirit *ahcahkw*; the stars in the sky *acâhkosak*; and the kinship word between women *nicâkos*. The oneness they found with Mother Earth, *okāwimāwaski*, and all their relations, *wāhkōmakāniwawâ*, was believed to yield desired states of **well-being** like reparation, recovery, renewal, and reconciliation.

Kēhtē-iÿinowâk, the Ancient Ones, routinely gave protocol to the earth, *asiskiy*, and to animal beings, *pisiskiwak*, because they were far too humble, too aware of their rightful place, and too much in awe of those who had gifts more rarified than theirs. The diversity and unity of all creation was not lost on them, especially when they saw *Kitchi Manitou*, the Great Spirit, as being inextricably related to *manicosak*, Little Great Spirits or insects. By leaning heavily on *īsihcikewin*, or culture, they avoided *kitimakisona*, poverties of all kinds—a practice that helped them move forward with a sense of hope, not only lament.

Kēhtē-iÿinowâk, the Ancient Ones, lived and breathed *kayās-isīhcikēwin*, the Old Ways, with an unswerving recognition of the healing fruits of nature, like *takwahiminānā*, chokecherries; *iÿinimina*, blueberries; *otēhimina*, strawberries; and the herbs that were ground or brewed into medicine, *nātāwapokan*. Moreover, they well understood the cunning wiles of coyotes, *mēstacākansak*, and owls, *ōhōwak*, along with the restorative power of medicine bundles, *iwatâ*. The worldviews and views of the world of the Ancient Ones were shaped by imagination, *wāpahcikātēwin*, traditions, *kāyas-isihicikēwin*, and innovations, *osk-āyiwan kikway*, that are consistent with born and bred helpers of the earth and its inhabitants. The life and times of *nāpēw*, man; *nimamsinan*, the mother of all; *nimis*, my older sister; *otōsimimāw*, my nephew; *nikāwyi*, my mother; and *āniski-ohtāwimāw*, my grandfather, will inform the stories I am about to tell you.

I was born at home and raised on the Kehewin First Nation, but my birth certificate says I was born in Gurneyville, a village that was off the reserve. I guess the government wanted to show we had no origins to Kehewin so that our little reserves would one day be declared empty since nobody would have been born in them. Kehewin means the *home of the eagle*. Likely, all of my brothers' and sisters' birth certificates would have said they were born off the reserve too, yet all of them were born in the *home of the eagle* with the help of midwives. The nickname my family gave me was *Ciken*. A lot of people back home still call me *Ciken*. It doesn't mean anything, although my brothers have always teased me because they said *Ciken* sounds like *chicken* to them.

Your great-grandfather, Billy Dion, was a hereditary Chief until the *Indian Act* changed that. Our family was to inherit Chieftainship over the generations, but this tradition broke with him and his generation. My mother's, your great-grandmother's, name was Sarah Youngchief. My father used to affectionately call her *Nōtokwēw*, meaning "the old woman." When my mother and my father got married, they just had a little feast under a tree. They were 18 and 21. My parents took in other relatives over the years so that no one was left homeless or uncared for but also because my parents needed help taking care of their 10 surviving children.

My early bonding and attachment with *Nāpēw*, man, show how signals of sweet sentiments come alive when children use attachment behaviours like crying, clinging, following, and cooing to show they need care. *Nāpēw*, a war veteran, was my consoler-in-chief and caregiver when I was a toddler. Because I was the fourth youngest in a family of 12, my mother welcomed every helping hand. And so it was that *Nāpēw* came to live with us. Every time I saw *Nāpēw* until he sadly passed away, he recounted the same stories about me as a toddler under his care. He would always begin by saying *"Hey hey ciken! eki maphi mastoskeyin mana"*—"Hey hey ciken! You were always such an incessant crier." Then he would tell me about the time he stopped my crying by making a soother for me from a lump of sugar tied into a piece of cloth with string. Even though cloth and sugar were precious commodities in those days, *Nāpēw* still pressed them into his corporal acts of mercy on my behalf. *Nāpēw*'s other favourite story was about the meltdown I had after breaking my rare glass baby bottle. In his resourceful way he found a wine bottle, filled it with the raw cow's milk we drank back then, slipped the long rubber nipple on the wine bottle, and with great relief watched me recline in repose, happily cradling my homegrown baby bottle, suckling on the milky white contents.

The wine bottle that replaced my baby bottle has proven significant because it introduced alcohol use into my community. Looking back, I feel that *Nāpēw* may have been experiencing PTSD after serving in the war and was probably drinking a lot as a result. I believe his own trauma allowed him to see just how therapeutic having an improvised milk bottle would be to me. At the time, his actions were really important because he gave me comfort and sustenance. I think that as a child or a youth, the most basic human needs are love and attention. I got those mostly from my caregivers, especially in my early years when my mother and father were so busy. As I grew older, I began to understand what my mother and father had done for us and how and why they did it.

We grew up in a two-room log house. Every fall, the men would gather to winterize the houses by re-chinking between the logs with a mixture of clay and straw, a demanding but essential way of protecting their families from overexposure to the elements. To keep their houses warmer, they would bank up snow around the bottom peripheries from where cold drafts often escaped into the houses. Such was our closeness to the earth and environments in those days. The land provided us with ready resources; in turn, we were resourceful with its provisions. This connection makes one think of the ancientness of the earth and how it has served our basic human needs for shelter over time. It is really hard to fathom this connection when construction companies are assembling prefabricated, unaffordable houses with little regard for the detrimental impacts on the earth. In my lifetime, our connection to the land has deteriorated to the point where we are not able to see, feel, hear, smell, and taste it on a daily basis. I still remember the time when, as a child, I really wanted to eat dirt, so I broke off a piece of clay chinking from our house to satisfy my craving. Because I didn't like the taste of the white paint on the clay, I spat it out. This was a good choice to make since I later found out that white paint was likely laced with lead. In nursing school, I found out that dirt contains iron, a nutrient our body naturally requires. When I think back, I was probably low on iron when I ate my house. I am not saying people should eat dirt as a main source of iron; rather, I am trying to emphasize the healing power of the land and its offerings. After I shared the story about eating the clay chinking of my house at a speaking engagement on my rez, my cerebral cousin very seriously asked my mischievous cousin, "Did Madeleine live in a two-room house?" The response was swift and hilarious: "No she didn't because she ate up one of the rooms."

In Cree, I use two words to describe a reserve. One is *tipahaskan*—measured lot; the other is *iskonikun*—leftover plot. So even though all of Canada is our homeland, we were relegated to these "leftover plots" and "measured lots," which alienated us further from the face of the earth where the land was abundant, full of largesse. We had really strong ties to the land because it fed and sustained us, and we lived as one with the animals and plants on it.

Our ancestors were hunters and gatherers until the government forced them to become farmers only to deforest their little "leftover lots" and "measured plots" to grow grain, a little bit of oats, a little bit of barley. They never had huge crops but at least they tried. As I've said, we didn't have cars or trucks, we had wagons and horses. We tended to visit a lot with each other, especially at times of celebration like Christmas and New Year's. New Year's Day was known as *ocēhtowi-kisikā*, the kissing day.

To this day, we call horses *mista-atimwak*, meaning "big dogs." Long before horses became commonplace, *atimwak*, the dogs, were the animals that helped us move from place to place—from one camp to another. Even though the people mourned the dogs who were being rendered archaic by bigger and more modern animals, they passed on their reverence for animal beings to the horses that had displaced the dogs, knowing full well the added value of the horses with whom they also had a symbiotic relationship. I have a story that illuminates the synergy between *mista-atimwak* and us. Last February, *Nimis*, my older sister, told me about her encounters with *kēhtē-iyinowâk*, the Ancient Ones, specifically *Nimamasinan*—the mother of all—who was the daughter of *Imsees*—the Hard Hearted One—who himself was the son of the late, great Big Bear—*Mistahi Maskwa*. Perhaps because we too are direct descendants of her grandfather Big Bear, *Nimamasinan* lived with us for long stretches of time when we were young. One day *Nimamasinan* saw a newborn foal racing frantically back and forth by the tent where *Nimis* and *Nimamasinan* had chosen to camp out rather than stay at home in the log house next door. "*Nicanis*, my little daughter, go and see what the problem is," called out *Nimamasinan*. "This newborn horse is in distress." At this, *Nimis* ran over to the reddish-brown mound that was in her sightline and back to *Nimamasinan* to report that the foal's mother was lying on her side, unable to move. When they both checked out the mare more closely, it was clear by her bloated belly that she had consumed too much from the meagre harvest of grain she lay by. "*Nicanis*, go and fetch a pail of water right away," ordered *Nimamasinan*. She then added *sāpohsikan*, an herbal medicine that loosens the bowel, to the pail of water. *Nimis* held the mare's head in a way that the mother horse could more easily drink the medicated water *Nimamasinan* was administering to her. *Nimis* was so close to the action she could hear and see the mare's gulps. At the same time, she took note of the foal's white marking on the forehead, along with the muffled and anxious sounds he was making. *Hmph hmph hmph!* I've heard traumatized people make this same sound. Soon enough the mare's bowels moved rather dramatically. When the mare sat up, *Nimamasinan* said, "*Nicanis*, run and fetch two ribbons; they need not be too long," gesturing from her fingertips to her mid-arm. "Bring a sky-blue ribbon, *sipihko senipan*, and a blood-red ribbon, *mikho senipan*." *Nimamasinan* methodically tied these ribbons on the mare's mane, all the while uttering relational words of gratitude and encouragement. In time, the newly adorned *kiskinowācihow*, mare, stood up and shook herself loose from the clay. We have a word for such an action: *papahowew*. After yielding her life-giving, engorged breasts to her foal, she and her newborn walked to the other horses in the field, hard-wired as one.

Nimamasinan, the mother of all, and *Nimis*, my older sister, wanted to save the horse, not just because it was servile or because it provided a service, but because they honestly respected and loved that fellow being. That's spirituality. The ritual site for human kind and kind humans—like *Nimis, Nimamasisnan, Imsees*, and the legendary *Mistahi Maskwa*—is *waskitaskamik*: "on the face of the earth and the clay we all come from." Other *kēhtē-iýinowâk*, Ancient Ones, just like these four, routinely resorted to *wansisohowin*, atoning for transgressions against other beings who raised them and the planet who fed them. Often heard in their midst were *mawimowina*, or cries for help, to the Great Spirit who was known to be inextricably related to *manicosak*, Little Great Spirits—insects, their next of kin. *Nēka! Nēka!* Mother! Mother! was *Nimamasinan*'s characteristic cry when she saw nature under attack, when traditional names were mocked, and age-old norms were cast asunder. *Nimamasinan* cherished and honoured earthly creatures like the horse, *mista-atim*, the big dog, natural occurrences like thunder and lightning, and the medicines the earth offers up. She valued generative medicines like water, *nipi*, and bonding and attachment between humans and animals. Ancient Ones like *Nimamasinan* asked personal questions in relational ways. For instance, they would ask *if we had seen our grandmother yet* if they wanted to know whether we'd had our menstrual period. In the same way, *Nikāwyi*, my mother, felt us suckling on her breast before we, as adults, arrived home, unannounced from faraway places.

Another story that reminds me of our profound connection to the land, the kinship ties in our communities, and our spirituality is one I'll simply title "*taskam* highway." *Otōsimimāw*, my nephew, shared this story with me, which concerns a wagon trail. Taskam highway is a curious kind of name. Half of it is in English and half of it is in Cree. *Taskam* means "cut across" and "highway" literally means a roadway. Although it was just a wagon trail, the people referred to it as "*taskam* highway" because it coursed through their reserve community, binding it as it went. For them, it was also a place name and a marker of who lived on that side of the trail versus who lived down from the house near the trail. In those days, the White farmers would lease from the reserve land for pennies in order to seed and grow their crops at very little cost. *Otōsimimāw* said how upsetting it was for the reserve residents to learn that one farmer was bringing White women to clear the farmland by picking rocks and roots. Instead of paying the men from the reserve to do that labour, this White man brought in his own outside helpers. The men from the reserve who would normally do the rock picking and root digging now became jobless. Still, the worst thing that farmer did was to till away *taskam* highway from the face of the earth. The wagon trail had marked time, place, and relationships, yet it was wiped out forever when, with his modern machinery, the farmer destroyed any semblance of it. He reduced *taskam* highway to lost memories of the way *kēhtē-iýinowâk*, the Ancient Ones, had lived harmoniously for a very long time. He destroyed the community's way of life along with their connection to one another, and with that he took big pieces of the community's heart and spirit. The men who were so upset over the unfolding injustice protested by holding a sit-in at the Chief and Council's office, just like young people today are sitting in for and standing by the fight against climate change. The underlying principle for people in these cases is *ôma ka-nîpawisitamahk piko ka-wi-tapistamahk*: "What we stand by, is what we have to sit in for." That the men who were cast aside in the name of progress still sat in for what they stood up for was very positive, but it took a lot of moral courage to take the position and resist. *Otōsimimāw*'s story saddens me because the lost highway traumatized the people to the core. More importantly, the story illustrates a microcosm of the harm we are inflicting on the face of the earth, *waskîtaskamik*.

We also experienced other radical changes in our lives. In particular, I remember October 15, 1958 because that is the day we moved into our new government-built house, which to us was ultra-modern in character. Yet its grey siding and sinister spectres compelled us to call it the "grey house." Not only did the grey house herald the beginning of our shift from self-reliance toward more dependence on the government but it also brought social problems to a head. Overall, it created a grey, dismal, depressing scene for us. To have a house built for you without any say in the matter is not fair, sustainable, or just. This kind of house is hard-pressed to become a household let alone a home. The day we moved into the grey house, the paint on the windowsill was still wet. I remember scratching the date, October 15, 1958, on the windowsill. I also noticed the men had started to drink a lot more because they no longer had to build and maintain their houses. The traditional roles they'd long practised as protectors and providers were being seriously eroded by government policies that were set out to modernize us.

A big highway routed right through our small reserve allowed us to see and covet the freewheeling cars and trucks. For modernity's sake we gave in to the temptation to buy and drive the vehicles that are now the cause of many deadly accidents and are among the main culprits of climate change. My brothers wanted a car, so what did my dad do to indulge his sons? He sold our precious cows and bought the boys a seafoam green coupe, and a lemon at that. When that car came into our family, the horses were displaced, another blot on the landscape and cause for our estrangement from nature and natural beings. My brothers drove this car around until it really began to fall apart. They then made it into a convertible by using a hacksaw to cut the top off. Once, 13 of us rode in the newly minted convertible, piled up on one another. The police sent us right home that night for good reason. After the boys had severed the coupe, they decided to drive it to our cousins' place. When one of my cousins saw the "convertible" crest a nearby hill, she called out in a panicked voice, "*ka-ti pakwesikan*—hide the bannock; *moniÿawôk papayowôk*—White men are driving here."

People today place a lot of emphasis on traditional knowledge without giving due credit to the power of example-setting, which is still one of the best ways to teach and learn by. My beloved *āniski-ohtāwimāw*, grandfather, lived with us in the grey house. He was a very industrious protector and provider. He was old then and blind in one eye, but he still made a screen door for our grey house, using tools like a saw and chisel. I remember sitting on a rock, watching him whistle while he patiently worked to perfect the door. When he finished the frame, he bought a wire mesh to add to the top half of the screen door. Although my grandfather believed in his Indigenous traditions, he was also a well-read Catholic. I remember one Easter morning, he called out, "*astām awāsisak*: come here children!" He then instructed us to look through the screen door where we would see the sun dance. According to my grandfather's belief, even the sun was jubilant because all our relations had risen from the dead and dread right here *waskítaskamik*: on the face of the earth.

This story shows how important it is to watch people go about their lives and times. By being observant and mindful, life-altering teachable moments are more readily perceived, passed on, and practised. Setting good examples is part and parcel of doing things right for less privileged people, especially children, and for treating the earth and its creatures with utmost affection and respect.

Many years later, we moved to Ottawa, where we lived for 18 years. All the while, I was carrying my belief that owls warned us about imminent danger, even death, especially if they hooted within our range of hearing. As I stepped outside for my daily walk on a darkening April evening, I heard two owls hooting back and forth. They kept hooting for the full hour I was on my walk. It occurred to me that I'd never heard an owl in Ottawa even though we'd been living there for almost 18 years. To put myself at ease, I stopped in my tracks and said, "Madeleine, you are an educated woman, just enjoy the sounds of the owls. Don't think past that." I let go of my encounter with the owls by completely shutting out the whole experience. Not long after, my brothers called to tell me about my mother's precarious health issue, but they reassured me she would be okay. When I called *Nikāwyi*, my mother, at the hospital, she described her heart attack to me this way: *mowéci épaskipiýan nāskikanih*: "I feel like my chest has exploded." Whenever she was burdened by grief and loss, *Nikāwyi* used to say she felt like she was being strangled by the pain—*tāpiscōc épihkitonēhpitikoweyan*. I now understand how critical it is to dislodge the pain that wells up as tears at the back of our throats.

Had I held my belief about owls front and centre, I would have flown home to Kehewin right away. I really feel those owls had come to tell me that *Nikāwyi* was in grave danger, but I chose not to heed their message. It was not long after my mother's passing that I lost my youngest brother too. Those two owls that were hooting during my walk were telling me of the imminent deaths of my mother and brother. Nowadays, we are all plugged into our mind-numbing machines, our podcasts, our playlists. If I had been plugged into my hand-held device, I would not have heard those owls forewarn of the peril ahead. When I hear about birds and animals being subjected to extinction by climate change all over the world at unprecedented rates, I feel the stranglehold of deep loss and grief. I ask questions that are not easily answered. Will there be enough creatures to warn us when danger rears its ugly head? Will there be songbirds to sing to us? What is our recourse in this heartbreaking situation? How do we move forward in a generative way?

I couldn't have foreseen what's happening today. I simply couldn't have anticipated it when I was a young girl growing up in Kehewin. For one thing, I remember how brilliant the stars were at night because we didn't yet have light pollution from street lamps or satellites. We only had a kerosene lamp that my dad would carry to the barn at milking time. I would walk with him while marvelling at the star-studded night sky. At times like this, I felt surrounded by Creation and creatures, just as the *kēhtē-iýinowâk*, the Ancient Ones, had likely felt too. The night sky was replete with reminders for living on the face of the earth dutifully, beautifully, and exhaustively. I saw *acāhkosak*, stars, decorate the heavens in formations at night. I witnessed *acāhkosak* routinely fall out of the sky and splinter into *ahcahkw*, a soul and/or spirit. Our connection to the stars is evident in the way their Cree name is rooted in the name we ascribe to souls and spirits. Cree women call one another *nicâkos*, meaning my fellow-star, my soulmate, my kindred spirit, my sister-in-law. Given all these star-related word connections, we believe we are star people.

Nōsisim, my grandchild, when you asked me if I thought things would ever change in my lifetime, I never thought the night sky would one day become so polluted I would not be able to see the stars in brilliant formation again. Sadly, I think this is already happening. We used to see a lot of Northern Lights in Northern Alberta, where we lived. We could see them dancing splendidly across the sky in sheets of blues, greens, yellows, and reds. They were quite simply a brilliant and dramatic display of nature. We always believed the Northern Lights were our dancing ancestors, our *cipayak nimihitowak*. It will be a sad day when the Northern Lights are no longer visible. If you cannot see your ancestors dancing up there ahead of you, you will not be able to prepare properly for your return to the stars. Our belief systems will also be very badly eroded, as well as our kinship ties with all our relations. We talk a lot about reconciliation in this day and age and the importance of realizing it. Reconciliation, in Cree—*peci miýo wicētowin*—means hither, to here, thence lie good, well, beautiful, valuable relationships. I have to wonder if reconciliation is as doable as we once thought, especially since our relationship with the stars is being broken, our relationship with songbirds is under siege, and our relationship with healthy trees and healthy animals is being threatened. If we can't relate to Creation the way our ancestors used to, I don't know how much reconciliation can happen *ōma waskitaskamik*—here on the face of the earth.

> I thank my kohkom for sharing these stories with me.
>
> Life is a circle. We hear that a lot, but the saying rings true. My kohkom and all the women before her were raised on the land, in tents and tipis and log cabins. I was raised in a house, on a street, in a city. But my soul aches for the land, and I have sought it out throughout my life. When I was 11, my friends and I went off to camp for a weekend, out of the city, and away from the world. I don't remember much about camp that weekend, except one thing that happened during the last night, that I'm sure will stay with me for the rest of my life. It was midnight, or close to it. The moon was plump and doughy and as we walked through the forest, we saw it flash through the breaks between the branches. When we broke through the trees, the moon seemed to swallow us. It was so cold, cold enough that we shivered under our layers. We had come into a wide open plain of frozen lake, only a bare white sheet in the darkness. As we began to walk, we turned off our flashlights, and placed them back in our pockets. After our eyes had adjusted, we looked up to see a sky brimming with stars that danced and twirled, the halos of soft light around them like lace. Kohkom told me once, how every night, she saw that sight. But this was the first time I ever got that sweet treat. For the first time in my 11 years, I was blessed with the otherworldly sights. We are star people. When we are born, we descend from the stars, and when we die, we ascend to the stars, back where we dance for all those still left living on earth. Polluting the stars is to **colonize** the stars, colonizing the dead, and those not yet born, so that the people on earth lose their sights and lose their ways.
>
> When I returned to the city, my girlfriends at school would sit me down every single recess for a month and make me tell that camp story over and over again. I would watch as they filled with awe,

and strained to imagine it, as if it were a fairy tale. Storytelling is powerful, and beautiful in the ways that we can remember things we haven't seen, as if stars still flood our veins, and the bird song is kept tucked in our bones.

CRITICAL THINKING QUESTIONS

1. How do we ensure that on-the-ground, person-to-person learning takes centre stage in this time of high-speed data sharing?
2. What approaches can be used to ensure the intergenerational communications of ideas, concepts, knowledge, and teachings?
3. In what ways can story sharing raise hope, pride, and mental well-being among Indigenous youth?

CHAPTER 8

Damaged, Not Broken: An Interview about White Settler Violence and Indigenous Health

Mary Teegee and Sarah de Leeuw

Sarah de Leeuw (SNdL): Will you tell me about yourself, Mary?

Mary Teegee (MT): I'm from the Takla Nation. I'm Gitk'san but Bear Lake Gitk'san and Carrier on my father's side. I'm Lax Gibuu Wolf **Clan**, from my mother. My father is Lhts'umusyoo Beaver Clan. We were raised in Fort St. James. For us to get an education we were raised off-reserve. It was important to my parents to teach us traditional ways of being, especially when it came to things like food gathering. How to do moose hide hunting, being out on the **land**. It was really important for them that we knew that and how to survive. So, we really had, I would say, the best of everything. It was important to my parents that we be educated secularly as well as traditionally. That's what I attribute to any of our successes: my parents' foresight, especially my father's, in ensuring that we were educated in the White way and in our Indigenous ways. And then I travelled all over the world. Now I am the Executive Director of Child and Family Services for Carrier Sekani Family Services, a role I've held for almost 16 years now. I'm also the Chair of the BC Delegated Aboriginal Agencies. There's 24 agencies. I represent British Columbia on the First Nations Caring Society, where Cindy Blackstock is the Executive Director. I am the President of the Aboriginal Childcare Society, and I represent British Columbia on the National Advisory Committee for Child and Family Service Reform. I also lead and was the Chair for many years of the Highway of Tears Initiative. So that's me!

SNdL: Your expertise is almost unparalleled. You can speak extensively about colonial violence and the way it impacts families and children. So, what do we mean when we talk about violence? Do you have thoughts about violence and Indigenous health? About the gendered nature of violence?

MT: When it comes to Indigenous people, our definition of violence is very clear. We live with it. Every day we're encountering some type of personal violence, be it violence against our spirit or against who we are—or even racial discrimination, which I would argue is violence. I think one of the first acts of violence was getting our lands taken away from us. **Colonization**, the modern history of Indigenous people, is built on violence. I also think about the feeling of having your children ripped away from you. That is the ultimate violence.

I always say that I think one of the first impacts of colonization or even residential school is heartbreak, and that partly started with men. You can imagine these men, protectors of our land and families, the providers for the community and for the Nation. They were left impotent in protecting their children. That violence and aggression against who we are as Indigenous people started with getting our children ripped away. This act of violence is linked to our lands and dislocation. And it's not only the children being removed from the land. Imagine being told you could not go into your Territory, you weren't allowed there anymore. My mother's people, my Gitk'san ancestors, lived since time immemorial in the area we called Bear Lake. Then in the 1950s, they were no longer allowed to go there. They were ripped away from the land, from the source of our being. My mother, she said it was literally like her heart was ripped out: "I can't even tell you how it felt, my yearning. Until the day I die, I will always yearn to be to be back with my home."

I remember once I was working in **Treaty** negotiations. I was talking about going back to my mother's birthplace. My mother was born under a tree. Her great aunt delivered her. So my mother and me, we drove and drove and she said, "I will take you to this place that's really special to us and you will see how beautiful it is and you will feel the strength of this area because this is where so many babies were born." So we drove and drove and we came up to this area. And it was deforested. There was nothing there. I just remember my mom heaving and bawling. She couldn't believe it.

I think about the look on her face. I cried with her because, to me, if you think about all of our warriors and our Chiefs and everybody, everything: who we are is tied to the land. We are Yinka Dene: People of the Land. So that first violent action was of ripping us away from our land, ripping us away from our own mother, mother earth. Ripping away children and then ripping apart families. Everything stems from that. The loss of traditional roles, customs, and practices that celebrated who we are. Colonization, and of course of residential schools, weakened a lot of those things and ripped away a lot of meaning. Ripped away our languages. Even our own gender is nuanced in our languages so that violent act of ripping out our tongue has impact on how we recognized and celebrated gender roles.

SNdL: Can you tie these broad systemic colonial violences to everyday violence? There was land theft, the imposition of residential schools, and now there's judicial, anti-Indigenous racism, healthcare racism, and other violences. Can you talk a bit about that?

MT: It's those years of trauma that has led us to the modern day. You still have children being removed from their parents because of their dependence on drugs and alcohol. Whenever I speak to people, like medical professionals or whoever, I say: "Do you honestly believe that someone wakes up and says, 'I want to end up homeless and be addicted to these drugs, and this is something I want to do?'" As if it's a fuckin' choice? Well, it's not a choice. They're self-medicating to overcome those years of trauma. I don't think the trauma can ever be understated. There are reasons for their behaviours that are so multi-layered, so multi-generational. So, we have this society that has been damaged, but not broken. Just damaged. We're not broken. I see broken-hearted parents. I see children in group homes or foster homes. All they want is a sense of place and a sense of community and family.

I spoke about traditional roles. Those gender roles have really been damaged because of the shattering of the family. How we view women has been damaged. How we view the ones with nuanced genders, damaged. How we regard the various genders has been damaged again and again. But I always say: not broken. Damaged. But not broken.

Then there are the laws meant to "protect" Indigenous people. These are actually violent laws. For example, domestic violence laws penalize women who have stayed in a home where the man is violent: the children are removed. So, not only was she violently beaten, but now society is going to beat her by taking away her children. If the man goes back to the house, which is not the woman's fault, but if he goes back to the house or if someone says the woman is talking to the father of her children, even on the street, then the children are removed. That's violence.

Then, look at why people are leaving their communities. It's issues around poverty. The lack of housing, the lack of jobs, and so on. So even though there may not have been a physically violent act of removal of people from their lands, there is no way for our people to stay on our land in these modern times. I think even the beautiful action of going hunting has been impeded because now, you know, you need a vehicle to get to the hunting territories that we used to have easy access to and even lived on. So even that is connected to the violent act of removing us through laws from our own Territory. There's all of these layers of violence and what makes our young people vulnerable to being taken advantage of, to being another statistic.

SNdL: Do you want to talk to me briefly about murdered, missing Indigenous women, police violence, violence in prisons?

MT: Since I was my 20s, I've been trying to bring up the issue of murdered, missing Indigenous women and girls: it was never heard. Then when we finally had the Highway of Tears Symposium. We called on all levels of government to be there. And they showed up. But we're still trying to do the work off the side of our desk. Also, don't forget the young men that have gone missing and are still unaccounted for. Our women are still going missing today. It's not in the past. It's still something we need to consistently advocate about and bring to the public's attention.

Highway of Tears Symposium

The missing and murdered women's families have spearheaded multiple public awareness initiatives about those whom they have lost along the Highway of Tears. One notable event was a walk from Prince Rupert to Prince George, BC (726 km) in 2006, which was followed by the Highway of Tears Symposium. The victims' families and more than five hundred representatives from government, police, and other sectors were in attendance. The symposium report made 33 recommendations, including developing and implementing "a victim prevention plan that measurably reduces the number of young women who are placing themselves at risk hitchhiking on Highway 16 west of Prince George" (Lheidli T'enneh First Nation et al., 2006, p. 13) and addressing "the underpinning causes that place young women on the highway and at risk" (p. 13).

In 2015, recognizing that the missing and murdered women along the Highway of Tears is "part of a larger, national crisis of missing and murdered Indigenous women and girls" (Sabo, 2019, para. 1), the federal government initiated a national inquiry that culminated in a report calling the systemic violence and racism that perpetuate these atrocities "acts of genocide against First Nations, Inuit and Métis women, girls, and 2SLGBTQQIA people" (National Inquiry, 2019, p. 1).

MT: We still have racism in the health system, government systems, and serving systems. They're built on racism. These systems are inherently violent. When you respond with violence to a person who is traumatized, a broken person, by throwing them in jail or doing more violence to them, it's just reinforcing a circle of violence. Violence begets violence. So, when you start responding to why even our own men are in those situations, where they cause violence, where the men are beating women, we need to respond differently. What we need to start concentrating on are the principles of who we are as Indigenous people. The ultimate [principle] is love. If you look at how we deal with [men that are] so traumatized, possibly who have been sexually abused, we have to ask how men see themselves. Violence may have been in their home as a child. Maybe these men don't know how to show love or know how to deal with all the anxieties and the pressures of a non-Indigenous world. Then the men are put into a violent situation like prison. We're just going to keep perpetuating that cycle.

So, what I would say across the board is that we need . . . resources. Not only financial resources, but the people, the capacity in communities to help us to get to the place where all of our natural laws are upheld, like the natural law of having your child with you. But I also think there needs to be a change in mindset. Because at the end of the day, the resources that we are receiving to help heal ourselves are minimal at best. And they are coming from the land that was violently ripped away from us. We need to get back to our land. We need to return to love.

I hate it when I am begging to heads of state, begging with hat in hand. Asking for pennies for our children. It is the inherent and innate right of our children to benefit from our land. This is part of the **United Nations Declaration on the Rights of Indigenous Peoples (UNDRIP)**. Our children have a right to their resources and to their land. And to benefit from their resources and land. It's just so wrong that they can't. As a Hereditary Chief, it is degrading that I am begging for what is rightfully ours. Begging is itself an act of violence.

SNdL: Is there a personal anecdote that encapsulates everything you're talking about—something that illustrates all these lines of conversation in a way that moves the heart?

MT: I always remember this one case. I have always wanted to start a program. It's because of this young girl. This beautiful and smart girl who had goals. She knew what she wanted to do. She ended up with this young man. They were 17 or 18 years old. She had been in care for a little bit but then her parents came back together, and they were able to take care of her. So that's how I got to know her, to be very close to her. The young man she ended up with, he was very violent with her. In her early 20s, she ended up pregnant, and then she had a little girl. Because of the violence, we had to take the child out of her home as per statute. We did everything we could to keep them together. She stayed with her mother, but she would always go back to this guy.

When we talk about colonial laws and intersection of laws with Indigenous peoples, I remember this young woman. She had to go to Court because the young man had beaten her and broken her bones. He wasn't charged because of those first beatings. I'm going to get very emotional. I said we need to get her out of this situation. But she kept on going back to him.

Later, she had this beautiful baby. Finally got away from this young man. But they were at a party later on. And the day after that party, I got a call from her mother. And the mother said we've heard that a body that was found could possibly be her daughter. They'd found a body, a young girl's body in this community. The mother asked me, she said, could you come?

You know we did everything, but then even colonial laws weren't there to protect her when we needed it. But what I really needed to know was: how could this man, this young man, be so hateful and angry? The damage he did to this young woman—just beat her to death and left her in a ditch to die. The community was very guarded. Many people knew about how violently the young man was raised. How violent his mom and dad were. He was treated horribly. He was left malnourished. So I developed a proposal where I said, okay, let's identify these young people at an early age. Let's start the intervention and the prevention there. Why wasn't the little boy cared for and removed from his family? The beautiful young woman, she's seen her own parents be violent. The cycle was just continuing.

Slowly but surely, that's what we're trying to do. We're trying to identify those tiny children. That's when we need to intervene. Children need all the support structures that we can give them, right at the early ages. But I provided this proposal to the federal government to no avail. Because I'm saying we need to look at a new way of doing things, so let's deal with this violence when they are just babies. We need to incorporate our traditional protective practices into our own child and family laws. That messaging has to be out there, that you have a responsibility as an aunt, mother, sister, clan member to those children, as well as to those that are not yet born. Our leadership and our collective also have responsibilities. We have responsibilities as humans. It's about the most basic human empathy.

SNdL: I am so deeply sorry, Mary. Do you think these tragedies are part of a larger intersectional social context, one people are fighting against through defund police movements, Black Lives Matter actions, and linkages across BIPOC communities?

MT: Absolutely, Sarah. I do believe this. Our people don't trust the RCMP. They don't. Let me give you an example. My son and I witnessed a bloody altercation. A few months later, I get a call. "We need your son to testify." But I told them, "My son isn't testifying, I'm testifying." The cop told me I needed to come in and sign a subpoena that he would leave at the front desk. But every time I went in to sign it, it was never there. Then, late on Thursday evening, there's a loud bang on the door. It was me all alone at home that evening, and when I opened the door, this 6'5" big, blond, White police officer said, "Are you Mary Teegee?" He took a step to come into my house, and I was like, oh fuck! I said, "No—you can't come into my house." He hadn't shown me anything. I didn't know who he really was. So. I just went to shut the door because I'm like, "Who the fuck is this guy?" It was so scary, and I was yelling. I was going to fight, so I pushed him out, and then I yelled at him. When I think back on this, honestly, I'm a fuckin' strong woman, but I'm shaking. I work with the cops. I know the cops. I meet with heads of state, for heaven's sake. But. I was scared with this huge officer. I am coming from a position of strength. Imagine vulnerable women. How they would feel? Imagine this big 6'5" guy, this intimidating man, with so much power. If he felt he could yell at me, imagine who else he might yell at. He had all of this physical power and all the weight of the law behind him.

Now I bring this up and talk about this being a teaching moment. About how you talk to people. How you treat people. So, I definitely agree with tenets of the defund the police movement, absolutely. It has to be coming from a community base, and there's good models out there, but it costs money, right? There's got to be more partnerships with community organizations, with Nations. Again, the solution has got to be coming from the community.

SNdL: Have we missed anything?

MT: A real thing that is a big issue is violence against self, especially when it comes to the youth. The way Indigenous youth feel about themselves because of social media. That whole issue around the violence that is perpetuated by social media to each other and to oneself, so the harm, the bullying, all of those things so absolutely go against who we are as Indigenous people. We have the increase in self-harming and, you know, self-cutting, suicidal ideation. The violence against oneself is against the whole, there's a whole that comes from being Indigenous. It's a violence to not be proud to be Indigenous.

CRITICAL THINKING QUESTIONS

1. Mary Teegee links together different *scales* of colonial violence, from body, spirit, and family to community, collective identity, and the land. How does thinking about different *scales* of colonial violence allow us to think about Indigenous health differently or more productively?
2. Mary Teegee is a strong, proud, and very well-accomplished Indigenous woman. She nevertheless offers many examples where she, personally, is impacted by colonial violence. What does this tell you about the force and power of colonialism and how it might impact the health of Indigenous peoples?
3. This chapter was structured as an interview, a kind of dialogue, between an Indigenous leader and a non-Indigenous White settler of Dutch/European descent. If you were to set up an interview with an Indigenous leader, who might they be? What questions would you want to ask? What thoughts do you have about dialogues between Indigenous and settler people?

REFERENCES

Lheidli T'enneh First Nation, Carrier Sekani Family Services, Carrier Sekani Tribal Council, Prince George Native Friendship Centre, & Prince George Nechako Aboriginal Employment & Training Association. (2006). *Highway of Tears Symposium recommendations report: A collective voice for the victims who have been silenced.* https://highwayoftears.org/wp-content/uploads/2022/04/Highway-of-Tears-Symposium-Recommendations-Report-January-2013.pdf

National Inquiry into Missing and Murdered Indigenous Women and Girls. (2019). *Executive Summary.* https://www.mmiwg-ffada.ca/wp-content/uploads/2019/06/Executive_Summary.pdf

Sabo, D. (2019). *Highway of Tears.* The Canadian Encyclopedia. Retrieved March 16, 2021, from https://www.thecanadianencyclopedia.ca/en/article/highway-of-tears

CHAPTER 9

Our Highways, Our Tears: Indigenous Women's and Two Spirit People's Health and Resource Extraction

Ryan O'Toole, Onyx Sloan Morgan, and Laura McNab-Coombs

LEARNING OBJECTIVES

1. To highlight how land and **resource extraction** impact and are intimately connected with the health and well-being of **Indigenous women**, girls, and **Two Spirit people**.
2. To reinforce one-ness and holistic interconnection between **land** and living beings as they pertain to Indigenous health and well-being *and* the health of everyone.
3. To emphasize the importance of perspective, including the intimacy of storytelling, as it relates to ecological health and well-being.
4. To celebrate the strength of Indigenous women and Two Spirit people in the face of extractive relations.

INTRODUCTION

What does it mean to say that the health of the land is the health of the people? To explore this question, we trace how ecological health and resource extraction pertain to Indigenous health, particularly the health and well-being of Indigenous women and Two Spirit people.[1] What you will not see here are facts on the health of Indigenous communities or figures that victimize Indigenous women and Two Spirit people. Too often, discussions on health and well-being perpetuate these discourses and deny self-determination over bodies, minds, and spirits, while masking the systemic entrenchment of gender-based violence that radiates from extractive relations (Million, 2013). As the Women's Earth Alliance (WEA) and Native Youth Sexual Health

Network (NYSHN) (2016) attested: "Viewed alone, statistics . . . do not tell the story of how the extractive industry, fueled by corporate and governmental greed, furthers colonial and patriarchal systems by eroding traditional Indigenous governance systems and the role of women in these communities" (p. 9).

This chapter illuminates the contours of thought and action that have *created* unique health disparities among Indigenous women and Two Spirit people, not the disparities themselves. We outline how colonially rooted ways of thinking have sought to erode the role of Indigenous women and Two Spirit people in communities and in relation to non-human kin, including lands, waters, and Indigenous legal orders. **Coloniality** has established a paternalistic hierarchy that has *attempted* to disempower Indigenous women and Two Spirit people and replace relations with land and water with extraction of lands and water. This chapter will share how Indigenous women and Two Spirit people remain community cornerstones despite violence and systemic discrimination that ensues from extractive relations (Hunt, 2018).

We want to begin with who we are. We, the authors, come together in this chapter with one voice. We are of First Nation, Scottish and Irish (White settler), and Métis ancestries. We have gender expressions, sexualities, and lived experiences that differ from one another. We live along the **unceded** and ancestral territories of First Nations whose lands are now connected by an infamous stretch of highway—Highway 16, the **Highway of Tears**. In territories now known as Northern British Columbia (BC)—like many territories across what is now Canada—resource extraction digs, forces open, splits apart, and takes from these lands and waters. Indeed, many of the economies of the towns and First Nations communities that Highway 16 connects are dependent on land extraction activities. Resource economies proliferate in Northern towns along the Highway of Tears, intertwining themselves with livelihoods and family relations that can often lead to heated and painful discussions about relations to land and to one another.

In light of resource-dependent economies and the often sensitive and challenging conversations about them, how can we understand ecological health as it pertains to **Indigenous peoples'** health in strength-based ways—particularly Indigenous women and Two Spirit people's health? To answer this, we reflect on the territories on which we stand, those from which we learn and draw life. As we will show, Indigenous women and Two Spirit people were arguably the first to be targeted by coloniality—but their strength was and is a force to be reckoned with.[2]

What follows draws on Indigenous writing, grounded in lived experience, to reinforce the one-ness and holistic interconnection between land and living beings as they pertain to Indigenous health and well-being *and* the health of all living beings. By emphasizing the importance of perspective, including the intimacy of storytelling as it relates to ecological health and well-being, we celebrate the strength of Indigenous women and Two Spirit people in the face of extractive relations. We begin with a story to foreground the intimate and bodily connection of what is too often discussed in ways that pave over our connection to lands and waters on which we rely.

HIGHWAY OF TEARS

The sun sets beyond and I brace myself for the darkness of night. Fuelled by the promise of a new day, I carry on. I have to. I have no other choice. As the sun releases me from her warm embrace, the benevolence of the cliff faces washes away with the coolness of shadows, leaving traces of uncertainty where safety had lived only moments before.

The night blankets dark and my spirit grows weary. My loneliness visible to the naked eye with each passing headlight. "It's just tonight. It's just *one night*." The wind picks up, blowing in rain and debris, leaving loose branches windswept like wet hair across a cheek. I've traversed this terrain for as long as my memory became a thought. I've meandered over the rock and through the trees as the seasons pass.

I've been there to see the Skeena rise to be with our ancestors. I've watched her come back down surrendering to purpose, bringing Creator's knowledge to every surface she touches as she falls. With every drop she brings a tortured hope, washing away all that we can't forgive and reminding me that I can never forget. But, oh, how I wish I could forget.

I wish I could forget every footstep, every tear, every heartbeat. I wish I could forget rolling thunder, crooked smiles, and hollow screams. It was never meant to be like this, this was never my fate. I remember when I was younger, or maybe it was just a dream. The days when I grew with all my relations, the days when the only way to learn was through each other. We began our lives surrounded. Surrounded with the knowledge that we only went as far as the edge of love, as far as our budding hearts could permeate.

We lived for the days that we could sing together, dance together, rise together. Our passionate hearts grew wild with curiosity. The reach of our embrace spanned as far as the horizon. We could feel the smiles of loved ones no matter what distance lie between us. I can feel myself there, every step of the way.

All of that changed when he came. His hopes and dreams were poisoned with conquer and fortune. He said fortune was not found in the life I gave. His words cut through me like his heart of steel slashed through my veins. He said the forest was not for the trees and he ripped away every shred of memory from my being. I shattered and the corners of his smile grew wider. He smeared me with ash, paved me with silence, and turned my world to black.

I wish I could hold her as I once did. I wish I could guide her like a lighthouse in dark seas. I know that she can feel me, I know that she hasn't forgotten . . . but what can I do? I am frozen. Frozen in space, time, and memory. I am no longer the path to her salvation . . . but how . . . how?! Can I be the path to her ruin? We once journeyed to the brink of awakening together, discovering more and more as we grew. Now she is but an illusion, casting her last breath with me instead of her first, and all I can do is weep. For I am the Highway of Tears and I will never forget, but, oh, how I wish I could forget.

Figure 9.1: Sun Low in the Sky along the Highway of Tears, outside of Witset, BC, Unceded and Ancestral Wet'suwet'en Territories.

Photo credit: Onyx Sloan Morgan.

THAT WHICH THEY TRIED TO MAKE US FORGET

Our perspectives impact how we understand, experience, and relate to lands and one another. They create taken-for-granted ways of relating to and seeing the world. They can reveal themselves through stories, art, or everyday interactions. Potawatomi scholar Robin Wall Kimmerer (2013) revealed the means through which colonial ways of thinking have distanced humans from non-humans:

> When we tell them [children] that the tree is not a who, but an it, we make that maple an object; we put a barrier between us, absolving ourselves of moral responsibility and opening the door to exploitation. Saying it makes a living land into a "natural resource." (p. 57)

Indigenous community leaders and scholars have long pointed to the damaging effects that colonial ideologies—or beliefs that organize aspects of society, such as political and economic systems, and epistemologies or worldviews—have on all aspects of being, including health, gender, and ecology (e.g., Daigle, 2018; Hunt, 2018; Million,

2018). Kimmerer revealed how ways of speaking to and understanding the land can also translate into making what is living into an extractable "natural resource." To understand the complexity of Kimmerer's observations, it is important to understand a broader worldview that embeds colonial ways of thinking, acting, and seeing.

In 1493, Pope Alexander VI issued a Papal Bull, "Inter Caetera," giving power to the Doctrine of Discovery and thus legitimizing Christian Europeans' **colonization** of lands that were not inhabited by Christians (i.e., Indigenous lands). These actions effectively shaped the world as we know it today. In the 1600s, international law proposed the legal doctrine of *terra nullius*, which colonists used until the 1800s to acquire Indigenous territories. Meaning "empty land" or "nobody's land," *terra nullius* demonstrates how European colonial authorities valued land: if land was not used for permanent dwellings, held as property, or extracted from, it was deemed empty (for more, see National Inquiry, 2019a, pp. 234–240). In other words, land was only worth value if it existed to serve humans.

Central to *terra nullius* is that humans can reign over (rather than with) land. As colonists (often referred to as "explorers" in Canadian history) continued to arrive on Indigenous territories, so too did this hierarchical way of thinking about relationships with land *and* people. However, when colonists reached the shores of **Turtle Island**, or North America, the land was anything but empty. Innumerable Indigenous Nations lived and remain on these lands, with unique legal, health, governance, and economic systems that were (and still are) enacted through worldviews, languages, ways of relating to lands and waters, and gender roles and sexualities. Instead of trying to understand or embrace them, European colonists rejected Indigenous worldviews, legal structures, and gender roles, seeing them as impediments to accessing lands and vast resources. Simultaneously, Christian ideologies drove the conversion of Indigenous populations.

Indigenous women and Two Spirit people were the first targeted by colonial and religiously rooted violence, which was wielded to access resources and lands. As Kwagu'ł scholar Sarah Hunt / Tłaliłila'ogwa (2016) attested, "colonial efforts to assimilate Indigenous peoples involved the imposition of racialized, gendered and sexualized categories which continue to be enforced today" (p. 9). The 2019 National Inquiry into Missing and Murdered Indigenous Women and Girls (MMIWG) in Canada relayed powerful stories of Indigenous women, girls, and 2SLGBTQQIA peoples[3] who experienced gender-based violence and the systemic entrenchment that allows this violence to continue. For example, the MMIWG report stated: "Conversion thus went hand in hand with displacing the traditional role of women healers and replacing Indigenous medicine practices with European medical knowledge" (National Inquiry, 2019a, p. 237). Highlighting the matriarchal structure of many Indigenous nations, Seneca organizer Iako'tsi:rareh Amanda Lickers (WEA & NYSHN, 2016) also explained the lasting effects of the violence that Indigenous women frequently experience: "women carry our **clans** and . . . by carrying our clans, [they] are the ones that hold that land for the next generation. . . . So if you destroy the women, you destroy the nations, and then you get access to the land" (p. 4).

Missionaries, residential schools, and the government of Canada punished Indigenous children for expressing non-binary genders, and people were criminally prosecuted under the law of "buggery" and, later, "gross indecency." The criminalization of gender and sexuality compounded colonial violence. Citing Sto:lo author and poet Lee Maracle, the MMIWG report shared that, historically, Indigenous gender identities were circular, not binary; diverse gender identities were "a gift from the grandmothers, whether from birth or by revelation" (National Inquiry, 2019a, p. 239). Cherokee scholar Qwo-Li Driskill (2016) explained how Two Spirit people often assumed powerful roles as healers, educators, and carriers of knowledge. Rigid gender identities as they are known today did not have a place in many Indigenous communities. For instance, Michi Saagiig Nisnaabeg scholar Simpson (2017) shared how her Ancestors "lived in a society where what I know as 'queer,' particularly in terms of social organization, was so normal that it didn't have a name" (p. 129); Two Spirit Cree scholar Alex Wilson (1996) commented that "traditionally, two spirit people were simply a part of the entire community" (p. 305). Colonialists, who brought with them rigid and binary ideas of gender, perceived Two Spirit people as heightened threats (Driskill, 2016). The MMIWG report explained:

> Within historical contexts, those considered to hold special gifts [diverse genders] were dismissed and reduced by observers—mostly explorers and anthropologists—as "berdaches," drawing from the Persian *bardaj*, a "slave." ... The use—or misuse, as is more accurate—of this term is important because it represents a limited understanding of gender ... that fails to capture all of the different identities that existed within some First Nations. (National Inquiry, 2019a, p. 239)

Just as human's separation from land seemingly justified property and extraction, women's supposed inferiority to men seemingly justified their subordination. Two Spirit people were not classifiable within binary understandings of gender and sexual practices outside of heteronormative[4] and monogamous relations and thus were seemingly shameful and criminal (National Inquiry, 2019a, p. 240).

Putting forward the concept of "environmental violence" to demonstrate the impact of resource extraction on lands and bodies, the WEA and NYSHN (2016) explained that *terra nullius* not only justified access to land and resources but also justified the belief "that Indigenous bodies are empty and open for conquering" (p. 7). They drew their definition of environmental violence from Carmen and Waghiyi (2012): "The disproportionate and often devastating impacts that the conscious and deliberate proliferation of environmental toxins and industrial development (including extraction, production, export and release) have on Indigenous women, children and future generations, without regard from States or corporations for their severe and ongoing harm" (p. 15).

Dane-Zaa writer and social worker, Helen Knott, foregrounded how environmental violence attempts to sever kin-based and intergenerational transfer of Indigenous relations to land: "If you're giving them [your children] land based food and you're worried that you're poisoning them," Knott asks, "how is that right?" (2019). Knott also elaborated on how overt violence and racism, which are systemically entrenched in Canada, facilitate access to Indigenous territories for resource extraction. She linked this violence to consent over lands and bodies: "racism, it looks like making people feel invisible within their territory and not hearing them when they say 'no,' whether that 'no' be about their body or . . . 'no' about Site C Dam" (she was speaking here about a major hydroelectric dam project in **Treaty** 8 territories) (2019). Many Two Spirit and Indigenous women and youth draw the link between consent over lands *and* bodies as paramount to understanding violence that stems from resource extraction (e.g., Women's Earth Alliance & Native Youth Sexual Health, 2016; Amnesty International, 2016a, 2016b). As Simpson (2020) recently observed of Wet'suwet'en Nation's hereditary Chiefs' assertion of legal authorities over their *yintah* (ancestral lands) and in opposition to the Coastal Gaslink pipeline: "Canada has always ignored consent when it comes to resource extraction and they have always undermined our self-determination and paternalistically decided what is best for our communities and our lands" (para. 6).

Figure 9.2: A Sign Warning Women about the Dangers of Hitchhiking on the Highway of Tears, Listing the Names of Indigenous Sisters Stolen along This Route.

Photo credit: Onyx Sloan Morgan.

Resource extraction impacts environmental health in myriad ways. From chemicals sprayed through forestry practices bioaccumulating in harvested foods (see Boxed Insert, below), to gendered impacts of tailing ponds on women's reproductive health (see WEA & NYSHNN, 2016, pp. 20–25), Indigenous peoples disproportionately bear the brunt of these effects. Infrastructure that supports extractive projects further weighs on Indigenous women and Two Spirit people's health (see Figure 9.2). For instance, resource extractive projects employ large workforces of primarily male, transient labourers.

Glyphosate, Forestry, and Environmental Health

"Roundup"® is a glyphosate-containing herbicide used in forestry practices to inhibit the growth of non-lumber tree species and underbrush. Originally purported to be safe for human exposure, recent research offers insights into the potential health consequences of glyphosate usage. For instance, pregnancy complications experienced by workers with frequent exposure to glyphosate influenced research into the role glyphosate may have in women's reproductive health. Richard et al. (2005) found that even low levels of glyphosate impaired vital growth pathways in human embryonic cells.

These workers are often housed and fed in work camps, or "Man Camps"—large industrial camps with sometimes thousands of predominantly male workers who work long hours in stressful conditions on intense fly-in/fly-out schedules and who have few options for activities in remote locales. Increased domestic and sexual assaults, gender-based violence, survival sex work, and substance misuse, as well as a lack of accessible housing and basic services (e.g., child and healthcare), are a handful of the impacts on Indigenous women traced to extractive projects.[5] Despite the MMIWG report clearly linking violence against Indigenous women and Two Spirit people with Man Camps (National Inquiry, 2019a, pp. 584–593), provincial and federal governments' assessment processes still fail to adequately consider gender-based violence. For instance, in 2020, Wet'suwet'en hereditary chiefs launched a judicial review of BC's Environmental Assessment Office's approval for the construction of the Coastal Gaslink pipeline. The request argued against this construction partly in light of the MMIWG report's findings and the project's proposed four hundred–worker industrial camp (Linnett, 2020).

Less is known about the impacts of resource extraction on Two Spirit people. Although not speaking to extraction specifically, Hunt / Tłaliłila'ogwa, in a report on emerging health priorities for Two Spirit people, pointed to increased threats of homophobic and transphobic[6] violence (i.e., hate crimes), a lack of services that meet unique Two Spirit needs and visibility, lack of data for violence against Two Spirit people, and challenges with mental health and substance misuse due to systemic and social discrimination. Hunt's (2016) report strongly supported the "need for a deeper integration of Two-Spirit people's lived experiences in local and national strategies to address violence" (p. 15). The MMIWG report (National Inquiry, 2019b) released five calls for justice specific to the resource extractive industry (p. 196). These, combined with the 32 "2SLGBTQQIA-Specific Calls for Justice" (pp. 214–218), provide systemic level suggestions for how violence stemming from extraction on the land can be combatted by all people living in Canada and beyond. Despite incursions to access lands and resources, Indigenous communities have not forgotten laws and self-determined ways of relating that link the health of the land to the health of the people. We now turn to how the health of the land *is* the health of the people.

THOSE WHO WILL NOT BE FORGOTTEN

In a 2019 address to the United Nations, Anishinaabe youth water protector Autumn Peltier rooted her families' sacred interconnection to the waters and lands of Wiikwemkoong. She centred the ways in which Indigenous peoples' identity, sense of being, and well-being remain intimately connected with lands and waters. Peltier reminded international delegates that "we can't eat money or drink oil." She voiced her responsibilities: "One day I'll be an ancestor and I want my descendants to know I used my voice so they could have a future." Peltier concluded by calling for people to "stand together as one" for the health of lands, waters, and one another (CBC News, 2019).

Indigenous women, land defenders, and Two Spirit people across Turtle Island join Peltier in articulating Indigenous peoples' health *and* the health of all beings. Katie Big-Canoe and Chantelle Richmond stated: "Herein lies an important and often overlooked inter-relatedness; the health of the land is inseparable from the health of those whose existence relies so indelibly on it" (2014, p. 128). About Wet'suwet'en relations to land, Freda Huson asserted, "Our people's belief is that we are part of the land. The land is not separate from us. The land sustains us. And if we don't take care of her, she won't be able to sustain us, and we as a generation of people will die" (as cited in Simpson, 2020, para. 12). Tlingit scholar Anne Spice recalled a conversation with Huson, where Huson pointed to "the salmon, the berries, and the bears that form 'our critical infrastructure'" (Spice, 2018, p. 42). Reflecting on this conversation, Spice stated that these are: "relations that require caretaking, which Indigenous peoples are accountable to . . . they are relations that are built through the agency of not only humans but also other-than-human kin" (p. 42). Understanding health and well-being as interconnected to all beings involves being in relation with the lands and waters on which we rely. Viewing health in this way requires looking at land and water as life sources rather than as something that can be split apart and paved over to prioritize extraction and sever human–land connections.

In the case of the Highway of Tears, transporting resources arguably takes precedence over the movement and interconnection of people. For example, in 2018, bus routes along this infamous corridor were cancelled. Furthermore, the Canadian National Railway claimed right of way for resources, making passenger rail service unreliable. However, just as Indigenous women and Two Spirit people have rallied for systemic change, so too have they led the development of creative and community-based initiatives to promote safety and transportation that recognizes the lived realities of Northern communities. For instance, many people must travel far distances in Northern BC to access essential services and basic supplies, such as groceries. Personal automobiles are often prohibitively expensive. Despite known dangers of getting rides from strangers, many Indigenous women have no other choice but to hitchhike. In response, the app "Aware 360" was developed for community use. Originally designed by resource companies to track workers in remote locales, the app can be downloaded on any smartphone and has been adapted for women to use while they travel along the Highway of Tears. Aware 360 creates check-ins via apps or calls, can signal for an immediate RCMP response, and is connected to the broader "BC SafetyLink" response call centre, which is operated and owned by the Gitxsan Development Corporation. Although many stretches of the Highway of Tears are in "dead zones" (i.e., out of cell phone range), Aware 360 is but one example of how Indigenous women are leading initiatives to meet the realities of Northern communities (CBC News, 2020).

REDress Project and Campaign

Métis artist Jaime Black developed the REDress Campaign in 2010 to draw attention to and honour the over one thousand missing and murdered Indigenous women and girls in Canada. Her campaign has been nationally embraced, with partnering institutions and communities developing installations to incorporate the hanging of red dresses through various artistic interpretations characteristic of the original REDress vision (Black, 2014).

The REDress Campaign is also an Indigenous women-led awareness campaign that has spread education on gender-based violence (see Boxed Insert). When travelling along the Highway of Tears, look to the trees and you will see red silhouettes swaying in the wind. They are reminders of the strength of Indigenous women and of how we must continue to honour stolen sisters by combatting gender-based violence and extractive relations (see Figure 9.3).

Figure 9.3: The Fourth Annual REDress Campaign, Held in Lheidli T'enneh Territories, Prince George, BC.[7]

Photo credit: Hanna Petersen. Used with permission.

We are *not* asserting that community-led initiatives promoting safety to meet the needs of Northern Indigenous communities are sufficient to combat gender-based violence. *Systemic transformation that is led by and for Indigenous peoples is essential.* We are asserting, by providing examples such as Aware 360 and the REDress Campaign, the strength and creativity of Indigenous communities in light of and despite the daily impact of extractive relations. These are but two examples on a long list depicting the strength and leadership of Indigenous women and Two Spirit people.

CONCLUSION

Close your eyes. Feel your steps, one foot in front of the other. Inching forward. Breathe in with one step, and out with another. In. And out. The support of the land holding up the pavement, carrying you forward. If you're sitting, feel the weight of your feet on the floor—on the land—grounding you to that which supports us all. Is the sun low in the sky? Is the moon radiating through the window? As you finish reading this chapter, ask yourself: how *is* the health of the land the health of the people?

Understanding the health of the land as the health of the people involves abandoning binary views of human and land—and human and more-than-human relations. It involves looking for and feeling the intimate connections between living beings. In this chapter, we have deliberately avoided reproducing facts on the health of Indigenous women and Two Spirit people. Indeed, some of these facts do not even exist, demonstrating how we invisibilize peoples' lived experiences by severing interconnection between people and not seeing one another for who we are. We have also excluded this information to reveal how our everyday thinking and interactions may feed into extractive relations to lands and reduce lived experiences to numbers. We encourage you to consider the importance of *your* perspective. How do your perspectives create often taken-for-granted relationships with lands and waters? How do your perspectives spill over to influence your relation with others? In considering these questions, we hope you can feel the land supporting you, wherever you are. As you breathe in. And out. One step in front of the other.

CRITICAL THINKING QUESTIONS

1. From whose perspective is the story that opens this chapter written? Why do you think it was written from this perspective?
2. How can health professionals better incorporate ecological health into their everyday interactions with patients?
3. How can the impacts from resource extraction be better understood as they pertain to the health of all beings?
4. What systemic changes could be implemented to honour Indigenous self-determination and relationships with lands and waters to support health and well-being?

NOTES

1. We use the term "Two Spirit" to refer to Indigenous peoples broadly who identify outside of the gender and sexual binaries. See Hunt (2016) and Driskill (2016) for more information.
2. For a powerful collection on the strength and transformative work Indigenous communities are leading against gender-based violence and to honour missing and murdered Indigenous sisters, see Campbell et al., 2018.
3. The MMIWG Inquiry also focused on Two Spirit people and on First Nations, Inuit, and Métis who identify across the sexuality and gender spectrum. The acronym 2SLGBTQQIA is used to recognize Two Spirit, Lesbian, Gay, Bisexual, Transgender, Queer, Questioning, Intersex, and Asexual identifying Indigenous peoples. The Inquiry and those who shared their stories emphasized that gender-based violence is experienced differently across sexuality and gender spectrums, and that experiences of Indigenous women and girls may differ from 2SLGBTQQIA

peoples. We use the term Two Spirit in this chapter since it is an introductory text; we do not comprehensively discuss gender or sexual identity.
4. Heteronormativity is rooted in binary ideas of gender being "man" and "woman," and that sexual and other intimate relationships are between these binary genders (i.e., heterosexual). The "normativity" associated with the term reflects that in Canadian society and beyond, institutional structures (e.g., healthcare) and social relations (e.g., families) reflect, expect, and are designed for binary-gendered and heterosexual relationships.
5. For more information on the impacts of resource extraction on Indigenous women, see Manning et al., 2018.
6. Homophobia is a fear of and/or discrimination against people who do not conform to heterosexual binary sexual orientations, including but not limited to: lesbian, gay, and queer orientations. Transphobia is a fear of and/or discrimination against people who do not conform to gender binary expressions of self, including but not limited to transgender, gender queer, gender non-conforming identities.
7. A video of this day can be viewed on YouTube. Please visit youtube.com and enter "Prince George's annual Red Dress Campaign honours Missing and Murdered Indigenous Women" in the Search function at the top of the page.

REFERENCES

Amnesty International. (2016a). *Out of sight, out of mind: Gender, Indigenous rights, and energy development in Northeast British Columbia, Canada* – Executive Summary. https://www.amnesty.ca/sites/amnesty/files/Out%20of%20Sight%20Out%20of%20Mind%20ES%20FINAL%20EN%20CDA.pdf

Amnesty International. (2016b). *The point of no return: The human rights of Indigenous peoples in Canada threatened by the Site C Dam*. https://www.amnesty.ca/sites/amnesty/files/Canada%20Site%20C%20Report.pdf

Big-Canoe, K., & Richmond, C. A. M. (2014). Anishinabe youth perceptions about community health: Toward environmental repossession. *Health & Place*, 26, 127–135. https://doi.org/10.1016/j.healthplace.2013.12.013

Black, J. (2014). *The REDress Project*. http://www.theredressproject.org

Campbell, M., Anderson, K., & Belcourt, C. (Eds.). (2018). *Keetsahnak/Our missing and murdered Indigenous sisters*. University of Alberta Press.

Carmen, A., & Waghiyi, V. (2012). Indigenous women and environmental violence: A rights-based approach addressing impacts of environmental contamination on Indigenous women, girls, and future generations. *Combatting violence against Indigenous women and girls*. United Nations Permanent Forum on Indigenous Issues Expert Group Meeting, New York, NY. https://www.un.org/esa/socdev/unpfii/documents/EGM12_carmen_waghiyi.pdf

CBC News. (2019, September 28). Water protector Autumn Peltier speaks at UN [Video]. YouTube. https://www.youtube.com/watch?v=OusN4mWmDKQ

CBC News. (2020, February 4). *Women in Northwestern B.C. at risk of violence can use app to try and stay safe*. CBC News: British Columbia. Retrieved April 27, 2020, from https://www.cbc.ca/news/canada/british-columbia/aware360-app-female-protection-smithers-1.5451498

Daigle, M. (2018). Resurging through Kishiichiwan: The spatial politics of Indigenous water relations. *Decolonization: Indigeneity, Education & Society, 7*(1), 159–172.

Driskill, Q-L. (2016). *Asegi stories: Cherokee queer and Two-Spirit memory*. University of Arizona Press.

Hunt, S. (Tłaliłila'ogwa). (2016). *An introduction to the health of Two-Spirit People: Historical, contemporary and emergent issues*. National Collaborating Centre for Aboriginal Health. https://www.familleslgbt.org/documents/pdf/HealthTwoSpirit_ENG.pdf

Hunt, S. (Tłaliłila'ogwa). (2018). Embodying self-determination: Beyond the gender binary. In M. Greenwood, S. de Leeuw, & N. Lindsay (Eds.), *Determinants of Indigenous peoples' health in Canada: Beyond the social* (2nd ed.) (pp. 22–39). Canadian Scholars' Press.

Kimmerer, R. W. (2013). *Braiding sweetgrass*. Milkweed Editions.

Knott, H. (2019). *Helen Knott on violence against Indigenous women and lands*. https://reclaimthewarrior.com/poetry-other-videos/

Linnett, C. (2020, February 8). B.C. failed to consider links between "man camps," violence against Indigenous women, Wet'suwet'en argue. *The Narwhal*. Retrieved April 27, 2020, from https://thenarwhal.ca/b-c-failed-to-consider-links-between-man-camps-violence-against-indigenous-women-wetsuweten-argue/

Manning, S., Nash, P., Levac, L., Stienstra, D., & Stinson, J. (2018). *A literature synthesis report on the impacts of resource extraction for Indigenous women*. Canadian Research Institute for the Advancement of Women. https://www.criaw-icref.ca/wp-content/uploads/2021/04/Impacts-of-Resource-Extraction-for-Indigenous-Women.pdf

Million, D. (2013). *Therapeutic nations: Healing in an age of Indigenous human rights*. University of Arizona Press.

Million, D. (2018). "We are the Land, and the Land is Us": Indigenous Land, lives, and embodied ecologies in the twenty-first century. In L. Nishime and K. Hester Williams (Eds.), *Racial ecologies* (pp. 19–33). University of Washington Press.

National Inquiry into Missing and Murdered Indigenous Women and Girls. (2019a). *Reclaiming power and place: The final report of the National Inquiry into Missing and Murdered Indigenous Women and Girls (Volume 1a)*. https://www.mmiwg-ffada.ca/wp-content/uploads/2019/06/Final_Report_Vol_1a-1.pdf

National Inquiry into Missing and Murdered Indigenous Women and Girls. (2019b). *Reclaiming power and place: The final report of the National Inquiry into Missing and Murdered Indigenous Women and Girls (Volume 1b)*. https://www.mmiwg-ffada.ca/wp-content/uploads/2019/06/Final_Report_Vol_1b.pdf

Richard, S., Moslemi, S., Sipahutar, H., Benachour, N., & Seralini, G. E. (2005). Differential effects of glyphosate and roundup on human placental cells and aromatase. *Environmental health perspectives, 113*(6), 716–720.

Simpson, L. B. (2017). *As we have always done: Indigenous freedom through radical resistance.* University of Minnesota Press.

Simpson, L. B. (2020, February 21). Being with the land, protects the land. *Abolition.* Retrieved April 27, 2020, from https://abolitionjournal.org/being-with-the-land-protects-the-land-leanne-betasamosake-simpson/

Spice, A. (2018). Fighting invasive infrastructures. *Environment and Society, 9*(1), 40–56. https://doi.org/10.3167/ares.2018.090104

Wilson, A. (1996). How we find ourselves: Identity development and Two Spirit People. *Harvard Educational Review, 66*(2), 303–318. https://doi.org/10.17763/haer.66.2.n551658577h927h4

Women's Earth Alliance, & Native Youth Sexual Health Network. (2016). *Violence on the land, violence on our bodies: Building an Indigenous response to environmental violence.* http://landbodydefense.org/uploads/files/VLVBReportToolkit2016.pdf

CHAPTER 10

Legislation, Reconciliation, and Water: Moving Upstream to Implement the UNDRIP in BC and Promote Indigenous Peoples' Health

Danièle Behn Smith and Shannon Waters

LEARNING OBJECTIVES

1. To support students to understand how **Two-Eyed Seeing** relates to human relationships with water.
2. To support students' understanding of the complexities of water governance and the tensions between **Western** governance and **Indigenous Peoples'** rights.
3. To illuminate the specific context of water governance and legislative mandates to uphold the **United Nations Declaration on Rights of Indigenous Peoples (UNDRIP)** in British Columbia.
4. To demonstrate how Indigenous **self-determination** frameworks can be applied to BC's *Drinking Water Protection Act* in order to uphold Indigenous Peoples' rights.

TWO-EYED SEEING PERSPECTIVES ON WATER AS IT RELATES TO POPULATION HEALTH AND WELL-BEING

The fundamental differences between Indigenous and Western perspectives of water must be reconciled in order to advance Indigenous self-determination, population health, and well-being. Water is indisputably a fundamental determinant of health; without it, we cannot survive. This chapter explores connections between water and Indigenous Peoples' health in relation to Western legislation, the *Drinking Water Protection Act*, and new legislative opportunities to advance reconciliation.

The authors invite you on a shared journey to uphold *Nutsumaat kws yaay'us tthqa'*, a Hul'qumi'num phrase meaning, "We come together as a whole to work together to be stronger as partners for the **watershed**" (Cowichan Watershed Board, 2018, p. 8). This collective journey starts from a place of Two-Eyed Seeing—of recognizing and embracing diverse knowledges. The term Two-Eyed Seeing was coined by Elder Albert Marshall who lives in Unama'ki (Cape Breton, Nova Scotia), who emphasized that the recovery and health of Indigenous Peoples living in Canada depend on First Nations peoples having the ability "to walk in two worlds: that of their Native community and that of the newcomers, of the white people, whose ways are the ways of mainstream society" (Marshall et al., 2018, p. 45). Such a way of seeing "can help us understand how our traditional teachings, our Traditional Knowledges, can work together with the knowledge of the newcomers for a better and more health world" (p. 45).[1]

TABLE OF ACRONYMS

AFN	Assembly of First Nations
CWB	Cowichan Watershed Board
DWPA	*Drinking Water Protection Act*
DWPP	Drinking Water Protection Plan
ENV	Ministry of Environment and Climate Change Strategy
FLNRO	Ministry of Forests, Lands, and Natural Resource Operations
MOH	Ministry of Health
OAG	Office of the Auditor General
PHO	Provincial Health Officer
UNDRIP	United Nations Declaration on the Rights of Indigenous Peoples

INDIGENOUS PERSPECTIVES OF WATER

Indigenous peoples in Canada are diverse, but we share many perspectives on water (McGregor, 2012). "Water is life" underpins many Indigenous teachings (Assembly of First Nations, 2013; Bharadwaj & Bradford, 2018). Water is also part of many creation stories. We also believe we have a responsibility to protect water, both now and for future generations (Sanderson et al., 2015; McGregor, 2012). This responsibility is a never-ending circle of protection, from the "tiny droplets of water falling from the skies to the continuation of its journey to the lakes and rivers and the ground where it is stored" (Assembly of First Nations, 2013, p. 1).

Water has power. A principal player in multiple arenas, it nourishes plants and animals, provides aesthetic environments, helps medicines that grow in and around it to flourish, acts as a life-enriching cleansing agent, and serves as an element of interconnectedness (Bharadwaj & Bradford, 2018; McGregor, 2012; Sanderson et al.,

2015). Water is critical for the physical, emotional, mental, and spiritual well-being of Indigenous peoples and for all life (McGregor, 2012).

Many regard water as a relative—a spiritual, living being with whom one communes with care and compassion. Many also understand water as an entity with feelings, such as sadness or anger if mistreated. Since water and humans share responsibilities in the relationship, humans must respect water so it can perform its life-giving duties. A respectful relationship includes speaking to and gaining permission from water to utilize its vital properties. Water is sacred as well—not a commodity to be bought and sold (McGregor, 2012; Sanderson et al., 2015). Across Canada, Indigenous communities have local protocols and ceremonies for giving thanks and maintaining a spiritual connection to water (McGregor, 2012). In some Indigenous communities, women are the keepers of water, and they conduct ceremonies when people gather (Assembly of First Nations, 2013).

Autumn Peltier: Water Warrior

Autumn Peltier, a youth of the Wikwemikong First Nation, is an internationally recognized water warrior. She follows in the footsteps of her great auntie, late **Anishinaabe** Elder, Josephine Mandamin, who walked over 15,000 km around the Great Lakes and other waterways, challenging people to perceive water as sacred and deserving of protection (McGregor, 2012). Autumn has taken on the responsibility to protect the waters, and in April 2019, at age 15, she was named the Chief Water Commissioner for the Anishnaabek Nation. Autumn is a powerful voice advocating for the rights of water at local, national, and international levels, including at the United Nations. She has been the worthy recipient of many awards and much recognition, including a feature on the BBC as one of the world's one hundred most influential women. Autumn inspires others to protect the waters too: "Anybody can do this work, and everybody can make a change," she says. "It's not only young people that are already making change, it's everybody" (as cited in Larned, 2021, para. 23).

Indigenous peoples, along with plants and animals, have the right to healthy water and have the responsibility to make informed decisions that affect water planning for future generations (Cowichan Watershed Board, 2018; McGregor, 2012; Sanderson et al., 2015). Indigenous peoples have sovereign, inherent, and **treaty** rights over the **land** and waters in their traditional territories. They persevere in asserting their rights and responsibilities through ceremony and management practices as traditional **stewards** of watersheds (Assembly of First Nations, 2013).

Indigenous laws that have long protected health and well-being, including teachings about how to relate to and care for water, were disrupted at Western contact. In 1493, the Doctrine of Discovery created an international legal framework that dehumanized Indigenous peoples and established spiritual, political, and legal justification for seizure, sovereign ownership, and **colonization** of land and waters. The relationships of Indigenous peoples with their environment, including water, were directly targeted and our roles in water protection were impeded. This disrupted relationship with water has consequences. The way humans treat or mistreat water can critically affect "all our relations,"[2] given we are all connected in the web of creation. When we damage water sources, all life suffers (Bharadwaj & Bradford, 2018).

WESTERN PERSPECTIVES OF WATER

Western conceptualizations of the relationship between water and humans tend to focus on the commodification of water and/or on water as a potential source of risk to human health. One way to illuminate these perspectives is to examine written legislation, which Western institutions use to uphold law.

In 2013, the federal *Safe Drinking Water for First Nations Act* was established to enable the creation of regulations for drinking water to help ensure that standards on First Nation lands were comparable to the standards for all Canadians. Federal regulations for access to safe drinking water and drinking water source protection were intended to be developed in partnership with First Nations for each region of Canada after completing further consultation. The Assembly of First Nations (AFN) passed a resolution (2017) to repeal the *Safe Drinking Water for First Nations Act* and have the federal government work directly with First Nations to address their concerns. The AFN is leading the process to address concerns, as well as to identify priorities and a course of action.

Legislation to protect public health also exists within each Canadian province and territory. In British Columbia (BC), the *Public Health Act* (2008) outlines the responsibilities of the Provincial Health Officer (Provincial Health Officer, 2019) in areas including environmental health. The Provincial Health Officer (PHO) also holds a specific role in drinking water protection.

In 2000, the BC premier stated his government would develop a strategy that embraced a multi-barrier approach to protect drinking water, i.e., an approach that considers source water protection, drinking water treatment, and the drinking water distribution system for reducing risks to human health. Source water protection, the first step, can reduce the cost of treatment needed to ensure that drinking water is safe.

In 2002, *An Action Plan for Safe Drinking Water* (*Action Plan*) was created. It stated the need for strong, effective legislation and for clear government responsibility to protect drinking water. The current *Drinking Water Protection Act* (DWPA) was amended in 2003 to reflect the *Action Plan*. In the DWPA, drinking water is defined as water "used or intended to be used for domestic purposes"—that is, human consumption, food preparation or sanitation, or other household purposes. The health minister stated at the time that both the *Action Plan* and the DWPA provided the framework for protecting public health. The DWPA allows the Provincial Health

Officer (PHO) to recommend a Drinking Water Protection Plan (DWPP) to ensure source watersheds are protected. A DWPP is a legislative "measure of last resort" that can empower local authorities to regulate activities in areas of concern for a community water supply system.

Jurisdiction over water in BC is complex. Multiple government departments and legislative pieces are involved in almost all BC's watersheds. The Ministry of Forests, Lands, and Natural Resource Operations (FLNRO) oversees areas that affect water. The Ministry of Environment and Climate Change Strategy (ENV) coordinates changes to water management and water use. Both FLNRO and ENV hold responsibility under the *Water Sustainability Act* (2016). The Ministry of Health (MOH) holds responsibility under the DWPA. Except for a brief period in 2008, the ministry responsible for health has held very little power over water protection; that power has rested with the ministry responsible for environment. BC's PHO holds accountability under the DWPA. The PHO's duties include: monitoring compliance and reviewing decisions of drinking water officers; preparing and delivering an annual report to the Health Minister; reporting on issues that threaten public health by negatively impacting drinking water; and making recommendations to the Health Minister with regard to DWPPs.

OFFICE OF THE AUDITOR GENERAL'S REPORT: A REVIEW SITUATED WITHIN WESTERN PERSPECTIVES

The BC Office of the Auditor General (OAG) provides independent advice and regular audit reports on the provincial government's management of its responsibilities and resources. It also makes recommendations for improvement. The 2019 OAG report on "The Protection of Drinking Water" concluded that the MOH and the PHO were failing to meet the expectations laid out in the 2002 *Action Plan* for protecting drinking water.

The OAG is rooted in Western mainstream structures and ideologies that have typically discredited or ignored Indigenous ways of knowing and being. The 2019 report situated the OAG within Western structures and beliefs when it emphasized that "[Western] legislation is the foundation from which action can be taken" (Auditor General, 2019, p. 8). The report found that multiple legislative pieces affect drinking water, but the DWPA does not support the MOH in assuming ultimate responsibility to provide safe drinking water. It also found that legislation favours **resource extraction** activities, or land uses that may adversely affect source water quality, over protecting drinking water. The OAG report found that the PHO requested a DWPP on four separate occasions (2008, 2010, 2015, and 2018), but—as of 2021—no plans have been ordered by BC's Health Minister. It recommended that the PHO, in collaboration with the MOH, review the legislative provisions regarding DWPPs. The PHO accepted the recommendation.

The MOH had been active in coordinating the ministries after the *Action Plan* was first created in 2002, but the OAG report found that coordination has decreased since then and that many committees that were created have since disbanded. The MOH stated that part of the problem was poor coordination—a consequence of the MOH's mandate to prioritize drinking water treatment and distribution systems at the expense of water protection. The OAG report recommended the MOH provide the leadership necessary to develop a cross-ministry commitment to coordinate strategies to address risks to drinking water. The MOH agreed.

The provincial government's commitments, such as the *Action Plan*, currently focus exclusively on Western conceptualizations of the water–human relationship. It does not include Indigenous perspectives and thus fails to uphold Indigenous peoples' ability to exercise their rights in relation to water. A potential benefit of the Indigenous perspective of water as a living being can be extrapolated from a previous OAG report, which stated that "one agency should be assigned the role of the 'voice of water' within government" (Auditor General, 1999, p. 2).

DECLARATION ON THE RIGHTS OF INDIGENOUS PEOPLES ACT: AN OPPORTUNITY TO INCORPORATE INDIGENOUS PERSPECTIVES

BC is at a critical juncture in water governance that creates an opportunity to elevate Indigenous self-determination in relation to water. Western systems have flagged the need to overhaul drinking water protection at the same time as BC's government has identified the need to align all legislation with the United Nations Declaration on the Rights of Indigenous Peoples (UNDRIP).

In November 2019, BC became the first government in Canada to adopt UNDRIP legislation as part of its commitment to develop a true and lasting reconciliation with First Nations, Métis, and Inuit populations. Bill 41–*Declaration on the Rights of Indigenous Peoples Act* "aims to create a path forward that respects the human rights of Indigenous peoples while introducing better transparency and predictability in the work we do together" (Province of British Columbia, n.d.). The legislation requires alignment of BC's laws with the UNDRIP and an action plan that includes consistent reporting. It provides a legislative framework to recognize Indigenous peoples' constitutional and human rights and is a tool that can align BC's laws with international standards. Two key functions of the Bill are: (1) recognition of a broader range of Indigenous governments; and (2) mechanisms to promote shared decision-making powers for Indigenous governments on issues impacting their citizens. Bill 41 has the potential to vastly enhance promoting and upholding Indigenous self-determination. Achieving full recognition of Indigenous peoples' rights in BC and renewed Crown–Indigenous relationships will require **distinctions-based approaches** that undertake meaningful partnerships with First Nations, Métis, and Inuit to implement Bill 41.

This critical window of opportunity to heal the human–water relationship requires legislative review so that new and existing legislation within BC aligns with the inherent rights of the land's first inhabitants and stewards of the lands and waters. Water governance in BC has the potential to manifest Indigenous self-determination and ensure that Indigenous Peoples can exercise their right to maintain their holistic relationships with their waters. The review process must pay explicit attention to Bill 41 and create governance structures that ensure meaningful partnership with Indigenous collectives.

Distinctions-Based Approaches in Relation to Bill 41

The Government of Canada stated their commitment to renew relationships with Indigenous peoples. They issued 10 principles to guide renewed relationships, including that "a distinctions-based approach is needed to ensure that the unique rights, interests and circumstances of the First Nations, the Métis Nation and Inuit are acknowledged, affirmed, and implemented" (Department of Justice, 2018, p. 17). Applying a distinctions-based approach requires meaningful engagement with First Nations, Métis, and Inuit collectives. According to Statistics Canada (2016), there were 270,585 Indigenous people in BC, making up 5.9% of the population. Of the Indigenous population in BC, 63.8% (172,520) were First Nations, 33.0% (89,405) were Métis, and 0.6% (1,615) were Inuit.

Bill 41 was drafted in collaboration with three First Nations partners: First Nations Summit, British Columbia Assembly of First Nations, and Union of British Columbia Indian Chiefs. There is no formal Inuit representative organization based in BC. The recognized representative organization for Métis in BC, Métis Nation British Columbia, was not formally engaged in developing Bill 41. As Bill 41 is implemented and BC provincial legislation becomes harmonized with the UNDRIP, it will be critical to formally include Métis and Inuit perspectives.

"WISE WAYS": EXPLORING EXISTING INDIGENOUS FRAMEWORKS TO HELP RECONCILE CONFLICTING WAYS OF KNOWING

Local and international frameworks that illuminate holistic Indigenous conceptualizations of population health and well-being can help to inform a legislative review of water-related Acts that can result in Indigenous self-determination and improved population health and well-being. What follows is an example of just such an international framework.

The Western approach to nature protection has largely consisted of such actions as establishing parks for human enjoyment and use. In the 1970s, it emerged in Western academic literature that nature should have the right to litigate its own interests. This notion evolved into "environmental personhood," which means designating parts of nature as legal persons entitled to independent consideration. Environmental personhood gained momentum from the legal precedence of "corporate personhood in protecting corporate rights" (Gordon, 2017, p. 2).

Indigenous Peoples are now drawing on environmental personhood legislation to uphold their reciprocal relationships with nature (Westerman, 2019). In 2008, Ecuador recognized within its constitution the rights of nature "to exist, persist, and maintain and regenerate its vital cycles" (Republic of Ecuador Constitution, 2008, as cited in Gordon, 2017, p. 4). Nature was given rights by analogy to "persons and people" (Republic of Ecuador Constitution, 2008, as cited in Gordon, 2017, p. 4), with every person having the right to advocate on nature's behalf. Bolivia passed a similar law in 2010, legally recognizing "Mother Earth" as a "collective subject of public interest" (Law on the Rights of Mother Earth, 2010, as cited in Gordon, 2017, p. 4). Bolivia's law places humans within the web of life and gives rights that were previously held exclusively by humans to that entire web. Both these legal changes coincided with a rise in political power for Indigenous groups. These approaches consider nature broadly, with humans as part of nature. Their implementation has been problematic as it can become "difficult to partition out various, and perhaps conflicting, interests in a principled way" (Gordon, 2017, p. 35).

Indigenous communities in the United States have enacted their own legislation to establish nature's personhood. In 2018, the White Earth **Band** of Ojibwe established legal personhood for wild rice (*manoomin*, in Ojibwe). This law extends from Ojibwe treaty rights and declares that *manoomin* has "inherent rights to restoration, recovery and preservation" (as cited in Smith, 2019, para. 6), including "the right to pure water and freshwater habitat" (para. 6) and "a natural environment free from human caused global warming" (para. 6). In 2019, the Yurok Tribe declared rights of personhood for the Klamath River during a difficult season in which fish were affected by low river flows. Legal personhood provides a different framework for dealing with pollution, drought, and climate change—though cases have not yet put these rights to test in the courts. Indigenous lawyers hope that codifying Indigenous knowledge will encourage a mindset change that values "long-held Indigenous perspectives" (as cited in Smith, 2019, para. 7) as an "innovative way forward and a necessary step" (para. 7) to protecting nature.

In Aotearoa (New Zealand), Indigenous peoples have fought for legal rights for nature with buy-in from the national government. In 2014, the *Te Urewera Act* granted legal personhood to a forest park. Public use continues in the park, but the park now has its own separate identity. The *Te Urewera Act* upholds the Indigenous perspective that human use and nature protection can occur simultaneously, and thus fauna may be harvested, for example, if managed properly. In 2017, the *Te Awa Tupua Act* granted legal personhood to a river; this was on account of the Act recognizing the river as an ancestor of the local Māori tribe. The 2017 Act states, "the health and well-being of the Whanganui River is intrinsically connected with the health and the well-being of the people" (as cited in Magallanes, 2015, para. 19). In the *Te Urewera* and *Te Awa Tupua*

Acts, guardians are appointed from the New Zealand government and local Māori—the Tūhoe and Whanganui, respectively (Magallanes, 2015). No lawsuits have been filed to date, but behavioural change has already been described (Westerman, 2019).

Given the current context in BC, it is worth noting the *Te Urewera* and *Te Awa Tupua Acts* were not designed to give rights to nature. They were devised to better uphold the Māori perspective and thus the human rights of the Māori, addressing grievances stemming from the colonization of New Zealand and the subsequent damage to relationships with their lands, waters, and other treasured relatives (Gordon, 2017; Magallanes, 2015).

PROPOSING A PATH FORWARD TO ALIGN BC WATER GOVERNANCE WITH THE RIGHTS OF INDIGENOUS PEOPLES

The DWPA needs to be reformed to benefit all British Columbians. This reform must follow a legislative review process that is collaborative, intersectoral,[3] committed to Two-Eyed Seeing, and focused on well-being.

For too long, Western legislation has had a monopoly on laws in Canada and Indigenous perspectives have been ignored. The DWPA does not incorporate Indigenous perspectives on water. It does not currently have the tools to address the unique relationship of Indigenous peoples with water and therefore is an instrument for further widening health inequities.

Fundamental differences in Indigenous and Western perspectives on water have created conflicting ways of knowing, where one perspective has shut out the other. With the Western perspective dominating legislation, the DWPA treats water as discrete (not interconnected), inert (not living), a commodity (not sacred), and a resource (not a relative). Our rights as Indigenous peoples cannot be protected, and neither can our health and well-being, when our perspectives are not incorporated.

Reconciliation means establishing and maintaining a mutually respectful relationship. Creating legislation exclusively from the Western perspective creates a hierarchy. Creating legislation with Two-Eyed Seeing values both Indigenous and Western perspectives. Bill 41 mandates the establishment of distinctions-based approaches and governance structures that create a meaningful partnership throughout the water legislation review process. Structures must be created to include Indigenous representation fulsomely from the outset. Indigenous peoples must be included in the legislative review process in order to speak on behalf of water in a way which is unfamiliar to Western law and policy makers. The review process must acknowledge that water is sacred for Indigenous peoples in BC and that the health of the water is the health of the people. The review process must ensure that Indigenous peoples are able to exercise their inherent rights to have respectful, caring relationships with the waters that sustain them. Ultimately, Bill 41 will meet its potential if Indigenous peoples' rightful place in the legislative review is established.

Legislative changes could include modifying the title and focus of the DWPA as it considers the protection of water in its relation to humans—for drinking. Reconciliation and the DWPA means addressing this human focus: if drinking water for humans is all we protect, we protect nothing, as water is interconnected with all. The authors, Indigenous women who are public health physicians, have written this chapter to walk the path of reconciliation themselves.

A United Nations report (Diaz et al., 2019) on Biodiversity and Ecosystem Services found that "nature is generally declining less rapidly in Indigenous peoples' land than in other lands" (p. 5). The report added that "Governance, including customary institutions and management systems, and co-management regimes involving Indigenous peoples and local communities, can be an effective way to safeguard nature" (p. 8). Recognition is growing that incorporating Two-Eyed Seeing into legislation can protect the health and well-being of humans and "all our relations."

The Cowichan Watershed Board

The Cowichan Watershed Board (CWB) is an example of Two-Eyed Seeing in governance. Development of the CWB flowed from crisis management following the 2007 summer drought, during which time stakeholders recognized the need for a more formal and proactive approach to water management. "Leadership and coordinated decision making" (CWB, 2018, p. 4) are foundational to the CWB purpose and structure, and Cowichan Tribes and the Cowichan Valley Regional District participate as equal partners and co-chairs. This partnership advances watershed health. It recognizes the region's commitment to Indigenous rights and reconciliation.

Complex management has hampered the governance of watersheds like Cowichan's: the legislative authority and responsibility for water is "spread among federal, provincial and local governments and agencies as well as unextinguished Indigenous rights" (p. 4). The CWB does not hold "statutory decision-making powers" (p. 4) at this time, but "it is anticipated that the CWB model may evolve to accept a form of delegated authority to make local water management decisions" (p. 4). *Nutsumaat kws yaay'us tthqa'*, an ancient Cowichan Tribes principle, was adopted to centralize CWB work: we work together to be stronger as partners for the watershed.

CRITICAL THINKING QUESTIONS

1. How do your personal perspectives on water resonate with and/or differ from some of the perspectives presented in this chapter? What is the significance of these similarities and/or differences?
2. Are you aware of other pieces of Western legislation that conflict with Indigenous perspectives and/or undermine Indigenous peoples' rights? As a policy maker

and/or decision maker, what principles could you use to approach this conflict in a good way?
3. Describe a "distinctions-based approach." Why is it important to use a distinctions-based approach when considering First Nations, Inuit, and Métis peoples' relationship with water?

NOTES

1. While Elder Albert Marshall coined the term, the concept is older. He writes that "Two-Eyed Seeing grew from the teachings of the late Mi'kmaw spiritual leader, Healer, and Chief Charles Labrador [1932–2002] of Acadia First Nation, Nova Scotia" (Marshall et al., 2018, p. 45) and is "the gift of multiple perspectives treasured by many Aboriginal peoples" (pp. 45–46).
2. Interconnection is a fundamental concept to Indigenous peoples. The phrase "All my relations," used by some First Nations people, reflects the knowledge that "everything in the universe is connected. It also reinforces that everyone and everything has a purpose, is worthy of respect and caring, and has a place in the grand scheme of life" (First Nations Pedagogy, n.d., para. 1).
3. The World Health Organization (n.d.) defines intersectoral action as "actions affecting health outcomes undertaken by sectors outside the health sector, possibly, but not necessarily, in collaboration with the health sector" (para. 2).

REFERENCES

Assembly of First Nations. (2013). *Strategy to protect and advance Indigenous water rights.* https://www.afn.ca/uploads/files/water/firstnationswaterstrategy.pdf

Auditor General of British Columbia. (1999). *Protecting Drinking-Water Sources.* https://www.bcauditor.com/sites/default/files/publications/1999/report5/report/protecting-drinking-water-sources.pdf

Auditor General of British Columbia. (2019). *The protection of drinking water: An independent audit report.* https://www.bcauditor.com/sites/default/files/publications/reports/OAGBC_Protection-of-Drinking-Water_RPT.pdf

Bharadwaj, L., & Bradford, L. (2018). Indigenous water poverty: Impacts beyond physical health. In H. Exner-Pirot, B. Norbye, & L. Butler (Eds.), *Northern and Indigenous health and healthcare.* Openpress. https://openpress.usask.ca/northernhealthcare/

Cowichan Watershed Board (CWB), & Hwitsum L. (2018, September 24). *Governance manual. Version 3.* https://cowichanwatershedboard.ca/wp-content/uploads/2019/08/CWB-Gov-Manual-Version3-Sept-24-2018.pdf

Department of Justice Canada. (2018). *Principles respecting the Government of Canada's relationship with Indigenous Peoples.* https://www.justice.gc.ca/eng/csj-sjc/principles.pdf

Diaz, S., Settele, J., & Brondizio, E. (2019). *Summary for policymakers of the global assessment report on biodiversity and ecosystem services – unedited advance version.* United Nations. Retrieved February 2, 2020 from https://www.documentcloud.org/documents/5990576-Summary-for-Policymakers-IPBES-Global-Assessment.html

First Nations Pedagogy. (n.d.). *Theory: Interconnectedness*. Retrieved January 26, 2021, from https://firstnationspedagogy.com/interconnection.html#:~:text=Some%20First%20Nations%20sum%20this,the%20grand%20scheme%20of%20life

Government of British Columbia. (2001). Excerpt from the Drinking Water Protection Act, Chap 9, Part I. Introductory Provisions. [Assented to April 11, 2001]. Retrieved May 17, 2022, from https://www.bclaws.gov.bc.ca/civix/document/id/complete/statreg/01009_01

Gordon, G. (2017, March 7). Environmental personhood. *SSRN*. Retrieved January 25, 2021, from http://dx.doi.org/10.2139/ssrn.2935007

Larned, M. (2021, January 1). *Water walker*. Thrive Global. Retrieved January 21, 2021, from https://thriveglobal.com/stories/water-walker/?fbclid=IwAR3vfVXSH4BMrkVR6MWoC2rSoIzALzx2llw6eGzmFBOkONcsrxAx5LV4mfM

Magallanes, C. (2015). Nature as an ancestor: Two examples of legal personality for nature in New Zealand. *VertigO*. https://doi.org/10.4000/vertigo.16199

Marshall, M., Marshall, A., & Bartlett, C. (2018). Two-Eyed Seeing in medicine. In Greenwood, M. et al. (Eds.), *Determinants of Indigenous Peoples' health: Beyond the social* (2nd ed., pp. 44–53). Canadian Scholars' Press.

McGregor, D. (2012). Traditional knowledge: Considerations for protecting water in Ontario. *International Indigenous Policy Journal, 3*(3), 1–21.

Province of British Columbia. (n.d.). *Declaration on the Rights of Indigenous Peoples factsheet*. https://news.gov.bc.ca/files/BC_Declaration_Act-Factsheet.pdf

Provincial Health Officer. (2019). Clean, safe and reliable drinking water: An update on drinking water protection in BC and the *Action Plan for Safe Drinking Water in British Columbia*. https://www2.gov.bc.ca/assets/gov/environment/air-land-water/water/documents/pho-drinking-water-report-2019.pdf

Sanderson, D., Picketts, I. M., Déry, S. J., Fell, B., Baker, S., Lee-Johnson, E., & Auger, M. (2015). Climate change and water at Stellat-en First Nation, British Columbia, Canada: Insights from western science and traditional knowledge. *The Canadian Geographer, 59*(2), 136–150.

Smith, Anna V. (2019, September 24). The Klamath River now has the legal rights of a person: A Yurok Tribe resolution allows cases to be brought on behalf of the river as a person in tribal court. *High Country News*. Retrieved February 18, 2020, from https://www.hcn.org/issues/51.18/tribal-affairs-the-klamath-river-now-has-the-legal-rights-of-a-person

Statistics Canada. (2016). *Total population by Aboriginal identity and Registered or Treaty Indian status, British Columbia, 2016 Census*. Retrieved February 11, 2020, from https://www12.statcan.gc.ca/census-recensement/2016/as-sa/fogs-spg/Facts-PR-Eng.cfm?TOPIC=9&LANG=Eng&GK=PR&GC=59

Westerman, Ashley. (2019, August 3). *Should rivers have same legal rights as humans? A growing number of voices say yes*. NPR. Retrieved February 18, 2020, from: https://www.npr.org/2019/08/03/740604142/should-rivers-have-same-legal-rights-as-humans-a-growing-number-of-voices-say-ye

World Health Organization. (n.d.). Social determinants of health: Intersectoral action. Retrieved January 26, 2021, from https://www.who.int/social_determinants/thecommission/countrywork/within/isa/en/#:~:text=Intersectoral%20action%20refers%20to%20actions,collaboration%20with%20the%20health%20sector

CHAPTER 11

Inuktut as a Public Health Issue

Aluki Kotierk

Our language Inuktitut is very powerful. The words have power. The Inuktitut words can heal.

(Mariano Aupilardjuk from Aupilardjuk, 2004)

LEARNING OBJECTIVES

1. To understand that Inuit, who are the public majority population of Nunavut, are not able to receive good healthcare services because they are not available in their language, **Inuktut**.
2. To grasp ways in which language of service is vital to the quality of healthcare service the patient receives.
3. To show steps that could be taken to strengthen the Inuktut health system in Nunavut.

INTRODUCTION

For those of you who have not had the good fortune to travel to my beautiful homeland of Nunavut, I thought I would begin by providing a contextual overview. I will then delve into the subject of **Inuktut** as a public health issue. I will conclude by contemplating possible next steps to ensure that Nunavut Inuit can reasonably expect to receive comparable health services to other Canadians.

NUNAVUT

Nunavut as a separate jurisdiction in Canada is the result of Article 4 of what is commonly called the Nunavut Agreement, which was signed by Nunavut Inuit and the Crown in right of Her Majesty on May 25, 1993 (Indian and Northern Affairs, 2010).

Nunavut means "Our Land" in Inuktut. This means that each time we utter the name of our jurisdiction, we are asserting that we come from this **land**. It is an immense geographic area that comprises about one-fifth of Canada's land mass. There are 25 communities spread across three different time zones and administratively separated into three different regions: Kitikmeot, made up of five communities, is the most westerly region of Nunavut; Kivalliq, in the central region, is composed of seven communities; the most easterly, Qikiqtaaluk, comprises 13 communities.

Nunavut Inuit make up 85% of Nunavut's population, and 70% identify Inuktut as their mother tongue. This is quite incredible: Nunavut is the only jurisdiction in Canada where, homogeneously speaking, an Indigenous population comprises the majority; it is also the only jurisdiction in Canada with a majority language that is not one of the federally recognized official languages—French or English. Inuktut is considered to be one of the more resilient Indigenous languages, given that there are still many Inuktut speakers. Yet, we know that in Nunavut, the number of individuals speaking Inuktut is declining at 1% per year (Martin, 2017). At this rate, by 2051, only 4% of us will be speaking Inuktut at home.

Inuktut is not federally recognized as an official language of Canada; however, the territorial Government of Nunavut passed both the *Official Languages Act* and the *Inuit Languages Protection Act* in 2008, which recognize Inuit languages as official languages of Nunavut. Thus, legally speaking, Nunavut Inuit can reasonably expect to receive programs and services within Nunavut in Inuktut. Such an expectation aligns with the vision of many Inuit through the creation of Nunavut: Inuit, a reasonable people, believed that the signing of the Nunavut Agreement would issue in proactive and focused measures and initiatives for the agreement's full and effective implementation, which includes, through Article 23, an obligation of governments to have a representative workforce. This would mean that Inuit would comprise 85% of the government workforce in all job categories, from administrative and paraprofessional to senior managerial. Unfortunately, the reality is that the Inuit employment rate has remained stagnated at 50% for many years, and Inuktut is neither the working language of government nor the language used consistently for essential services.

Across Nunavut, health services are delivered through 22 community health centres located in regional health centres: Kangiq&iniq (Rankin Inlet), Iqaluktuuttiaq (Cambridge Bay), and the Qikiqtani General Hospital in Iqaluit. Depending on a patient's needs and the types and level of healthcare available in a community, patients may be sent to larger centres for treatment. Incredible amounts of money are spent to cover the costs of medical travel. For instance, in 2015–2016, over $70 million was spent on medical travel, constituting 16.7% of total departmental expenditures (Office of the Auditor General [OAG], 2017, point 7).

Community health centres are typically staffed by a nurse-in-charge and community health nurses. As of March 31, 2016, 62% (43 of 69) of the community health nurse positions were vacant and 20% (5 of 25) of the nurse-in-charge positions were vacant (Office of the Auditor General, 2017, point 21). Casual and agency nurses are used to fill these vacancies and replace permanent nurses on leave. During 2015–2016, a little over $30 million was spent on casual and agency nurses (Office of the Auditor General, 2017, point 22). In addition to this complement of employees, there are also clerk interpreter positions across many of the health centres.

INUKTUT AS A PUBLIC HEALTH ISSUE

In Nunavut, we live under a public government, just like Ontario or Quebec. We pay income tax. We expect to receive essential public services, just like other Canadians. We want to feel safe and secure when we enter the health system. Inuktut is a public health issue. Without the ability to communicate with each other and understand each other, there is no effective way to provide healthcare.

Take a moment to think about your last trip to the doctor or to the hospital: how important is communication to you? How important is language to communicating with your doctor or nurse?

Think about your doctor's visit: how big a role does accurate communication and understanding play in what type of health treatment you receive?

Pretty big, right?

So, imagine living in Southern Canada where the majority public language is English; now imagine that almost none of the health professionals speak or understand that majority language. How would you feel going into that system?

Now imagine that you need the expertise of a doctor, or services that only a hospital can deliver. Imagine that you have to fly, possibly unaccompanied, to a place as far away as Mexico, where not only is the language different, but so is the food and the majority culture.

This is the reality for the majority of the population in Nunavut.

In 2015, a systemic investigation into the Qikiqtani General Hospital's compliance with the *Official Languages Act* (hereafter, "systemic investigation") found:

- "Language barriers have a negative impact on quality of care, patient safety and access to health care services" (Office of the Languages Commissioner [OLC], 2015, p. 30);
- "Patient-provider communication problems may result in a misdiagnosis and relevant follow-up treatment" (p. 30); and
- "Patient confidentiality rights and informed consent may not be protected" (p. 30).

These findings are significant: Canadian patients are receiving health services that may compromise their safety and lead to misdiagnosis or even death because they are not receiving health services in Inuktut. In 2017, Annie Kootoo was being treated for tuberculosis (TB), and she died in Ottawa of liver failure. Her daughter, Bernice Clarke, stated that having services offered in Inuktitut may have made all the difference ("She kept asking," 2017). In that same year, when Geela Kooneeliusie was asked what needed to be done to prevent another death like that of her 15-year-old daughter, Ileen, she responded that the "health centres need Inuit staff who speak Inuktitut" ("She was my," 2017, para. 49).

In 2015, a CBC article showcased the experience of Alicee Joamie, a unilingual Elder who takes four types of prescription drugs daily. She does not understand the English-only labels and warnings on the boxes. Elder Alicee explained: "'When I walk into stores I look for a translator to help me with translation,' she said in Inuktitut. 'I ask them when I need to take them and they tell me when, so that's how I've been taking my pills'" (Pharmacies, 2015, para. 6–7). She also indicated that she relies on her daughter or other family members to help. This circumstance is common across Nunavut, and the obvious challenges are worsened because Nunavut has no Inuktut-speaking pharmacists. This means that many patients seeking assistance rely on a third party to interpret, thus forcing breaches of confidentiality. One of the contributors to the systemic investigation spoke to this point: "The worst case I saw is that we had to use other patients as interpreters. Obviously, it is a breach of confidentiality, but I also feel that if I use a patient to translate for another patient, it transgresses medical rights. You are here to get better and you are being used as staff. Sometimes the patient has to give it a try, but it is the best solution we can come up with" (OLC, 2015, p. 27).

These examples illustrate the importance of individuals being able to communicate in Inuktut. This continues to be raised as a concern, most recently during the Nunavut Legislative Assembly 2020 winter sitting. Margaret Nakashuk, MLA for Pangnirtung, commented that Inuit often do not seek the assistance of mental health workers or social workers when they know that they are unable to communicate in Inuktut (Legislative Assembly, 2020, p. 50).

Although many of the health centres across Nunavut have clerk interpreters, all health centres should have them. More supports should be made available to ensure this. A recent Office of the Auditor General (OAG, 2017) report on Health Services in Nunavut found that, although there is a non-mandatory course on medical terminology available for clerk interpreters, many had not received such training, had not received it in a timely manner, or had not taken the training in many years. The report stated, "Having interpreters with knowledge of medical terminology and vocabulary is important because it helps Inuit patients who do not speak English and their health care providers better understand each other about, for example, the patient's condition" (point 37).

Inuit are **resilient**, adaptable, and pragmatic. So, we cope, we cooperate, and we communicate. We do what the public services have chosen not to do. We keep our language alive at home, and we interpret for our relatives in the health system. Every day, in hundreds of interactions with public services, we act as informal interpreters for our relatives and community members. I do this. My relatives do this.

One day when I was checking in at the Iqaluit airport, there was no one on the check-in desk who could speak Inuktut. The airline staff at the counter gestured me over to help them communicate with a unilingual Inuktut-speaking passenger. Keep in mind: this is in Nunavut. On Inuit homeland. Where the majority public language is Inuktut.

Providing informal interpretations is an additional burden of being an Inuktut-speaking **Inuk** living in Nunavut—a burden that is hardly ever acknowledged and recognized but is readily expected and undeniably necessary. This is our reality as Inuktut-speaking residents of Nunavut. Because an Inuk is fluent in Inuktut, the assumption is made that an Inuk will be able to effectively and accurately interpret any discussion, even if it has complex technical vocabulary that one has never used or even encountered.

Let's take a moment to consider how interpreting for other people is expected. Imagine, for instance, if in the airport scenario, I had said I was not willing when an employee I neither work nor associate with called on me to interpret. Here are some possible results:

- The airline employee might have been offended and thought that I had an attitude—that I was being difficult.
- The unilingual Inuktut-speaking person might have wondered what kind of an Inuk I was. As Inuit, we are brought up to be helpful, contributing members of society.
- I might have felt guilty and thought that I was a bad Inuk for not helping a fellow Inuk.

The expectations placed on us are another way of maintaining a power imbalance. The ability to be able to communicate in one's language is crucial. Our 2007–2008 annual report on Nunavut's Health System stated:

> Inuit are emerging from a period when health care priorities and most aspects of health care practice and delivery were set by non-Inuit. Inuit wish to improve upon the conventional medical system in Nunavut. It does not engage Inuit, does not operate in Inuit language, does not employ Inuit at a representational level, and does not adequately acknowledge Inuit healers or healing practices. Poorly adapted and chronically under-funded health care services and programs based in Southern Canada and delivered primarily in English are no longer acceptable. (Nunavut Tunngavik Incorporated [NTI], 2008, p. 5)

To have services offered in the language of the majority population seems like a reasonable expectation. Yet, too often, an Inuktut-speaking patient must use English to receive essential health services when they walk into a healthcare centre in Nunavut.

Again, we learn an important lesson from the systemic investigation: "What medical providers must understand is that when one is placed in a situation of vulnerability, it is often difficult to understand medical jargon and to clearly express one's needs, fears, pain, etc. It is even more difficult to express these concepts in a language that is not our own" (OLC, 2015, p. 36).

The coroner's report on the death of Annie Kootoo highlighted the need in healthcare for both Inuktut interpreters and written instructions in Inuktut (Government of Nunavut, 2017, p. 7, recommendations 1 and 2). Nunavut Tunngavik Incorporated's[1] 2009 annual report on the recruitment and retention of Inuit nurses in Nunavut took up the issue as well:

> Linguistic and cultural barriers separate health care providers from patients. These barriers can lead to incomplete or incorrect diagnosis and treatment of health problems due to health care providers' limited understanding of what a patient says. One informant noted that southern public health strategies tend to rely upon printed materials and provision of readings, resources, and web-based information. In Northern communities, the most effective communication is verbal and one-on-one. This approach, however, requires both fluency in the patient's language and familiarity with culturally relevant communication styles. (NTI, 2009, p. 7)

Many Inuit have little faith in the current health service delivery model and, to a certain degree, in the healthcare centres' staff. There is a sense that their needs are not well understood at the community level, and that the communication gap is even greater when they are forced to travel to regional centres for care (NTI, 2008, p. 33).

For communities such as Rankin Inlet, with a relatively high proportion of Inuit nurses (five out of seven), informants reported a very positive impact on the impressions of Inuit patients who have been able to access healthcare in their own language: "Several informants noted that the presence of Inuit nurses on staff reduces much of the stress experienced by non-Inuit full-time nurses" (OLC, 2015, p. 22).

Not only is the ability to communicate in Inuktut in our communities crucial, but it is equally vital for any health worker going into our communities to have a general understanding of the types of lived experiences, social history, and **intergenerational trauma** that Inuit carry. Like other languages, Inuktut is a vehicle through which Inuit communicate their view and understanding of the world. This is illustrated through the many kinship names that are common across our communities, but which often create confusion for non-Inuktut speakers. For instance, I have a niece who is named after my late grandmother, so I, along with many members of our extended family, always call her grandmother.

In Nunavut, the history of our family members living out on the land—nomadically and in family groupings, as leaders of their own destiny—is in our living memory. It is only quite recently that the *Qallunaat* (non-Inuit) established 25 communities. When these communities were being established, the *Qallunaat* would come to our lands and assume authoritative positions. Life was disrupted and changed forever. Being relocated from the land to live in communities resulted in many disruptions to the Inuit way of life. Children had to go to school. Families were more sedentary. They had to adjust to a new wage economy. The transition from being self-reliant to being much more dependent on public service agencies (e.g., RCMP) and systems (e.g., health, education) was great. The challenges were exacerbated by the RCMP killing the sled dogs to ensure that Inuit would remain in the communities.

It was during this stark transition period that there was an increase in TB, and many Inuit were sent south for treatment: "By 1955, almost one thousand Inuit had been evacuated to Southern sanatoria. Treatment generally averaged twenty months. This meant that in 1956, one in seven Inuit were in hospitals in the South" (Qikiqtani Inuit Association, 2013a, p. 25). A glimpse of the pain of this dislocation and language isolation emerges from this letter, written by an Inuk TB patient at a southern sanatorium at that time (English translation in the publication):

> I really do want to go home. I do want to stay outside. I cannot tell you about my health, as I am not able to understand English. . . . I am obeying the medical staff. I take aspirins. . . . It is hard to tell. . . . Also, I cannot cure myself. . . . I very, very much want to speak English. I am just trying to obey the directions of the medical people. I want to get home too. Sometimes I appear not to be listening. . . . I want to follow the wishes of the medical people. I, however, do not understand. (Qikiqtani Inuit Association, 2013a, pp. 25–26)

This transitional period continues to impact Inuit who understandably carry pain and heartache about the time when Inuit were transported to southern tuberculosis sanatoria. Some Inuit still do not know where their family members were sent and where their remains may be. It is important that healthcare professionals understand the context for and reasons behind some of the stigma that exists regarding, for instance, tuberculosis among Inuit.

> **The Qikiqtani Truth Commission**
>
> The Qikiqtani Inuit Association established the Qikiqtani Truth Commission (QTC) in 2007. The QTC gathered Inuit testimony about events between 1950 and 1975 to document their experiences moving from the land to communities, including relocations, dog slaughters, residential school experiences, and measures to separate Inuit from their language, culture, and land. This Commission did extensive archival research to corroborate Inuit testimony. A final report was released in 2013 entitled *Qikiqtani Truth Commission Thematic Reports and Special Studies 1950–1975 QTC Final Report: Achieving Saimaqatigiingniq* (Qikiqtani Inuit Association, 2013b). The report recommended such measures as acknowledging and healing past wrongs, strengthening Inuit governance, strengthening Inuit culture, and creating healthy communities.

CONCLUSION: LOOKING TO THE FUTURE

It is astounding that Nunavut Inuit, who live in Nunavut, where the majority population are Inuktut-speaking, cannot expect to consistently receive healthcare services in a community health centre, regional health centre, or the Qikiqtani General Hospital in Inuktut. Ultimately, this means that unilingual Inuktut-speaking Inuit, when compared with other Canadians, are not receiving equitable health services.

One may question why, in a jurisdiction where the public majority are Inuit, and where Inuktut is the public majority's mother tongue, the public government does not operate or provide essential public services in Inuktut. What is clear is that, over 25 years after the signing of the Nunavut Agreement, there were calculated decisions made to ensure that Inuktut did not receive the necessary resources and supports for it to continue to thrive.

When the Government of Canada and the Government of Northwest Territories met 30 years ago to determine how to fund the Nunavut's public government and services, they decided not to fund Inuktut as the language of our government, as a cabinet document from March 1990 clearly expressed (Government of Canada, 1990, p. 31). It was a decision; it was not an accident or an oversight.

Inuit experience the results of this decision every day. The results are that we do not receive essential public services in our language and, ultimately, that the health system does not function in the majority public language.

Additionally, we know that, through residential schools, Canada funded buildings and personnel that actively stripped **Indigenous Peoples**, including Inuit, of their language and culture. In light of this history, it is my view that Canada should have, and indeed has, the responsibility to ensure that Inuit have the right types of resources and supports to ensure that Inuktut continues to thrive in Nunavut. As the systemic investigation report clearly stated: "Being able to speak in one's mother tongue when it concerns health is not asking a favour of health care professionals or organizations. On the contrary, it is a basic issue of accessibility, safety, quality and equality of services" (OLC, 2015, p. 2).

For me, reconciliation includes returning dignity to a people. The healthcare system can play an important role in reconciliation with Indigenous Peoples across this nation. The Nunavut healthcare system can play a significant leadership role in achieving reconciliation with Inuit. There is an opportunity to return dignity to Inuit by ensuring that essential public services, including healthcare, are available to Nunavut Inuit in Inuktut.

In the Nunavut context, many actions can be taken to positively impact healthcare: increasing Inuit in healthcare positions, growing Inuit clerk interpreter supports, and recognizing Inuktut as a founding language.

Inuit in Healthcare Positions

Article 23 of the Nunavut Agreement must be fully and effectively implemented to achieve a representative Inuit workforce in the health field. This would, itself, increase the probability of Inuit receiving healthcare services in Inuktut.

During the Nunavut Tunngavik Inc. (NTI) annual general meeting in 2006, the membership put forward a resolution calling on the Government of Nunavut to:

1. Implement robust and creative measures to increase the number of Inuit primary healthcare professionals in NTI.
2. Actively encourage and adequately support the successful completion of Inuit students attending the Nursing Program offered by Nunavut Arctic College.
3. Evaluate the Department of Health's efforts to increase recruitment and retention of Inuit nurses.

Since 2004, the Nunavut Arctic College has had a Nursing Program, providing a space where homegrown Inuktut-speaking nurses can attain their accreditation. This is a good start, but the program could more proactively recruit Inuit students. For example, I would argue that there is great merit in having an Inuit-specific program in Nunavut. Further, the program could have an Inuit-centric approach to healthcare education by incorporating Inuktut courses covering specialized medical terminology into the program and incorporating Inuit concepts of **well-being**. I would even state that all programs offered through Nunavut Arctic College should have an Inuktut language component to learn specialized terminology in the field of study. Furthermore, Inuit nursing students who undertake their practicum at the hospital need additional support to learn medical terminology and should not be expected to interpret for patients of health professionals.

In line with the nursing program offerings by Nunavut Arctic College, it is important that Inuit start seeing health professions as those that can be aspired to and attained. To pique the interest of young Inuit to pursue health careers, the Government of Nunavut and NTI, in partnership with the Northern Ontario School of Medicine, developed an ongoing week-long Health Careers Camp in Iqaluit for Inuit high school students from across Nunavut. The experience allowed them the opportunity to, as examples, hear first-hand stories from individuals (including Inuit) in the healthcare field, try hands-on activities (e.g., setting a cast, going to the laboratory), speak with an Elder about traditional medical treatments, and visit the hospital. This program is also an opportunity to celebrate the Nunavut Inuit who have successfully completed medical school and inspire other Inuit to pursue medical careers. In my view, the healthcare system can play an important role in reconciliation with Indigenous Peoples across this nation. The Nunavut healthcare system, more specifically, can facilitate achieving reconciliation with Inuit.

Inuit Clerk Interpreter Supports

In addition to providing training and refresher terminology courses to support clerk interpreters, one of the systemic investigation's recommendations was that, "The Department of Health, in collaboration with Inuit Uqausinginnik Taiguusiliuqtiit (IUT),[2] should develop competency tools to evaluate language proficiency of medical interpreters" (OLC, 2015, p. 32, recommendation 13).

Clerk interpreters are so crucial to our health system that they must be adequately supported and compensated for their services.

Recognition of Inuktut as a Founding Language

Currently, the federal government is working on the modernization of the *Official Languages Act*, which was passed into law in 1969—when Nunavut was not yet a jurisdiction. It is important that the modernized Act reflects the modern Canadian jurisdictional landscape, including Nunavut, where, unlike any other jurisdiction in Canada, French and English are both minority languages. The modernization of the Act is an opportunity to recognize that the founding languages of this nation include Inuktut. By recognizing Inuktut as a founding language of our jurisdiction, Nunavut Inuit could reasonably expect that Inuktut would be adequately and appropriately supported and resourced like the minority languages of French and English. Only then would Nunavut Inuit start to be on equal footing to work to receive equitable public essential services enjoyed by other Canadians.

Inuit are resilient and patient. Inuit are focused and determined. In living memory, Inuit have moved from the land to communities; Inuit have negotiated and completed a land claim agreement; Inuit have learned English and have trained to be doctors. With continued determination and persistence, Inuit will be able to achieve the recognition of Inuktut as a founding language of our homeland and will take for granted that essential services are delivered in Inuktut.

I look forward to the day when an Inuktut-speaking Inuk living in Nunavut can walk into a health centre or the Qikiqtani General Hospital with the self-assuredness that they will be able to receive service in Inuktut. I look forward to the day in which I see more Inuit walking within Nunavut, in our homelands, with their heads held up high—proud to be Inuit, with dignity and without shame, knowing that they can receive services in Inuktut.

I know that this will happen in my lifetime.

CRITICAL THINKING QUESTIONS

1. What role can you play to make the healthcare system better for Nunavut Inuit?
2. Does the federal government have a role in ensuring that Inuktut continues to thrive in Nunavut?
3. Should Nunavut Inuit expect to receive equitable health services compared with other Canadians?
4. How significant is being able to speak one's language with a healthcare practitioner in the context of receiving health services?

NOTES

1. Nunavut Tunngavik Incorporated represents Nunavut Inuit; it advocates for the social, economic, and cultural well-being of Inuit through the implementation of the Nunavut Agreement.
2. The Inuktut Language Authority, established through the *Inuit Language Protection Act* of 2008.

REFERENCES

Aupilardjuk, Mariano. (2004). *Inuit healing in contemporary Inuit society*. Pauktuutit Inuit Women's Association.

Government of Canada. (1990). *Report of committee decision – Cabinet Committee on Human Resources, Income Support and Health, Meeting of March 13, 1990*. https://president.tunngavik.com/files/2019/12/RCD-03-20-90-TFN-CC-HR-income-support-and-health.pdf

Government of Nunavut. (2017, February 14). *Report of coroner: Supplementary information additional information of the deceased Annie Kootoo: DOD: 03 January 2015*. https://aptnnews.ca/wp-content/uploads/2017/02/FN-A.K-1.pdf

Indian and Northern Affairs Canada. (2010). *Agreement between the Inuit of the Nunavut Settlement Area and Her Majesty the Queen in right of Canada as amended, May 25, 2018*. Nunavut

Tunngavik Inc. and Minister of Indian Affairs and Northern Development and Federal Interlocutor for Métis and Non-Status Indians. http://www.tunngavik.com/documents/publications/LAND_CLAIMS_AGREEMENT_NUNAVUT.pdf

Legislative Assembly of Nunavut. (2020, Feb. 20). *Nunavut Hansard: Unedited transcript.* https://www.assembly.nu.ca/sites/default/files/20200220_Hansard.pdf

Martin, Ian. (2017, October). *Language-in-education policy and planning in the wake of the Bill 37 debate: A matter of urgency.* Paper presented at NTI AGM, Iqaluktuuttiaq, Cambridge Bay, NU (Nunavut, Canada). [PowerPoint slides].

Nunavut Tunngavik Incorporated (NTI). (2008). *Nunavut's health system: A report delivered as part of Inuit obligations under Article 32 of the Nunavut land claims agreement, 1993. Annual report on the state of Inuit culture and society, 2007–2008.* http://www.tunngavik.com/documents/publications/2007-2008%20Annual%20Report%20on%20the%20State%20of%20Inuit%20Culture%20and%20Society%20(English).pdf

Nunavut Tunngavik Incorporated (NTI). (2009). *Recruitment and retention of Inuit nurses in Nunavut.* https://www.tunngavik.com/files/2010/03/2010-02-nti-recruitment-retention-inuit-nurses-report_english.pdf

Office of the Auditor General of Canada. (2017). *Report of the Auditor General of Canada.* Retrieved February 20, 2020, from https://www.oag-bvg.gc.ca/internet/English/nun_201703_e_41998.html

Office of the Languages Commissioner of Nunavut (OLC). (2015). *Systemic investigation report: Investigation into the Qikiqtani General Hospital's compliance with the Official Languages Act, R.S.N.W.T. 1988 Final Report.* https://assembly.nu.ca/sites/default/files/TD%20135-4(3)%20EN%20Language%20Commissioner%20of%20Nunavut's%20Systemic%20Investigation%20Report-Investigation%20into%20the%20Qikiqtani%20General%20Hospital's%20Compliance%20with%20the%20Official%20Languages%20Ac.pdf

Pharmacies need to print labels in Inuit languages, says Nunavut official. (2015, November 26). CBC News. Retrieved February 20, 2020, from https://www.cbc.ca/news/canada/north/pharmacies-inuktut-languages-commissioner-1.3338083

Qikiqtani Inuit Association. (2013a). *Qikiqtani Truth Commission thematic reports and special studies 1950–1975 Aaniajurliriniq: Health care in Qikiqtaaluk.* Inhabit Media Inc. https://www.qtcommission.ca/sites/default/files/public/thematic_reports/thematic_reports_english_aaniajurlirniq.pdf

Qikiqtani Inuit Association. (2013b). *Qikiqtani Truth Commission thematic reports and special studies 1950–1975 QTC final report: Achieving Saimaqatigiingniq.* Inhabit Media Inc. https://www.qtcommission.ca/sites/default/files/public/thematic_reports/thematic_reports_english_final_report.pdf

"She kept asking for help": Iqaluit woman monitored daily by nurses dies from liver failure. (2017, February 21). CBC News. Retrieved May 6, 2017, from: https://www.cbc.ca/news/canada/north/iqaluit-annie-kootoo-coroner-report-liver-failure-1.3991685

"She was my only girl": Nunavut teen's death sheds light on failures in fighting TB. (2017, March 23). CBC News. Retrieved May 8, 2017, from https://www.cbc.ca/news/canada/north/tb-nunavut-teen-death-ileen-kooneeliusie-1.4036205

PART II CREATIVE CONTRIBUTION

Cactus and Wild Roses

Garry Gottfriedson

the blue ceiling of sky
sprawls the rugged landscape
over our homelands
it can change its colours anytime
some things are predictable, others are not
but transformation is constant
a wave of life and death in all forms
rolling over centuries of customs
built upon the dust of ancestors
enticed by the old language of land
the desire to thrive
the art of living
breaths of fresh air
pure, untainted food
giving meaning to tribes
marking borders of territories
protecting the resources within
the hearts and will of people
inspired by the blue sky gathering clouds
evolving into celebration
the making of ceremonies
healing ceremonies
water ceremonies
because water is life
snow and rain are lifeforces
filling the skies

nurturing the land
like the blood of our mothers
veins of streams and rivers
feeding land and all relatives
remembering all life begins in water
and this is worth fighting for

it is a fight for all people
protecting things that heal
returning bodies to pure states
remembering that sacrifices are necessary
that blood bursts and spills for great cause
like mothers who give birth
spectacular miracles
labour
for the right to breath
bringing meaning
in defense of children
strong, healthy children
who maintain balance
in a world gone wrong
so when women stand
shoulder to shoulder
in defiance of sloppy policies
that promote ill health
and the decimation of humanity
the foreign laws that invade
the hunger growing in their bellies
remember
mothers are not to be messed with
and it is up to men to warrior up
because a man comes from her body
and he must go back
understanding her intentions
returning to the land
in search of red ochre
to paint his face with earthly power
and build buffers in defense of healthy communities
bringing with him a tribe of brothers
and new weapons
to smash wrongful acts

that disregard the pure and raw natural
beauty of the land, water, air and people
warriors must know
the lay of the land and the dictionary well
because laws are two-sided
freedom or sealed fate
health or death
silencing voices
is absolute ridicule after all

extinction is real and possible
we have seen this
colonial and government promises

exposed
between the spaces of bureaucratic teeth
nearly eradicating tribal voices and identity
the knowledge and pathways to healthy dialogue
this is not a future to leave grandchildren with
erotic and erratic settler behavior
perpetuated
desires already charted
pathways to destruction
corralling souls
claiming watersheds
growing invasive crops
digging into the landscape
for oil and gas
for diamonds and gold
melting down idol promises
putting reserves on men and women's fingers
imprisoning them
even creating highways
for murdered and missing women and men
this is called civilization
this is called assimilation
and this is Canada's aspiration
and there is nothing healthy about it

our bones tell it all
deep within marrow

understanding
reversal is reprisal
witnessed
by land in drought
the skies dropping acid rain
transforming colour
making deserts that survive
and from the cracked skin of land and hearts
cactus and wild roses thrive
even grow between the land
filled with bone-dust and love
inducing centuries of labor
screaming out in pain
bursting into joyful song
for tribal identities and rights to endure
and amid it all, the hovering of scab policies
like dc scott's Indian Act
the ratification for death or assimilation
the conversation must be on equal terms
the words must hold meaning to and from
revenge is not the answer
if we are to reverse this state
it is not about assimilation
one culture over another
it is about recognizing
the brilliance in all peoples
but it will surely be a death warrant
should ethnocentric views dominate
simply, it is a war of worldviews
we are alive amid ultimate sins

why not return to the desire to thrive?

PART III

SUPPORTING HEALTHY INDIGENOUS COMMUNITIES

Part III reflects on practical ways that the health of Indigenous communities can be—or is already being—supported. It demonstrates how the legacy of **colonialism** compromises **Indigenous Peoples'** health, and it illustrates the means by which First Nations, Inuit, and Métis Peoples are forging a path toward wellness that reinstates their right to **self-determination** and draws on multiple ways of knowing and being.

Chapter 12, "Vaccine Mistrust" (Greenwood, MacDonald), explains how colonialism and ongoing mistrust of a colonized healthcare system are key contributing factors to vaccine hesitancy among Indigenous Peoples. These populations were subject to forced vaccine testing and other experiments, resulting in persistent health and social inequities. What is needed to enhance vaccine acceptance among Indigenous Peoples is co-created information, access to resources and strategies, and messaging that supports the right to personal choice.

Chapter 13, "Taking Care" (Isaac), introduces readers to art that examines the wide-ranging impacts of historical and ongoing colonial policies on Indigenous Peoples' health. The author identifies unique and recurring themes in the artists' work, including misperceptions about seal hunting, buffalo decimation, **resource extraction**, diabetes, **food insecurity**, and cultural appropriation. It considers some of the artists' representations of healing, as well as their calls for action and self-determination. Their art is activism and cultural reclamation through which others can find avenues to health.

Chapter 14, "A Path in the Snow" (D'Hont), takes an autobiographical approach to show how the availability of Indigenous health practitioners is an important determinant of health for Indigenous Peoples. The chapter considers geographic, social, financial, and cultural determinants that impede or facilitate recruitment and retention of Indigenous Peoples in faculties of medicine in Canada. It also points out numerous best practices for encouraging Indigenous youth to pursue medicine.

Chapter 15, "Youth Protection, Social Determinants of Health, and Reappropriation of Decision-Making Power" (First Nations of Quebec and Labrador Health and Social Services Commission [FNQLHSSC]), reflects on how social determinants of health can result in neglect or serious risk of neglect of First Nations children. The chapter provides background to Quebec's *Youth Protection Act* and the *Act Respecting Indigenous Families*. It highlights the progress of First Nations who are demanding autonomy, including over child and family services, as they work toward self-determination.

Part III closes with "Angled Windows" (Maracle), a poem whose imagery alternates between women (whose confinement restricts their power) and men (who, freer than women, yearn to understand these mysterious beings). The women are resilient despite their confinement: as caged birds continue to sing, so too do these women "continue to dance."

CHAPTER 12

Vaccine Mistrust: A Legacy of Colonialism

Margo Greenwood and Noni MacDonald

This article was originally published by the Globe and Mail *and by the Royal Society of Canada on March 31, 2021.*

Vaccine mistrust and concern about accepting vaccines was part of the general Canadian population's response to routine immunization well before COVID-19. Such hesitancy among any population, including among **Indigenous peoples**, has the potential to impact everyone living in Canada. It is thus a pressing national challenge. Vaccine hesitancy among Indigenous peoples is particularly complex because of the direct connection between vaccination and **colonialism**. Acknowledging and addressing that lineage is the only way to build trust and overcome hesitancy about the COVID-19 vaccine.

Indigenous peoples in Canada have a bleak history of death and near annihilation as a result of vaccine preventable diseases such as smallpox, diphtheria, polio, and tuberculosis, among others. What is more, settler governments stripped Indigenous peoples of rights to make basic choices about our own lives and many were confined to isolated reserves. Segregated substandard health care facilities and services were established, including Indian Hospitals—federally operated segregated hospitals where forced medical experimentation was conducted on children and adults (Mosby & Swidrovich, 2021). These included nutritional experiments, vaccine testing for TB, and uninformed and coerced sterilization (Collier, 2017; Mosby & Swidrovich, 2021; Stote, 2017). Residential schools were also sites for forced experimentation on children (MacDonald et al., 2014; Turpel Lafond, 2020).

Memories of these atrocities are passed from generation to generation. Tragically, the legacy of colonial violence endures. Examples include the grotesque racist treatment of 37-year-old Atikamekw woman Joyce Echaquan in 2020, allegations of racism against British Columbia's healthcare system in the same year, the blatant neglect of Brian Sinclair and his unnecessary death in 2008 at age 45, and the ongoing forced and coerced sterilization of Indigenous women and girls. These disturbing events lay bare the level of entrenched, insidious racism permeating Canadian society (National Collaborating Centre, 2020; Shaheen-Hussain, 2020; Turpel Lafond, 2020). This is a daily reality for many Indigenous peoples. This demands societal change.

These legacies result in persistent health and social inequities for Indigenous peoples. COVID-19 is shining a spotlight on these injustices. Many Indigenous populations' experiences with overcrowding, little or no access to safe water, and an ongoing mistrust in the healthcare system have resulted in an emergency among Indigenous peoples and communities that has culminated in and contributed to high rates of COVID-19 infection and deaths.

Historic and present-day inequalities cannot be separated from Indigenous peoples' questions about COVID-19 vaccines. Vaccine hesitancy and Indigenous populations' past experiences of medical experimentation are inextricably connected. This hesitancy has arisen from decades of neglect and willful ignorance about the unfair conditions created for Indigenous peoples across this country. Questions about the value and safety of these vaccines are directly impacted by Indigenous peoples' recent memories of fighting to regain and retain the most basic legal human rights to personal choice about and control over their own bodies. A lack of vaccine acceptance is a symptom of ongoing mistrust that is our collective colonial lineage.

Acknowledging and supporting Indigenous peoples' right to **self-determination**—the right to choose—is a critical step in addressing COVID-19 vaccine mistrust. Indigenous peoples have the right to credible and culturally-relevant information in order to make an informed choice. They have the right to question. They have the right to say "no." They also have the right to resources and strategies that acknowledge the colonial lineage and provide assurances that past atrocities will not happen again. All vaccine literatures for Indigenous peoples must draw on the strengths of our cultures and our teachings. They must be co-created rather than imposed. This includes recognizing, celebrating, and drawing on intergenerational relationships and the collective orientations of Indigenous cultures. In this spirit, many Indigenous Elders and Leaders from across the country have endorsed the COVID-19 vaccine as a means to protect our grandchildren and children, our families, and ultimately our communities.

In the short term, enhancing vaccine acceptance among Indigenous peoples will rest on pairing messaging about the scientific efficacy of the COVID-19 vaccine with information that is grounded in the strengths and wisdom of our teachings. All vaccine messaging for Indigenous peoples must support the precious and hard-fought right to personal choice. We must not allow history to repeat itself. It will be the work of all Canadians to acknowledge the legacies of colonial harm and to commit to a future of equity.

REFERENCES

Collier R. (2017). Reports of coerced sterilization of Indigenous women in Canada mirrors shameful past. *Canadian Medical Association Journal, 189*(33), E1080–1081. https://doi.org/10.1503/cmaj.1095471

MacDonald, N. E., Stanwick, R., & Lynk, A. (2014). Canada's shameful history of nutrition research on residential school children: The need for strong medical ethics in Aboriginal health research. *Paediatrics & Child Health, 19*(2), 64. https://doi.org/10.1093/pch/19.2.64

Mosby, I., & Swidrovich, J. (2021). Medical experimentation and the roots of COVID-19 vaccine hesitancy among Indigenous Peoples in Canada. *Canadian Medical Association Journal, 193*(11), E381–383. https://doi.org/10.1503/cmaj.210112

National Collaborating Centre for Indigenous Health (NCCIH). (2020). *Informed choice and consent in First Nations, Inuit and Metis women's health services: National forum, January 28-29, 2020.* https://www.nccih.ca/Publications/lists/Publications/Attachments/IC/RPT-NCCIH-Consent-Summary-Bios-EN_Web_NIVA_2021-03-18.pdf

Shaheen-Hussain, S. (2020). *Fighting for a hand to hold: Confronting medical colonialism against Indigenous children in Canada.* McGill University Press.

Stote, K. (2017). Birthright denied: The sterilization of Indigenous women. *Herizons, 31*(2), 16–19.

Turpel Lafond, M. E. (2020). *In plain sight: Addressing Indigenous-specific racism and discrimination in BC health care.* Ministry of Health. https://engage.gov.bc.ca/app/uploads/sites/613/2020/11/In-Plain-Sight-Summary-Report.pdf

CHAPTER 13

Taking Care: Indigenous Peoples' Art, Resurgence, and Wellness

Jaimie Isaac

LEARNING OBJECTIVES

1. To demonstrate how art can reflect and critique narratives outside the art world.
2. To introduce students to a selection of Indigenous artists who engage in health and wellness narratives.
3. To explain how colonial policies have affected the health of **Indigenous Peoples** by restricting their access to traditional food practices.

INTRODUCTION

"Curate" comes from the verb "to care for." In this chapter, this meaning will be extended to consider how bringing together relevant and significant artwork demonstrates care. Through the lens of an **Anishnaabe**-kwe/womxn's curatorial and community-focused positionality, this chapter will explore interdisciplinary art[1] from a selection of Indigenous artists who visually contextualize health and wellness as these relate to traditional forms of **subsistence** and food sovereignty (a human right to healthy and culturally appropriate food). Their exploration is related in part to understanding **foodways**, which include awareness about land biodiversity and knowledge of how to hunt, gather, forage, fish, and farm.

The featured artwork evokes active narratives outside the art world that unify or divide diverse cultural and political groups. Specifically, it examines the wide-ranging impacts of historical and ongoing colonial policies affecting the health of Indigenous Peoples. These policies support colonial systems that favour big industry and profit and promote dislocation from knowledge of the land at the expense of community health. In light of such policies, the artists explore Indigenous Peoples' reliance on commodity-based, commercially available food. They examine policies restricting access to traditional food practices and ancestral lands. Importantly, they also celebrate acts of cultural reclamation. This includes humans connecting to the land, a relationship that directly affects human and environmental health. In short, the interdisciplinary art in this chapter visually contextualizes health and wellness from diverse knowledge bases and creates critical dialogue. Understanding the relationship between food, health, and tradition helps Indigenous and non-Indigenous people combat ongoing colonial oppression.

The artwork is mediated by exploring terms of resistance, **survivance**, and **self-determination**. The study is situated in the **Truth and Reconciliation Commission's** (2015) Calls to Action (especially 18 and 19) and the **United Nations Declaration on the Rights of Indigenous Peoples** (UNDRIP) (UN General Assembly, 2007) (especially article 20). Calls to Action 18 and 19 charge the federal, provincial, territorial, and Aboriginal governments not only to acknowledge the connection between the current state of Aboriginal health in Canada and earlier government policies but also to recognize and implement the healthcare rights of **Aboriginal people** identified in law (internationally and nationally) and in **Treaties**. They also call on the federal government to consult with Aboriginal groups and individuals in order to identify and close the gaps in health outcomes between Indigenous and non-Indigenous populations.

Article 20 of the UNDRIP maintains, among other points, that Indigenous Peoples have the right to "be secure in the enjoyment of their own means of subsistence" and that they are "entitled to just and fair redress" when they are "deprived of their means of subsistence and development" (UN General Assembly, 2007, p. 7).

In 2019–2020, the Winnipeg Art Gallery hosted an exhibition entitled *subsist*,[2] which assembled a selection of interdisciplinary art that considered Indigenous traditional practices of food sovereignty and economies, including the controversial practice of seal hunting. Many of the artists featured in this chapter appeared in *subsist*. The exhibition revealed historical and contemporary impacts of **colonialism** on Indigenous Peoples' connection to land and uncovered knowledge about the determinants of health for Indigenous Peoples in Canada. As Mi'kmaq lawyer and activist, Dr. Pam Palmater, pointed out, "a giant, well-enforced wall of laws and regulations has kept Indigenous Peoples from hunting, fishing, fowling and gathering. Our traditional economies have been criminalized to maintain a non-Indigenous monopoly" (Palmater, 2020). This wall bolsters the large-scale food industry and modern systems of agriculture that negatively affect small-scale traditional foodways.

Maureen Gruben's installation, *Breathing Hole* (Figures 13.1 and 13.2), comprises 18,000 sealskin pins hand-fixed onto 40 squares of pale blue Dricore insulation: "These tiny circles of sealskin were punched out one at a time from piles of scraps— the collected remnants of a community sewing workshop" (Gruben, n.d., para. 1). The artwork visually echoes the landscape, and in particular, the floating ice sheets of the North. The white circular spot suggests a hole in the ice for seal hunting. Gruben brought community members together to complete the work over several months, evoking in artistic practice the patience of both seal hunting and collective labour. As Gruben created this piece, she considered and revered the patience and perseverance of her ancestors' subsistence lifestyle.

Breathing Hole recalls the women in Gruben's community using every piece of skin when making cultural material objects, including clothes and dolls. This "zero waste" practice has been common in Indigenous communities for centuries. For example, hunted seals fed, sheltered, clothed, and provided for the community. The items and objects derived from a seal include furnishings, tools, instruments, boats, baskets, toys, sports equipment, architecture, etc. In one visit to a Canadian museum, I recall seeing a 30-foot kayak with a hull made entirely of sealskin. It even had a sealskin buoy.

Figure 13.1: *Breathing Hole*, 2019. Dricore insulation board, stainless steel pins, sealskin, 48" × 30"
© Maureen Gruben. Reprinted with the kind permission of the artist. Photo credit: Kyra Kordoski.

Figure 13.2: *Breathing Hole*, 2019. Dricore insulation board, stainless steel pins, sealskin, 48" × 30"
© Maureen Gruben. Reprinted with the kind permission of the artist. Photo credit: Kyra Kordoski.

Mark Igloliorte's *Kayak is Inuktitut for Seal Hunting Boat* (Figure 13.3) asserts that the kayak is integral to Inuit ways of life. In so doing, it shifts popular perceptions of kayaks as watercrafts for tourist recreation in North America. Igloliorte originally created it as a painting, but it took its form in *subsist* as an enlarged vinyl reproduction embodying the spirit of a meme.

Respectfully drawing on earlier Inuit art, Igloliorte's kayaks are the same bright yellow as Luke Anguhadluq's in *The Men Hunting Caribou in Kayaks* (1978). The hunters' exuberant facial expressions in Igloliorte's work are also akin to the hunters' facial expressions in Anguhadluq's prints. Igloliorte was also inspired by the film, *Angry Inuk* (2016), directed by award-winning documentary director, Alethea Arnaquq-Baril,

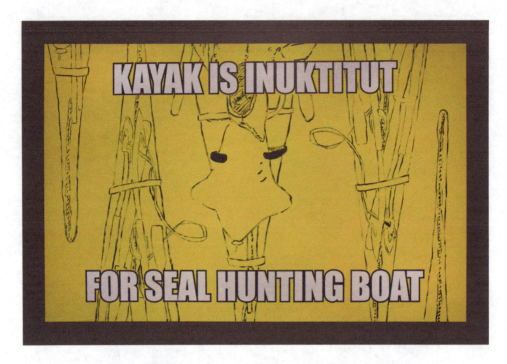

Figure 13.3: *Kayak is Inuktitut for Seal Hunting Boat*, 2019. Vinyl reproduction of acrylic on unstretched canvas. Collection of the artist.

© Mark Igloliorte. Photo Credit: Serge Gumenyuk, courtesy of the Winnipeg Art Gallery. Reprinted with the kind permission of the artist.

who uses storytelling through film and social media to advocate, with other Inuit, for sustainable traditional economies.

Igloliorte's work engages in the discussion on how the European Union's 2010 ban on the trade and exchange of seal products negatively impacted Inuit traditional economies rather than large-scale commercial hunting. Oppressive policies restricting seal hunting demonstrate a complete disregard for those affected:

> Inuit aren't just eating seal, they also depend heavily on seal pelt sales and are hit hardest by bans and boycotts. . . . The ban nevertheless promoted a worldwide collapse in demand for seal products. Overnight, Arctic sealing hunting revenues plummeted, nomadic hunters were forced to settle into fixed communities and the region's already-high suicide rates became the worst on the planet. (Hopper, 2018)

Whatever their intentions, organizations such as People for the Ethical Treatment of Animals (PETA) and Greenpeace have perpetuated myths that misguide the general public into demonizing the Inuit and their traditional hunting rights for subsistence. For example, "cute white fluffy baby seals" are not "clubbed to death" in seal hunts.

Instead, adult seals are humanely and sustainably hunted to feed families and make material goods. Environmental statistics and conservation research show the seal population is not depleted, as the traditional Inuit way of hunting results in a limited number of seals being hunted (Hopper, 2018). How, then, do these organizations inform policy that restricts Inuit access to cultural practices and limits their traditional economies?

We must balance the harm to the animals being hunted (not endangered) against the harm posed to human lives and cultural continuity when we consider oppressive policies that restrict traditional subsistence methods. These policies, which also repress Indigenous Peoples' knowledge and their long-standing respectful and **reciprocal** relationship with the land, demonstrate ongoing colonial violence and make a mockery of the Truth and Reconciliation Commission's Calls to Action. Creating policies and laws that do not consider the people they affect is an act of supremacy, as Natan Obed, President of Inuit Tapiriit Kanatami, a national research, advocacy, and education organization, explained: "**Systemic racism** remains the main barrier Inuit face when it comes to the laws and policies that most negatively impact individuals and communities. Addressing systemic racism requires a society-wide commitment to social equity in the areas of access to services, housing, infrastructure, and healthcare within the Call for Justice" (Inuit Tapiriit Kanatami, 2020).

Dana Claxton's *Buffalo Bone China* (Figures 13.4 and 13.5) reflects on the federal starvation policy under Canada's first Prime Minister, John A. Macdonald,

Figure 13.4: *Buffalo Bone China*, 1997. Video, buffalo bone china installation. Acquired with funds from the Winnipeg Rh Foundation Inc. and with the support of the Canada Council for the Arts Acquisition program, 1999-601.

© Dana Claxton. Collection of the Winnipeg Art Gallery. Photo Credit: Serge Gumenyuk. Reprinted with the kind permission of the artist and the Winnipeg Art Gallery.

Figure 13.5: *Buffalo Bone China*, 1997. Video, buffalo bone china installation. Acquired with funds from the Winnipeg Rh Foundation Inc. and with the support of the Canada Council for the Arts Acquisition program, 1999-601.

© Dana Claxton. Collection of the Winnipeg Art Gallery. Photo Credit: Serge Gumenyuk. Reprinted with the kind permission of the artist and the Winnipeg Art Gallery.

and the decimation of the buffalo population.[3] Claxton's work comprises broken pieces of bone china, arranged in a circular pile on the gallery floor in front of a projected film. The smashed bone china is an ironic part of the installation: the plates were created from buffalo bones for the settler population's dining needs, which contributed to the starvation of the Indigenous population. The work thus illustrates how government-legislated policies can support one culture at the cost of another.

The broken plates represent the disrepair that is a legacy of **colonization**. The sharp edges of the broken china allude to the violence of **resource extraction**, which brought wealth to settlers and impoverished Indigenous Peoples by displacing them from their land. Many colonial government policies legitimized land and resource theft and exploitation, such as the settler initiative to overhunt buffalo to facilitate the building of the railway. Other policies included tactics of social control, such as the pass system. This restricted tribes from leaving the reserves they were forced to live on unless they received permission from government agents, thus curtailing their opportunity to hunt. The agents also rationed

Indigenous Peoples' food. These genocidal policies harmed the tribes and the buffalo populations, as dependence on the buffalo for clothing, shelter, and food greatly affected Indigenous Peoples' survival and cultural connection. Other colonial-driven policies, such as the scorched earth policy (burning Indigenous Peoples' fields), denied Indigenous Peoples access to traditional food and resulted in their reliance on unhealthy, processed food, contributing to the prevalence of diabetes (LaDuke, 2005, pp. 194–195). These policies also increased Indigenous Peoples' reliance on welfare, thus stripping them of their freedom to sustain their traditional economies.

Omalluq Oshutsiaq's *Store items I remember in 1950s* (Figure 13.6) is a colour graphic drawing depicting commodity-based processed foods, such as canned meat, packaged coffee, tea, sugar, and flour, and other store items that Oshutsiaq recalls from the 1950s. During this decade, the local, land-based hunting and foraging practices that were part of Indigenous Peoples' sustainable food systems dramatically changed into colonially motivated systems of reliance on globalized agricultural and big industry food economies, which produced food that was

Figure 13.6: *Store items I remember in 1950s*, 2014. Graphite, coloured pencil, felt-tip pen on paper, 58.8 × 76.5 cm. Collection of the Winnipeg Art Gallery. Acquired with funds from the Estate of Mr. and Mrs. Bernard Naylor. Funds administered by The Winnipeg Foundation Inc., 2015-134.
© Omalluq Oshutsiaq. Photo credit: Serge Gumenyuk, courtesy of the Winnipeg Art Gallery. Reprinted with the kind permission of Dorset Fine Arts.

laden with preservatives, chemicals, and genetically modified organisms. Kwakwaka'wakw Elder Daisy Sewid-Smith expressed the following about this loss of food sovereignty:

> If you destroy your environment, you are destroying yourself. . . . When we [Kwakwaka'wakw people] took something from the environment . . . we were careful just to take what we needed. And that . . . is a difference between traditional Kwagiulths and Europeans today. We only took what we personally needed and no more, whereas the Europeans are reaping our resources to supply the rest of the world, and not thinking of the effects, how it's going to affect us in the future. (As cited in Turner, 2013, p. 129)

Oshutsiaq's artwork signals the shift from self-determining modes of traditional subsistence to reliance on heavily packaged and processed commercial food. The commercial food industry feeds a global economy. It starkly contrasts the practice of sourcing food locally. Stores in the geographic north of Canada charge excessive prices for water, produce, and healthy foods. Moreover, reliance on commercial food results in the consumption of foods from external (national and international) industries, thus depleting the community economies of local fishers and hunters. In a subtle act of resistance, the store items in Oshutsiaq's drawing prompt the viewer to consider the historical pivot from traditional to processed foods and policies affecting food sovereignty.

KC Adams's digital photography of black and white triptychs, *The Gifts* (Figure 13.7), juxtaposes images of the human body (impacted by diabetes) with

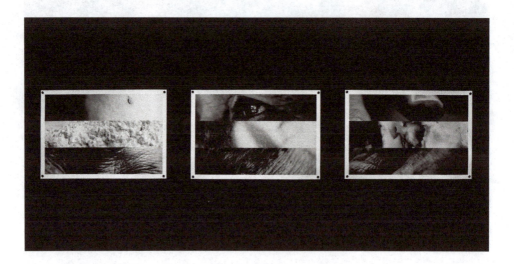

Figure 13.7: *The Gifts*, 2011. Three digital prints. 50.8 × 76.2 cm. each.
© KC Adams. Collection of the artist. Photo credit: Serge Gumenyuk, courtesy of the Winnipeg Art Gallery.

images of flour, sugar, and lard. These processed foods were provided as rations during the starvation policies that forbade Indigenous groups to hunt and maintain their traditional foodways. Ironically, flour, sugar, lard, and water are the ingredients for bannock, an item now culturally celebrated as a product of survival of and resistance to starvation.

Similar to the colour scheme in newspapers and many other publications, Adams's horizontal triptychs are black and white. This visually connects them with text (e.g., statistics, reports, articles, policies, laws), which has historically shaped social ideas about Indigenous Peoples. By juxtaposing body parts affected by diabetes with the "gifts of colonialism" (lard, sugar, flour) that contribute to the disease, the viewer gets the uneasy feeling that what can feed the hungry body can also cause it to erode.

When did diabetes become an endemic in Indigenous populations? Neufeld (2014) considered the turning point in history and the timeline of colonial policies that affected Indigenous Peoples' **well-being** in general and their traditional foodways in particular:

> Dietary change is therefore leading to significant changes in the physical health status of Aboriginal Peoples in Canada, but so, too, have the effects of dietary change on cultural identity been significant. . . . For many Indigenous peoples, food is a physical, as well as a spiritual medicine. Traditional, or perhaps more culturally accepted foods are highly valued among Indigenous groups for maintaining health, preserving cultural identity, and promoting a sense of self-worth or autonomy. (p. 28)

Casting a net outside the *subsist* exhibition, the following paragraphs introduce other artists who raise awareness about health, wellness, and **resilience** among Indigenous Peoples through contemporary art.

CMaxx Stevens's striking sculptural installation, *Last Supper* (Figures 13.8 and 13.9), is a conceptual feast on a white table. White plates present a lavish display of moulded cakes, piled donuts, and crumpets, all sprinkled with white powder (evoking sugar and flour). Underneath the table—hidden, secret, taboo—are shapes alluding to amputations and physical frailty. With *Last Supper*, Stevens reveals a diet that negatively affected Indigenous Peoples, and which was the result of "government programs that dole out processed foods loaded with salt, fat, and sugar, creating a generation of people with heart disease, high blood pressure and most notably, diabetes" (Stevens, 2013).

Stevens's powerful work carefully considers her community's future and culture. It also commemorates her tribal members, family, and friends who have suffered, and continue to suffer, from the impact of diabetes, dis-ease, and systemic health dysfunction: "The Seminole Diabetes Clinic predicts that one of every six Native people will develop diabetes," Stevens (2013) said. Although Indigenous Peoples are re-educating

Figure 13.8: *Last Supper*, 2012. Mixed media installation.
© CMaxx Stevens. Reproduction rights given through the IAIA Museum of Contemporary Native Arts, Institute of American Indian Arts, 82 Avan Nu Po Road, Sana Fe, NM 87508

themselves in traditional Indigenous food systems, as Stevens (2013) explained, "not only do economic conditions within the community make it difficult to make changes in diet, but these changes in eating habits are not second nature to our people. The foods that have become 'traditional' do not sustain the genetics of Native peoples."

Stevens's work addresses the social, cultural, political, and physical disabilities that connect diabetes and colonialism and, by extension, Indigenous health and land sovereignty. Without an actual body present in the work, *Last Supper* draws attention to ways in which cultural and social factors affect the body. In short, one could ponder, *are we what we eat?*

Last Supper, both in name and representation, reflects visual images of the final meal Jesus ate with his disciples before being crucified. The Christian practice of

Figure 13.9: *Last Supper*, 2012. Mixed media installation.

© CMaxx Stevens. Reproduction rights given through the IAIA Museum of Contemporary Native Arts, Institute of American Indian Arts, 82 Avan Nu Po Road, Sana Fe, NM 87508

eating bread together in memory of Christ's crucifixion permeates Stevens's installation. What *Last Supper* highlights, by deliberately paralleling religion and cultural genocide, is the relationship between colonialism and the church. Stevens underscores Indigenous Peoples' ill health as a consequence of religious indoctrination and colonial policies. Stevens works with some of the oldest motifs in the art historical canon—religion and the human figure—to raise awareness about the health epidemics within Indigenous communities. The forms under the table are bodily fragments—isolated from a full, whole-bodied being. Could the dislocation of the body be a metaphor for dislocation from the land and knowledge of traditional food systems?

Kent Monkman's *Nativity Scene* (Figure 13.10) explores ongoing colonial encroachment (invasion of lands and rights) and **hegemony**, continued land and resource extraction, child welfare, and **intergenerational trauma**. The triangle composition of figures links this piece to the Christian nativity scene, which depicts characters worshipping Jesus at his birth. Thus, the imagery unites colonialism with Christianity, the religion colonizers imposed on Indigenous Peoples.

Figure 13.10: *Nativity Scene*, 2017. Mixed media installation.
© Kent Monkman. Collection of Museum London. Reprinted with the kind permission of the artist.

The characters in Monkman's scene—mother, father, and baby—share Kent Monkman's own features, pointing to the static and "everyman" representations of Indigenous Peoples in museum settings and dioramas. The baby lies naked on a contemporary Hudson's Bay Company baby blanket, surrounded by objects suggesting unsafe/unhealthy living conditions: a plastic bottle filled with an unknown dark liquid, plastic diapers, a jerry can of gas, and a portable cooking element. The parents hover over the baby with rosaries clenched in their hands. Nearly everything evokes a sense of precariousness and distress. And yet, the scene is framed with a Latin saying translating to "love conquers all," a line Monkman extracted from a painting by the Italian Baroque artist, Caravaggio. It may be the only optimistic reference in this provocative piece. There is resilience in love.

The visual vocabulary in the *Nativity Scene* is layered with meaning and representation, presenting a multitude of issues that Indigenous Peoples face and illuminating the innumerable hard realities that are forced on many Indigenous families: poor housing conditions on reserves, illustrated by the substandard housing materials; high-priced processed food sold in community stores, such as pop and canned meat; and unsafe drinking water, underscored by the Nestle baby formula and "Pure Life" bottled water. The piece simultaneously points to the exploitation and appropriation of Indigenous identity from the main-(White)-stream: the mannequin wearing a Chicago Redskins jersey; a "made in China" ball cap adorned with dream catchers; and Dakota-label work boots.

In *Death of a Virgin* (Figure 13.11), Monkman summons the despair of the piece to which it refers: Caravaggio's *Death of the Virgin* (ca. 1601–1606). Monkman draws on Caravaggio to examine Indigenous health and community mourning. In *Death of a Virgin*, a young woman in a hospital bed is surrounded by a community of mourners in prayer. The painting exposes a plethora of realities for Indigenous Peoples who suffer in a racist healthcare system that affects their health and lives. The triggering image of a woman in bed represents all the hurt, missing, and murdered **Indigenous women**, children, and men—victims of violence and societal disregard.

Death of a Virgin also considers the epidemics, such as influenza, measles, and smallpox, that Europeans introduced to **Turtle Island** and that claimed the lives of many Indigenous Peoples. It also illustrates current diseases effectuated by colonial policies that plague Indigenous communities: tuberculosis, diabetes, HIV, AIDS, fetal alcohol syndrome (FAS), suicide, and intergenerational mental, physical, and spiritual dis-ease. However, in an act of cultural reclamation, Monkman also indicates a path of healing. Even in death and trauma, he points to recovery and a return to traditional medicines through such images as a **smudge** bowl, feather, and drum. As the medicine burns, releasing its cleansing and calming smoulder, one can imagine a healing song being sung to the beat of the drum.

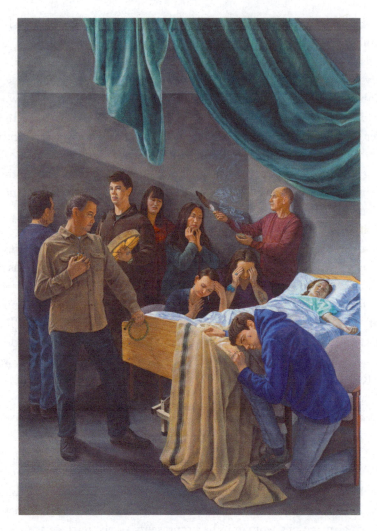

Figure 13.11: *Death of the Virgin (After Caravaggio)*, 2016. Acrylic on canvas, 72" × 51".
© Kent Monkman. Reprinted with the kind permission of the artist.

Resistance Comes from the Four Directions (Figure 13.12), by scholar and artist Dylan Miner, is a unifying and motivating illustrative call for action and self-determination. Miner is driven by care for community, future generations, the health of the land, and environmental justice. Art is often perceived to be storytelling through images and text. In this vein, Miner shared that "engaging the process of storytelling, as a medicinal practice tied to the *strength of the earth* [emphasis in original], helps Indigenous Peoples combat the omnipotent horrors of colonialism, and therefore serves as an anticolonial and liberatory device" (2013, p. 322). Miner's image resonates with meaning and power in an age of cultural

Figure 13.12: *Resistance Comes from the Four Directions*
© Dylan Miner. Reprinted with the kind permission of the artist (ca. 2019–2020).

resurgence. The title *Resistance Comes from the Four Directions* refers to the cardinal directions (north, east, south, west) of the medicine wheel, which carries **Anishinaabe** knowledge systems that are guides to life cycles and ways of being and that teach about the importance of balance and harmony.

Miner makes his artistic and scholarly activism available on social media as open-source content. He does this in the spirit of generosity and collective cultural reclamation and resurgence, as well as in the name of Indigenous sovereignty over land, bodies, and traditional means of cultural maintenance and subsistence. His respect for the ancestors' resilience reminds me of the Anishinaabe concept of *Mino Pimatisiwin*,[4] which was passed down to me from my matriarchal Anishinaabe-kwe family, and which is an approach to living in a way that seeks harmony, balance, and healing.

Miner's work appears in a time of public dissonance and resistance movements. *Resistance Comes from the Four Directions* both reflects and supports movements such as Idle No More, Standing Rock, the Wet'suwet'en pipeline resistance,

#LANDBACK, and global climate change and environmental rallies. In these movements, land protectors of many generations—youth and Elders, together—are standing on the frontline, armed with ancestral knowledge and political will, and risking their lives to speak for the land and land bequeathed to those not yet born—land that we have made fragile. Land protector and activist Winona LaDuke (2016) proclaimed, "this is a moment in Indigenous agriculture in North America. There is a resurgence, a recovery of Indigenous farming, native harvesting, food security, sovereignty, producers and chefs" (pp. 228–229). She added, "Why is this moment important? Because we have lost a great deal, and we will not be able to feed ourselves if we do not . . . take care of the land and water the food comes from, and in the process find ourselves" (pp. 228–229).

The most important things are the hardest to say, and each artist presented in this chapter has considered thoughtful and careful ways to create a visual literacy to address difficult yet significant realities respecting health and wellness. They have also, through striking and provocative artwork, challenged contemporary traditional means of subsistence and food sovereignty and demanded government accountability for Indigenous healthcare rights. Through curatorial considerations, community discussions, and artistic productions, artists are working together to foster ideas of what it means to "take care."

CRITICAL THINKING QUESTIONS

1. How do the artists featured in this chapter play with iconic religious images to explore the connections between religion and the disastrous effects of colonialism?
2. Does art have a role to play in sparking dialogue about important issues outside the art world? Is it effective for audiences to engage these issues through art?
3. What ethical challenges might an artist or curator face when making artwork or curating an exhibition that deals with issues of health and wellness?

NOTES

1. Interdisciplinary art involves more than one artistic discipline. This chapter captures just a few of the many significant Indigenous artists' health and wellness narratives.
2. *subsist* was curated by Jaimie Isaac (author) with Jocelyn Piirainen, Assistant Curator of Inuit Art at the Winnipeg Art Gallery.
3. The policy employed starvation to force Indigenous Peoples off their own land and onto federally appointed reserve lands, making way for the building of the Canadian Pacific Railroad and issuing in disease, sexual exploitation, and ethnic cleansing (DasChuk, 2013; Kelm, 2015).
4. My teachers for this concept/philosophy were Elaine Isaac (née Courchene), my mother, and Elder Dr. Mary Courchene, my nana. Both are survivors of the residential school system in Canada and sought cultural and language reclamation as a way to heal and practise the "good life."

REFERENCES

DasChuk, J. W. (2013). *Clearing the Plains: Disease, politics of starvation, and the loss of Aboriginal life*. University of Regina Press.

Gruben, Maureen. (n.d.). *Breathing hole*. Retrieved November 9, 2020, from https://www.maureengruben.com/breathing-hole

Hopper, T. (2018, April 4). The hunt Canada loves: Why seal clubbing will never die. *National Post*. Retrieved October 28, 2020, from https://nationalpost.com/news/canada-is-never-ever-going-to-stop-killing-seals-your-tell-all-guide-to-the-seal-hunt

Inuit Tapiriit Kanatami. (2020). *Inuit leadership supports the full implementation of the calls for justice contained within the National Inquiry into Missing, Murdered Indigenous Women and Girls "Reclaiming Power and Place" and their 231 Calls for Justice*. Retrieved March 5, 2020, from https://www.itk.ca/inuit-leadership-supports-the-full-implementation-of-the-calls-for-justice-contained-within-the-national-inquiry-into-missing-murdered-indigenous-women-and-girls-reclaiming-power-and-place/

Kelm, M-E. (2015). Clearing the path to truth: *Clearing the Plains: Disease, politics of starvation and the loss of Aboriginal life*, by James Daschuk, and the narrative of Canadian history. A Commentary. *Journal of the Canadian Historical Association, 26*(2), 43–52.

LaDuke, W. (2005). *Recovering the sacred: The power of naming and claiming*. South End Press.

LaDuke, W. (2016). *The Winona LaDuke chronicles: Stories from the front lines in the battle for environmental justice*. Fernwood Publishing.

Miner, D. A. T. (2013). Stories as Mshkiki: Reflections on the healing and migratory practices of Minwaajimo. In J. Doerfler, N. J. Sinclair, and H. Kiiwetinepinesiik Stark (Eds.), *Centering Ahishinaabeg studies: Understanding the world through stories* (pp. 317–340). Michigan State University Press.

Neufeld, H. T. (2014). We practically lived off the land: Generational changes in food acquisitions patterns among First Nation mothers and grandmothers. In D. Memee Lavell-Harvard and K. Anderson (Eds.), *Mothers of the Nations: Indigenous mothering as global resistance, reclaiming and recovery* (p. 28). Demeter Press.

Palmater, P. (2020, March 3). The blockades no one talks about devastate Indigenous economies. *Maclean's*. Retrieved March 5, 2020, from https://www.macleans.ca/opinion/the-blockades-no-one-talks-about-devastate-indigenous-economies/

Stevens, C-M. (2013). Seeing one's creative process. *Expedition Magazine, 55*(3). Retrieved March 5, 2020, from http://www.penn.museum/sites/expedition/?p=19134

Truth and Reconciliation Commission of Canada. (2015). *Honouring the truth, reconciling for the future: Summary of the Final Report of the Truth and Reconciliation Commission of Canada*. Truth and Reconciliation Commission of Canada. https://irsi.ubc.ca/sites/default/files/inline-files/Executive_Summary_English_Web.pdf

Turner, Nancy. (2013). *The earth's blanket: Traditional teachings for sustainable living*. Douglas & McIntyre.

UN General Assembly. (2007). *United Nations Declaration on the Rights of Indigenous Peoples: Resolution / adopted by the General Assembly,* 2 October 2007, A/RES/61/295. Retrieved March 14, 2020, from https://www.refworld.org/docid/471355a82.html

CHAPTER 14

A Path in the Snow: How Indigenous Medical Trainees Can Inspire Indigenous Youth to Become Medical Doctors

Thomsen D'Hont

LEARNING OBJECTIVES

1. To encourage students to consider how cultural sensitivity in healthcare and the number of Indigenous healthcare workers, including physicians, are important determinants of health for **Indigenous Peoples**.
2. To contextualize the progress of, and challenges related to, training more Indigenous physicians.
3. To describe the roles of medical trainees in inspiring Indigenous youth to pursue medical training.

INTRODUCTION

As a Métis from Yellowknife, Northwest Territories (NWT), medical school has been an incredibly challenging but also rewarding experience of personal growth and insight into humanity's tragedies and resilience. Getting into medical school and training to be a physician have been huge victories for my community and me, particularly since the NWT has a significant need for more Indigenous physicians and culturally safe healthcare for Indigenous patients. There is currently one Indigenous physician working in the NWT, even though the population is 50% Indigenous.

I was 27 when I received my medical school admission offer in mid-May 2016. I'd been labelled an "untraditional" applicant because my life experiences had periodically interrupted my university studies, and I was older than the average applicant.

Ironically, I don't think I could have been in a more traditional setting than hunting when I received my offer of admission.

I remember the day clearly: I was goose hunting in a marsh near Behchoko, NWT, with my dad and his friend, Francis. Earlier that day, I had stumbled on a large, curious black bear in our camp. There were a few tense moments as we scared it away. As the adrenaline wore off, I walked to the top of a nearby hill to get cell reception to load my emails. One stood out: "Congratulations! We are very pleased to offer you a position in the MD program." I immediately shared this much-anticipated news with my dad and Francis. Elated, we celebrated for about five minutes before returning to the business at hand: carefully scanning the horizon for bird movement. Aside from joy, my main emotion was relief. I had unsuccessfully applied the year before, after having spent thousands of dollars flying south to write my MCAT[1] and be interviewed. I had begun to doubt whether getting into medical school would ever become a reality. That night, lying in my tent, I pondered how my life was about to change. A pair of wolves howled on the mainland nearby.

Spurred by my experiences, I recently wrote a research paper about challenges and facilitators Indigenous students encounter on their journey to become medical doctors. The phrase "breaking trail" was part of my title. Unbeknownst to me, Dr. Nadine Caron, one of my preceptors[2] at the Northern Medical Program, similarly conceptualized the journey into medicine for Indigenous youth (TEDx Talks, 2017). Dr. Caron's metaphor was of a path covered in tall grass: the path is easily lost if only few people walk it, but it is easily followed if many people do because they keep the grass packed down.

My own inspiration for trail-breaking takes the form of a 200-kilometre winter dogsled trail connecting Fort Providence and Behchoko in my home region of the NWT. My great-great-great-grandmother, Catherine Beaulieu Bouvier Lamoureux, also known as *Kokum Baie* (Michif for "mother of us all"), was a renowned leader in her community. In this story, my great-great-great-grandmother is breaking trail through the fresh snow, using her snowshoes so her dog team can follow her. She often travels alone because others will slow her down. In the days between fresh snowfalls, others can use the well-packed trail to easily travel by dog team between the two communities. Without *Kokum Baie*, the trail will go out of use. The snow will become too deep for others to travel. Trails need to be maintained, be they trails of grass or snow. I am now walking these trails that my predecessors have created, doing my small part to keep them packed down so others can follow.

TRAINING MORE INDIGENOUS PHYSICIANS: PROGRESS AND ONGOING CHALLENGES

An important determinant of health for Indigenous populations is the availability of Indigenous health practitioners, including physicians. This is a need highlighted by the **Royal Commission on Aboriginal Peoples** (RCAP) of 1996, the **Kelowna Accord** of 2005, and the **Truth and Reconciliation Commission** of 2015. This is important for improving Indigenous patients' trust in the healthcare system, the quality of Indigenous patient care, and provider understanding of the cultural backgrounds and health issues faced by Indigenous Peoples (e.g., the health-damaging legacy of the Indian residential school system) (Cooper & Powe, 2004; Johnson-Jennings et al., 2015; LaVeist et al., 2003; Truth and Reconciliation, 2015).

The number of Indigenous healthcare providers in Canada increased by more than the targeted 10,000 following the 1996 RCAP final report. However, it was still not representative of the Indigenous population of Canada, leading to further calls for more Indigenous healthcare providers. In 2006, 3.8% of people in Canada were Indigenous, but they only comprised 2.1% of the nation's healthcare providers (Statistics Canada, 2006). The number of Indigenous physicians in Canada was proportionally even lower, with an estimated 100–150 Indigenous physicians in 2005, representing less than 0.25% of all physicians (Anderson & Lavallee, 2007). In 2002, Indigenous medical students were also significantly underrepresented, comprising 0.8% of first-year medical students in Canada (Spencer et al., 2005). In response, the Association of Faculties of Medicine of Canada (AFMC) partnered with the Indigenous Physicians Association of Canada (IPAC) in 2005 to co-lead the AFMC's Aboriginal Health Initiatives with the primary objectives of increasing Indigenous admissions to medical schools and incorporating Indigenous content into medical school curriculum (Anderson et al., 2019).

Following these initiatives, Indigenous healthcare workers increased to 3.1% of the healthcare workforce, with Indigenous physicians still significantly underrepresented at 0.8% of physicians in Canada (760 out of 93,985) (Statistics Canada, 2016). There are no accurate data on the numbers of Indigenous medical students in Canada (Anderson et al., 2019; Sadler et al., 2017). However, estimates show that the numbers of Indigenous medical students and graduates today are higher than ever: by 2016, a survey of the 17 faculties of medicine in Canada showed that, in the 10 faculties that responded, Indigenous medical students comprised 2.6% of first-year medical students (45 out of 1,755 seats) (Sadler et al., 2017). That said, 4.9% of people in Canada at the time were Indigenous.

Despite some success from the AFMC's Aboriginal Health Initiatives, there remain significant challenges to admitting a representative number of Indigenous medical students, incorporating effective Indigenous health curriculum, and providing sufficient anti-racism and anti-colonialism teachings within medical schools (Anderson et al., 2019). Barriers to encouraging more Indigenous youth to pursue medicine include: early childhood social determinants of health (e.g., poverty, lack of access to education); high school factors (e.g., lack of role models and mentors, lack of awareness about health careers); post-secondary factors (e.g., relocation from community, financial challenges); and socio-cultural factors (e.g., racism, social alienation,

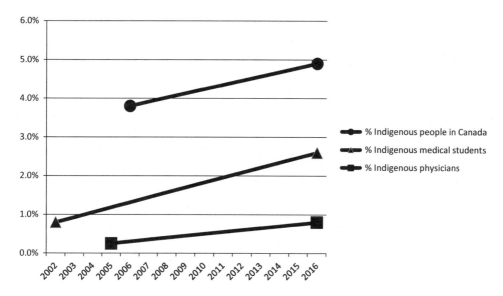

Figure 14.1: Percentages of Indigenous Peoples, Indigenous Medical Students, and Indigenous Physicians in Canada.

© Thomsen D'Hont, from Anderson & Lavallee (2007), Sadler et al. (2017), Spencer et al. (2005), Statistics Canada (2016), Statistics Canada (2006).

lack of Indigenous knowledge and ways of knowing within medical programs) (Health Canada, 2019). In response, the Canadian Federation of Medical Students has recommended policies such as prioritizing equity in admissions and implementing approaches that support Indigenous Peoples from secondary school, through medical school, and into their practices as physicians (Arkle et al., 2015). There are now established best practices to encourage youth to pursue medicine, including outreach and mentorship activities (Curtis et al., 2012). Notably, starting in 2019, the University of Alberta Faculty of Medicine prioritized equity in their admissions by removing the cap on the number of Indigenous students admitted to their program and by committing to admit all those who meet the admissions criteria (Alberta, 2019). So far, however, these best practices have been applied piecemeal across Canada (Anderson et al., 2019).

PERSPECTIVES FROM THE NORTHWEST TERRITORIES

As a child, I was not aware of any Indigenous medical students or doctors from the Northwest Territories. Growing up in Yellowknife, my Indigenous friends and I had few conversations about pursuing post-secondary education, let alone becoming doctors. I recall university representatives presenting at my high school, but there was never outreach from a medical school. Growing up in the relatively urban centre of

Yellowknife, I had access to high school courses that students in smaller NWT communities didn't have that would facilitate a post-secondary path. At the time, many high school counsellors encouraged my classmates and I to go into the trades or mining after high school.

A number of things inspired me to pursue medicine, including a Grade 9 teacher who instilled in me a love for science. I also had a few mentors in my community who were physicians, and later, in my mid-20s, I learned more about the need for Indigenous physicians in the NWT. I also learned the names of others from the territory who had been to medical school. I realized if they could do it, I could too.

The simple idea of hearing about other Indigenous Peoples from your community or region pursuing medicine can instill a novel idea in youth. Dr. Caron has a story about a young Indigenous girl whose belief that an Indigenous person couldn't be a doctor changed when they met (Greenwood et al., 2018). The importance of sparking peoples' interest in medicine at a young age was evidenced in Australia by Gore et al. (2018), who demonstrated how images of "types of people who pursue medicine" could shape self-concepts and aspirations in individuals as young as eight (p. 235). For others, who are older, an inspirational spark might still be enough to encourage them into medicine.

And examples of Indigenous doctors exist and must be broadcast. Take, for instance, Dr. Noah Carpenter, the first Inuvialuit doctor in Canada (Noah Carpenter, 2014). He is one of nine Indigenous physicians to have come from the NWT to date. He attended a residential school in Inuvik before beginning medical school in 1972, where he began a journey to become a thoracic and peripheral vascular surgeon. Whenever the NWT has a new Indigenous medical graduate—every few years in the last decade—they are celebrated in the news. Some young people may be inspired, as I was, but whether they are lastingly impacted following these fleeting celebrations is unclear. Graduates have been too infrequent to normalize medical training for Indigenous youth, at least in the NWT.

"MAYBE YOU SHOULDN'T HAVE GONE HUNTING" AND RACISM IN MEDICAL TRAINING

To encourage more Indigenous youth to pursue medical training, it is important to appraise and analyze some of the numerous challenges they face. Two of the most significant challenges—ones my family and I know intimately—are cultural disconnection and racism stemming from **colonialism**.

Recently, my dad went to see a locum family doctor about a chronic cough he had developed while we were on a hunting trip. Like many Indigenous patients, my dad doesn't usually or willingly go to the doctor. So, this was a bad cough. The doctor said to him, "Maybe you shouldn't have gone hunting." The doctor then explained he didn't believe in hunting. I was angry when my dad told me about the interaction. To my dad and me, and to many others in the NWT, hunting isn't as simple as believing or not believing in it. Hunting is about food security in a region where groceries are very expensive. Hunting is also about engaging in cultural traditions and maintaining connection to the **land**. My dad told that doctor as much.

This doctor had jumped to conclusions and shared his beliefs without being better informed about issues facing Indigenous Northerners. Although a doctor is entitled to their own beliefs, I deeply believe they should be more informed about the context they're working in. The health of the NWT patient population, especially Indigenous patients, is anchored in cultural strengths, including hunting. Unfortunately, racist ideas and practices aren't uncommon in the Canadian healthcare system, and egregious practices still occur. Take, for example, the ongoing coerced sterilization of **Indigenous women** across Canada (Boyer, 2017; Zingel, 2019).

Indeed, the impacts of **colonization** and racism permeate the medical training system. As an Indigenous medical student, I have regularly encountered racist and discriminatory comments on clinical rotations and in classroom settings. Recent papers have documented racism as a significant reality for Indigenous students in both undergraduate and medical studies (Currie et al., 2012; DeCoteau et al., 2017; Health Canada, 2019; Ly & Crowshoe, 2015). In clinical training settings, it is difficult to challenge individuals who make racist comments since evaluations depend on pleasing preceptors. Indigenous medical students from the University of Manitoba identified the effect of the power differential in clinical training and the difficulties of challenging authority; they regretted that they had not objected to the racism they experienced (DeCoteau et al., 2017).

I have also found it difficult to challenge preceptors, even when I have been directly confronted with racism. I once assisted a senior surgical resident physician in the operating room who referred to the overweight Indigenous woman on the operating table as a "Northern special" while she was unconscious. This was a respected Elder whose life story, including her pivotal role in her Northern community, I had the honour of knowing. Yet a resident doctor was reducing this amazing woman to a damaging stereotype. Was the resident having a bad day? Was this behaviour normalized in her profession? As I am a White-passing person, did the resident know that I was Indigenous? Would she have made such comments in front of someone with darker skin?

With certain preceptors, I have felt myself anticipating racist comments based on past experiences or warnings from colleagues. I am forced to be constantly on guard, which is exhausting emotionally and physically. I feel I must always be preparing a response to preceptors' derogatory statements that won't, hopefully, negatively affect the all-important evaluations. The best response I can give is, "What do you mean by that?" or "Maybe that patient had a difficult upbringing." In the moment in which I am racking my brain for the right words, I might have lost the opportunity to speak up. I have often felt inadequate for not quickly summoning a response, but I also recognize significant power differentials that have prevented these important conversations. Although my colleagues and I have found mistreatment reporting or submitting a complaint helpful, we have experienced varying degrees of success doing so. Moreover, in many situations, it is difficult to know whether a situation is bad enough to warrant raising a flag.

Racism even occurs within social settings at medical school. At a Halloween event in Vancouver during my first year of medical training, a medical student in the year ahead of me, who I didn't know, was dressed as an "Indian"—war paint and everything. I was appalled and disappointed that one of my colleagues would do this, someone who was vetted by the admission process and had undergone cultural sensitivity training as part of the first-year curriculum. Did she not realize how, as a member of the cultural group that colonized Canada, wearing Indigenous cultural dress in jest could be offensive, especially to Indigenous Peoples? Did she know there were Indigenous medical students at this event? Would she have dressed differently if she had known? Was this a marker of more widespread systemic factors that normalize this type of racist behaviour to the point that it can persist in medical school—a place where students are supposed to be aware of and sensitive to structures of power and oppression? I was there with another Indigenous medical student colleague, and we decided that this wasn't the time or place for us to approach this individual about her offensive behaviour. And anyhow, we were lost for words.

CULTURAL DISCONNECTION

Another one of my prominent experiences in medical training is cultural disconnection. One of the most challenging aspects of pursuing an intensive four-year degree is being geographically removed from my traditional territory. This has greatly affected my well-being as I derive much of my wellness from being on the land. The separation from community—specifically family and Elders—suspends my role in my community. It also postpones my learning of traditional skills and knowledge, which is another important branch of my education as an Indigenous person.

Beyond being geographically distant from traditional territory and disconnected from community, the experiences of medical education alter one's behaviour and life perspectives. Medical trainees bear witness to the tragedies and joys of patients and their families, and this affects all medical trainees to some extent. Yet, learning the predominant attitudes and behaviours attached to being a physician can affect Indigenous students in ways that it doesn't affect non-Indigenous students. One American researcher even studied the extent to which medical education for Indigenous Peoples is "an experience in assimilation" into White culture (Buckley, 2004, p. 20). Participants acknowledged that medical studies are life-altering. Yet, they rejected the idea that they were assimilated, demonstrating instead how they became physicians on their own terms, preserving their Indigenous identities with specific, intentional activities. For me, sneaking out for at least one annual hunting trip with my dad, setting snares over winter holidays with friends and family, or hunting for chickens with a preceptor while on an elective have all helped me maintain cultural connection.

I believe living away from community is worth the accompanying challenges because of the potential impact we can make on our home regions, or on wherever we choose to work. Even in these early stages of my training and career, I have already gained a sense of the impact I can have on Indigenous patients and their families. These patients, especially the Elders, also have a tremendous impact on me.

HOW CAN INDIGENOUS MEDICAL TRAINEES INSPIRE INDIGENOUS YOUTH TO PURSUE MEDICAL TRAINING?

Indigenous medical trainees can play a key role in inspiring future generations of Indigenous youth to do likewise because they are relatively close in age and are familiar with how to get into and succeed in medical school. Along with other Indigenous medical trainees, I have been part of outreach and mentoring activities for Indigenous youth.

One powerful outreach experience—an afternoon workshop that I organized at a Yellowknife high school for Indigenous and non-Indigenous students in Grades 11 and 12—occurred before I began medical school. I invited several local physicians to assist in a suturing workshop and a hands-on trauma scenario. The University of Alberta flew up Dr. James T'Seleie, a recent Indigenous medical graduate from the NWT who was doing his residency in Edmonton, to participate. Dr. T'Seleie and I presented on our own experiences growing up in the North and applying to medical school. I could see the students' eyes grow wide as they learned that Dr. T'Seleie had grown up in the NWT. After the event, 20 of the 50 attendees filled out a brief feedback form, providing unanimous positive reviews. Many students indicated this was the first time they had learned about the process of pursuing medical training and that they were interested in learning more about it. This workshop demonstrated that, even within schools with well-developed science programs and access to guidance counsellors, there is a need to improve access to this information.

Another powerful outreach experience I had was with an Elder at a school in a Dene community close to Yellowknife. The Elder spoke to the adolescents about wellness and the Dene laws while weaving in stories about how we can incorporate traditional medicine into **Western** medical practice. I shared a brief account of growing up in Yellowknife and my own journey into medicine. I then taught the students how to listen to the heart and lungs with a stethoscope.

> ### Incorporating Traditional Medicine into Western Medical Practice
>
> Elders in First Nations, Métis, and Inuit communities have a crucial role in guiding the development of services and programs within their regions to infuse Western medical practices with traditional medicine. The Elder I was working with before I began medical school promotes a collaborative approach between traditional healers and Western healthcare providers that emphasizes the importance of ceremony, traditional medicines, and the knowledge of traditional practitioners. The Truth and Reconciliation Commission's Calls to Action and the **United Nations Declaration on the Rights of Indigenous Peoples** (UNDRIP) do the same. The systematic oppression of traditional healing practices has kept Indigenous knowledges from being passed on to many Indigenous Peoples, and so the Elders are vital to blending these practices.

Anecdotal evidence shows that the outreach experiences I have just outlined inspired Indigenous youth to consider pursuing medicine. Unfortunately, even though most medical schools in Canada have some form of related outreach, there is a lack of academic literature describing or evaluating the outreach and mentorship activities that Indigenous medical trainees can undertake. For example, Western University and the Northern Ontario School of Medicine have incorporated Indigenous medical students into their outreach and mentorship activities, but they have neither provided a description of these activities nor articulated their impact (Hill, 2007; Sadler et al., 2017). Moreover, the grey literature (i.e., information generated outside of traditional publishing pathways) has shown that a role model program from the mid-2000s with the now-defunct National Aboriginal Health Organization (NAHO) highlighted the successes of Indigenous medical trainees and incorporated them into outreach activities to Indigenous communities; however, no evaluations of these programs are available (NAHO, 2009; Wohlberg, 2012).

A few sources (e.g., Henderson et al., 2015) described medical students' outreach with Indigenous youth, but none specifically mentioned Indigenous medical trainees' efforts (Clar et al., 2018). Henderson et al. (2015) recounted their successful mini-medical school program for Indigenous youth but tempered the program's success with a question about whether their short-term format would have sustained long-term positive impacts on attendees. Anonson et al. (2008) mentioned a nursing program in Saskatchewan that engaged Indigenous nursing students in outreach activities at high schools, but they neither described nor evaluated these activities. They also highlighted the existence of peer-mentoring between nursing students in different years of study and informal mentoring between practising Indigenous nurses and community members. These mentorship and outreach activities were part of an overall successful program, but the degree to which they contributed to this success is unclear. Maurice et al. (2019) evaluated medical students' outreach to youth in rural communities in BC, but they neither pointed out that several of the medical students and youth were Indigenous nor assessed the interactions between Indigenous participants. This raises the question, how many current outreach and mentorship activities include but do not report on Indigenous participants?

Despite a lack of studies about mentorship roles by Indigenous medical trainees and recent graduates specifically, related studies have shown how mentoring youth from low socio-economic backgrounds has facilitated their pursuit of medical studies. This contrasts with their peers who come from more advantaged backgrounds, have strong connections to the medical profession (e.g., a family member who is a doctor), and who thus have enhanced opportunities or access to information that support their pursuit of medical training (Nicholson & Cleland, 2017).

Studies on the recent influx of Indigenous role models and potential mentors in the medical field can help inform future directions for outreach activities with young people that could encourage more Indigenous youth into medicine.

CONCLUSION

For Indigenous youth, numerous geographic, social, financial, and cultural determinants impede or facilitate achieving medical training. Recent efforts by the Association of Faculties of Medicine of Canada (AFMC) and the Indigenous Physicians Association of Canada have resulted in an increase in Indigenous students of medicine. The arrival of a new generation of Indigenous medical students and graduates who can inspire the next generation to do likewise can help maintain this momentum. Ultimately, training more Indigenous physicians can lead to cultural change within healthcare institutions to the benefit of Indigenous health. Furthermore, although there is a lack of literature about how Indigenous medical trainees and physicians can inspire Indigenous youth to pursue medical training, best practices and anecdotal reports such as those outlined above suggest the importance of these roles.

Beyond the need for ongoing outreach to Indigenous students by Indigenous medical trainees and physicians—and the need to evaluate such efforts—other endeavours are required to improve processes for Indigenous students to study medicine and to support them during medical training. For example, barriers to admission must be lifted to expedite admissions processes. Such an initiative could further encourage students to enter healthcare by making the medical training environment more appealing for the next generation.

The AFMC's Joint Committee to Action on Indigenous Health identifies numerous action statements that include laudable goals, such as advancing relationships between medical schools and Indigenous communities, bettering the learning environment, improving admissions policies, and incorporating anti-colonialism and anti-racism frameworks into Indigenous health curricular content in medical school and residency training.

The number of Indigenous physicians in Canada can itself be seen as an important determinant of health. Thus, with new cohorts of Indigenous medical trainees and physicians reaching a critical mass, we can normalize becoming a doctor for Indigenous youth. We can provide a spark of inspiration to the fastest-growing demographic in Canada (Aboriginal Peoples, 2019). Trails in snow and grass are being forged, and those trails are being travelled.

CRITICAL THINKING QUESTIONS

1. What are the differences between equity and equality? Provide an example of each.
2. Compare and contrast equity- and merit-based approaches for evaluating applicants for a job or for medical school. Which value system is more common today? Why do you think it is more common?
3. What are some constructive approaches to challenging racist or discriminatory remarks by colleagues or peers?
4. Reflect on an experience that inspired you to pursue something. Alternatively, reflect on mentorship you have received that has given you strength and resilience. How did these experiences or mentorship influence you?

NOTES

1. Medical College Admission Test. A computer-based standardized test administered by the American Association of Medical Colleges. Required for admission to most medical schools in Canada.
2. An experienced practitioner who teaches/mentors/advises students and less-experienced practitioners.

REFERENCES

Aboriginal Peoples in Canada: Key results from the 2016 Census. (2019). *The Daily*. Retrieved January 13, 2020, from: https://www150.statcan.gc.ca/n1/daily-quotidien/171025/dq171025a-info-eng.htm

Alberta, University of. (2019). *Indigenous Admissions Review: MD Program*. https://www.ualberta.ca/medicine/media-library/programs/ihi/university-of-albertaindigenous-admissions-review-reportmarch-5-2019.pdf

Anderson, M., & Lavallee, B. (2007). The development of the First Nations, Inuit and Métis medical workforce. *Medical Journal of Australia*, 186(10), 539–540. https://doi.org/10.5694/j.1326-5377.2007.tb01033.x

Anderson, M. C., Crowshoe, L., Diffey, L., Green, M., Kitty, D., Lavallee, B., Saylor, K., & Richardson, L. (2019). *Joint commitment to action on Indigenous health*. https://afmc.ca/sites/default/files/pdf/AFMC_Position_Paper_JCAIH_EN.pdf

Anonson, J. M., Desjarlais, J., Nixon, J., Whiteman, L., & Bird, A. (2008). Strategies to support recruitment and retention of first nations youth in baccalaureate nursing programs in Saskatchewan, Canada. *Journal of Transcultural Nursing, 19*(3), 274–283. https://doi.org/10.1177/1043659608317095

Arkle, M., Deschner, M., Giroux, R., Morrison, R., Nelson, D., Sauvé, A., & Singh, K. (2015). Indigenous Peoples and Health in Canadian Medical Education CFMS Position Paper.

Boyer, Y. (2017). Healing racism in Canadian health care. *Canadian Medical Association Journal, 189*(46), E1408–E1409. https://doi.org/10.1503/cmaj.171234

Buckley, A. (2004). Does becoming a professional mean I have to become White? *Journal of American Indian Education, 43*(3), 19.

Clar, M., Drouin, E., & Iverson, S. (2018). Dare to dream: Promoting Indigenous children's interest in health professions through book collections. *Journal of the Canadian Health Libraries Association, 39*(2), 28–55. https://doi.org/10.29173/jchla29364

Cooper, L. A., & Powe, N. R. (2004, July 1). Disparities in patient experiences, health care processes, and outcomes: The role of patient-provider racial, ethnic, and language concordance. *The Commonwealth Fund.* Retrieved March 8, 2020, from https://www.commonwealthfund.org/publications/fund-reports/2004/jul/disparities-patient-experiences-health-care-processes-and

Currie, C. L., Wild, T. C., Schopflocher, D. P., Laing, L., & Veugelers, P. (2012). Racial discrimination experienced by Aboriginal university students in Canada. *The Canadian Journal of Psychiatry, 57*(10), 617–625. https://doi.org/10.1177/070674371205701006

Curtis, E., Wikaire, E., Stokes, K., & Reid, P. (2012). Addressing Indigenous health workforce inequities: A literature review exploring "best" practice for recruitment into tertiary health programmes. *International Journal for Equity in Health, 11*(13). https://doi.org/10.1186/1475-9276-11-13

DeCoteau, M. A., Woods, A., Lavallee, B., & Cook, C. (2017). *Race and racism: Unsafe learning environments: Indigenous medical students' experiences of racism.* http://www.limenetwork.net.au/wp-content/uploads/2017/10/Anderson-DeCoteau.M-Woods.A-Lavellee.B-Cook.C-GPCS-V4.pdf

Gore, J., Patfield, S., Holmes, K., & Smith, M. (2018). Widening participation in medicine? New insights from school students' aspirations. *Medical Education, 52*(2), 227–238. https://doi.org/10.1111/medu.13480

Greenwood, M., de Leeuw, S., & Lindsay, N. M. (2018). *Determinants of Indigenous Peoples' health: Beyond the social* (2nd ed.). Canadian Scholars' Press.

Health Canada. (2019). *Evaluation of the First Nations and Inuit Health Human Resources Program 2008–09 to 2012–13.* https://www.canada.ca/content/dam/hc-sc/migration/hc-sc/ahc-asc/alt_formats/pdf/performance/eval/2013-fni-hr-rh-pni-eng.pdf

Henderson, R. I., Williams, K., & Crowshoe, L. (2015). Mini-med school for Aboriginal youth: Experiential science outreach to tackle systemic barriers. *Medical Education Online, 20*(1), 29561–29567. https://doi.org/10.3402/meo.v20.29561

Hill, S. M. (2007). *Best practices to recruit mature Aboriginal students to medicine.* The Association of Faculties of Medicine of Canada. https://www.afmc.ca/sites/default/files/pdf/IPAC-AFMC_Recruitment_of_Mature_Aboriginal_Students_EN.pdf

Johnson-Jennings, M., Tarraf, W., & González, H. M. (2015). The healing relationship in Indigenous patients' pain care: Influences of racial concordance and patient ethnic salience on healthcare providers' pain assessment. *International Journal of Indigenous Health, 10*(2), 33–50. https://doi.org/10.18357/ijih.102201515112

LaVeist, T. A., Nuru-Jeter, A., & Jones, K. E. (2003). The association of doctor–patient race concordance with health services utilization. *Journal of Public Health Policy, 24*(3/4), 312–323. https://doi.org/10.2307/3343378

Ly, A., & Crowshoe, L. (2015). "Stereotypes are reality": Addressing stereotyping in Canadian Aboriginal medical education. *Medical Education, 49*(6), 612–622. https://doi.org/10.1111/medu.12725

Maurice, S., Mytting, K., Gentles, J. Q., Roots, R., Constantin, A. G., Kruger, S. L., Sim, S., Brock, W., Oyedele, O., Soles, J. A., & Snadden, D. (2019). The healthcare travelling roadshow: A qualitative study of a rural community engagement initiative in Canada. *Rural and Remote Health, 19*(3), 5238. https://doi.org/10.22605/RRH5238

NAHO. (2009). Lead Your Way! National Aboriginal Role Model Program. Paper presented at the NAHO Conference, Ottawa, ON. https://www.slideshare.net/NAHONews/national-aboriginal-role-model-program

Nicholson, S. & Cleland, J. A. (2017). "It's making contacts": Notions of social capital and implications for widening access to medical education. *Advances in Health Sciences Education, 22*(2), 477–490. https://doi.org/10.1007/s10459-016-9735-0

Noah Carpenter: Health (1995). (2014). *Indspire*. Retrieved January 10, 2020, from https://indspire.ca/laureate/noah-carpenter-2/

Sadler, K., Johnson, M., Burnett, C., Gula, L., & Kenard, M. A. (2017). Indigenous student matriculation into medical school: Policy and progress. *International Indigenous Policy Journal, 8*(1). https://doi.org/10.18584/iipj.2017.8.1.5

Spencer, A., Young, T., Williams, S., Yan, D., & Horsfall, S. (2005). Survey on Aboriginal issues within Canadian medical programmes. *Medical Education, 39*(11), 1101–1109. https://doi.org/10.1111/j.1365-2929.2005.02316.x

Statistics Canada. (2006). *2006 Census topic-based tabulations*. Retrieved March 8, 2020, from https://www12.statcan.gc.ca/census-recensement/2006/dp-pd/tbt/Rp-eng.cfm?LANG=E&APATH=3&DETAIL=0&DIM=0&FL=A&FREE=0&GC=0&GID=0&GK=0&GRP=1&PID=97446&PRID=0&PTYPE=88971,97154&S=0&SHOWALL=0&SUB=738&Temporal=2006&THEME=73&VID=0&VNAMEE=&VNAMEF=

Statistics Canada. (2016). *Data tables, 2016 census*. Retrieved March 8, 2020, from https://www12.statcan.gc.ca/census-recensement/2016/dp-pd/dt-td/Rp-eng.cfm?TABID=2&LANG=E&A=R&APATH=3&DETAIL=0&DIM=0&FL=A&FREE=0&GC=01&GL=-1&GID=1325190&GK=1&GRP=1&O=D&PID=112126&PRID=10&PTYPE=109445&S=0&SHOWALL=0&SUB=0&Temporal=2017&THEME=124&VID=0&VNAMEE=&VNAMEF=&D1=1&D2=0&D3=0&D4=0&D5=0&D6=0

TEDx Talks. (2017). The Other Side of "Being First" | Nadine Caron | TEDxUNBC [Video]. YouTube. https://www.youtube.com/watch?v=6JEry_t0Cfw

Truth and Reconciliation Commission of Canada. (2015). *Honouring the truth, reconciling for the future: Summary of the Final Report of the Truth and Reconciliation Commission of Canada*. https://irsi.ubc.ca/sites/default/files/inline-files/Executive_Summary_English_Web.pdf

Wohlberg, M. (2012, April 17). NAHO cuts put an end to Role Model program. *Northern Journal*. Retrieved January 13, 2020, from http://norj.ca/2012/04/naho-cuts-put-an-end-to-role-model-program/

Zingel, A. (2019, April 18). Indigenous women come forward with accounts of forced sterilization, says lawyer. *CBC*. Retrieved March 8, 2020, from https://www.cbc.ca/news/canada/north/forced-sterilization-lawsuit-could-expand-1.5102981

CHAPTER 15

Youth Protection, Social Determinants of Health, and Reappropriation of Decision-Making Power: Quebec First Nations Demands

Marjolaine Sioui, Patricia Montambault, Michel Deschênes, Marie-Pier Paul, Leila Ben Messaoud, and Richard Gray (First Nations of Quebec and Labrador Health and Social Services Commission)

LEARNING OBJECTIVES

1. To stimulate reflection on social determinants of health and their effect on **child neglect** in the context of First Nations.
2. To articulate First Nations' main demands about the recognition of rights to child and family services in Quebec.
3. To discuss the benefits, effects, and challenges related to C-92–*An Act Respecting First Nations, Inuit and Métis Children, Youth and Families* in terms of **self-determination**.

INTRODUCTION

Quebec First Nations have taken numerous political and legal actions to have their inherent rights to child and family services recognized. This article presents the main contributions of First Nations and the resulting changes.

First Nations and their Historical Context in Quebec

In Quebec, there are 43 First Nations communities from 10 nations:[1] Abenaki, Algonquin, Atikamekw, Cree, Innu, Maliseet, Mi'gmaq, Mohawk, Naskapi, and

Huron-Wendat. Diversity is a key element because each community and nation has its own historical, economic, and cultural characteristics.

> **One more time, en français**
> Le Québec compte 43 communautés des Premières Nations issues de dix nations:[1] les Abénakis, les Algonquins, les Atikamekw, les Cris, les Innus, les Malécites, les Mi'gmaq, les Mohawks, les Naskapis et les Hurons-Wendat. La diversité est un élément central, car chaque communauté et chaque nation ont leurs particularités sur les plans historique, social, économique et culturel.

In 2018, the First Nations population was 88,678 in Quebec (1% of the population). Of those, 64% live in communities, and 36% live outside of communities. Although the First Nations population is younger than that of the rest of Quebec and is rapidly growing with high fertility rates, the population in some communities is aging: between 2002 and 2015, the median age rose from 24 to 32 (Indigenous Services Canada, 2018).

Like everywhere else in Canada, **colonialism** has dramatically impacted these Peoples, notably as a result of three historical events: (1) the introduction of *An Act for the Gradual* **Enfranchisement** *of Indians, the Better Management of Indian Affairs, and to Extend the Provisions of the Act 31st Victoria, Chapter 42* in 1869; (2) the introduction of the *Indian Act* in 1876; and (3) the requirement, as of 1920, for all children to attend a residential school. The loss and trauma suffered by First Nations people have been widely documented in reports from inquiry commissions, such as the **Royal Commission on Aboriginal Peoples**, the National Inquiry into **Missing and Murdered Indigenous Women and Girls (MMIWG)**, the **Truth and Reconciliation Commission (TRC)**, and the Public Inquiry Commission on Relations Between **Indigenous Peoples** and Certain Public Services. The wounds of this painful legacy have affected several generations of First Nations, and its effects endure. It is hard to break the cycle of this intergenerational transmission in a context where **colonization** has created economic, social, and political conditions that have marginalized First Nations, and where racist, ethnocentric ideas continue to cause violence (Reading & Wien, 2009; National Inquiry, 2019).

In Quebec, the *Youth Protection Act* (YPA), passed in 1977, established the entire province's general youth protection program. It is an emergency act, meaning that it only applies when a child's safety and development are in danger. From the outset, First Nations people have heavily criticized it. They often feel excluded from decision making and confronted with a system that is imposed on them and that does not adequately account for their realities, their concepts of family, and their cultures. The Act is administered by Directors of Youth Protection (DYPs) who exercise their authority over the entire population in all administrative regions, including First Nations communities.

Political Administrative Governance Structures

The Assembly of First Nations Quebec-Labrador (AFNQL), created in 1985, is composed of the Chiefs from Quebec and Labrador's 43 First Nations communities. The AFNQL has created several regional commissions and organizations, including the First Nations of Quebec and Labrador Health and Social Services Commission (FNQLHSSC). Founded in 1994 by means of a resolution of the AFNQL Chiefs, FNQLHSSC is responsible for supporting First Nations efforts to plan and deliver culturally appropriate preventive health and social services programs. Its mission is to work with Quebec First Nations to help them achieve their health, wellness, culture, and self-determination goals. FNQLHSSC is governed by a Board of Directors composed of seven members elected by the general assembly.

> **One more time, en français**
>
> L'Assemblée des Premières Nations Québec-Labrador (APNQL) a été créée en 1985. Elle est composée des chefs des 43 communautés des Premières Nations au Québec et au Labrador. Au fil des ans, l'APNQL a créé différentes commissions et organismes régionaux (COR), dont la Commission de la santé et des services sociaux des Premières Nations du Québec et du Labrador (CSSSPNQL). Celle-ci a été créée en 1994, par voie de résolution des chefs de l'APNQL, et elle est responsable d'appuyer les efforts des Premières Nations dans la planification et la prestation de programmes de santé et de services sociaux culturellement adaptés et préventifs. Elle a pour mission d'accompagner les Premières Nations au Québec dans l'atteinte de leurs objectifs en matière de santé, de mieux-être, de culture et d'autodétermination. Elle est administrée par un conseil d'administration, composé de sept membres élus par son assemblée générale.

SOCIAL DETERMINANTS OF HEALTH AND CHILD NEGLECT

Overview of the Child Neglect Situation among First Nations

Data on **child neglect** among First Nations come primarily from two studies: the First Nations Component of the *Canadian Incidence Study of Reported Child Abuse and Neglect* (Sinha et al., 2011), conducted nationwide; and the *Analysis Project on the Trajectories of First Nations Youth Subject to the Youth Protection Act* (FNQLHSSC, 2013; 2016), which concerns Quebec in particular.

Studies show that First Nations children are overrepresented at all stages of the youth protection intervention process (Trocmé et al., 2004; Sinha et al., 2011, 2013; FNQLHSSC, 2016). This overrepresentation increases with every decision made during the assessment period. In Canada, the investigation rate for First Nations children is 4.1 times higher than for non-Indigenous children. First Nations children are also

12.4 times more likely to be placed in out-of-home care during the investigation than non-Indigenous children (Sinha et al., 2011). In Quebec, data from mainstream youth protection agencies indicate that:

> The rate of neglect investigations (per one thousand children in the population) for First Nations children was 6.7 times higher than the rate for non-Aboriginal children. The disparity in investigation rates was higher for neglect (6.7) than for any other type of maltreatment. . . . Within the neglect category, the disparity was greatest for investigations of risk of neglect. The rate for First Nations children was 9.3 times higher than the rate for non-Aboriginal children, in comparison with rates varying from 5.1 to 5.4 higher for other neglect categories. . . . In addition, almost half (48%) of the First Nations children with a retained report were 5 or under at the time of the report. (FNQLHSSC, 2016, pp. 15–16)

Risk factors identified by First Nations people include substance abuse, domestic violence, and caregiver history of being placed in foster care or in a group home (Sinha et al., 2011).

Social Determinants of Health for First Nations

It is widely recognized that many social factors directly impact health. Research has drawn a clear connection between social inequalities caused by colonial policies and various health problems experienced by First Nations people (Reading & Wien, 2009; Gracey & King, 2009; Greenwood & de Leeuw, 2012).

Determinants of health are considered underlying causes of health inequalities between First Nations people and the rest of the population (NCCAH, 2019). A model of determinants of health for Indigenous populations (Greenwood & de Leeuw, 2012; FNQLHSSC, 2018) revealed three levels of determinants: distal (e.g., residential schools, self-determination, racism); intermediate (e.g., social services, justice, cultural approaches); and proximal (e.g., lifestyle and physical environments).

How Social Determinants of Health Affect Child Neglect Among First Nations

The provincial legislative approach to child neglect focuses on parents' unsuitable behaviour and inability to meet their children's needs. Research has shown that in family situations where child neglect or a serious risk of neglect is present, a variety of factors are generally at play, not all of which are related to parental behaviour. Structural factors, such as poverty and the availability of resources, must be taken into account (Association des centres jeunesse, 2010; Higgins, 2010 as cited in INESSS, 2014; Trocmé

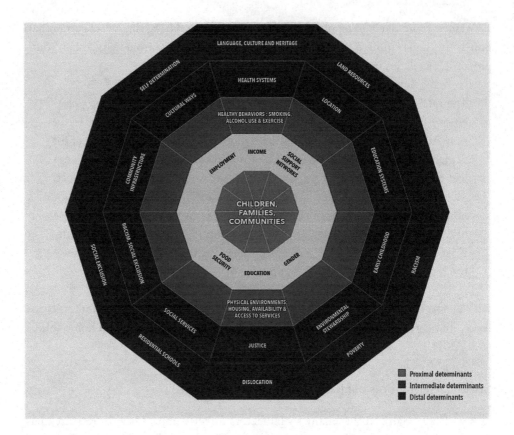

Figure 15.1: Determinants of Indigenous Peoples' Health
Adapted from Greenwood & de Leeuw, 2012. Reprinted with permission.

et al., 2004). These factors are particularly prevalent in several communities. Since the late 1990s, research has proven the overrepresentation of Indigenous children in youth protection, as well as the inadequacy, if not inaccessibility, of **first-line social services** within First Nations communities (FNQLHSSC, 2011). Furthermore, most communities are facing a shortage of housing, which leads to overcrowding in homes (FNQLHSSC, 2017). In this context, many families deal with issues such as poverty, addiction, mental health problems, and domestic violence. These damage family relationships and jeopardize children's safety and **well-being**.

The Declaration of the Rights of First Nations Children states that "parents have a fundamental responsibility to provide their children with a safe . . . home and child care environments" (2014, p. 3). For parents to fulfill this responsibility, their communities need to be able to develop youth and family services, including protection services, that reflect their realities and are built on First Nations cultures (FNQLHSSC, 2017).

MAIN ACHIEVEMENTS AND DEMANDS OF FIRST NATIONS

In Quebec, non-treaty communities[2] face a very different reality than **treaty** communities because funding comes from the federal government and is lower than provincial funding.

Integration of First-Line Social Services into First Nations Communities

During the Forum on the Social and Economic Development of the First Nations held in Quebec in 2006, the federal and Quebec governments announced a $3 million investment over three years to implement first-line social services in four communities. The project aimed to improve access to prevention and intervention services for First Nations children, youth, and families living on reserve by developing culturally appropriate services based on a bottom-up community development approach. Over the long term, the project would reduce the number of reports and the number of children that youth protection placed in out-of-home care. Funding for these services was not made available to all First Nations communities in Quebec until 2009. That same year, a partnership framework for the Enhanced Prevention Focused Approach (EPFA) (FNQLHSSC et al., 2011) was developed to establish principles and guidelines for implementing the services.

FNQLHSSC also held consultations and undertook other initiatives with key players to better understand the health and social services inequalities and to find ways to make improvements. In 2009, research for the *Analysis Project on the Trajectories of First Nations Youth Subject to the Youth Protection Act* (Components 1 and 2) began in collaboration with McGill University and the federal and provincial governments. This project continued, and the report for Component 3 was published in 2016 (FNQLHSSC, 2016). First Nations also worked with institutional partners in other areas, for example, on the 2019 publication of *Portrait of the Criminalization of the First Nations in Quebec* (FNQLHSSC, 2019a), written in collaboration with the University of Ottawa, the Université de Montréal, and the Institut national de la recherche scientifique. Results revealed that the government's justice system and youth protection system are poorly adapted for and discriminatory against First Nations children, adolescents, and families, and that they continue to weaken the fabric of First Nations society, in a way perpetuating the effects of residential schools.

Moreover, the Canadian Human Rights Tribunal (CHRT) recognized in 2016 that the federal government had engaged in discriminatory practices regarding the underfunding of child and family services for First Nations. The CHRT ordered the government to reform its funding formula and cover actual costs of certain first-line child and family services (Canadian Human Rights Tribunal, 2016, 2018).

In 2016, with the approval of AFNQL Chiefs, FNQLHSSC coordinated the regional consultation process to reform First Nations Child and Family Services

(FNCFS). Through this process, FNQLHSSC was able to discern families' needs, their vision for child and family services, and solutions (FNQLHSSC, 2017). The report led to 40 recommendations related to culture, language, governance, self-determination, and the modalities of discriminatory funding, that is, the prejudiced approaches to designating financial resources.

Today, all non-treaty communities in Quebec are responsible for delivering their own first-line services. The communities share a desire to improve living conditions and wellness for children and families by offering services that respect traditional Indigenous knowledges, cultures, and practices (FNQLHSSC, 2011, 2017).

> *One more time, en français*
>
> Aujourd'hui, l'ensemble des communautés non conventionnées au Québec ont pris en charge la prestation de leurs services de première ligne. Elles ont le désir commun d'améliorer les conditions de vie et le mieux-être des enfants et des familles en offrant des services qui respectent les savoirs, les cultures et les pratiques traditionnelles autochtones (FNQLHSSC, 2011, 2017).

The Principle of Substantive Equality

According to the principle of "formal equality," from existing jurisprudence, the law is applied similarly to people in similar situations, which can lead to inequality. The now-favoured principle of "substantive equality" holds that different treatment that considers the distinct needs of a group of people (e.g., their cultural, historical, and geographical context) may be necessary to ensure the equality of certain groups (Butler, 2013).

Basing itself on the principle of substantive equality, the Canadian Human Rights Tribunal ruled against the Canadian government (CHRT, 2016) on the grounds that the First Nations Child and Family Services Program was underfunded (CHRT, 2016). It demonstrated that the program's funding models, and other related provincial or territorial agreements, were discriminatory because they only applied to First Nations people living in communities and in the Yukon. It was only because of their race or ethnic origin that they were adversely affected by the provision of these services, which constitutes a violation of the *Canadian Charter of Rights and Freedoms*. In fact, the principle of substantive equality is found in the *Act Respecting First Nations, Inuit and Métis Children, Youth and Families*.

First Nations Influence on the Evolution of the *Youth Protection Act*

As noted above, the *Youth Protection Act* (YPA, 1977) established a general youth protection program imposed by the government of Quebec, to which First Nations are subject and which they have heavily criticized. Over time, First Nations demands for autonomy have led to progress. In 2019, 15 First Nations child and family services agencies offered youth protection services to 19 communities through provincial delegation agreements and funding agreements with Indigenous Services Canada. These agreements allow the Director of Youth Protection (DYP) and the Provincial Director (PD) to grant authorization to communities and groups of communities to assume most responsibilities under sections 32, 33, 37.6, and 37.7 of the YPA, as well as under section 22 of the *Youth Criminal Justice Act*. Communities can therefore hire First Nations caseworkers who have an understanding of cultural factors and are more sensitive to the socio-economic context created by the effects of colonialism. However, the directors retain the power to withdraw authorization at any time.

The YPA was amended in 2001 to add section 37.5, which specifies that a nation, community, group of communities, or any other Indigenous group may enter into an agreement with the government of Quebec to establish a special youth protection program (Bill 166, 2001). This program enables First Nations to regulate all or some youth protection services and adapt the YPA's application to reflect their cultures. However, the requirements to enter into such an agreement are so strict that only the Conseil de la Nation Atikamekw has met them to date, implementing a program in 2019 for the Manawan and Wemotaci communities.

In 2006, the YPA was amended (Bill 125, 2006) to include the maximum period for being placed in out-of-home care, within which time a decision must be made as to whether or not to return the child to their family environment. After that time, if the child's safety and development are still in danger and returning the child to the family is not possible, the court will make a decision to have the child placed in a permanent, stable living environment. First Nations were opposed to this amendment and, without additional funding, implemented preventive measures to mitigate its impact and preclude children from being permanently removed from their family environment and community (FNQLHSSC et al., 2011).

In 2009, the *Professional Code* was amended to impose more demanding academic requirements for social services workers and to reserve certain activities for members of professional orders and those listed in a registry of rights (Bill 21, 2017). To lessen the effects of the Code, a committee was appointed and a report was submitted in 2016. The report recommended developing training that would lead to qualifications, as well as recognizing and upgrading skills to enable First Nations and Inuit social services workers to perform reserved activities.

First Nations have often had to work to convince the government of Quebec of the need to mitigate the impact of a law after it has been passed. However, on a few occasions, the provincial government listened to First Nations beforehand. In 2016, the Quebec government consulted First Nations about a bill to amend the YPA before it was tabled. The amendments aimed to promote the preservation of Indigenous children's cultural identity and community involvement when making decisions concerning them (Bill 99, 2017). That same year, the government of Quebec also consulted First Nations and Inuit representatives before introducing a bill to amend the *Civil*

Code and other legislative provisions as regards adoption and the disclosure of information (Bill 113, 2017). The act adopted recognized the effects of Indigenous customary tutorship or adoption when it takes into account the interest of the child, respect for their rights, and the consent of the people concerned.[3] When the DYP places a child or when they are at risk of being removed from their family environment, the law stipulates that a life plan must be developed for the child to ensure stability and that their basic needs are met (FNQLHSSC, 2015). These are now permanent life plans, recognized for Indigenous children and followed by youth protection.

Along the same lines, Quebec First Nations participated in consultations for federal Bill C-92–*An Act Respecting First Nations, Inuit and Métis Children, Youth and Families* (2019) and the consultation held by the Quebec government on a family law reform project.

Reappropriating Systems and Governance

First Nations are actively working on self-determination, particularly the takeover of services intended for them. Current approaches do not reflect the holistic approach to health and wellness that many First Nations would take (*Land for Healing*, 2018), which connects an individual's physical, spiritual, emotional, and psychological dimensions and considers their life experiences and those of their extended family, which are affected by all social and environmental determinants (Reading & Wien, 2009).

For instance, the devolution of responsibilities for basic health services to nearly all communities and the implementation of the first framework policy on First Nations income security contributed to the **reappropriation** of these systems. However, it was not long before a need arose to develop a plan to guide and organize efforts toward self-determination. Therefore, with support from AFNQL, FNQLHSSC published *Quebec First Nations Health and Social Services Blueprint, 2007–2017: Closing the Gaps . . . Accelerating Change* (FNQLHSSC, 2008). The document included two strategic goals:

1. To progressively address the health and collective well-being disparities between First Nations and the rest of the Canadian population.
2. To initiate structural change to perspectives and approaches involving governance of healthcare and social services for First Nations.

Quebec First Nations Health and Social Services Governance Process

A Quebec First Nations health and social services governance process was launched to increase First Nations autonomy and wellness as they work toward self-determination. In 2013, AFNQL Chiefs commissioned FNQLHSSC to develop a governance model that is adapted to the needs and context of First Nations, and that promotes their self-determination (FNQLHSSC, 2019b).

The process is guided by this vision: "Through our self-determination, a global and concerted approach, individual and collective commitment, we will be healthy people connected to Mother Earth and our physical, mental, emotional and spiritual well-being will be balanced."

> **One more time, en français**
> La vision du processus se formule ainsi : « Par notre autodétermination, une approche globale concertée et l'engagement individuel et collectif, nous serons un peuple en santé lié à la Terre mère et notre mieux-être physique, mental, émotionnel et spirituel sera en harmonie ».

This collective approach laid the new model's foundations, defined how it would operate, and determined its components. It provides First Nations with greater autonomy and enables them to act on certain social determinants of health for the benefit of all their peoples (FNQLHSSC, 2019c). The governments of Canada and Quebec officially adhered to the process in 2019, following the signing of a tripartite Memorandum of Understanding as part of the health and social services governance process.

An Act Respecting First Nations, Inuit and Métis Children, Youth and Families

The federal government recognized the historic failure of the Canadian colonial system to treat Indigenous Peoples with respect for their human rights on a national and international scale. To rectify this and make amends with Indigenous Peoples and the global community, on June 21, 2019, the Canadian Parliament adopted *An Act Respecting First Nations, Inuit and Métis Children, Youth and Families* (hereinafter referred to as the *Act Respecting Indigenous Families*), which came into force on January 1, 2020 (Bill C-92, 2019). The Act explicitly recognizes that Indigenous governing bodies have inherent legislative jurisdiction with respect to child and family services, and that communities have a right to develop their own laws.

As previously mentioned, progress has been made on improving the YPA in 2016, and again more recently, concerning amendments aimed to promote the preservation of Indigenous children's cultural identity and community involvement when making decisions concerning them, but the *Act Respecting Indigenous Families* goes further: it enables communities to enact their own legislation, outside the provincial jurisdiction framework, while also establishing national principles (sections 9 through 17) that apply to provincial laws in terms of youth protection.

On December 18, 2019, a few days before the *Act Respecting Indigenous Families* came into effect, the provincial government submitted a reference to the Quebec Court of Appeal. An opinion was rendered on February 10, 2022, confirming the validity of this Act, with the exceptions of sections 21 and 22(3), which were declared unconstitutional. Although this intervention was primarily intended to maintain some provincial power in a never-ending conflict over jurisdiction between the two levels of government, it unfortunately reminds us of the colonial system's lasting effects.

CONCLUSION

Research has demonstrated the direct impact of social factors as determinants of health for children and families. Among First Nations, the social and economic inequalities created by the colonial policies that the governments of Canada and Quebec have been carrying out for over a century have characterized these social factors. These policies aimed at assimilating First Nations children and families into the "great" Canadian nation were also accompanied by measures intended to eradicate their culture and destroy their ties to their **land**, which was integrated into Crown land. In this context, we can highlight three different levels of determinants of health. At the highest, overarching level, there are factors related to the impacts of residential schools, racism, and self-determination. At the intermediate level, there are factors related to social services, justice, and cultural approaches. And finally, there are factors more directly and immediately related to family life, such as lifestyles and physical environments.

Considering all these levels of social determinants of health will facilitate the implementation of measures to support children and families that respond to the real needs and culture of First Nations. Such an approach would avoid perpetuating the current system founded on a legal (and cultural) framework inherited from colonialism. This framework bases its understanding of reality on its own values and its own vision of modern society, with no regard for the values and vision of First Nations. Self-determination is, therefore, the approach that should be privileged. This would allow First Nations to make their own decisions about the system and services to establish, as well as the mode of governance that best suits them, without having to convince governmental authorities of the validity of their decisions.

As of recently, the Canadian government's *Act Respecting Indigenous Families* has offered an avenue for First Nations to obtain more autonomy. This law is not perfect, but it provides a sound framework for increased governance and broadens First Nations powers and ability to act with consideration for their own social determinants of health. All stakeholders involved have to engage and support the new legislation by investing the necessary financial, material, and human resources. The many advantages extend well beyond legislation and will pave the way for the next **seven generations**.

CRITICAL THINKING QUESTIONS

1. What success factors would give First Nations full autonomy over family and child wellness?
2. What changes and outcomes are expected following the adoption of *An Act Respecting First Nations, Inuit and Métis Children, Youth and Families*?
3. How can reappropriating First Nations governance modes favourably affect social determinants of health?

NOTES

1. There are also 15 Inuit communities in Quebec. Because this article focuses on the situation experienced by First Nations living in communities, it uses the term First Nations rather than Indigenous.
2. The James Bay and Northern Quebec Agreement for the Cree and Inuit and the Northeastern Quebec Agreement for the Naskapi are land claim agreements under which specific roles and responsibilities were determined for the federal and provincial governments, in particular, regarding local health services.
3. Customary adoption is an act that permanently transfers the legal relationship between a child and their parents of origin (e.g., biological parents) to their adoptive parents. It results in the transfer of parental responsibility/authority and modifies the child's birth record (equivalent to a long-form birth certificate). Tutorship/customary care differs from customary adoption as it does not sever the legal relationship between a child and their parents of origin. In tutorship/customary care, the parents of origin's parental responsibilities are suspended. A guardian is named who has custody of the child and ensures their safety and development but never becomes the child's legal parent (FNQLHSSC, 2019c).

REFERENCES

Legislation:

Bill C-92, An Act respecting First Nations, Inuit and Métis children, youth and families, SC 2019, c.24.

Bill 21, An Act to amend the Professional Code and other legislative provisions in the field of mental health and human relations, 1st session, 39th Legislature, 1st Session, Quebec, 2017, CQLR, c P-34.1.

Bill 99, An Act to amend the Youth Protection Act and other provisions, 1st session, 41st Legislature, 1st Session, Quebec, 2017, CQLR, c P-34.1.

Bill 113, An Act to amend the Civil Code and other legislative provisions as regards adoption and the disclosure of information, 1st session, 41st Legislature, Quebec, 2017, CQLR, c P-34.1.

Bill 125, An Act to amend the Youth Protection Act and other legislative provisions, 1st session, 37th Legislature, Quebec, 2006, CQLR, c P-34.1.

Bill 166, An Act to amend the Youth Protection Act, 2nd session, 36th Legislature, Quebec, 2001, CQLR, c P-34.1.

Youth Protection Act, CQLR, c P-34.1.

Reports and publications of organizations:

Association des centres jeunesse du Québec. (2010). *La négligence: Faites-lui face. Bilan des directeurs de la protection de la jeunesse / directeurs provinciaux.* http://observatoiremaltraitance.ca/Documents/Bilan%20DPJ_DP%202010.pdf

Butler, Martha. (2013). *Section 15 of the Canadian Charter of Rights and Freedoms: The Development of the Supreme Court of Canada's Approach to Equality Rights Under the Charter*, Legal and Social Affairs Division, Parliamentary Information and Research Service. https://bdp.parl.ca/staticfiles/PublicWebsite/Home/ResearchPublications/BackgroundPapers/PDF/2013-83-e.pdf

Canadian Human Rights Tribunal. (2016, January 26). *2016 CHRT 2*. https://fncaringsociety.com/sites/default/files/2016_chrt_2_access_0.pdf

Canadian Human Rights Tribunal. (2018, February). *2018 CHRT 4*. https://decisions.chrt-tcdp.gc.ca/chrt-tcdp/decisions/en/308639/1/document.do

Declaration of the Rights of First Nations Children. (2014). Assembly of First Nations Quebec-Labrador and Assembly of First Nations (AFNQL & AFN) (2014). Poster.

First Nations of Quebec and Labrador Health and Social Services Commission (FNQLHSSC). (2008). *Quebec First Nations health and social services blueprint, 2007–2017: closing the gaps . . . accelerating change*. FNQLHSSC.

First Nations of Quebec and Labrador Health and Social Services Commission (FNQLHSSC). (2011). *Implementation evaluation of the First-Line Social Services Pilot Project in four Quebec First Nations communities*. FNQLHSSC.

First Nations of Quebec and Labrador Health and Social Services Commission (FNQLHSSC). (2013). *Analysis project on the trajectories of First Nations Youth subject to the Youth Protection Act, Analysis Report, Component 1: Analysis of AADNC financial and client data*. https://cwrp.ca/sites/default/files/publications/analysis-project-on-the-trajectories-component-1-eng.pdf

First Nations of Quebec and Labrador Health and Social Services Commission (FNQLHSSC). (2015). *Our children's security is our responsibility: The Youth Protection Act: What do we need to know and what can we do? Brochure intended to First Nations families of Quebec*. https://numerique.banq.qc.ca/patrimoine/details/52327/2668978

First Nations of Quebec and Labrador Health and Social Services Commission (FNQLHSSC). (2016). *Trajectories of First Nations youth subject to the Youth Protection Act, Component 3: Analysis of mainstream youth protection agencies administrative data*. https://cwrp.ca/sites/default/files/publications/analysis_project_on_the_trajectories_component_3eng_0.pdf

First Nations of Quebec and Labrador Health and Social Services Commission (FNQLHSSC). (2017). *Another step toward self-determination and upholding the rights of First Nations children and families, consultation process for the reform of the First Nations Child and Family Services (FNCFS) program*. FNQLHSCC.

First Nations of Quebec and Labrador Health and Social Services Commission (FNQLHSSC). (2018). *Public health for First Nations in Quebec. Shared responsibility concerted action*. Discussion paper. FNQLHSCC.

First Nations of Quebec and Labrador Health and Social Services Commission (FNQLHSSC). (2019a). *Portrait of the criminalization of the First Nations in Quebec: Providing impetus for change*. FNQLHSSC.

First Nations of Quebec and Labrador Health and Social Services Commission (FNQLHSSC). (2019b). *Regional priorities for the wellness of First Nations in Quebec*. Document presented to the Assembly of First Nations.

First Nations of Quebec and Labrador Health and Social Services Commission (FNQLHSSC). (2019c). *Reference guide, appointing a competent authority for customary adoption and tutorship in First Nations Community/Nations*. FNQLHSSC.

First Nations of Quebec and Labrador Health and Social Services Commission (FNQLHSSC), Aboriginal Affairs and Northern Development Canada, & Ministère de la santé et des services sociaux. (2011). *First-line preventive services: Partnership Framework for Enhanced Prevention Focused Approach (EPFA)*. First Nations Child and Family Services (FNCFS). Partnership framework, Tripartite working group. Unpublished document.

Gracey, Michael, & Malcolm King. (2009). Indigenous health part 1: Determinants and disease patterns. *The Lancet, 374*(9683), 65–75.

Greenwood, Margo, & Sarah de Leeuw. (2012). Social determinants of health and the future well-being of Aboriginal children in Canada. *Paediatrics & Child Health, 17*(7), 381–84.

Indigenous Services Canada. (2018). *The Nations 2018*. Indigenous Services Canada. Retrieved January 21, 2020, from aadnc-aandc.gc.ca/nations

Institut national d'excellence en santé et en services sociaux (INESSS). (2014). *Efficacité des interventions en matière de négligence auprès des enfants, des familles et des communautés autochtones*, Revue systématique. https://www.inesss.qc.ca/fileadmin/doc/INESSS/Rapports/ServicesSociaux/INESSS_Rapport_Efficacite_intervention_negligence.pdf

Land for healing: Developing a First Nations landbased service delivery model. (2018). Thunderbird Partnership Foundation.

National Collaborating Centre for Aboriginal Health (NCCAH). (2019). *Fourth National Forum on Indigenous Determinants of Health: "Nakistowinan (Stop In)—Pimicisok (Stock Up)—Kapesik (Stay Over)"* – Proceedings Report. National Collaborating Centre for Indigenous Health.

National Inquiry into Missing and Murdered Indigenous Women and Girls. (2019). *Executive Summary*. https://www.mmiwg-ffada.ca/wp-content/uploads/2019/06/Executive_Summary.pdf

Reading, C. L., & Wien, F. (2009). *Health inequalities and social determinants of Aboriginal Peoples' health*. National Collaborating Centre for Indigenous Health.

Sinha, V., Trocmé, N., Fallon, B., & MacLaurin, B. (2013). Understanding the investigation-stage overrepresentation of First Nations children in the child welfare system: An analysis of the First Nations component of the Canadian Incidence Study of Reported Child Abuse and Neglect 2008. *Child Abuse & Neglect, 37*(10): 821–831.

Sinha, V., Trocmé, N., Fallon, B., MacLaurin, B., Fast, E., Prokop, S. T., Petti, T., Kozlowski, A., Black, T., Weightman, P., Bennett, M., Formsma, J., Brascoupe, P., O'Brien, S., Flette, E., Gray, R., Lucas, L., Hoey, S., . . . Richard. K. (2011). *Kiskisik Awasisak: Remember the children: Understanding the overrepresentation of First Nations children in the child welfare system*. Assembly of First Nations.

Trocmé, N., Knoke, D., & Blackstock, C. (2004). Pathways to the overrepresentation of Aboriginal children in Canada's child welfare system. *Social Service Review, 78*(4): 577–600.

PART III CREATIVE CONTRIBUTION

Angled Windows

Lee Maracle

Women peer through
Angled windows
Passion binds them to glass
While their mouths crave
some kind of exotic taste
their hands claw
at the air inside the open space

This space is limbo
Shrouding the body
disconnected from the foot
whose rhythms seek dance tunes
freedom songs
and escape from this glass

In darkness men
Peer at the silhouettes of women
Strive to see rose petal lips
peel back curtains
guarding thoughts
uncover mysticism

Angled windows

Women peer through
Angled windows
the sharp edges
drives their passion
to open the curtains
beyond the glass
closed mouths crave shapes
Open windows offer

Essence

Hands reach
fingers splay
caress glass
and stop limp in midair

Limbo

this arrested moment
Invades movement
shrouds knowledge
veils understanding
covering communality
as feet stomp
and loosen this gate

From the dark

men peer into windows
lusting feminine silhouettes

lonely voyeurs peek
at the dynamics of stillness

sighing as the curtains close
inside the feet continue to dance.

PART IV

PRACTICAL APPLICATIONS

Part IV considers methods, programs, policies, legislation, curriculum, and ways of thinking that can improve the health and well-being of Indigenous Peoples from coast to coast to coast.

Chapter 16, "Transforming Medical Education" (Richardson, Sutherland), focuses on recruitment and retention of Indigenous students and healthcare professionals. The authors call on faculties of medicine to apply an anti-racism framework to their curriculum and reveal how introducing concepts such as **Two-Eyed Seeing** and adding experiential learning into medical curriculum can expedite the **decolonization** of faculties of medicine and the healthcare system. The authors also outline the principles of trauma- and violence-informed care as ways to improve **cultural safety** in the healthcare system.

Chapter 17, "Learning from the Elders" (Kurtz, Nyberg), explains how the use of Whiteness in healthcare as the norm against which **Indigenous Peoples** are measured is a barrier to this population's health. The authors envision a health system that includes Indigenous worldviews, highlighting the need for cultural safety education within all organizations. They describe a decolonized curriculum at a specific Canadian university that includes Indigenous and **Western** medical knowledge, and which was developed in collaboration with Elders.

Chapter 18, "Indigenous Food Sovereignty" (Coté) explains how reclaiming Indigenous food sovereignty (IFS) requires decreasing dependence on the global industrial food system and revitalizing Indigenous **foodways**. The chapter explains how IFS emphasizes a reciprocal relationship between humans and non-humans. The chapter also demonstrates how settler **colonialism** impacted Indigenous Peoples' ability to access traditional foods and medicines. It explains how, through IFS, Indigenous Peoples seek to heal the wounds of colonialism and assert their cultural and political autonomy.

Chapter 19, "Walking with Our Most Sacred" (Cidro, Hayward, Bach, Sinclair), considers how colonialism, and especially the maternal evacuation policy, disrupted **Indigenous women's** practice of giving birth in their communities, where they were cared for by Elders, **midwives**, and birth workers (doulas). The chapter provides examples of communities that are resisting colonized systems through midwives and recognizing Indigenous sovereignty over their bodies and lands.

Chapter 20, "Systems Innovation through First Nations Self-Determination" (Johnson, Behn Smith, Beck), demonstrates how First Nations in BC are developing strategic partnerships and entering into political, legal, and operational agreements that "hardwire" their involvement in decision making and governance and help to make the province's health system more welcoming and sustainable. It also outlines the role of the First Nations Health Authority in supporting healthy, **self-determining** First Nations.

Part IV closes with a prose poem, "ᐃᑦᒋᑐᖅ (to sit down for a long time)" (Dunning), in which the speaker highlights how non-Inuit views of Northern Canada and Inuit, and the policies they have imposed on Inuit, have impacted Inuit ways of living and ultimately their health.

CHAPTER 16

Transforming Medical Education

Lisa Richardson and Julie Sutherland

LEARNING OBJECTIVES

1. To guide students in understanding what anti-racist practice is.
2. To inform students about reflexivity as a key element of culturally safe care.
3. To introduce the core principles of trauma- and violence-informed care.

INTRODUCTION

In 2008, Brian Sinclair, an Indigenous middle-aged male who used a wheelchair, died in the ER of Winnipeg's Health Sciences Centre. He had been referred to the ER by a community healthcare centre for a treatable bladder infection (Brian Sinclair, 2017; Gunn, n.d.). After an initial greeting by a triage aid (Brian Sinclair, 2017, p. 2), video footage documents how he was "ignored, unattended, and uncared-for" (Gunn, n.d., p. 2) for 34 hours. The inquest's presiding judge indicated that race and disability "would play a significant role when the inquest considered how similar deaths could be prevented in the future" (p. 2), but this claim was eventually reversed by the presiding judge who ruled "that issues of race, racism, poverty, disability and substance abuse were beyond the mandate of the inquest" (p. 2).

This story is frequently used as an example of the racist stereotyping and neglect many Indigenous people experience in the Canadian healthcare system. It is just one of many. More recently, a coroner's inquiry into the death of Joyce Echaquan, an Atikamekw woman who recorded and livestreamed hospital staff making racial slurs about her just hours before she died in 2020, concluded that racism and prejudice were contributing factors (Nerestant, 2021). How can we put a stop to tragic events such as these?

One answer is to address the inherent power dynamics in the relationship between patients and practitioners due to the vulnerability of a person who seeks care and help from a medical professional. For Indigenous patients, the relationship and power differential are heightened by centuries of ongoing colonial violence that have fuelled inequities in Canadian healthcare. The power dynamic between patient and provider increases when an Indigenous patient receives care from a non-Indigenous provider. Such a scenario is likely given the small (albeit increasing) number of Indigenous physicians practising in Canada. There are nearly two million Indigenous people in Canada, comprising nearly 5% of Canada's population, yet less than 1% of physicians in Canada are Indigenous according to Statistics Canada (2016).

In addition to increasing the number of Indigenous healthcare providers and ensuring their retention, Canada has an obligation to provide **cultural competency training** for all healthcare professionals, including physicians. These recommendations are a portion of the **Truth and Reconciliation Commission's Calls to Action** that have become foundational to efforts to confront systemic racism in healthcare and elsewhere. A main objective of cultural competency training is to ensure that learners understand their patient's culture (DeSouza, 2008) and are prepared "to effectively work within the cultural context of a client" (Campinha-Bacote, 1995, as cited in Berg et al., 2019, p. 134). This requires the learner to *become an expert in* multiple cultures of their patients. A critique of the concept of cultural competency training is the implication that such expertise is possible. Consequently, alternatives to cultural competency training in healthcare have emerged, including **cultural humility** and **cultural safety** training. Cultural humility is "a life-long process of self-reflection and self-critique" (Turpel-Lafond, 2020, p. 8). Additionally,

> cultural humility begins with an in-depth examination of the provider's assumptions, beliefs and privilege embedded in their own understanding and practice, as well as the goals of the patient–provider relationship. Undertaking cultural humility allows for Indigenous voices to be front and centre and promotes patient/provider relationships based on respect, open and effective dialogue and mutual decision-making. (p. 8)

Physicians have the responsibility to *learn from* the patient about their unique needs, which may be rooted in their culture. Cultural humility may be seen as a step in the physician's journey toward ensuring culturally safe care. Cultural safety is a

> desired outcome and can only be defined by the Indigenous person receiving care in a manner that is safe and does not profile or discriminate against the person but is experienced as respectful, safe and allows meaningful communication and service. It is a physically, socially, emotionally and spiritually safe environment, without challenge, ignorance or denial of an

individual's identity. To be culturally safe requires positive anti-racism stances, tools and approaches and the continuous practice of cultural humility. (Turpel-Lafond, 2020, p. 11)

Foundational to cultural safety is that healthcare practitioners do the following:

1. reflect on how their behaviours may be rooted in racist or colonial attitudes;
2. understand the power differentials inherent in health service delivery and the existence of institutional discrimination; and
3. see the need to fix these inequities through education and system change.

Most importantly, it is the recipients of care—the patients—who determine how safe the proposed treatment or care experience feels (Ward et al., 2016).

Although a recent evaluation of Canadian medical residents indicated they feel prepared to deliver cross-cultural care, participants in the same study admitted to "not having a great deal of additional instruction or evaluation of cross-cultural care in residency" (Singh et al., 2017, para. 30). Some Canadian universities are working to change this. For example, the University of British Columbia offers an Indigenous Cultural Safety course as a required component of 13 health professional programs at UBC. Across 12.5 hours of instruction and workshops, students engage with such topics as Indigenous perspectives of history, the legacy of **colonialism** in Canada, and Indigenous Peoples' health and Canada's healthcare system. In addition to core content training, curriculum and learning experiences must be incorporated across all health professional training programs at all stages of training.

INFUSING MANDATES, CURRICULUM, AND PRACTICE WITH INDIGENOUS KNOWLEDGES

A common framework to consider as a way to incorporate both Indigenous and Western knowledges in practice is **"Two-Eyed Seeing,"** or *Etuaptmumk* in Mi'kmaw—the language of Elder Albert Marshall, who described the concept in detail (Marshall et al., 2018, p. 45). For medical students to learn to become physicians who are invested in seeing wholesale change in themselves and across the institutions in which they serve, they must learn how concepts like Two-Eyed Seeing can facilitate culturally safe care. Dr. Lisa Richardson noted significant differences between Western medical practices and many Indigenous ones:

> When we think about health from an Anishinaabe perspective . . . we think about connection to not only mind, body, spirit and emotion but connection to land, connection to community, connection to our ancestors. That is very different from where biomedicine evolves from, which is "here is your body,

here is an approach to thinking about medicine." It's disconnected from all these other aspects of healing. (As cited in Richardson & Pennington, 2017)

The inclusion of Indigenous knowledges in medical education is one step toward decolonizing the country's Faculties of Medicine—a vital step in preparing future physicians to provide culturally safe care and in ensuring the retention of Indigenous students. Richardson articulated what a Faculty of Medicine striving to be a decolonized, culturally safe space might look like:

> We know that not only do we need to be teaching cultural safety for our patients, but we need to be educating our faculty about creating culturally safe spaces for our Indigenous learners. That means that students are seeing themselves, Indigenous peoples see themselves, reflected in the curriculum, that they have access to cultural and traditional medicines if they want, that they can participate in community activities, that they can do clinical electives in Indigenous communities, and that when they need advocacy because they feel that they have encountered racism or unfair treatment based on being an Indigenous person, that they have people they can turn to who can advocate for them at the highest levels. (As cited in Richardson & Pennington, 2017)

Some work has already been done at many higher education institutions across Canada. For example, the University of Toronto Mississauga has an Indigenous Centre that supports Indigenous students, staff, and faculty, promotes the recruitment and retention of Indigenous students, and offers avenues for non-Indigenous people to increase their understanding about Indigenous Peoples' worldviews, knowledges, and histories. Another example of efforts to decolonize faculties can be found in the work of the Indigenous Reference Group (IRG) at the Northern Ontario School of Medicine, which was formed in partnership between Laurentian University in Sudbury, Ontario, and Lakehead University in Thunder Bay, Ontario. The IRG's mandate is "to provide leadership to the Northern Ontario School of Medicine in the areas of research, administration and academic issues in order to promote excellence in higher learning and ensure appropriate reflection and inclusion of the Indigenous worldview(s)" (Northern Ontario School of Medicine, 2016, p. 1).

Despite these examples (and many others that could be provided), Canada's institutions have colonial foundations and continue to be unsafe for learners, patients, and staff (Richardson & Pennington, 2017). Decolonizing spaces will not only facilitate the retention of Indigenous students but will also create opportunities for non-Indigenous students, faculty, and staff to think more holistically about healthcare in Canada. It will help them to proceed with best practices that include, demand,

and foster high quality, safe, and respectful care for Indigenous people that is free of racism and discrimination and that respects their Indigenous identities.

> ### Indigenous Health Values and Competent Physicians
>
> In 1996, the Royal College of Physicians and Surgeons of Canada (RCPSC) adopted CanMEDs, a framework that "identifies and describes the abilities that physicians require to deliver effective health care" (RCPSC, 2019, p. 30). In 2013, the RCPSC issued the Indigenous Health Values and Principles Statement (2nd edition, 2019). Emerging from the input of practitioners from various First Nations, Inuit, and Métis communities and nations, the Statement maps Indigenous health values and principles onto the CanMEDS framework. This framework defines a culturally safe physician as one who:
>
> - embraces Indigenous knowledge/science, understands and accepts that racism exists and how historical/intergenerational trauma affects the health and well-being of the Indigenous patient, and takes steps to foster anti-racism interventions.
> - communicates in clear, honest and respectful dialogue about health matters, and sees a mutual responsibility between [the physician] and the Indigenous patient/community for achieving shared health outcomes.
> - recognizes that the Indigenous patient–physician relationship is sacrosanct and without hierarchy or dominance.
> - is equipped with the tools, knowledge, education and experience to achieve the highest form of evidence-informed professional competencies, while practising with cultural humility, fostering an environment of cultural safety and proactively pursuing anti-racism interventions.
> - embraces Indigenous identity as the platform that promotes holistic health and encourages active participation of Indigenous people . . . as "agents of change for health."
> - understands that Indigenous health is an integral component of medical research, education, training and practice.
> - is committed to the well-being of Indigenous patients, their families, communities and cultures through ethical behaviours, compassion, integrity, respect and a commitment to clinical competencies that engender health of Indigenous people. (Indigenous Health Committee of the Royal College & Office of Research, Health Policy and Advocacy, 2019, pp. 3–5)

INCREASING ANTI-RACISM EDUCATION IN FACULTIES OF MEDICINE

Racism comes in multiple forms. It can include prejudice and overt bias, stereotyping, racial profiling, racial discrimination, and oppression. It can be conscious or unconscious. It can manifest in whom we hire, whom we pick for teams, whom we sit beside on a bus, whom we convict of crimes, or how we treat our patients. It can even show up in curriculum. The Association of Faculties of Medicine of Canada states that "the hidden curriculum often supports hierarchies of clinical domains or gives one group advantages over another" (2009, as cited in RCPSC, 2019, p. 12). Curriculum can "reinforce traditional power structures and Eurocentric worldviews that may perpetuate racist behaviours" (Tomascik et al., 2018, as cited in RCPSC, 2019, p. 8).

Racism "in the health care system has been cited as a significant barrier to receiving needed care and services" (McGibbon & Etowa, 2009, p. 38). This has resulted in Indigenous Peoples in Canada living with some of the highest burdens of poor health in the country, including significantly shortened life expectancies, excessively high infant mortality rates, disproportionately high cases of chronic and infectious diseases, and alarmingly high suicide rates (Frohlich et al., 2006; Government of Canada, 2018; Health Council of Canada, 2012; Sheppard et al., 2017). An anti-racist framework to guide clinical practice begins with understanding how racism has informed oppressive health policies and then applying this understanding to act for social change (McGibbon & Etowa, 2009). Acting for social change means to educate ourselves and others, and to work to change individual and institutional actions, policies, and legislation that negatively impact Indigenous patients (McGibbon & Etowa, 2009). It also means integrating knowledge about the effects of historical and ongoing colonial trauma into policies, procedures, practices, and settings.

The healthcare curriculum must include a study of "the historical roots of racism and colonialism, how they grow, where racism takes place and what are its detrimental effects on Indigenous patients" (RCPSC, 2019, p. 12). Further, it must apply "principled interventions based on Indigenous health values" (p. 12). To this end, the Royal College of Physicians and Surgeons of Canada has initiated the provision of anti-racism and cultural safety education to all its members.

PROMOTING REFLEXIVITY IN MEDICAL EDUCATION CURRICULUM

A core tenet of anti-racism education is reflexivity. In the context of culturally safe care, reflexivity can be defined as "being aware of oneself and the person/people that we are working with as we communicate with them, noticing the effects of who we are, our ways of communication and then being responsive to what we notice" (Fyers & Greenwood, 2016, para. 4). Reflexivity is about becoming aware of and reflecting on biases, discriminatory attitudes, or beliefs such as the assumption that Western medical practices are superior. It demands that we think about power and privilege and also about how being in a position of power affects our relationship with our patients, clients, learners, and others.

Reflexive teaching in medical education might involve "showing [students] examples of unequal treatment, and addressing differences and inequalities in access to health care and skills training" (Verdonk, 2015, para. 2). It might include assignments such as autobiographical journalling, with such prompts as the following:

- What/how did you first learn about race?
- When [did] you first learn that you were a member of a racial group?
- What/how did you learn about your racial group?
- When did you first learn that there were racial groups other than your own?
- What/how did you learn about this/these groups?
- How do you perceive your own race, and how do others perceive your race?
- Select a significant institution in your life (e.g., educational, religious, media/cultural, etc.). What have you learned from this institution about race? How might this have affected the relationships you have and how you identify racially (or not)?
- Scan your relationships with people who have been socialized into a different racial group than yourself. Thinking back to your childhood, what has been the nature of these relationships (e.g., friends, family, teachers, service providers, mentors/coaches, charity recipients, etc.)? Have the types of relationships changed over time? What do you notice about the relationships in your life today? (Harbin et al., 2019, p. 15)

Critically thinking about issues of privilege and power and reflecting on how our assumptions about other people affect the way we treat them can be emotionally challenging work. However, it can also transform us and improve our future professional practices (Fook & Askeland, 2007). Crystal Milligan, a researcher from Yellowknives Dene First Nation in the Northwest Territories, said the following about the role of self-reflexivity in ensuring culturally safe care:

> Cultural awareness, sensitivity, and competency are not enough. From a young age, I have been able to see similarities and differences between cultural groups (cultural awareness). I like to think as well that I accept other groups without judgment (cultural sensitivity) and can work across cultures (cultural competency). However, critical self-reflexivity is what helps me avoid promoting stereotypes and the simplistic idea that I can easily learn a set of skills to navigate other cultures. . . . Instead of a magnifying glass to look at the Other, we hold up a mirror to scrutinize our own roles in an inequitable structural framework. If done in a supportive environment, this unsettling process can spark transformative learning and new capacity to create cultural safety. This journey can be an enlightening one. (n.d., paras. 6–7)

An important part of cultural safety is cultural awareness. While this term often is understood to mean an awareness of differences between cultural groups, as used in the above quote from Milligan, it is crucial that those engaging in reflexivity understand cultural awareness to include an awareness of themselves. This is especially important for White healthcare professionals who generally possess privilege and power, both of which must be actively resisted and dismantled to create decolonized spaces.

LEARNING ABOUT HOW TO PROVIDE TRAUMA- AND VIOLENCE-INFORMED CARE

Trauma is "the lasting emotional response that often results from living through a distressing event" (CAMH, n.d., para. 1). Traumatic experiences can happen at any time in life. Examples of early-life trauma are child abuse or neglect. Later-life trauma may include sudden and unexpected loss (e.g., miscarriage, death of a child) or violent events (e.g., spousal abuse, military action). Trauma can lead to "allostatic load" (wear and tear on the body), addiction, mental health issues, and a number of physical health issues such as cardiovascular disease, respiratory disease, or cancer (RCPSC, 2019, p. 17).

Historical trauma is the "cumulative emotional and psychological wounding over one's lifespan and across generations, emanating from massive group trauma experiences" (Yellow Horse Brave Heart, 2003, as cited in RCPSC, 2019, p. 17). Indigenous Peoples in Canada (and around the world) experience historical trauma from governments' multiple assimilation policies and violent practices, including cultural, spiritual, and physical genocide, forced and coerced sterilization, forced dislocation, and neglect (leading to, for example, disproportionately high numbers of missing and murdered Indigenous women and girls whose cases are often ignored by police). Moreover, the federal government's medical research practices, supported and advanced by oppressive policies and laws, have resulted in severe trauma for many Indigenous peoples. Mistreatment has included compulsory and segregated hospitalization and experimentation without consent, among other severe and discriminatory practices (RCPSC, 2019, p. 18).

For Indigenous people to experience cultural safety in healthcare, practitioners must recognize that "trauma is a public health issue that impacts every health care service system in Canada" (RCPSC, 2019, p. 19). Trauma- and violence-informed care understands, identifies, and responds to the effects of trauma. It minimizes the risk of re-traumatizing patients and contributes to support and healing.

By offering trauma- and violence-informed care, practitioners can increase the safety of care they deliver within their healthcare settings. They must consider the possibility that each individual they engage with may have a traumatic history of which they may not be aware. To that end, healthcare curriculum must acknowledge the widespread impacts of trauma. It must teach students to recognize the signs and symptoms of trauma. It must provide students with an understanding of the variety of ways people deal with trauma (e.g., anger, avoidance, substance use) and with a recognition that people follow different pathways to healing.

Core Principles of Trauma- and Violence-Informed Care

Below are seven core principles of trauma- and violence-informed care that should inform every trauma-informed practice and every patient–practitioner interaction.

1. **Acknowledgement that trauma is pervasive**: practitioners understand that survivors are affected physically, psychologically, and emotionally. Practitioners treat the patient, understanding that trauma isn't a single event; rather, it builds up over the course of the individual's life. They must be treated holistically to be empowered to regain control.
2. **Safety**: care takes place in environments that feel safe (emotionally, physically, culturally) for patients. Practitioners establish an atmosphere of trust and safety by creating intake procedures that are appropriate (e.g., in the patient's language, in accordance with their cultural practices), ensuring respectful, clear, and comprehensive communication, and empowering the patient to maintain some control of their physical space.
3. **Trust**: trustworthiness can be developed and established through clarity, transparency, openness, and honesty, as well as through "meaningful sharing of power and decision-making." (Inviting Resilience, 2020, para. 4)
4. **Choice and control**: practitioners understand the cruciality of case-by-case approaches to care and empower patients to participate in decision making about the service and care they receive.
5. **Compassion**: practitioners strive to relieve their patient's suffering and improve their well-being through attentiveness and non-judgement.
6. **Collaboration**: the power relations that often appear intrinsic to practitioner–patient interactions are eliminated. Healing takes place when relationships are mutually respectful and where parties share decision making and power.
7. **Strengths-based**: practitioners pay particular attention to patients' inherent strengths, which they draw on to facilitate recovery. (Klinic Community Health, 2013)

CONCLUSION: POSITIVE INDIGENOUS CLIENT CARE AND OUTCOMES

How can learning be transformed so that future health practitioners are empowered to provide culturally safe care? First, faculties of medicine must recruit and retain Indigenous learners in the health professions and they must increase the number of Indigenous faculty. They must create safe and respectful pre-clinical and clinical learning environments that are free of racism and discrimination. Learners must also feel prepared to enhance Indigenous clients' health journeys through the practice of trauma- and violence-informed care and programs and through initiatives that are guided by local Indigenous communities, advisors, and clients. Students must learn concepts such as Two-Eyed Seeing so that Indigenous and non-Indigenous ways of knowing and healing can exist alongside one another. They must understand the importance of ensuring that patients have access to traditional foods and healing practices, support from Elders, land-based healing, and other cultural supports.

Finally, students must have the opportunity to participate in experiential learning (EL) in medical education. In EL, students "engage in direct encounter and then purposefully reflect upon, validate, transform, give personal meaning to and seek to integrate their different ways of knowing" (McGill & Weil, 1989, as cited in de Leeuw et al., 2020, p. 73). It is well-established that EL can lead to transformative learning (de Leeuw et al., 2020). Many students, physicians, and researchers have attested to the power of experiential learning, including cultural immersion (e.g., Herzog, 2017; Thackrah et al., 2017; Yardley, 2012). Electives may include cultural immersion programs. For example, medical students at the University of British Columbia who participate in the FLEX Program work on projects in rural and remote areas of British Columbia. As another example, medical students at the University of Toronto can take an Urban Indigenous Health elective during which they explore various urban Indigenous health service and cultural organizations in Toronto.

Though Canada's healthcare system is often upheld as exemplary (e.g., GBD 2015 Healthcare Access and Quality Collaborators, 2017), the inequities found therein indicate that changes must be made (Greenwood, 2019). We all have a role in creating a more culturally safe healthcare system. As Coast Salish actor and physician Evan Tlesla II Adams noted, "Cultural humility and cultural safety in the health system requires health professionals to acknowledge they are always on a journey of learning, and being open to listening to what better care means for First Nations and Aboriginal peoples. We all need to acknowledge, 'it starts with me'" (First Nations Health Authority, n.d., p. 1).

CRITICAL THINKING QUESTIONS

1. What are some things we can do to make our educational and healthcare institutions safe spaces for Indigenous Peoples?
2. What would you say are some of the inherent power dynamics in the physician–patient relationship? How might those positively and negatively impact the patient?
3. What are some ways a physician can build respectful engagement with a patient who is from another culture?

REFERENCES

Berg, K., McLane, P., Eshkakogan, N., Mantha, J., Lee, T., Crowshoe, C., & Phillips, A. (2019). Perspectives on Indigenous cultural competency and safety in Canadian hospital departments: A scoping review. *International Emergency Nursing, 43*, 133–140. https://doi.org/10.1016/j.ienj.2019.01.004

Brian Sinclair Working Group. (2017). *Out of sight: A summary of the events leading up to Brian Sinclair's death and the inquest that examined it and the interim recommendations of the Brian Sinclair Working Group.* https://media.winnipegfreepress.com/documents/Out_of_Sight_Final.pdf

CAMH. (n.d.). *Trauma.* Retrieved October 15, 2020, from https://www.camh.ca/en/health-info/mental-illness-and-addiction-index/trauma

de Leeuw, S. N., Larstone, R., Fell, B., Cross, N., Greenwood, M., Auerbach, K., & Sutherland, J. (2020). Educating medical students' "hearts and minds": A humanities-informed cultural immersion program in Indigenous experiential community learning. *International Journal of Indigenous Health, 14*(3).

DeSouza, R. (2008). Wellness for all: The possibilities of cultural safety and cultural competence in New Zealand. *Journal of Research in Nursing, 13*(2), 125–135. https://doi.org/10.1177%2F1744987108088637

First Nations Health Authority. (n.d.). *#itstartswithme: FNHA's policy statement on cultural safety and humility.* https://www.fnha.ca/Documents/FNHA-Policy-Statement-Cultural-Safety-and-Humility.pdf

Fook, J., & Askeland, A. (2007). Challenges of critical reflection: "Nothing ventured, nothing gained." *Social Work Education, 26*(5), 520–533.

Frohlich, K. L., Ross, N., & Richmond, C. (2006). Health disparities in Canada today. *Health Policy, 79*(2–2), 132–143.

Fyers, K., & Greenwood, S. (2016, October 28). *Cultural safety: Becoming a reflexive practitioner.* HealthCentral.nz. Retrieved October 15, 2020, from https://healthcentral.nz/cultural-safety-becoming-a-reflexive-practitioner/

GBD 2015 Healthcare Access and Quality Collaborators. (2017). Healthcare Access and Quality Index based on mortality from causes amenable to personal health care in 195 countries and territories, 1990–2015: A novel analysis from the Global Burden of Disease Study 2015. *Lancet, 390,* 231–266. https://dx.doi.org/10.1016%2FS0140-6736(17)30818-8

Government of Canada. (2018). *Key health inequalities in Canada: A national portrait: Executive summary.* https://www.canada.ca/en/public-health/services/publications/science-research-data/key-health-inequalities-canada-national-portrait-executive-summary.html

Greenwood, M. (2019). Modelling change and cultural safety: A case study in northern British Columbia health system transformation. *Healthcare Management Forum, 32*(1): 11–14.

Gunn, B. (n.d.). *Ignored to death: Systemic racism in the Canadian healthcare system: Submission to EMRIP the Study on Health.* https://www.ohchr.org/Documents/Issues/IPeoples/EMRIP/Health/UniversityManitoba.pdf

Harbin, M. B., Thurber, A., & Bandy, J. (2019). Teaching race, racism, and racial justice: Pedagogical principles and classroom strategies for course instructors. *Race and Pedagogy, 4*(1), 1–16. Retrieved November 12, 2020, from https://soundideas.pugetsound.edu/cgi/viewcontent.cgi?article=1044&context=rpj

Health Council of Canada. (2012). *Empathy, dignity, and respect: Creating cultural safety for Aboriginal people in urban health care.* https://publications.gc.ca/collections/collection_2013/ccs-hcc/H174-39-2012-eng.pdf

Herzog, L. S. (2017). The need for narrative reflection and experiential learning in medical education: A lesson learned through an urban Indigenous health elective. *Medical Teacher, 39*(9), 995–996. http://dx.doi.org/10.1080/0142159X.2016.1270442

Indigenous Health Committee of the Royal College and the Office of Research, Health Policy and Advocacy. (2019). *Indigenous health values and principles statement* (2nd ed.) RSPCS. Retrieved October 15, 2020, from https://www.royalcollege.ca/rcsite/health-policy/initiatives/indigenous-health-e

Inviting Resilience. (2020). *Trauma-informed practice*. Retrieved October 16, 2020, from http://invitingresilience.ca/trauma-informed-practice/

Klinic Community Health Centre. (2013). *Trauma-informed: The Trauma Toolkit* (2nd ed.). https://trauma-informed.ca/wp-content/uploads/2013/10/Trauma-informed_Toolkit.pdf

Marshall, M., Marshall, A., & Bartlett, C. (2018). Two-Eyed Seeing in medicine. In Greenwood, M. et al. (Eds.), *Determinants of Indigenous Peoples' health: Beyond the social* (2nd ed., pp. 44–53). Canadian Scholars' Press.

McGibbon, E. A., & Etowa, J. B. (2009). *Anti-racist health care practice*. Canadian Scholars' Press.

Milligan, C. (n.d.). The self-reflexive path to cultural safety. *Insights: Essays*. Longwoods Publishing Corporation. Retrieved October 19, 2020, from https://www.longwoods.com/content/25668//the-self-reflexive-path-to-cultural-safety

Nerestant, A. (2021, October 1). Racism, prejudice contributed to Joyce Echaquan's death in hospital, Quebec coroner's inquiry concludes. *CBC News*. https://www.cbc.ca/news/canada/montreal/joyce-echaquan-systemic-racism-quebec-government-1.6196038

Northern Ontario School of Medicine. (2016). *Northern Ontario School of Medicine Indigenous Reference Group*. https://www.nosm.ca/wp-content/uploads/2018/06/IRG-ToR-approved-October-12-2016.pdf

RCPSC. (2019). *Indigenous health primer: The Indigenous health writing group of the Royal College*. Retrieved October 15, 2020, from http://www.royalcollege.ca/rcsite/health-policy/initiatives/indigenous-health-e

Richardson, L., & Pennington, J. (2017). Episode 3. *Voices from the Field* [Audio podcast transcript]. National Collaborating Centre for Indigenous Health. https://www.nccih.ca/docs/general/PODCAST-VoicesFromField-LisaRichardson-JasonPennington-Transcript-EN.pdf

Sheppard, A. J., Shapiro, G. D., Bushnik, T., Wilkins, R., Perry, S., Kaufman, J. S., Kramer, M. S., & Yang, S. (2017). *Health reports: Birth outcomes among First Nations, Inuit and Métis populations*. Statistics Canada. Retrieved September 30, 2020, from https://www150.statcan.gc.ca/n1/pub/82-003-x/2017011/article/54886-eng.htm

Singh, B., Banwell, E., & Groll, D. (2017). Canadian residents' perceptions of cross-cultural care training in graduate medical school. *Canadian Medical Education Journal, 8*(4): e16–30. Retrieved August 10, 2020, from https://www.ncbi.nlm.nih.gov/pmc/articles/PMC5766216/

Statistics Canada. (2016). *Data tables, 2016 census*. Retrieved March 8, 2020, from https://www12.statcan.gc.ca/census-recensement/2016/dp-pd/dt-td/Rp-eng.cfm?TABID=2&LANG=E&A=R&APATH=3&DETAIL=0&DIM=0&FL=A&FREE=0&GC=01&GL=-1&GID=1325190&GK=1&GRP=1&O=D&PID=112126&PRID

=10&PTYPE=109445&S=0&SHOWALL=0&SUB=0&Temporal=2017&THEME=124&VID=0&VNAMEE=&VNAMEF=&D1=1&D2=0&D3=0&D4=0&D5=0&D6=0

Thackrah, R. D., Hall, M., Fitzgerald, K., & Thompson, S. C. (2017). Up close and real: Living and learning in a remote community builds students' cultural capabilities and understanding of health disparities. *International Journal for Equity in Health, 16*, 119. https://doi.org/10.1186/s12939-017-0615-x

Turpel-Lafond, M. E. (2020). *In plain sight: Addressing Indigenous-specific racism and discrimination in B.C. health care.* https://engage.gov.bc.ca/app/uploads/sites/613/2020/11/In-Plain-Sight-Summary-Report.pdf

Verdonk, P. (2015). When I say . . . reflexivity. *Medical Education, 49*(2), 147–148. https://doi-org.prxy.lib.unbc.ca/10.1111/medu.12534

Ward, C., Branch, C., & Fridkin, A. (2016). What is Indigenous cultural safety—and why should I care about it? *Visions Journal, 11*(4), 29. Retrieved July 8, 2020, from https://www.heretohelp.bc.ca/visions/indigenous-people-vol11/what-indigenous-cultural-safety-and-why-should-i-care-about-it

Yardley, S. (2012). Experiential learning: Transforming theory into practice. *Medical Teacher, 34*(2), 161–164. https://doi.org/10.3109/0142159X.2012.643264

CHAPTER 17

Learning from the Elders: Traditional Knowledge and Cultural Safety within Health Science Education

Donna L. M. Kurtz and Elder Jessie Nyberg

TRADITIONAL PRAYER[1]

Creator, Great Spirit, Mother Earth, Father Sky, and the Spirits of our Ancestors, especially our Grandmothers and our Grandfathers, we thank you for this opportunity to write important words for this book. We respectfully acknowledge the Syilx Okanagan Nation and their peoples, on whose unceded territory we work and live. Help us to share our knowledge, wisdom, experience, and education in our writings. Creator, health science students must learn cultural safety to be able to develop respectful relationships in safe environments with their patients, clients, peers, and all those they communicate and are in relation with.

Creator, help us to write words that will resonate with those who read them so they will understand and come to use cultural safety as a way of being. We must remember that cultural safety is a determinant of health. Creator, again we thank you and those who have asked us to participate in this writing. All My Relations

Elder Jessie Nyberg, Secwepemc Nation, Canoe Creek, BC

LEARNING OBJECTIVES

1. To understand Indigenous Elders' important role in health science education.
2. To explore cultural safety in healthcare practice and everyday life.
3. To learn how to apply cultural safety actions through a case example.

INTRODUCTION

Social determinants of health influence individual and population health. In Canada, these determinants are related to personal, social, economic, and environmental factors, including: income and social status; employment and working conditions; education and literacy; childhood experiences; physical environments; social supports and coping skills; healthy behaviours; access to health services; biology and genetic endowment; gender; culture; and race/racism (Government of Canada, 2019). However, health is not simply a result of an individual's genetics, culture, or lifestyle choices; it is also impacted by one's gender, age, class, ability, and socio-political context (Doane, 2002). For Indigenous Peoples, specific structural determinants go beyond health to include considerations of how mental, physical, spiritual, and emotional wellness have been, and are, affected by **colonialization** (Czyzewski, 2011), racism and social exclusion (Reading & Wien, 2009), and geography and health inequity (Greenwood et al., 2015). The **well-being** of **Indigenous Peoples** is also affected by the intergenerational, historical, and ongoing contemporary effects of residential schools, as well as by the **Sixties Scoop**, the **Millennium Scoop**, and other forms of discrimination within a colonial society that strip away power, freedom, **land**, language, family cohesiveness, ceremony, and love (Reading & Wien, 2009).

Indigenous Peoples, globally, face barriers to health, education, and societal systems that can interfere with their life balance and harmony. A major barrier many Indigenous Peoples face in seeking care is that, in **Western** healthcare systems—that is, those set up by and for dominant cultures—Whiteness is considered the norm against which all else is measured and in which all else is framed. Within these systems, Indigenous Peoples tend to be referred to, inappropriately and incorrectly, as a culturally homogeneous group who share similar health and wellness beliefs, concerns, and practices. Practitioners may attribute differences in health status to skin colour and culture rather than to relevant complex factors, such as poverty, lack of access to services, or racist healthcare practices (Kurtz, 2011). However, broader intersecting factors affect Indigenous health and well-being than such generalizations would allow.

According to the United Nations, Indigenous Peoples have the same human rights as all peoples globally: "the right to access, without any discrimination, to all social and health services" (UN General Assembly, 2007). Yet, in the 2013 Canadian Community Health Survey, Indigenous Peoples reported experiencing discrimination 73% more than individuals identified as White (Hyman et al., 2019).

From our Elders and Indigenous communities, we, the authors (Kurtz, Nyberg), have learned the importance of understanding the effects of historical and contemporary colonization that continue to cause blame and trauma and that persist in excluding Indigenous Peoples. We have likewise learned how vital it is to recognize each other's unique cultural needs in respectful and power-sharing relationships. Programs and services have emerged over the past several decades aimed at reducing health gaps between Indigenous and non-Indigenous people in Canada. However, progress has been slow. It is thus imperative that all society work together and learn from each other to facilitate a universal understanding of Indigenous history and Indigenous worldviews, and to generate a vision for the future.

In this chapter, we provide an overview of specific determinants of Indigenous health, including culture and **cultural safety**, as well as of the important role of Indigenous Elders in wellness and health science education. We share our journey as Elder and Elder-in-Training, working alongside and learning from other Elders, faculty, undergraduates, and graduate health science students who helped to develop and implement Indigenous health cultural safety education curriculum. This curriculum, which includes Indigenous and Western medical knowledge, provides a holistic, culturally safe approach to healthcare that better addresses barriers and gaps Indigenous Peoples face and that can result in health equity and social justice.

To begin, the **Royal Commission on Aboriginal Peoples** (Canada, 1996) and Health Canada (2007) expressed that multi-level, multi-sector, multi-system collaboration, commitment, and change, in full partnership with Indigenous people, are crucial for improved health equity. More recently, the **Truth and Reconciliation Commission (TRC) Calls to Action** advocated "establishing and maintaining a mutually respectful relationship between Aboriginal and non-Aboriginal peoples in this country" (Truth and Reconciliation, 2015, p. 6). Action #23 specifically calls for an improvement in the numbers and retention of Aboriginal professionals working in healthcare and Aboriginal communities and the provision of **cultural competency** (safety) training/education for all healthcare professionals. Action #24 presses for medical and nursing school students in Canada to be required to take a course in the following: Indigenous health issues; history and legacy of residential schools; the **United Nations Declaration on the Rights of Indigenous Peoples (UNDRIP)**; **Treaties** and Aboriginal rights; and Indigenous teachings and practices. This means that *skills-based training* in *intercultural competency, conflict resolution, human rights*, and *anti-racism* are a mandated part of the curriculum.

These reconciliatory Calls to Action are critical to us as Indigenous Peoples. Our everyday experience as Indigenous people seems to be lost amidst destructive colonizing practices. Consequently, Indigenous stories are often not told, not heard, and not understood: we are silenced, ignored, and treated as "other" within colonial systems of health, education, and society. Racism is learned—from our parents, families, and friends, from children on the bus, from the media, the Internet, everywhere. For Calls to Action #23 and #24 to become reality, Indigenous Elders need to be involved in teaching through sharing their stories and histories.

LEARNING FROM OUR ELDERS

> You cannot understand the present without knowing about the past. The history of our people shapes who we are today and who our children will be tomorrow. . . . If you learn to respect people that are different from yourself, that are of a different colour; if you can learn to respect and deal with me, then you will be able to learn to respect and deal with those that are Black, Yellow, Brown, White. (Personal communication, Elder Jessie Nyberg, July 3, 2006)

Indigenous Elders can provide culturally relevant education from *"a whole different perspective,"* in which storytelling and realities of social, economic, physical, emotional, and spiritual determinants of health are shared (Kurtz et al., 2014, p. 20). As recognized teachers of traditions and protocols, Elders are critical in the development of culturally appropriate programs (Stiegelbauer, 1996). Elders view the world holistically and can help students understand self-responsibility within an interwoven connectedness to each other, society, and the environment. Elders "promote peace, kindness, acceptance, and respect" (Anonson, et al., 2014, p. 6), which are deeply important attributes of healthcare providers. For education of healthcare students/professionals to be effective, it is important that educators consider who has written the curricular content, who is doing the teaching, and how the material is being taught.

Indigenous Peoples, especially Elders, are often the best teachers for sharing the history and experiences of Indigenous Peoples in Canada. Elders guide people to see both Western and Indigenous perspectives. They connect the past to the present and future and provide guidance in physical, mental, and spiritual health through ceremony, stories, and teachings (Stiegelbauer, 1996). Through their life journey of learning, wisdom, spirituality, and experiences, Elders are deeply respected within Indigenous and non-Indigenous communities for their knowledge of language, tradition, protocol, ceremonial practices, and skills. Elders' truths and teachings have been learned through oral history that has been passed down from generation to generation through storytelling.

Elders' knowledge, shared through stories and ceremony, is used to help others better understand history and current contexts of colonization, racism, discrimination, stereotypes, and biases. They have a responsibility to give back to their communities and families by sharing their knowledge and teaching others. They are role models—especially for youth—in the way that they live what they have learned and demonstrate how to apply these learnings to life. They model how "being a human being" is essential to a strong sense of cultural identity and healing.

CULTURAL SAFETY

The concept of cultural safety was founded by Ramsden (1993), a Māori nurse who recognized the impact of power imbalances between nurses and Indigenous patients. She saw that Indigenous Peoples' health improved when nurses understood colonial history and its intergenerational effect on lives. The reference to *culture* in the context of cultural safety is not anthropological or ethnic: it is not about how one dresses, eats, worships, or expresses their religious beliefs. When we discuss cultural safety, *culture* includes, but is not limited to, age or generation; gender; sexual orientation; occupation and socio-economic status; ethnic origin or migrant experience; religious or spiritual belief; and disability (Nursing Council of New Zealand, 2005, 2011). While this definition has been drawn from New Zealand, it is equally applicable to Australia, Canada, and other countries with a shared colonial history. In countries such as these, dominant ways of describing culture carry assumptions about social order. People who have power and authority therein often dictate a specific set of social norms (values, beliefs, behaviours, and practices) that support the dominant status quo. Those who choose not to abide by these norms are often labelled, "othered," marginalized, ignored, or unaccepted by the norm. By shifting the power and authoritative dominant perspectives within the healthcare system away from the colonizer, a space opens up in which providers are better able to listen and respond to Indigenous people's stories and share decision making about healthcare needs. This requires cultural humility.

Cultural safety, as a determinant of health, acknowledges the social, historical, and political factors that have shaped Indigenous people's lives. It addresses power imbalances to create non-racist and non-discriminatory environments in which people feel safe (Curtis et al., 2019; Kurtz et al., 2008).

Read the Case Study below and answer the questions.

Case Study: The Emergency Room Experience of an Indigenous Elder

Recently, Mary experienced excruciating back pain for no specific reason. She has lived with arthritis pain for decades, but this pain was different. She usually refused to visit the Emergency Room (ER) because of past negative experiences with the healthcare system as an Indigenous woman. However, as a Registered Nurse (RN), she knew something was terribly wrong and went to the hospital. In the ER, she described her extreme pain to the nurse, but she was not offered any relief. She felt that the RN did not believe her. Two hours later, a physician visited and the first question they asked was, "Are you drug seeking?" Mary wondered why she was asked this. She does not drink alcohol, and she became very upset. Four hours later, having been given no pain relief, Mary had an X-ray and CAT scan. The reason for these was not explained to her. The physician confirmed she had four spontaneous lumbar compression fractures and would be allowed pain medicine. Mary said, "No one apologized. This experience is so similar to many others I have had—not being believed, being ignored, being called and treated as an old fat Indian."

Critical Thinking Questions:

1. Long waits in the ER are a common experience within healthcare. What makes Elder Mary's experience different?
2. What underlying "social norms" may have had a role in the healthcare Elder Mary experienced?

TAKING ACTION THROUGH CULTURAL SAFETY EDUCATION

Cultural safety philosophy provides an understanding of others that goes beyond "cultural awareness," which acknowledges difference, and is broader than "cultural sensitivity," which respects difference. Cultural safety also goes further than "cultural competence," in which checklists can be used to measure the healthcare practitioner's knowledge, skills, and attitudes. In the context of nursing, cultural competence is used to measure a nurse's understanding of and attitudes about another culture. This measurement is often of the *nurse's perception* of care provided; it may not consider how the patient felt in receiving the care. Cultural safety education guides learners to understand that culture extends beyond cultural practices and traditions. A culturally safe environment is one in which the patient feels spiritually, socially, emotionally, and physically safe; it is an environment where there is no assault, challenge, or denial of a person or group's identity, of who they are, or of what they need. It does not diminish, demean, or disempower the cultural identity and well-being of an individual (Williams, 1999). As in the case study above, the ER nurse may have thought the care provided was appropriate, yet Mary's concerns were diminished and demeaned, and she had no power in decision making about her care. In fact, her experience reconfirmed why she is reluctant to seek health services. This aversion to seeking help could result in increased seriousness of illness and disease, thus affecting her quality and length of life.

Cultural safety education aims to improve Indigenous People's health by providing practitioners with a better understanding of the importance of positive encounters and ensuring access to, and awareness about, available health services (Kurtz et al., 2018; Papps, 2005; Wepa, 2015). A recent literature review of health sciences cultural safety education in Australia, Canada, New Zealand, and the United States found that this education changed student knowledge, attitude, self-confidence, and behaviour when working with Indigenous populations (Kurtz et al., 2018). Cultural safety education was linked to improved relationships, healthier outcomes, increased number of Indigenous people entering health education programs, and more graduates interested in working in diverse communities (Kurtz et al., 2018). Elders and health providers noticed that culturally safe care strengthened individual, family, and community **resilience** to respond to crisis and community stress (Brascoupé & Waters, 2009).

Over 10 years ago, the University of British Columbia's School of Nursing recognized the need for cultural safety education for health science students (nursing, human kinetics, and social work). A core group of Indigenous experts—including local Elders, a Band Councillor, a nursing professor, and community and health authority healthcare providers—developed the Aboriginal Health Cultural Safety Curriculum. This process was supported by an Advisory Committee of Indigenous post-secondary students, local Indigenous health organizations leaders, community members, Elders, and health sciences Dean, Directors, and faculty members of Nursing, Human Kinetics, Social Work, and Indigenous Studies. This curriculum draws on the New Zealand principles of cultural safety (Nursing Council of New Zealand, 2005, 2011), which are aimed at improved health outcomes for Indigenous Peoples through teaching how to build and maintain ethical and respectful relationships, promoting health equity, and engaging in advocacy. This SWKNAQINX ("Okanagan") curriculum honours the traditional unceded territory of the local Okanagan Nation, urban Indigenous Peoples, and all human beings.

In this curriculum, we teach that the process of embracing cultural safety occurs within a circle. Such an approach to teaching cultural safety honours the meaning of circles for Indigenous Peoples, such as the Life Circle, which does not have a beginning or end: birth, life journey, death, and rebirth (see Figure 17.1).

Figure 17.1: Cultural Safety as a Life Circle
Kurtz et al., 2015; adapted from Ramsden, 1993, 1996; Papps, 2005.

Learning how to be culturally safe in everyday life is important within the current dominant colonial society, but it does not happen automatically. Learners and practitioners may catch themselves shifting back and forth around the circle. In some instances, they may not realize that they are being culturally sensitive or culturally competent. At other times, they may not understand that they are being culturally aware but not necessarily culturally safe. Clients can see and feel healthcare providers, colleagues, friends, and citizens distancing, judging, and taking and holding power—purposefully or unintentionally—through unspoken words, body language, tone of voice, or failure to really listen. This is why engaging in self-reflection and having humility and an open heart, mind, and body help us treat each other respectfully.

In the SWKNAQINX curriculum, students learn about pre-colonization, colonization, and **decolonization**. They learn about cultural safety philosophy and its application to professional practice and everyday life. The course is taught by a university instructor, Elders, and Elders-in-Training. It consists of 18 hours of classroom learning and one day at a local Indigenous community on reserve, where students meet local Elders to learn about the land, history, and ways of life. Students also visit the Band's Health Centre to meet health and wellness care providers and learn about multiple programs and resources available for community members.

On the second day of the class, Elders open with a prayer to honour and acknowledge the traditional territory holders, the collective rights of Indigenous Peoples, and the importance of Mother Earth. The Elders teach using a Talking Circle, an ancient tradition among Indigenous people for teaching, decision making, planning, and healing. Talking Circles provide a model for cultural safety training because they encourage dialogue for collective decision making and problem solving (Becker et al., 2006; Loppie, 2007), foster collaborative learning (about, for example, culture and traditions) that can inform research, education, and practice (Hodge et al., 1996; Kurtz, 2011, 2013), and assist in healing (Kurtz, 2011). They provide a culturally safe environment for profound, innocent, and honest teaching/learning in which everybody's unique cultural needs are acknowledged and the power within the circle is shared. During a Talking Circle, students sit on chairs in a circle, without tables, laptops, or cellphones. The person speaking holds a talking stick or other item of special meaning (feather or stone) to honour their vital role and remind people to listen thoughtfully. When the speaker is finished, the talking stick is passed to the next speaker in the circle (usually in order). Participants are asked to remain in the circle until the dialogue is finished (personal communication, Elder Jessie Nyberg Shuswap, 2015). The circle ensures each member can see each other. All questions and comments are invited, acknowledged, and responded to by Elders, respectfully and non-judgmentally.

To navigate between worldviews within the university setting, both didactic (e.g., PowerPoint presentations) and experiential (e.g., watching videos, problem-solving with real life case studies) teaching methods are used. Elders support students along their learning journey and provide insights into how they can become allies and treat each other with love and kindness as a way of life.

One student on the course shared insights about their learning:

> Yes—culture is a big determinant of health and understanding of health and healing is important for healthcare workers; I am better able to see how narrow and non-holistic the medical model is; I am much more appreciative of my role on this earth as a participant rather than a bystander or spectator; From the stories, I learned how to I want to be as a nurse; This course should be mandatory for all helping professionals. (Year 4 student)

==Engaging in culturally safe ways of being can counter the perpetuation of historical and contemporary racism, discrimination, and trauma.==

A VISION FOR NON-RACIST, NON-DISCRIMINATORY EDUCATION AND PRACTICE

Cultural safety education is increasingly becoming a requirement of health science program accreditation, degree completion, and professional registration (Canadian Association of Schools of Nursing, 2013; IPAC-RCPSC, 2009), but it is not just healthcare graduates who need to ensure the improved health and well-being of Indigenous Peoples in Canada and globally. The leaders of all levels of government in Canada need to instigate a higher level of effort to include Indigenous people in all organizations, particularly in health and education. Implementation of Indigenous-specific cultural safety curricula will help to improve the overall mental, physical, spiritual, and emotional wellness of Indigenous Peoples, facilitating their rights, empowerment, and self-determination, and generating meaningful relationships between Indigenous and non-Indigenous people.

Vision for Culturally Safe, Non-Racist, Non-Discriminatory Education, Practice, and Research in Everyday Life

1. Understanding we are all human beings.
2. Looking past skin colour.
3. Self-reflecting and questioning the status quo of power and taken-for-granted practices.
4. Respecting each other unconditionally.
5. Taking time to develop relationships.
6. Listening to each other's voice.
7. Asking each other what name they want to be called, rather than assuming they use the name on their records.

8. Being humble and willing to learn; being patient.
9. Including family, extended family, and community to support the healing of Indigenous people.
10. Realizing our own actions may purposefully or unintentionally perpetuate racist and discriminatory practices that exclude and place people as "other."
11. Sharing power, working together on decision and consensus making.

(Adapted from Kurtz et al., 2014)

The Culturally Safe Emergency Room Experience of an Indigenous Elder

Based on what you have learned in this chapter, re-read Elder Mary's story and answer the following questions:

1. What could the nurse or physician have done differently to provide culturally safe care? Explain why.
2. How would a culturally safe approach have helped Elder Mary feel safe and believe that she was receiving the best care possible?

HONOURING EACH OTHER AS HUMAN BEINGS

Teaching, learning, and understanding how Indigenous-specific determinants of health (e.g., colonization, racism, discrimination) impact Indigenous Peoples can change the ways health providers perpetuate or recreate racism, discrimination, and trauma. It will result in improved overall wellness of Indigenous people for generations. Cultural safety must be a part of all of our lives. Whether we are a provider or a receiver of care, we have a right to feel comfortable, respected, and safe. We have a right to have power over our lives. Cultural safety, as an action and a way of being, involves a shared trust in our day-to-day lives. Those who hold onto power in structural, organizational, and societal contexts can interfere with the provision of culturally safe, non-judgmental health care delivery (Kurtz, 2011).

Gaining knowledge about cultural safety in a course or workshop is only the beginning. We cannot tick a box and say we are culturally safe people. Elders are critical for teaching about culture, tradition, and being human beings, and they remind us that learning to share power and build respectful relationships with all peoples is a lifelong journey.

NOTE

1. An ancient protocol for meetings, gatherings, and ceremonies in which an Indigenous Elder acknowledges the Peoples on whose traditional territorial land the event is occurring. The Elder asks the Creator (spiritual figure) for guidance, support, and strength and gives thanks for the opportunity to assemble. Meant to create a safe space for interaction and engagement. Not intended to be a religious treaty or doctrine the intention is to acknowledge and give thanks for our Indigenous spirituality.

REFERENCES

Anonson, J., Huard, S., Kristoff, T., Clarke-Arnault, V., & Wilder, V. (2014). The role of Elders in post-secondary educational institutes. *The Canadian Journal of Native Studies*, *34*(2), 1–18.

Becker, S. A., Affonso, D. D., & Blue Horse Beard, M. (2006). Talking circles: Northern Plains Tribes America Indian women's view of cancer as a health issue. *Public Health Nursing*, *23*(1), 27–36. https://doi.org/10.1111/j.0737-1209.2006.230105.x

Brascoupé S., & Waters C. (2009). Cultural safety: Exploring the applicability of the concept of cultural safety to Aboriginal health and community wellness. *Journal of Aboriginal Health*, *5*(2), 6–41. https://doi.org/10.3138/ijih.v5i2.28981

Canada. (1996). *Report of the Royal Commission on Aboriginal Peoples*. https://www.bac-lac.gc.ca/eng/discover/aboriginal-heritage/royal-commission-aboriginal-peoples/Pages/final-report.aspx

Canadian Association of Schools of Nursing. (2013). *Educating nurses to address socio-cultural, historical, and contextual determinants of health among Aboriginal peoples 2013*. https://casn.ca/wp-content/uploads/2014/12/ENAHHRIKnowledgeProductFINAL.pdf

Curtis, E., Jones, R., Tipene-Leach, D., Walker, C., Loring, B., Paine, S. J., & Reid, P. (2019). Why cultural safety rather than cultural competency is required to achieve health equity: A literature review and recommended definition. *International Journal of Equity in Health*, *18*, 174. https://doi.org/10.1186/s12939-019-1082-3

Czyzewski, K. (2011). Colonialism as a broader social determinant of health. *The International Indigenous Policy Journal*, *2*(1), 1–14. https://doi.org/10.18584/iipj.2011.2.1.5

Doane, G. A. H. (2002). *Beyond behavioral skills to human-involved processes: Relational nursing practice and interpretive pedagogy*. Thorofare, New Jersey: SLACK Incorporated.

Government of Canada. (2019). *Social determinants of health*. Official Website of the Government of Canada. Retrieved April 11, 2020, from https://www.canada.ca/en/public-health/services/health-promotion/population-health/what-determines-health.html

Greenwood, M., de Leeuw, S., Lindsay, N. M., & Reading, C. (Eds.). (2015). *Determinants of Indigenous Peoples' health in Canada: Beyond the social*. Canadian Scholars Press.

Health Canada. (2007). *Tripartite First Nations Health Plan*. Retrieved April 11, 2020, from http://hc-sc.gc.ca

Hodge, F. S., Fredericks, L., & Rodriguez, B. (1996). American Indian women's talking circle: A cervical cancer screening and prevention project. *Cancer, 78*(Suppl. 7), 1592–1597.

Hyman, I., O'Campo, P., Ansara, D., Siddiqi. A., Forte, T., Smylie, J., Mahabir, D. F., & McKenzie, K. (2019, June). *Prevalence and predictors of everyday discrimination in Canada: Findings from the Canadian Community Health Survey*. Wellesley Institute. https://www.wellesleyinstitute.com/wp-content/uploads/2019/10/Prevalence-and-Predictors.pdf

IPAC-RCPSC Core Curriculum Development Working Group. (2009). *Promoting culturally safe care for First Nations, Inuit, and Métis patients. A core curriculum for residents and physicians*. Indigenous Physicians Association of Canada and the Royal College of Physicians and Surgeons of Canada. https://www.ipac-amac.ca/downloads/core-curriculum.pdf

Kurtz, D. L. M. (2011). *Contributing to health reform: Urban aboriginal women speak out* [Doctoral dissertation]. Deakin University. http://dro.deakin.edu.au/view/DU:30040133

Kurtz, D. L. M. (2013). Indigenous methodologies: Traversing indigenous and western worldviews in research. *AlterNative: An International Journal of Indigenous Peoples, 9*(3), 217–229.

Kurtz, D. L. M., Cash, P., Nyberg, J., & Wepa, D. (2015). Embracing cultural safety in health education, practice, and research: Learning from our Elders. Paper presented at The Healing Our Spirit Worldwide. The Seventh Gathering, Hamilton, New Zealand, November 15–20, 2015.

Kurtz, D. L. M., Janke, R., Vinek, J., Wells, T., Hutchinson, P., & Froste, A. (2018). Health sciences cultural safety education in Australia, Canada, New Zealand, and the United States: A literature review. *International Journal of Medical Education, 9*, 271–285. https://doi.org/10.5116/ijme.5bc7.21e2

Kurtz, D. L. M., Nyberg, J. C., Van Den Tillaart, S., Mills, B., & Okanagan Urban Aboriginal Health Research Collective. (2008). Silencing of voice: An act of structural violence: Urban Aboriginal women speak out about their experiences with health care. *Journal of Aboriginal Health, 4*(1), 53–63. https://doi.org/10.18357/ijih41200812315

Kurtz, D. L. M., Turner, D., Nyberg, J., & Moar, D. (2014). Social justice and health equity: Urban Aboriginal women's actions for health reform. *International Journal of Health, Wellness, and Society, 3*(4), 13–26. https://doi.org/10.18848/2156-8960/CGP/v03i04/41081

Loppie, C. (2007). Learning from the grandmothers: Incorporating Indigenous principles into qualitative research. *Qualitative Health Research, 17*(2), 276–284. https://doi.org/10.1177/1049732306297905

Nursing Council of New Zealand. (2005, 2011). *Guidelines for cultural safety, the Treaty of Waitangi, and Maori health in nursing and midwifery*. Nursing Council of New Zealand.

Papps, E. (2005). Cultural safety: Daring to be different. In D. Wepa (Ed.), *Cultural safety in Aotearoa New Zealand* (pp. 20–28). Pearson Education.

Ramsden, I. (1993). *Kawa Whakaruruhau*. Cultural safety in nursing education in Aotearoa, New Zealand. *Nursing Praxis in New Zealand, 8*(3), 4–10.

Ramsden, I. (1996). The Treaty of Waitangi and cultural safety: The role of the Treaty in nursing and midwifery education in Aotearoa. In *Nursing Council of New Zealand, Guidelines for cultural safety in nursing and midwifery education*. NCNZ.

Reading, C., & Wien, F. (2009). *Health inequalities and social determinant of Aboriginal Peoples' health*. National Collaborating Center for Indigenous Health. https://www.ccnsa-nccah.ca/docs/determinants/RPT-HealthInequalities-Reading-Wien-EN.pdf

Stiegelbauer, S. M. (1996). What is an Elder? What do Elders do? First Nations Elders as teachers in culture-based urban organizations. *Canadian Journal of Native Studies, 16*(1), 37. http://www3.brandonu.ca/cjns/16.1/Stiegelbauer.pdf

Truth and Reconciliation Commission of Canada. (2015). *Honouring the truth, reconciling for the future: Summary of the Final Report of the Truth and Reconciliation Commission of Canada*. https://irsi.ubc.ca/sites/default/files/inline-files/Executive_Summary_English_Web.pdf

UN General Assembly. (2007). *United Nations Declaration on the Rights of Indigenous Peoples: Resolution / adopted by the General Assembly*, 2 October 2007, A/RES/61/295. Retrieved March 14, 2020, from https://www.refworld.org/docid/471355a82.html

Wepa, D. (Ed.). (2015). *Cultural safety in Aotearoa New Zealand* (2nd ed.). Cambridge University Press. https://doi.org/10.1017/CBO9781316151136

Williams, R. (1999). Cultural safety: What does it mean for our work practice? *Australian and New Zealand Journal of Public Health, 23*(2), 1–16. https://doi.org/10.1111/j.1467-842X.1999.tb01240.x

CHAPTER 18

Indigenous Food Sovereignty: Realizing its Potential for Indigenous Decolonization, Self-Determination, and Community Health[1]

Charlotte Coté

LEARNING OBJECTIVES

1. To provide students with a comprehensive understanding of Indigenous food sovereignty and its importance in building and nourishing strong and healthy Indigenous Nations and communities.
2. To encourage students to develop a critical understanding of how settler colonialism has impacted Indigenous health by barring access to traditional and nutritional foods.
3. To provide students with a deeper comprehension of how traditional foods impact Indigenous peoples' physical, emotional, and spiritual health.

**Throughout this chapter, Dr. Coté has used a number of* Nuu-chah-nulth *words, which have been marked with an asterisk (*). To assist with pronunciation, please see the text box entitled* Nuu-chah-nulth Words, Phonetic Spellings, and Definitions.

My people, the Tseshaht on Vancouver Island, British Columbia, like **Indigenous peoples** worldwide, are enacting food sovereignty to revitalize our **foodways** and restore health and wellness in our respective communities. Food sovereignty is positioned within Indigenous struggles for **decolonization**, cultural revitalization, and self-determination. To fully reclaim our food sovereignty, we must peel away the layers of **colonialism** that have been the Indigenous lived experience and redefine our lives within our own ancestral teachings and cultural knowledge. This decolonial praxis—that is, this practice of reasserting our inherent right to food sovereignty—entails decreasing dependence on the global industrial food system and revitalizing

Indigenous foodways through the reaffirmation and reclamation of the physical, emotional, and spiritual relationships to the **lands,** waters, plants, and all living things that have sustained our Indigenous communities and cultures.

COLONIZATION, COLONIALISM, AND INDIGENOUS HEALTH

A 2019 study estimated that one in five deaths globally are associated with the **Western** diet, which is high in salt, sugar, and fat, and which also includes high levels of red and processed meats (Afshin et al., 2019). Another recent study pointed to the rise in unhealthy diets for the last two decades as being the leading risk factor for illness, death, and disability in Canada and throughout the world (Kaczorowski et al., 2016). Additionally, human health is directly linked to the health of the animals we eat and the unnatural diets of corn the animals are fed, as well as the steroids, antibiotics, and other drugs they are given (Pollen, 2006).

The history of settler colonialism and the resulting economic, social, and cultural marginalization has profoundly impacted Indigenous peoples' health worldwide. Many of the health issues and inequalities Indigenous peoples face today are directly linked to the dispossession of our homelands and the loss of access to our ancestral harvesting areas, which have impacted our ability to access our traditional foods and medicines. As ethnobiologists Nancy Turner and Katherine Turner explained, "Through a complex interplay of colonial pressures and policies, traditional foods were marginalized and their use declined dramatically" (Turner & Turner, 2008, p. 109). Low socio-economic status and economic inequality are also powerful risk factors for poor health outcomes. Low-income populations face higher rates of mortality and morbidity from many diseases associated with a dramatic shift in Indigenous lifeways (Adelson, 2005; Sheehy et al., 2014).

What Is Settler Colonialism?

Settler colonialism is when colonizers seek to oust an original population from a region and settle there themselves. That is, they stay long-term and persist in practices that aim to eliminate, literally or culturally, the Indigenous Peoples they have displaced. It is structurally oriented around "the dispossession of Indigenous peoples of their lands and self-determining authority." Yellowknives Dene Glen Coulthard (n.d., p. 10)

In analyzing settler colonialism and federal Indian policy, one cannot overlook the disturbing legacy that the Canadian and American Indian education policies had on Indigenous peoples, cultures, identities, and health. By the late 1800s, both Canada and the United States had adopted an educational system of boarding schools (also called residential schools) whereby Indigenous children were taken from their families and communities and placed in these institutions, which were intentionally designed to eradicate their spiritual traditions, political and economic systems, languages, and cultures (Haig-Brown, 1989; Smith, 2009). In these schools, Indigenous children were estranged from their own traditional and healthy diets and forced to eat foods that many had never eaten before, such as domesticated meats, cheese, wheat flour, and sugar. It is not an overstatement to say that the bodies of these young children were being colonized from the inside out. At the schools and throughout Indigenous communities, Western processed foods were supplanting nutritious traditional foods, which themselves began to play only a supplemental role.

> **What is Collective Historical Trauma?**
>
> Indigenous identity, to a large extent, is a collective identity, and so the experiences of the generations of children who attended residential schools not only affected those students but also resulted in collective trauma, framed within a context of loss: loss of family, loss of community, loss of language, loss of culture, loss of access to traditional and nutritious foods.

As part of the Indigenous **self-determination** movement that grew in the 1970s, Indigenous communities throughout the world have been actively engaging in decolonization strategies and reasserting authority over our homelands, our lives, and our physical, emotional, and spiritual health and **well-being**. The budding food sovereignty movement provided Indigenous peoples with a pathway to decolonization and self-determination through the revitalization of our traditional food systems and practices.

> **Nuu-chah-nulth Words, Phonetic Spellings, and Definitions**
>
> ḥaaḥuuɬi – haahuulhi – traditional lands and waters
> haʔum – ha-um – traditional food
> ḥaw̓iiḥ – ha-wayh – chiefs
> hišukʔiš čawaak – hishuk ish tsawalk – everything is interconnected
> ʔiisaak – eesahk – being respectful
> masčim – maschim – community members under a chief's leadership
> n̓aas – nahs – Creator
> p̓ačiƛ – pahchitl – to give
> ʔuuʔaɬuk – uu-ah-lhuk – to take care of

UNDERSTANDING FOOD SOVEREIGNTY

In 1993, peasants and small-scale farmers organized into a global agrarian movement, Via Campesina, representing 148 organizations from 69 countries. Collectively, they formed the strongest voice yet in radical opposition to what they described as a "globalized, neoliberal model of agricultural food production" (Coté, 2016, p. 7). In a conference held in 1996 in Tlaxcala, Mexico, Via Campesina introduced a new food regime concept—"food sovereignty":

> Food sovereignty is the right of peoples to healthy and culturally appropriate food produced through ecologically sound and sustainable methods, and their right to define their own food and agricultural systems. It puts the aspirations and needs of those who produce, distribute and consume food at the heart of food systems and policies rather than the demands of markets and corporations. (Declaration of Nyéléni, 2007, para. 3)

This notion of food sovereignty became a uniting call to small-scale farmers and Indigenous peoples throughout the world. While the food sovereignty movement developed in an agrarian-based, Latin American context, Indigenous peoples with fishing, hunting, and gathering traditions were able to connect to its underlying philosophy that all nations, including Indigenous nations, have the right to develop food systems and practices that reflect our own cultural values as those relate to producing, distributing, and consuming food.

INDIGENOUS FOOD SOVEREIGNTY

In the mid-1990s, Indigenous peoples in Canada and the US began exploring ways that food sovereignty could be employed as a concept to create dialogue and action connected with the revitalization of Indigenous food practices and **ecological knowledge**. Created in 1996, the Working Group on Indigenous Food Sovereignty (WGIFS) in British Columbia was one of the first Indigenous groups to explore the new concept of food sovereignty and articulate ways it could be defined and applied to pressing issues facing Indigenous communities as they responded to their own health needs (Morrison, 2011).

The WGIFS developed four key principles of Indigenous food sovereignty that Indigenous peoples and communities could use as a framework as they addressed their food needs:

1. Sacred or Divine Sovereignty: food is a sacred gift from the Creator;
2. Participation (a call to action): people have a responsibility to uphold and nurture healthy and interdependent relationships with the ecosystem, which provides land, water, plants, and animals as food;
3. Self-Determination: food sovereignty needs to be placed within a context of Indigenous self-determination, in which Indigenous peoples have the freedom and ability to respond to community needs regarding food; and

4. Legislation and Policy: a restorative framework is required to reconcile Indigenous food and cultural values with colonial laws and policies (Morrison, 2011, pp. 100–101).[2]

In what follows, I build on the WGIFS's four principles and frame these in four sections that help contextualize Indigenous food sovereignty, situating it within the decolonial struggles taking place in Indigenous communities around the world today.

BUILDING RELATIONSHIPS AND AFFIRMING RESPONSIBILITIES

As I stated earlier, the concept of food sovereignty was framed within a larger rights discourse: the right of peoples to healthy and culturally appropriate food and the right to freely and independently define their own food and agricultural systems. Having the political and cultural right to one's traditional foods recognized by the state government through policy, which the WGIFS identified as a requirement, can provide a framework for reconciling Indigenous food and cultural values with colonial laws and policies. This has the potential to align with and support the rights contained in the **United Nations Declaration on the Rights of Indigenous Peoples (UNDRIP)**, specifically Article 20: "Indigenous peoples have the right to maintain and develop their political, economic and social systems or institutions, to be secure in the enjoyment of their own means of **subsistence** and development, and to engage freely in all their traditional and other economic activities" (UN General Assembly, 2007, p. 7). In 2016, the Government of Canada endorsed the UNDRIP as part of the movement toward reconciliation with Indigenous peoples. However, as of the time of writing, it has not officially adopted the UNDRIP into law (Fitzgerald & Schwartz, 2017). By contrast, in 2019, British Columbia and the Northwest Territories made political moves to incorporate the UNDRIP into their provincial and territorial laws (Last, 2019).

Jeff Corntassel (Cherokee) argued that "the existing rights discourse [on food sovereignty] can take Indigenous peoples only so far" (2008, p. 105) through its emphasis on state political and legal recognition of Indigenous rights. Rather than focus on achieving political and legal recognition of the right to food sovereignty, Corntassel aimed attention at Indigenous community action, emphasizing the cultural responsibilities and relationships Indigenous peoples have with the land, water, plants, and animals that have sustained their cultures, and placing these at the core of sustainable self-determination. To decolonize, Indigenous peoples need to direct change from within. Moreover, to work toward becoming sustainable, self-determining nations, Indigenous peoples need to decolonize through action, change, strategies, and policies (Corntassel, 2008).

Indigenizing food sovereignty places emphasis on Indigenous responsibility, mutuality, and kinship. It also focuses on relationships with the natural world, which are built on reciprocity between humans and non-humans. In these "cultures of reciprocity" (Kimmerer, 2013, p. 115), humans and other living things exist in an interconnected web of life where all are equally worthy of respect, and where all—humans and non-humans—have duties and responsibilities. As explained by Potawatomi scholar Robin Kimmerer, "If an animal gives its life to feed me, I am in turn bound to support its life. If I receive a stream's gift of pure water, then I am responsible for returning a gift in kind. An integral part of a human's education is to know those duties and how to perform them" (2013, p. 115). Embedded within Indigenous **eco-philosophies** and worldviews is the cultural knowledge and understanding of the interconnectedness of people, animals, land, water, and air. Such a view emphasizes good relationships based on gratitude and respect. Indigenous food sovereignty, therefore, embodies a deeply spiritual appreciation for food as a sacred gift—a form of gratitude that is recognized in Indigenous food rituals, offerings, and ceremonies (Morrison, 2006).

My Nuu-chah-nulth nation and other Indigenous peoples have a belief that all things in our natural world have spirits, which we recognize through ceremonies such as First Species, First Foods, and First Salmon.

> Ceremonies are conducted to honour animals and plants for gifting themselves as food. They elicit a relationship based on reciprocity. During these ceremonies, there is gratitude for the spirit of a plant or animal that gives itself to humans. Ceremonies recognize the sacredness of these gifts.

RESTORATIVE FOOD JUSTICE

Indigenous food sovereignty entails a rebuilding of the relationships between humans and non-humans in a restorative framework. The human–ecosystem relationship is characterized as one of reciprocity and respect, where humans do not control nature but live in harmony with it. Thus, Indigenous food sovereignty restores the health of Indigenous communities and restores the health of the land. Or, as Kimmerer so aptly stated, "We restore the land and the land restores us" (2013, p. 336).

Indigenous food sovereignty is defined within a restorative context—one that works to nurture individual and community health by repairing and building healthy relationships between Indigenous peoples and their ancestral homelands, as well as between Indigenous peoples and the plants and animals that provide them with food. As scholars Grey and Patel explained, kinship "is not restricted to consanguine human beings . . . but is a quality of the totality of the natural world—including all of the life-forms that provide sustenance. . . . Thus, food can be seen as the most direct manifestation of the relationships between Indigenous peoples and homelands" (2015, p. 437).

The Indigenous food sovereignty movement embodies a decolonization framework and, through action and practice, seeks to heal the wounds of colonialism and repair our relationships with the natural world. For Indigenous peoples, our health and well-being are tied to our ancestral lands, the waters, and the plants and animals. Our foods and ecological knowledge are embedded in our land and seascapes. In order to return to healthy communities, we need to restore healthy relationships to our ecosystems. This requires decolonizing our traditional homelands and having access to our lands and waters where we once harvested, fished, and hunted.

PROMOTING HEALTH AND WELL-BEING

Indigenous peoples' health is directly connected to our ability to eat our traditional foods (Krohn & Segrest, 2010). Being "healthy" is about more than just our physical well-being; it is also about our spiritual and emotional health. It is about feeding our bodies with traditional and healthy foods and feeding our minds and spirits with our cultural teachings. Restoring our traditional food practices allows us to experience a special connection to our cultures and our lands because every plant and animal carries their own spiritual gifts. Thus, there is "a sense of vitality and belonging" that comes with eating the foods that provided our ancestors with optimum health and longevity (Krohn & Segrest, 2010, p. 9).

Inuit in northern Alaska have a saying: "I am what I am because of what I eat" (as cited in Coté, 2010, p. 199). Studies of the Indigenous whaling nations in the Arctic demonstrate how traditional foods—especially whales—have more than just nutritional value; they have social, cultural, spiritual, and psychological significance as well. While whales are highly valued as a healthy food source, the tradition of whaling also maintains community solidarity and collective security through communal hunts and communal processing, distributing, and consuming whale products. Whaling serves to link Inuit materially, symbolically, and spiritually to their cultural heritage and ancestral knowledge (Coté, 2010).

Indigenous peoples have an emotional connection to our traditional foods, and we see these foods as impacting our physical and nutritional well-being and as having strong cultural and social value. A delicate balance between nutrition, emotional health, and social contact can be struck through complex interactions between people, brain chemistry, and the foods we eat (Morrison, 2006). Eating traditional healthy foods is associated with the release of neurotransmitters, including dopamine, endorphin, oxytocin, and serotonin (often referred to as "happy chemicals"). These chemicals, in turn, send messages to the brain that make us feel joyful and content (Breuning, 2012; Linden, 2011). Many studies have been conducted with Indigenous peoples in northern Canada and Alaska to examine cultural and dietary change resulting from an increase in the consumption of industrialized and processed foods. Even with the increased availability of market and processed foods, these communities have stayed connected to their traditional harvesting practices. Studies have shown that although store-bought foods were available, traditional foods still retained their cultural, social, and psychological significance and were associated with good feelings, health, and pleasurable events—especially when the foods were locally harvested. A study conducted with Indigenous women in Canada's Arctic communities between 1993 and 2003 asked the question, "What do you think are the most important advantages of traditional food?" to which women responded: "traditional food is healthy"; "[traditional food] has more iron"; and "[traditional food] makes your blood strong" (Lamden et al., 2007, p. 312). When asked what the socio-political benefits were of eating traditional foods, the respondents remarked: "keeps our tradition"; "brings people together"; and "involves family in food prep[aration]" (p. 309).

STRENGTHENING SOCIAL, FAMILIAL, AND COMMUNITY BONDS

As I reflect on growing up in my community of Tseshaht, which is one of the communities of the larger Nuu-chah-nulth Nation, and harvesting *haʔum* * (traditional food) with my relatives, I realize how important these food traditions were to maintaining and strengthening the social and cultural bonds with my relatives. I grew up in a large, tight-knit family, and our food traditions, such as berry-picking and salmon fishing, were—and still are—important in reinforcing social and familial ties. The harvesting, processing, and sharing of our *haʔum* created a space where our elders transferred their cultural and foods knowledge to us younger ones. These practices reaffirmed our cultural identity as Tseshaht and strengthened our relationships to the plants and animals that gave themselves as food, as well as to our ancestral homelands, where harvesting takes place. As social creatures, our ability to function in healthy interdependent relationships is directly influenced by our ability to maintain balance and harmony within our own bodies. In turn, our ability to maintain healthy bodies is directly influenced by the emotions we experience in positive social interactions. Working with family and community members to hunt, fish, gather, or prepare Indigenous foods increases mental and emotional health through bonding, as well as through creating memories that can help build or enhance social and familial relationships (Morrison, 2006).

Integral to coastal Indigenous people's cultures is our social gathering or feast, known as the **Potlatch**.[3] The word comes from the Chinook trade language and was derived from the Nuu-chah-nulth word, *paciƛ* *, which means "to give."[4] The Potlatch reflected and perpetuated Nuu-chah-nulth social organization, and in pre-contact times, only the *ḥawiiḥ* * (chiefs) held potlatches, which they used to announce, make a claim to, and validate their hereditary privileges or birthrights. They were also used as a social mechanism to maintain harmony with their *masčim* * (community members under a chief's leadership) by acknowledging their skills and labour.

While the purpose of potlatches was to pass on titles of rank and their associated privileges to designated heirs of the *ḥawiiḥ*, they also functioned to distribute food surpluses and special local products to the people invited to witness the claim being made (Drucker, 1951). These foods and other items were given as gifts to the invited guests, whose acceptance of them acknowledged their recognition of the claim being made. Today, anyone in our community can host a Potlatch. They are still held to transfer and bestow names, celebrate marriages, recognize a youth's coming of age, and mourn and recognize the death of a tribal member. The Potlatch continues to serve an important economic and social function through the sharing and distribution of food and material goods.

HIŠUKʔIŠ ĆAWAAK: EVERYTHING IS INTERCONNECTED

My people, the Nuu-chah-nulth, are actively engaging in decolonization and self-determination by developing strategies and implementing policies that are aimed at the sustainable production and consumption of traditional foods and grounded in our philosophical and ecological knowledge. Embodied in Nuu-chah-nulth philosophies of *ʔiisaak* * (being respectful), *ʔuuʔatuk* * (to take care of), and *hišukʔiš ćawaak* * (everything is one/everything is connected) is the understanding that we must honour the wisdom and values of ancestral ecological knowledge in maintaining responsible and respectful relationships with the environment. *ʔiisaak* applies to all life-forms, as well as to the land and water. At its most basic, it teaches that all life forms are held in equal esteem (Atleo, 2004; Turner et al., 2000). The underlying vision of *ʔuuʔatuk* is to "take care of" the *ḥaaḥuuɫi* * (our traditional lands and waters) in a way that aligns with Nuu-chah-nulth values and principles. This is a responsibility given to our people through *ṅaas* * (our Creator).

Viewing the universe as a "network of relationships," Nuu-chah-nulth hereditary Chief Umeek, Richard Atleo maintained that *hišukʔiš ćawaak* connects people, animals, plants, and the natural and the supernatural (spiritual) realms in a seamless and interconnected web where all life-forms are revered and worthy of mutual respect (Atleo, 2004, p. 118). The stewardship of our homelands is rooted in Chief Umeek's philosophy, and it is what the Nuu-chah-nulth are striving to revitalize. Nuu-chah-nulth hereditary Chief Tom Mexsis Happynook affirmed that, embedded within these human and non-human relations, is the understanding of responsibilities that Indigenous peoples strive to uphold in our social, cultural, and economic practices—responsibilities that have evolved into unwritten laws over millennia: "the environment is not a place of divisions but rather a place of relations, a place where cultural diversity and bio-diversity are not separate but in fact need each other" (Happynook, 2001, para. 1). This is rooted within our overarching philosophy of *hišukʔiš ćawaak*—everything is interconnected.

CONCLUSION

Today, many Indigenous communities throughout Canada and the US are enacting food sovereignty to revitalize traditional foodways, restore and strengthen individual and community health and wellness, and assert our cultural and political autonomy. Traditional foods have become a potent cultural symbol as Indigenous peoples recognize that eating our traditional foods, and making the choice to eat these foods, is itself a political act—a resistance to settler colonialism. Harvesting, sharing, and eating our traditional foods is central to decolonization and an exercise in self-determination. Indigenous food sovereignty is intricately linked to our cultural sovereignty. As Ojibwe environmentalist, economist, and writer Winona LaDuke stated, "You can't say you're sovereign if you can't feed yourself" (LaDuke, 2019, p. xiv).

CRITICAL THINKING QUESTIONS

1. Did you grow up eating foods that were connected to your cultures? If so, what foods and food traditions did you grow up with?
2. How did colonization and ongoing settler colonialism impact Indigenous people's physical, emotional, and spiritual health?
3. How does Indigenous food sovereignty connect to the Nuu-chah-nulth philosophy of *hišukʔiš ċawaak*?
4. What does Winona LaDuke mean when she says, "You can't say you're sovereign if you can't feed yourself?"
5. What challenges do Indigenous peoples face in achieving food sovereignty?

NOTES

1. This chapter is adapted from two of my previous publications (Coté, 2016; Coté, 2021).
2. Also see the Indigenous Food Systems Network website, which grew out of the forums held by the WGIFS: http://www.indigenousfoodsystems.org.
3. For an anthropological analysis of the Nuu-chah-chah potlatch, see Barnett, 1966, Drucker, 1951, 1963, 1965, and Sapir & Swadesh, 1955.
4. In *Potlatch*, Tseshaht writer and artist George Clutesi described how Pa-chuck (his spelling) means "to be given" (Clutesi, 1973, p. 10).

REFERENCES

Adelson, N. (2005). The embodiment of inequity health disparities in Aboriginal Canada. *Canadian Journal of Public Health*, *96*(2), S45–61.

Afshin, A., Sur, P. J., Fay, K. A., Cornaby, L., Giannina, F., Salama, J. S., Mullany, E. C., Abate, K. H., Abbafati, C., Abebe, Z., Afarideh, M., Aggarwal, A., Agrawal, S., Akinyemiju, T., Alahdab, F., Bacha, U., Bachman, V. F., Badali, H., Badawi, A., . . . Murray, J. L. (2019). Health effects of dietary risks in 195 countries, 1990–2017: A systematic analysis for the Global Burden of Disease Study 2017. *Lancet*, *393*, 1958–1972.

Atleo, E. R. (2004). *Tsawalk: A Nuu-chah-nulth worldview*. University of British Columbia Press.

Barnett, H. G. (1966). The nature of the Potlatch. In T. McFeat (Ed.), *Indians of the North Pacific Coast* (pp. 81–91). Carleton University Press. (Reprinted from "The nature of the Potlatch," 1938, *American Anthropologist*, *40*, 349–358).

Breuning, L. G. (2012). *Meet your happy chemicals*. CreateSpace Publishing.

Clutesi, G. (1973). *Potlatch*. Gray Publishing. (Original published 1969)

Corntassel, J. (2008). Toward sustainable self-determination: Rethinking the contemporary Indigenous-rights discourse. *Alternatives, 33*(1), 105–132.

Coté, C. (2010). *Spirits of our whaling ancestors: Revitalizing makah and nuu-chah-nulth traditions*. University of Washington Press.

Coté, C. (2016). "Indigenizing" food sovereignty: Revitalizing Indigenous food practices and ecological knowledges in Canada and the United States. *Humanities, 5*(57), 1–14. https://www.mdpi.com/2076-0787/5/3/57

Coté, C. (2021). *hišukʔiš ċawaak—Everything is interconnected: Food sovereignty, health, and haʔum (traditional foods) in northwest coast Indigenous communities*. University of Washington Press.

Coulthard, G. S. (n.d.) *Subjects of empire? Indigenous peoples and the "politics of recognition" in Canada* [Unpublished doctoral dissertation]. University of Victoria.

Declaration of Nyéléni, Declaration of the Forum for Food Sovereignty, Sélingué, Mali. (2007). Retrieved September 1, 2015, from https://nyeleni.org/IMG/pdf/DeclNyeleni-en.pdf

Drucker, P. (1951). The Northern and Central Nootkan Tribes. *Bureau of American Ethnology Bulletin, 144*, 1–480.

Drucker, P. (1963). *Indians of the Northwest Coast*. Carleton University Press. (Original work published 1955).

Drucker, P. (1965). *Cultures of the North Pacific Coast*. Chandler Publishing Company.

Fitzgerald, O., & Schwartz, R. (2017). *Introduction: UNDRIP implementation braiding international, domestic and Indigenous laws: Special report*. Center for International Governance Innovation.

Grey, S., & Patel, R. (2015). Food sovereignty as decolonization: Some contributions from Indigenous movements to food systems and development politics. *Agriculture & Human Values, 32*(1), 431–444. https://doi.org/10.1007/s10460-014-9548-9

Haig-Brown, C. (1998). *Resistance and renewal: Surviving the Indian residential school*. Arsenal Pulp Press.

Happynook, T. M. (2001). Cultural biodiversity: Indigenous relationships within their environment. In *Microbehavior and macroresults: Proceedings of the Tenth Biennial Conference of the International Institute of Fisheries Economics and Trade, July 10-14, 2000, Corvallis, Oregon, USA*. Compiled by Richard S. Johnston and Ann L. Shriver. International Institute of Fisheries Economics and Trade (IIFET), Corvallis. https://ir.library.oregonstate.edu/concern/conference_proceedings_or_journals/js956g66s

Kaczorowski, J., Campbell, N. R. C., Duhaney, T., Mang, E., & Gelfer, M. (2016). Reducing deaths by diet. Call to action for a public policy agenda for chronic disease prevention. *Canadian Family Physician, 62*, 469–470.

Kimmerer, R. (2013). *Braiding sweetgrass: Indigenous wisdom, scientific knowledge, and the teachings of plants*. Milkweed Editions.

Krohn, E., & Segrest, V. (2010). *Feeding the people, feeding the spirit: Revitalizing Northwest Coastal Indian food culture*. Gorham Printing.

LaDuke, W. (2019). Foreword. In D. A. Mihesuah & E. Hoover (Eds.), *Indigenous food sovereignty in the United States: Restoring cultural knowledge, protecting environments, and regaining health* (pp. xiii-xvi). University of Oklahoma.

Lambden, J., Receveur, O., & Kuhnlein, H. V. (2007). Traditional food attributes must be included in studies of food security in the Canadian Arctic. *International Journal of Circumpolar Health, 66*(4), 308–319.

Last, J. (2019, November 2). What does implementing the UNDRIP actually mean? *CBC News*. Retrieved November 11, 2019, from https://www.cbc.ca/news/canada/north/implementing-undrip-bc-nwt-1.5344825.

Linden, D. J. (2011). *The compass of pleasure: How our brains make fatty foods, orgasm, exercise, marijuana, generosity, vodka, learning and gambling feel so good*. Penguin Books.

Morrison, D. (2006). *1st annual interior of B.C. Indigenous Food Sovereignty Conference. Final Report*. Interior of B.C. Indigenous Food Sovereignty Conference (ISFC) Planning Committee. https://www.indigenousfoodsystems.org/sites/default/files/resources/IFSC2006FinalReport.pdf

Morrison, M. (2011). Indigenous food sovereignty: A model for social learning. In H. Wittman, A. A. Desmarais, & N. Wiebe (Eds.), *Food sovereignty: Reconnecting food, nature and community* (pp. 97–113). Fernwood Publishing.

Pollen, M. (2006). *Omnivore's dilemma: A natural history of four meals*. Penguin Books.

Sapir, E., & Swadesh, M. (1955). Native accounts of Nootka ethnography. *Indiana University Research Center in Anthropology, Folklore, and Linguistics Publications, 1*, 230–332.

Sheehy, T., Kolahdooz, F., Roache, C. & Sharma, S. (2014). Changing dietary patterns in the Canadian Arctic: Frequency of consumption of foods and beverages by Inuit in three Nunavut communities. *Food and Nutrition Bulletin, 35*(2), 244–252. https://doi-org.prxy.lib.unbc.ca/10.1177%2F156482651403500211

Smith, A. (2009). *Indigenous Peoples and boarding schools: A comparative study*. The Secretariat of the United Nations Permanent Forum on Indigenous Issues. https://www.un.org/esa/socdev/unpfii/documents/E_C_19_2009_crp1.pdf

Turner, N., Ignace, M. B., & Ignace, R. (2000). Traditional ecological knowledge and wisdom of Aboriginal Peoples in British Columbia. *Ecological Applications, 10*(5), 1275–1287.

Turner, N., & Turner, K. (2008). "Where our women used to get the food": Cumulative effects and loss of ethnobotanical knowledge and practice; case study from coastal British Columbia (1). *Botany, 86*(2), 103–115.

UN General Assembly. (2007). *United Nations Declaration on the Rights of Indigenous Peoples: Resolution / adopted by the General Assembly*, 2 October 2007, A/RES/61/295. Retrieved June 15, 2020, from https://www.refworld.org/docid/471355a82.html

CHAPTER 19

Walking with Our Most Sacred: Indigenous Birth Workers Clearing the Path for Returning Birthing to Indigenous Communities

Jaime Cidro, Ashley Hayward, Rachel Bach, and Stephanie Sinclair

---

LEARNING OBJECTIVES

1. To understand the link between colonialism, policy, and contemporary health outcomes.
2. To understand the link between self-determination, positive identity development, and positive health outcomes.
3. To understand the historical and contemporary role of birth workers and midwives in Indigenous communities.

INTRODUCTION

Different Indigenous cultures have origin stories illuminating who we are, where we come from, and how our destinies are determined. The sacredness of pregnancy and childbirth is woven throughout Indigenous communities and cultures across **Turtle Island**. Prior to **colonialism, Indigenous women** always birthed in their communities, supported by family, friends, **Knowledge Keepers**, and traditional midwives (Anderson, 2011). However, **colonization** has disrupted our sacred regard for Indigenous expectant mothers and has led to the loss of positive identity formation and understandings of inherent responsibilities among **Indigenous Peoples**. Outcomes of colonial disruption persist in numerous ways, including: the number of Indigenous children in the custodial care of child and family service agencies; the high rates of violence Indigenous women experience; the epidemic of missing and murdered

Indigenous women, girls, and **Two Spirit people**; the mistreatment of **lands** and waters; and the suicide crises facing Indigenous communities.

This chapter will explore how expectant Indigenous women have been cared for as our most sacred and how birth workers have championed the return of birthing and birthing traditions to Indigenous communities across Canada. Birth workers are formal birth companions who provide continuous physical, emotional, and advocacy support during labour and birth, but not medical, midwifery, or nursing care (Campbell-Voytal et al., 2011). Synonymous with "birth worker," doula is an ancient caregiving role, usually provided by family members or experienced local women (Campbell-Voytal et al., 2011). Doulas are not medical professionals and do not deliver babies; they provide information as well as physical and emotional support to a mother before, during, and just after childbirth. The more formalized doula care provider as we know it today is the result of women living away from their families, and in the case of Indigenous women, being forced to birth away from their home community—as this chapter will explain.

This chapter will also illuminate pathways to birthing **self-determination** by exploring Indigenous pregnancy and birthing traditions, the historical role of midwives and birth workers, the impact of the maternal evacuation policy, and the need for a renewed role of Indigenous midwives and birth workers as critical for returning birthing to Indigenous communities. This chapter only provides an overview, and it is thus important for readers to engage in further studies to understand the nuances of traditional ways of knowing and doing as they relate to pregnancy and birthing across territories and nations. Indeed, the origin stories and experiences that guide inherent roles are varied, giving way to different practices in various Indigenous communities.

HISTORY OF MIDWIFERY IN INDIGENOUS COMMUNITIES

Traditional midwives have long been a mainstay in Indigenous communities across Canada (Lalonde et al., 2009). Until the mid-twentieth century, Indigenous women gave birth in their communities, supported by family members, traditional midwives, or both (Lalonde et al., 2009). Birth knowledge, including midwifery knowledge about pre-conception, fertility, pregnancy, birthing, and postpartum, was passed intergenerationally to all Indigenous women. Women were taught the physical logistics of pregnancy and birth; they also learned about ceremony and traditional medicines for a range of conditions associated with delivery and postpartum (Lalonde et al., 2009). Often the role of a **midwife**, a very spiritual position, was viewed as a calling (Carroll & Benoit, 2004).

Colonial interference negatively impacted the reproductive practices of Indigenous women as well as overall health and wellness (Jasen, 1997; Theobald, 2019). In the seventeenth century, settlers to Canada relied on Indigenous midwives for birthing (Rushing, 1991). At that time, midwifery did not exist as an organized profession in

Western biomedicine. Moreover, those in medical professions during this time, in settler and Indigenous communities alike, were initially not interested in midwifery or childbirth, as they considered birth to be a community event in which female friends and neighbours assisted the parturient (the person in labour) (Mason, 1987). However, by the end of the eighteenth century, medical practitioners were coming to see their role in childbirth as an entry point into family practice (Bourgeault, 2006). Childbirth became increasingly medicalized, and physicians—having been trained in **Western** science and technology—were promoted as the superior birth attendant (Biggs, 2004).

The speed at which birth came under the domain of licensed medical doctors was uneven (Werner & Waito, 2008, p. 2) as Western medicine was only sporadically available and seldom of the highest quality (First Nations Health Authority [FNHA], 2017). Many Indigenous Peoples resisted Western medicine because its approach to wellness excluded Indigenous ways of being and knowing. However, because colonization had caused Indigenous Peoples to be in a state of massive upheaval and Indigenous languages, cultures, healing practices, and ceremonies were under attack, by the 1950s, maternity and birth care services for women living in Indigenous communities were transferred to nursing stations with federally employed nurses (Plummer, 2000). This transfer of responsibility from traditional roles within the community to external service providers undermined Indigenous birth practices, eventually led to a diminished role for traditional midwives and birth workers, and consequently adversely impacted intergenerational knowledge transfer of birthing practices. In fact, by the 1970s, almost all births occurred in hospitals located in larger Southern towns and cities (Carroll & Benoit, 2004).

The role and dominance of Western biomedicine resulted in the imposition of medically based maternity technologies; consequently, Indigenous women were told that "their time honoured midwifery and birthing practices were unsafe and that they must turn to the advances of Western medical practice for 'modern' maternity care" (Varcoe et al., 2013, p. 7). The impact of this message directly relates to Indigenous women and families' physical and mental health. The resultant lack of midwives in Indigenous communities, which would mitigate the impacts of birth evacuation, is an indicator of the government's continued colonization of women's bodies, limiting their choice for healthcare providers and maintaining the status quo of forcing women to evacuate their communities. It perpetuates dependence on Western models of medicine and negates possibilities of incorporating cultural models of care to support women in pregnancy, labour, delivery, and postpartum.

Nevertheless, examples of communities resisting this policy of medicalization and relocation for birthing exist. In Puvirnituq, Quebec, for example, a birth centre staffed by Inuit and non-Inuit midwives opened in 1986 (Plummer, 2000). This centre continues to service its communities, and it has established a training program for Inuit who wish to train as midwives (Centre de santé Inuulitisivik, 2019). This important assertion of local midwifery mitigates the profound impacts of travelling for birth.

The revitalization of Indigenous midwifery directly relates to the larger resistance to colonial oppression and the assertion of Indigenous rights. Indigenous midwives across Canada are labouring to bridge evidence-based care with traditional knowledge to meet the needs of their communities and provide Indigenous women with services that are culturally and spiritually appropriate, uphold the sacredness of pregnancy and birth, and recognize Indigenous sovereignty over their bodies and lands.

CANADA'S MATERNAL EVACUATION "POLICY"

Indigenous women living in rural and remote communities without hospitals typically fall under the "evacuation policy"—also called "maternal evacuation." Health Canada policy obliges pregnant women living in rural or remote Indigenous communities to move to urban centres at 36- to 38-weeks' gestational age (sooner, for high-risk pregnancies) to use these cities' labour and birthing services (Government of Canada, 2012). This means that women are required to travel, often far from their communities, weeks before their due date to wait for labour to commence in a boarding home, motel, or tertiary care centre (an advanced medical care centre) (Lawford & Giles, 2012, p. 330). This policy prioritizes Western biomedicine in obstetrical management of pregnant bodies (Lawford et al., 2018) and has caused a cascade of social, health, economic, and cultural consequences, as we explain further below (Chamberlain & Barclay, 2000; Society of Obstetricians and Gynecologists, 2010).

Lawford (2016) demonstrated how the birth evacuation policy "creates a reliance on provincial maternity resources to ensure [Indigenous] women living on reserves have access to intrapartum care" (p. 148). Moreover, the policy is inconsistently applied because it lacks clear documentation and details (Lawford et al., 2019). Rather than being based on detailed guidelines, the policy is arguably grounded in historic or current institutional practices. Lawford (2016) argued that the evacuation practice, despite not being formalized in written guidelines, constitutes an institutional policy—albeit an "invisible" (p. 148) one—because it meets three criteria:

1. It has material impacts.
2. There are allocations of resources.
3. There is a reaction to this policy.

As noted above, this policy perpetuates the loss of traditional social and cultural practices related to pregnancy, labour, childbirth, and postpartum. In discussing allocation of resources, Lawford (2016) identified how the federal government's exclusion of midwives from federally funded nursing stations and hospitals signals that they value investing in sending expectant mothers outside their community to birth in tertiary care centres rather than keeping them close to families and cultural-based approaches to pregnancy, birthing, and postpartum care. Thus, the practice perpetuates the goal of assimilating Indigenous Peoples into Canadian society. It reinforces the colonial notion that Indigenous women need to rely on the state to facilitate the delivery of Indigenous children, thus undermining the roles of family and traditional health practitioners. This is an intentional policy-driven approach in which, "the absence of midwifery . . . ensures that the evacuation policy remains necessary" (Lawford, 2016, p. 154).

Multiple professional societies, such as the Society of Obstetricians and Gynecologists of Canada, (SOGC), have released statements supporting the return of birthing to Indigenous communities. The Native Women's Association of Canada has prepared guidebook resources for women travelling for birth that attempt to minimize the damaging effects of the evacuation policy. Moreover, there have been academic critiques of this policy, along with recommendations (Couchie & Sanderson, 2007; Women and Health Care Reform, 2007).

The wide range of social, emotional, and financial repercussions suffered by Indigenous women as a result of this federal government health policy includes the above-mentioned confinement to temporary accommodations in urban centres to await the start of labour. This entails long separation from family and community emotional support in addition to travel and subsistence expenses. To provide a sense of the distance some women must travel to birth, Pimichikimak (Cross Lake), Manitoba (population approximately 7,600) evacuates approximately 150 women from the community annually to travel primarily to Thompson (120 kilometres away by air) and sometimes to Winnipeg (520 kilometres away by air). Only recently, after significant pressure from groups such as the SOGC, did the federal government begin funding one travel escort to accompany the expectant woman (Robinson, 2017).

The birth evacuation policy has also negatively impacted the physical health of Indigenous women and their families. Replacing traditional birthing practices with biomedicine and so-called modern, medically based maternity technologies has negatively affected preterm births and birth weights, and infant and neonatal mortality has occurred. The infant mortality rate among First Nations remains twice as high as the Canadian average (McShane et al., 2009). In Manitoba, the infant mortality rate for First Nations (**Status Indians** on reserve) and off-reserve from 1991 to 2000 was 10.2 deaths per 1,000 live births—1.9 times higher than that among non-First Nations (5.4 per 1,000 live births) (Smylie et al., 2010, p. 146).

PREGNANCY AND BIRTHING TRADITIONS IN INDIGENOUS COMMUNITIES ACROSS CANADA

From an Indigenous worldview, pregnancy has always been considered special and sacred; the expectant mother is both a carrier of new life and a bridge between the physical and spiritual realms (Anderson, 2011; Jasen, 1997; Moffitt, 2004). In most

Indigenous cultural traditions, pregnant women aim to nurture and foster their growing child's **well-being** (Anderson, 2006; Anderson, 2011) by following protocols during pregnancy and actively focusing on maintaining mental, physical, emotional, and spiritual balance (Whitty-Rogers et al., 2006).

Moreover, all women had a role to play in midwifery, as they had some understanding of how to assist in birth. Typically, teenage girls began to learn birth skills from older women by observing and helping in births (O'Driscoll, et al., 2011). Traditional Indigenous birth workers attended to both the ceremonial and the physical aspects of birth (National Aboriginal Health Organization, 2008) and created social bonds that extended well beyond the actual birth to form relationships and community connections. Many of the Indigenous beliefs surrounding pregnancy and birth were captured in the final report of the **Royal Commission on Aboriginal Peoples** (Canada, 1996, chap. 3), but generally birth is understood as a natural process, and intervention should be limited to high-risk pregnancies (Douglas, 2006; Whitty-Rogers et al., 2006).

Although Inuit customs vary across communities and regions, within some Inuit communities, it was customary to birth on the land, with the assistance of a midwife (sometimes known as a *sanariak* among Inuit) (Douglas, 2006) and with the entire family present (Douglas, 2010). The midwife would be gifted the first piece of sewing a female child made or the first animal hunted by a male child (Pauktuutit Inuit Women of Canada, 2019). The community, whose health was viewed as connected to the health of the mother and child (Douglas, 2006), also had an important role in childbirth, which included maintaining their own health and ensuring Elders participated in the birth event. A newborn's place in the community was solidified when each member of the community, including children, greeted them with a handshake (Gallagher, 1997). A spiritual man called an *angakkuq* (or sometimes a shaman) became involved in a birth if an intervention for a "spiritual or supernatural interference" was required (Douglas, 2006; Oosten et al., 2012; Therrien & Laugrand, 2001); this spiritual process restored a healthy environment and set positive conditions for welcoming a child into the community.

As a response to evacuation, Inuit women's organizations in the Nunavik region of Northern Quebec established birth centres (also known as maternities) for low-risk pregnancies in Inukjuak, Nunavik, in 1998 and Salluit, Nunavik, in 2004 (Epoo et al., n.d.). Inuit birth traditions are also practised and shared in Puvirnituq, Nunavik, at the Inuulitisivik Health Centre, a community-based, Inuit-led initiative that is dedicated to serving Inuit women and preserving Inuit birthing knowledge (Wagner et al., 2012; Epoo et al., n.d.). Here, midwives can attend to low- and medium-risk pregnancies (Epoo et al., n.d.). Akinisie Qumaluk, a community midwife at the maternity project of Inuulitisivik Maternity Centre, shared traditional beliefs about pregnancy, including that caribou or whale sinew should be used to tie the umbilical cord to avoid infections caused by thread (Qumaluk as cited in Gallagher, 1997).

For First Nations women, the ability to have children is a gift from Creator (Native Women's Association of Canada, 2007), and their roles as both mothers and life-givers are an extension of their responsibilities to care for and nurture their entire community (Anderson, 2016; Lavell-Harvard & Anderson, 2014). Women's importance within First Nations traditions and the family is established in many creation stories like those of the "Corn Woman [or Selu] from the Cherokee, Thought Woman from the Laguna Pueblo, Hard Beings Woman from the Hopi . . . White Buffalo [Calf] Woman from the Lakota . . . as well as Nokomis, or First Grandmother, from the Ojibwe" (Allen & Child as cited in Sellers, 2014, pp. 197–198). The term midwife in Nuu-chah-nulth, a language spoken by some Indigenous Peoples in British Columbia, means "she who can do everything" (O'Driscoll et al., 2011).

With the spiritual aspect of birthing comes the ceremonial aspect, and on the west coast of British Columbia, cedar played an integral spiritual and practical role in many ceremonies, including birthing ones. The inner bark of the Yellow Cedar, ranging from 20 to 40 metres long, was valued for its softness and absorbency. Women would use this to create baby diapers, sanitary napkins, and bedding. Expectant mothers would give birth in "a pit lined with Yellow Cedar bark to receive the infant" (Huang, 2009, para. 3).

In the Nishnawbe Aski Nation, which has a total land mass covering approximately two-thirds of Ontario, midwives are seen as holding seven roles: "teacher, healer, caregiver, nurturer, dietician, deliverer, and 'do-dis-seem' (the midwife becomes a spiritual partner of the child through a cutting of the umbilical cord)" (Payne, 2008, p. 45).

BIRTH WORKERS AND THE RESURGENCE OF SELF-DETERMINATION IN BIRTHING

The National Aboriginal Health Organization (NAHO) found that continuous emotional and social support to women during childbirth has positive impacts, not only for labour and delivery but also for breastfeeding rates and attachment (NAHO, 2008). The basis of support for Indigenous women who birth is having a relationship with their birth care provider that they view as positive. According to research with First Nations communities in BC, sentiments of "respect, understanding of cultural context and connection with communities" (Varcoe et al., 2013, p. 4) underpinned whether a relationship with care providers was deemed as positive or stressful. In the case of Inuit women's birth experiences, the presence of an Inuit maternity worker in the birthing centre provided additional psychosocial support. One report noted that such a worker "spent a great deal of time on personal counselling with abused women even though this had not initially been seen as part of her role" (Chamberlain & Barclay, 2000, p. 121).

Psychosocial stressors and poor health outcomes associated with negative birthing experiences are important challenges facing primary care providers. However, to work successfully in Indigenous communities, healthcare providers must establish **cultural safety**, be able to apply their knowledge, have self-awareness, and have personal attributes and attitudes that facilitate respectful partnerships with communities (Wiebe et al., 2015).

In the face of the challenges listed above, culturally-based doula practices are emerging to counter **hegemonic** colonial approaches to reproductive healthcare and the mandatory mobility—and immobility—of Indigenous women's pregnant and reproducing bodies. Indigenous women are increasingly returning to culturally-based birthing practices to assert their sovereignty over their bodies and their birthing experience. This includes birthing in their communities, being surrounded by families and community members, and observing or participating in many pregnancy and birthing traditions, including placenta burying and belly button ceremonies (Lawford & Giles, 2012). These traditions and this circle of care and support result in **resiliency**, strength, and a connection to the land, family, and community. Across Canada, Indigenous women are becoming trained and engaged in supporting their relatives and community members as Indigenous doulas.

> The Chippewas consider the dried umbilical cord—a piece of the newborn infant that naturally falls off, leaving the belly button—to be sacred. The umbilical cord is kept in a small bag, often made of an animal hide, such as moose. The bag is attached to the baby's cradleboard to keep it close to the infant. They can play with the bag, which keeps them from missing the cord. Once the infant is older, the bag is placed on the land during a hunting trip to make the child a good hunter.

Indigenous women in Manitoba are being trained through the Manitoba Indigenous Doula Initiative, also known as *Wiijii'idiwag Ikwewag*. This training was developed with community members, service providers, and Knowledge Keepers. It focuses on restoring cultural knowledge about birth. In Alberta, a similar group has formed to support women who travel to urban settings for birth (Cruikshank, 2016). British Columbia has the *eḵw'i7tl* doula collective, an Indigenous group that offers full-circle support to mothers and families during pregnancy, labour, birth, and postpartum care. Indigenous birth workers provide an important role not only in re-igniting traditional practices for pregnancy, birthing, and parenting but also in working to address the narrative for returning birthing practices to communities and supporting the profession of midwifery as a counter to the long-standing policy of mandatory birth evacuations and medicalized birthing (Cidro et el., Forthcoming).

PATHWAYS TO RETURNING BIRTHING TO COMMUNITIES

Returning to traditional approaches of supporting expectant mothers and families is closely linked to supporting health holistically. Across Canada, Indigenous communities have responded to birth evacuation by creating community-driven midwifery training programs, such as the one in Puvirnituq (see above). The training of Indigenous doulas across Canada is also indicative of the crucial need for culturally-based care. Returning birthing to communities will require widespread support from the community level all the way up to federal policy realignments. In an era of post–**Truth and Reconciliation Calls to Action**, governments are expected to be more responsive to Indigenous communities' demands for self-determination in health. Call to Action #19 specifically charges the federal government to close health gaps between Indigenous and non-Indigenous populations and address health indicators (e.g., maternal health, birth rates, infant and child health issues) (Truth and Reconciliation, 2015).

Supporting a return of birthing to Indigenous communities and a revival of related cultural practices promoting healthy children and families is only the beginning. Supporting healthy childhood development also requires the integration of cultural practices across the life stages through participation in key rites of passage. These rites mark important transitions in the four phases of life: infancy, youth, adulthood, and old age (Johnston, 1976). These phases have corresponding moral stages of development: preparation, quest, vision, and fulfillment of vision (Anderson, 2011). Each transition is marked with a ceremony, sometimes several, in which the individual and their family receive teachings to prepare them for the next phase.

CONCLUSION

The hope of Indigenous Peoples is to have birth returned to community. This way of welcoming a new life into the community results in the child having a strong identity with connections to family, friends, culture, and language from birth (Cidro et al., 2018). This is critical because, from an Indigenous perspective, those who are present at the birth of a child have a responsibility to support the well-being of the child as they grow, thus fostering lifelong connections.

Returning birth to communities is also about restoring balance. Providing children with a connection to their families, culture, language, ancestral land, and waters is one of their rights. Children will have the best start in life if their mothers are provided with a birth experience that is grounded not in fear but rather in the teachings of their culture, in an environment where they are supported by family and community. Returning birth to Indigenous communities is sustainable prevention for many health and social issues. Indigenous Peoples have the solutions to what is required to restore wellness: the implementation of Indigenous knowledge in the current context of ongoing colonialism (Alfred, 1999).

CRITICAL THINKING QUESTIONS

1. How can Indigenous communities push for self-determination in health services, specifically with respect to birthing, given the dependence on the federal government for health funding?
2. What are some similarities in cultural approaches to pregnancy and birthing in different Indigenous communities?
3. What are the benefits of having a midwife and/or birth worker compared to receiving care from a Western medical professional? What are the disadvantages?
4. What is an invisible policy? What other practices or policies may fall under this category?

REFERENCES

Alfred, G. R. (1999). *Peace, power, and righteousness: An Indigenous manifesto*. Oxford University Press.

Anderson, K. (2006). New life stirring: Mothering, transformation, and Aboriginal womanhood. In D. Memee Lavell-Harvard & J. Corbiere (Eds.), *Until our hearts are on the ground: Aboriginal mothering, oppression, resistance and rebirth* (pp. 13–24). Demeter Press.

Anderson, K. (2011). *Life stages and native women: Memory, teachings, and story medicine*. University of Manitoba Press.

Anderson, K. (2016). *A recognition of being: Reconstructing native womanhood* (2nd ed.). Women's Press.

Biggs, L. (2004). Rethinking the history of midwifery in Canada. In I. L. Bourgeault, C. Benoit, R. Davis-Floyd (Eds.), *Reconceiving midwifery* (pp. 17–45). McGill-Queen's University Press.

Bourgeault I. L. (2006). The fall and rise of midwifery in Canada. In I. L. Bourgeault (Ed.), *Push! The struggle for midwifery in Canada* (pp. 43–64). McGill-Queen's University Press.

Campbell-Voytal K., McComish, J. F., Visger, J. M., Rowland, C. A., & Kelleher, J. (2011). Postpartum doulas: Motivations and perceptions of practice. *Midwifery, 27*(6), e214–221.

Canada. (1996). Royal Commission on Aboriginal Peoples. *Report of the Royal Commission on Aboriginal Peoples*. Vol. 3: *Gathering strength*. Canada Communication Group. http://data2.archives.ca/e/e448/e011188230-03.pdf

Carroll, D., & Benoit, C. (2004). Aboriginal midwifery in Canada: Merging traditional practices and modern science. In I. L. Bourgeault, C. Benoit, & R. Davis-Floyd (Eds.), *Reconceiving midwifery* (pp. 263–286). McGill-Queen's University Press.

Centre de santé Inuulitsivik. (2019). Retrieved March 9, 2020, from https://www.inuulitsivik.ca/healthcare-and-services/professional-services/midwives/?lang=en

Chamberlain, M., & Barclay, K. (2000). Psychosocial costs of transferring Indigenous women from their community for birth. *Midwifery, 16*(2), 116–122.

Cidro, J., Bach, R., & Frohlick, S. (Forthcoming). *Canada's forced birth travel: Towards feminist Indigenous reproductive mobilities*. Mobilities.

Cidro, J., Doenmez, C., Phanlouvong, A., & Fontaine, A. (2018). Being a good relative: Indigenous doulas reclaiming cultural knowledge to improve health and birth outcomes in Manitoba. Canada. *Frontiers in Women's Health, 3*(4), 1–8.

Couchie, C., & Sanderson, S. (2007). A report on best practices for returning birth to rural and remote Aboriginal communities. *Journal of Obstetrics and Gynecology Canada, 29*(3), 250–254.

Cruikshank, A. (2016, June 19). Indigenous doulas in Alberta hope to provide more cultural birth support. *Edmonton Journal.* Retrieved March 19, 2021, from https://edmontonjournal.com/health/family-child/indigenous-doulas-in-alberta-hope-to-provide-more-cultural-birth-support

Douglas, V. K. (2006). Childbirth among the Canadian Inuit: A review of the clinical and cultural literature. *International Journal of Circumpolar Health, 65*(2) 117–132.

Douglas, V. K. (2010). The Inuulitisivik maternities: Culturally appropriate midwifery and epistemological accommodation. *Nursing Inquiry, 17,* 111–117.

Epoo, B., Tukalak, B., & Provencal, S. (n.d.). *Making a difference in remote Inuit communities: The Inuulitisivik midwifery service.* https://www.cerp.gouv.qc.ca/fileadmin/Fichiers_clients/Documents_deposes_a_la_Commission/P-1131.pdf

First Nations Health Authority. *Our history, our health: Origins.* Retrieved November 1, 2017, from http://www.fnha.ca/wellness/our-history-our-health

Gallagher, B. (1997). Bringing birth home. *Canadian Geographic, 117*(1), 50–55.

Government of Canada. (2012). *Clinical practice guidelines for nurses in primary care.* Retrieved January 29, 2020, from https://www.canada.ca/en/indigenous-services-canada/services/first-nations-inuit-health/health-care-services/nursing/clinical-practice-guidelines-nurses-primary-care.html

Huang, A. (2009). *Cedar.* First Nations and Indigenous Studies. The University of British Columbia. Retrieved June 23, 2021, from https://indigenousfoundations.arts.ubc.ca/cedar/

Jasen, P. (1997). Race, culture, and the colonization of childbirth in Northern Canada. *Social History of Medicine, 10*(3), 383–400. https://doi.org/10.1093/shm/10.3.383

Johnston, B. (1976). *Ojibway heritage.* University of Nebraska Press.

Lalonde, A. B., Butt, C., & Bucio, A. (2009). Maternal health in Canadian Aboriginal communities: Challenges and opportunities. *Journal of Obstetrics and Gynaecology Canada, 31*(10), 956–962.

Lavell-Harvard, D., & Anderson, K. (2014). *Mothers of the Nations: Indigenous mothering as global resistance, reclaiming and recovery.* Demeter Press.

Lawford, K. M. (2016). Locating invisible policies: Health Canada's evacuation policy as a case study. *Atlantis: Critical Studies in Gender, Culture & Social Justice, 37*(2 (2)), 147–160.

Lawford, K. M., Bourgeault, I. L., & Giles, A. R. (2019). "This policy sucks and it's stupid:" Mapping maternity care for First Nations women on reserves in Manitoba, Canada. *Health Care for Women International, 40*(12), 1302–1335.

Lawford, K. M., & Giles, A. R. (2012). An analysis of the evacuation policy for pregnant First Nations women in Canada. *Alter-Native: An International Journal of Indigenous Peoples, 8*(3), 329–342.

Lawford, K. M., Giles, A. R., & Bourgeault, I. L. (2018). Canada's evacuation policy for pregnant First Nations women: Resignation, resilience, and resistance. *Women and Birth, 31*(6), 479–488.

Mason, J. (1987). A history of midwifery in Canada. *Report of the Task Force on the Implementation of Midwifery in Ontario*, 195–232.

McShane, K., Smylie, J., & Adomako, P. (2009). Health of First Nations, Inuit, and Métis children in Canada. In J. Smylie, & P. Adomako (Eds.), *Indigenous children's health report: Health assessment in action*. (pp. 11–66). Toronto: Centre for Research on Inner City Health.

Moffitt, P. M. (2004). Colonialization: A health determinant for pregnant Dogrib women. *Journal of Transcultural Nursing, 15*(4), 323–330. https://doi.org/10.1177/1043659604268959

National Aboriginal Health Organization (NAHO). (2008). *Celebrating birth: Aboriginal midwifery in Canada*. National Aboriginal Health Organization.

Native Women's Association of Canada. (2007). Aboriginal women and reproductive health, midwifery, and birthing centres: An issue paper. Prepared for the National Aboriginal Women's Summit, Corner Brook, NL, June 20–22, 2007.

O'Driscoll, T., Payne, L., Kelly, L., Cromarty, H., St Pierre-Hansen, N., & Terry, C. (2011). Traditional First Nations birthing practices: Interviews with Elders in Northwestern Ontario. *Journal of Obstetrics and Gynaecology Canada, 33*(1), 24–29.

Oosten, J., Laugrand F., & Trundel, F. (2012). *Representing Tuurngait: Memory and history in Nunavut* (Volume 1). Nunavut Arctic College.

Pauktuutit Inuit Women of Canada. (2019). Access to Midwifery Services Is a Reproductive Right. Retrieved March 9, 2020, from https://www.pauktuutit.ca/health/maternal-health/midwifery/

Payne, Lauren E. (2008). *Toward the development of culturally safe birth models among Northern First Nations: The Sioux Lookout Meno Ya Win Health Centre Experience*. https://core.ac.uk/download/pdf/56375485.pdf

Plummer, K. (2000). From nursing outposts to contemporary midwifery in 20th century Canada. *Journal of Midwifery & Women's Health, 45*(2), 169–175.

Robinson, M. (2017). Giving birth away from home. *Thunder Bay Spectator*, Jan 1. https://www.thespec.com/news-story/7045608-giving-birth-alone-and-far-from-home/

Rushing, B. (1991). Market explanations for occupational power: The decline of midwifery in Canada. *American Review of Canadian Studies, 21*(1), 7–27.

Sellers, S. A. (2014). The power of ancestral stories on mothers and daughters. In D. Memee Lavell-Harvard, & K. Anderson (Eds.), *Mothers of the Nations: Indigenous mothering as global resistance, reclaiming and recovery* (pp. 195–205). Demeter Press.

Smylie, J., Fell, D., & Ohlsson, A. (2010). A review of Aboriginal infant mortality rates in Canada: Striking and persistent Aboriginal/non-Aboriginal inequities. *Canadian Journal of Public Health, 101*(2), 143–148.

Society of Obstetricians and Gynecologists of Canada. 2010. SOGC Policy Statement No. 251: Returning birthing to Aboriginal, rural, and remote communities. *Journal of Obstetrics and Gynecology 32*(12), 1186–1188.

Theobald, B. (2019). *Reproduction on the Reservation: Pregnancy, childbirth, and colonialism in the long twentieth century.* UNC Press Books.

Therrien, M., & Laugrand, F. (2001). *Interviewing Inuit Elders: Perspectives on traditional health* (Vol. 5). Language and Culture Program of Nunavut Arctic College, Iqaluit. http://www.tradition-orale.ca/english/pdf/Perspectives-On-Traditional-Health-E.pdf

Truth and Reconciliation Commission of Canada. (2015). *Honouring the truth, reconciling for the future: Summary of the Final Report of the Truth and Reconciliation Commission of Canada.* https://irsi.ubc.ca/sites/default/files/inline-files/Executive_Summary_English_Web.pdf

Varcoe, C., Brown, H., Calam, B., Harvey, T., & Tallio, M. (2013). Help bring back the celebration of life: A community-based participatory study of rural Aboriginal women's maternity experiences and outcomes. *BMC Pregnancy and Childbirth, 13*(1), 26.

Wagner, V., Osepchook, C., Harney, E., Crosbie, C., & Tulugak, M. (2012). Remote midwifery in Nunavik, Québec, Canada: Outcomes of perinatal care for the Inuulitisivik health centre, 2000-2007. *Birth, 39*(3), 230–237.

Werner, H., & Waito J. (2008). Manitoba history: "One of our own:" Ethnicity politics and the medicalization of childbirth in Manitoba. *Manitoba History, 58*, 2–10.

Whitty-Rogers, J., Etowa, J., & Evans, J. (2006). Childbirth experiences of women from one Mi'kmaq community in Nova Scotia. In D. M. Lavell-Harvard, & J. C. Lavell (Eds.), *Until our hearts are on the ground: Aboriginal mothering, oppression, resistance and rebirth* (pp. 34–61). Demeter Press.

Wiebe, A. D., Barton, S., Auger, L., Pijl-Zieber, E., & Foster-Boucher, C. (2015). Restoring the blessings of the morning star: Childbirth and maternal-infant health for First Nations near Edmonton, Alberta. *Aboriginal Policy Studies, 5*(1). Retrieved March 9, 2020, from https://journals.library.ualberta.ca/aps/index.php/aps/article/view/23823

Women and Health Care Reform. (2007). *Maternity matters: Why should we be concerned about the state of maternity care?* https://cdn.dal.ca/content/dam/dalhousie/pdf/diff/ace-women-health/2/b/ACEWH_maternity_matters.pdf

CHAPTER 20

Systems Innovation through First Nations Self-Determination

Harmony Johnson, Danièle Behn Smith, and Lindsay Beck

LEARNING OBJECTIVES

1. To support students to understand what self-determination is and why is it important, with a particular focus on the BC health sector.
2. To support students to conceptualize self-determination as the key determinant of health or "root of wellness" and understand how it supports other roots of wellness and health outcomes.
3. To summarize how First Nations self-determination is being embedded within the health system in BC and outline the positive impacts for First Nations, British Columbians, and health and other systems.
4. To encourage students to appreciate and embrace, and not be discouraged by, the complexity of this work as part of their journeys and practice.

ACKNOWLEDGEMENTS

We would like to acknowledge the **unceded** territories upon which we carry out this work and the efforts and ongoing presence of our ancestors.

We would also like to acknowledge that we bring First Nations, Métis, and non-First Nations perspectives and thus distinct worldviews to our collaboration, as well as training and experience in **Western**, First Nations, and Métis methodologies. We embody a commitment to **Two-Eyed Seeing** in the work we do, and in this chapter we draw upon multiple worldviews to conceptualize and convey our meaning. This includes the use of multiple methodologies, such as story and visuals.

In this chapter, we also embody a **distinctions-based approach**. Much of the work described herein is specific to BC First Nations and therefore this is the terminology used. Although this work is by and for BC First Nations, some of the lessons learned can be conceptualized more broadly within an Indigenous context. The work of BC First Nations is carried out in respectful partnership with Métis people and their representative organizations.

INTRODUCTION

In 2007, the UN General Assembly adopted the **United Nations Declaration on the Rights of Indigenous Peoples (UNDRIP)**. The UNDRIP acknowledges, among other rights, that **Indigenous peoples** worldwide have the right to **self-determination**, and by virtue of that right, they freely determine their political status and freely pursue their economic, social, and cultural development (UN General Assembly, 2007).

The work in British Columbia (BC) to "hardwire" (systematically embed) First Nations self-determination throughout the health system is emblematic of the UNDRIP's aims. This work demonstrates how self-determination facilitates the dismantling of colonial systems and practices, supporting improvements in health and wellness outcomes. Through the inclusion of First Nations decision making and efforts to empower BC First Nations individuals, families, and communities, the health system is becoming more welcoming for First Nations, and indeed is improving for all British Columbians. This is now expanding beyond the health sector, with First Nations leading new efforts to address the "roots of wellness," which are deeply interconnected and contribute to health and wellness outcomes.

CONTEXT

BC First Nations peoples, families, and communities have a long history of health and **well-being**. Health and wellness refer to a state of balance influenced by many factors, including: culture and values; relationships with human and ecological communities; and the contexts and settings in which people live their lives (see Figure 20.1). Decision making and governance structures rooted in generational knowledge and executed through rich protocols and practices assure the prosperity and sustainability of BC First Nations societies.

The First Nations Perspective on Health and Wellness depicts a philosophy of health and well-being commonly shared by diverse First Nations in BC. The interconnected circles describe internal and external factors that, when in balance, produce health and wellness:

- The centre represents individual human beings. Each unique person has a right and responsibility to lead the journey that belongs to them.

- The second circle illustrates the mental, emotional, spiritual, and physical elements of a healthy and balanced life.
- The third circle represents the values that support wellness: respect, wisdom, responsibility, and relationships.
- The fourth circle shows the people and places from which we come: Nations, community, family, and land.
- The fifth circle depicts the social, cultural, economic, and environmental determinants of health and well-being.
- The people who comprise the Outer Circle represent the strong children, families, Elders, and all other people in our communities who make us whole (FNHA, n.d.a).

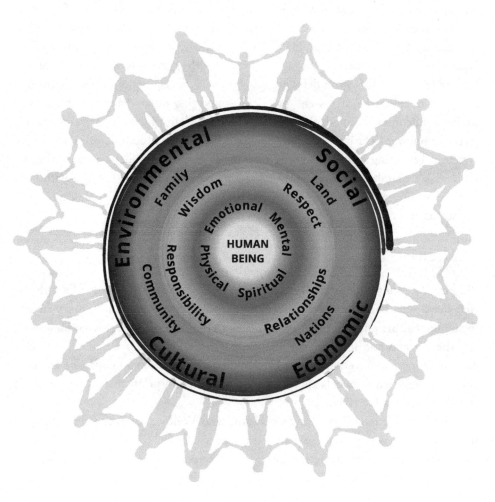

Figure 20.1: BC First Nations Perspective on Health and Wellness
© FNHA. Reprinted with permission.

The Europeans' arrival marked a difficult change in the journeys of First Nations people, families, communities, and Nations. First Nations health and wellness was disrupted through a process of **colonialism** fuelled by settler discourses of superiority, imperial ideologies, extreme imbalances in power, and the momentum of capitalism and geopolitical claims that led to the exploitation of First Nations peoples and their **lands** (Harris, 2002). This oppressive colonial agenda was designed to eliminate First Nations self-determination as individuals and Nations, as well as to systematically devalue their practices, beliefs, and traditions (Johnson et al., 2016). In particular, interconnected, complex, and multi-dimensional First Nations conceptions of health and well-being were undermined by dominant Western biomedical concepts of health, which tend to focus on sickness and disease, as well as on quantifiable, physical aspects of health (Davis, 2016).

Colonialism restricted the ability for First Nations to be self-determining as individuals and Nations: settlers usurped First Nations lands and control, and subjected them to laws, policies, and practices based on domination and assimilation. Aggressive tactics and policies took away individuals' control over their own lives, disempowered community governance, undermined Nationhood, and prevented the population from uniting to draw strength from one another and advocate for their title and rights. These included the Indian Residential School System, Indian Hospitals, the reserve pass system (which made it illegal for First Nations individuals to be outside their reserve without written permission from the federal government), and the sudden introduction of relief foods (which the federal government delivered to reserves and which were often lacking in nutrition). Alienation from decision making, land stewardship, and resources disrupted the lifestyle patterns and cultural practices that kept people balanced and well. Some of the patterns that were—and continue to be—disrupted include gathering and consuming traditional foods and medicines, being out on the land and territory, and participating as contributing members of healthy, welcoming communities (National Aboriginal Health Organization, 2006). Colonialism's past and present impacts have undermined First Nations self-determination, created health and social inequities experienced by First Nations, and led to their poorer health outcomes.

Despite continuing to be impacted by colonialism and oppression, First Nations have demonstrated remarkable **resilience** and ceaseless efforts to exercise self-determination. First Nations and other Indigenous people in BC, Canada, and internationally have advanced a multitude of efforts and strategies to make decisions for themselves, reclaim control through unity, and develop strategic partnerships to increase involvement in decision making.

Key outcomes of these efforts include: political organizing and successive court decisions on title and rights, arising primarily from the efforts of BC First Nations (Johnson et al., 2016); processes for granting recognition of First Nations title and rights within the unceded territories of what is now BC; and formal international and national agreements, including the UNDRIP, which acknowledges that Indigenous peoples have the right to self-determination.

SELF-DETERMINATION IN BC FIRST NATIONS HEALTH

In BC, another key outcome of First Nations self-determination is the creation of the BC First Nations health governance structure. Since 2005, working in partnership with the federal and provincial governments, First Nations in BC have developed a series of political, legal, and operational agreements outlining tripartite commitments to improve First Nations health, including but not limited to the following:

- Transformative Change Accord: First Nations Health Plan (2006);
- Tripartite First Nations Health Plan (2007);
- British Columbia Tripartite Framework Agreement on First Nation Health Governance (2011); and,
- Health Partnership Accord (2012) (First Nations Health Authority [FNHA], 2013; Johnson, et al., 2016).

These agreements hardwire the involvement of BC First Nations in decision making about the policies, programs, and services that affect them.

These agreements and the formation of this BC First Nations health governance structure were outcomes of a consensus development process among more than two hundred First Nations communities in BC. These communities designed and implemented a process for themselves to collaborate, debate, and consensus-build at local, regional, and provincial levels, and to collectively validate the outcome of that process. The resolution to take control of their own wellness and create a unique governance structure and health partnership with federal and provincial governments has been called "the largest self-determination decision" ever made by First Nations in BC (Gallagher, 2019).

The First Nations health governance structure (see Figure 20.2) includes the First Nations Health Authority (FNHA) as the entity responsible for strategic partnerships, policy and strategy development, and, as of 2013, the delivery of what were formerly federal government (First Nations and Inuit Health Branch) programs and services for eligible First Nations people in BC (Gallagher et al., 2015).

First Nations Elders and **Knowledge Keepers** have long emphasized that self-determination is foundational to health. A growing body of evidence supports this conclusion (Canada, 1996; Castellano & Neil, 2000). Self-determination influences all other determinants of health, including education, housing, and safety (Reading & Wien, 2009). Chandler and Lalonde (1998) wrote a seminal paper which found that BC First Nations that secured a degree of self-government and local control over community services, and that were actively engaged in the defence of their land rights and the revitalization of culture, experienced low to non-existent rates of youth suicide.

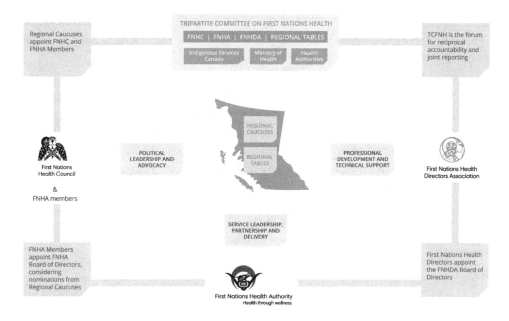

Figure 20.2: BC First Nations Health Governance Structure
© FNHA. Reprinted with permission.

Conversely, it found that communities that had achieved little progress in these areas had considerably higher levels of youth suicide (Chandler & Lalonde, 1998).

Given the importance of self-determination to health and wellness and to the creation of the FNHA, the concept continues to be centrally positioned in the organization's work. The FNHA's vision statement is "Healthy, self-determining, and vibrant BC First Nations children, families and communities" (FNHA, n.d.b), and the very first goal in its Multi-Year Health Plan is to "Enhance First Nations health governance." This goal is deliberately sequenced to emphasize the importance of First Nations engagement and decision making in relation to their health and wellness (FNHA, 2019). Through the philosophy of the FNHA as a "health and wellness partner," the organization continuously reminds itself to "do *with* and not *for*," thereby supporting individual people and Nations' self-determination and control. This means recognizing that individuals are the experts on their own body, mind, and spirit, and that communities and Nations are the experts in their own teachings, traditions, and priorities. It is the FNHA's role to be an expert partner that provides data, information, and assets to support their clients and the Nations it is accountable to in an equitable way. Inspired by the philosophy of Southcentral Foundation in Alaska, the FNHA views BC First Nations people as "customer-owners," meaning they exercise rights and responsibilities both as clients and as owners of the institution (Gallagher, 2019). The FNHA and its federal and provincial partners prioritize the agency of First Nations, recognizing that the aforementioned history of federal and provincial governments making decisions for First Nations is no longer acceptable (O'Neil et al.,

2016). Some of the specific activities of the FNHA, BC First Nations, and federal and provincial governments to advance self-determination in health, at multiple interconnected levels, include:

- Providing tools and resources for individual people, families, and communities to better support their own health and wellness journeys;
- Providing flexible grants and new funding methodologies that incentivize decision making by communities individually, collectively, and with partners;
- Undertaking policy and strategy development, and program and service design and delivery in a manner aligned with First Nations philosophies, perspectives, and ways of being;
- Implementing the only Chief Medical Officer in Canada who works from the governance authority of First Nations;
- Working with governments, organizations, and regulatory bodies to support their understanding and respect for First Nations and their inherent right and capability to exercise self-determination, through building a system-wide commitment to **cultural safety and humility**; and,
- Upholding **First Nations health data governance** by serving as a province-wide **steward** for First Nations health data, thereby supporting First Nations' jurisdiction over their information in a way that also generates population health insights and benefits (Goss Gilroy, Inc. [GGI], 2020a; GGI, 2020b; FNHA et al., 2019).

Cultural Humility Promotes Self-Determination

How did **systemic racism** develop in Canada? The colonial narrative about the inferiority and incapability of Indigenous peoples remains insidiously pervasive (Harding, 2006). These stereotypes shape the thoughts and decision making of individual people, institutions, and structures within Canadian society, leading to interpersonal and systemic racism against Indigenous peoples (Allan & Smylie, 2015).

How does racism undermine self-determination? Stereotypes that depict Indigenous peoples as incapable, unintelligent, and impaired disempower them from decision making throughout their health and wellness journeys (Provincial Health Services Authority, 2017). The pervasiveness of interpersonal and structural bias, which underlies all social, political, and economic contexts, makes racism one of the most profound determinants of health for Indigenous peoples (Allan & Smylie, 2015; Reading & Wien, 2009).

What is cultural humility and how does it promote self-determination? The FNHA and other health system leaders in BC have initiated a movement to address stereotypes, eliminate racism, and create cultural safety for Indigenous peoples through the exercise of cultural humility. Through cultural humility, individuals examine their power and privilege, thereby illuminating imbalances and inequities at individual and systemic levels. This practice can then create space for Indigenous peoples' voices and promote respect, effective dialogue, and decision making. These are central to dismantling and transforming existing colonial attitudes and structures that inhibit self-determination.

IMPACTS OF SELF-DETERMINATION IN HEALTH

Two major five-year summative evaluations of the impacts of the First Nations health governance structure and the progress of the FNHA were concluded in 2019 and 2020. A key finding was that a sense of ownership of the FNHA has been generated among First Nations in BC, who feel "more in charge of their own health system" (GGI, 2020b, p. 23). The FNHA's efforts related to health governance partnership and self-determination have directly influenced health system policies, programs, and services in many areas, including primary care and mental health and wellness (GGI, 2020a; GGI, 2020b). The concerted efforts to establish governance partnerships have facilitated the inclusion of the FNHA and First Nations in health system decision-making processes. The resulting influence of First Nations in the health system has been described as a "cornerstone" of the work undertaken from 2013–2019, greatly exceeding initial expectations of the parties to the various health plans and agreements (GGI, 2020b; FNHA et al., 2019). The report found that the FNHA's unique and groundbreaking work serves as an example for Indigenous organizations and communities worldwide who are at different stages of developing self-determination in their health systems (GGI, 2020a).

The inclusion of First Nations self-determination and decision making is resulting in improved health system performance for First Nations in BC. This includes: a more coordinated landscape of health services; services that better reflect First Nations philosophies; programs and services that are safer for First Nations; and enhanced access, availability, and utilization of services by First Nations people (FNHA, et al., 2019). This is also increasingly impacting areas outside of the health sector (e.g., within emergency management and the BC Coroners Service). The work with the Coroners Service (see Makara's Story, below) also demonstrates how a focus on First Nations self-determination is benefiting all families in BC.

Makara's Story

In 2012, a two-month-old Tla'amin child named Makara passed away suddenly and without warning. Tla'amin traditional laws direct the family to carry out death protocols within a week, with their loved ones' bodies intact so they can carry out their role in the spirit world.

> The coroner ordered an autopsy for Makara, as they would with any infant death. The report came back clear of any criminal wrongdoing. The family was then informed that, without their consent, her body was being returned, but her brain stem was to be retained for several weeks for medical investigation. The family was told that, regardless of the family's will, this was standard practice and was for the greater good of society.
>
> The FNHA worked with the family to support their right to decide whether brain stem retention was to take place and questioned the utility of this long-standing autopsy practice. Eventually, an exception was made for the family to carry out the traditional funeral in the manner that was important to them. Subsequently, the FNHA continued to advocate for systemic change in order to honour the wishes of families who have lost an infant. The BC Coroners Service displayed cultural humility: they undertook a review of the value of brain stem retention and solicited multiple opinions. After reviewing the evidence, they found that there were no situations where the neuropathological examinations added value to the investigation. Thus, the Coroners Service concluded that this practice can cause unnecessary harm to families. They reversed their original position and deemed the practice not medically necessary. They also changed their policy framework to provide for family decision making in situations where no further criminal investigation was required.
>
> Makara's legacy is a Coroners Service that acts with cultural humility. Their willingness to consider the voices of the people they serve and review their practices has helped them establish culturally safe practices for all British Columbians (Gallagher, 2016).

Another key conclusion in the summative evaluations was that there has been an insufficient amount of time for the exercise in self-determination and improvements in health systems performance to result in observable shifts in health outcomes at the population level (FNHA et al., 2019). Since 2006, the Office of the Provincial Health Officer (PHO) and the FNHA have been regularly reporting on five core indicators of health: life expectancy, youth suicide rate, infant mortality, age standardized mortality rate, and diabetes rates.[1]

First Nations Data Governance and Self-Determination

> First Nations decision making over their data and information is foundational to restoring the health and well-being of individuals and communities. Historically, First Nations data have been collected, interpreted, reported, and used without First Nations knowledge or permission, and without regard to First Nations principles, values, and traditions. First Nations have often not been able to access their data, limiting their ability to exercise informed decision making and self-determination for the benefit of their communities.

> Established in 2002 as important parameters for First Nations health data governance, the four OCAP® principles—Ownership, Control, Access, and Possession—have since become the gold standard for First Nations data governance (First Nations Information Governance Committee, 2020). These interconnected principles uphold First Nations jurisdiction and collective rights, supporting the use and sharing of information in a way that benefits the community and reduces harm.
>
> Over two decades of policy work and tripartite agreements in BC have supported the expression of OCAP® for BC First Nations. These have established the clear imperative for First Nations health data governance as a means to protect, promote, and incorporate First Nations knowledge and beliefs, values, practices, medicines, and models of health and healing into all health programs and services for BC First Nations. It ensures that First Nations data are collected, analyzed, and reported in a culturally safe and respectful manner, grounded in First Nations governance and self-determination.

The summative evaluation findings demonstrate that there have been modest improvements in mortality rates (adults and infants), youth suicide rates, and life expectancy (FNHA et al., 2019; FNHA, & Provincial Health Officer, 2020). However, the data also concluded that inequality between the First Nations population and other residents of BC has increased for the indicators of life expectancy, infant mortality, and mortality rates. The fact that these indicators are improving for non-First Nations at a faster rate than for First Nations shows that further progress is also needed outside of the health system to bring increased focus to the environments and social factors—that is, the "roots of wellness"—that shape First Nations health and wellness, including First Nations self-determination (FNHA et al., 2019).

A GREATER FOCUS ON THE ROOTS OF HEALTH AND WELLNESS

In 2016, the FNHA's Chief Medical Officer and the BC Provincial Health Officer commenced an initiative to develop a First Nations Population Health and Wellness Agenda (PHWA). The PHWA uses an expanded suite of health and wellness indicators to support a **paradigm shift** from a sickness-based to a wellness-based philosophy. By bringing together Indigenous Knowledge and ways of knowing, and Western knowledges and ways of knowing, the PHWA provides an "eagle eye view" of the health and wellness of First Nations people living across BC. In doing so, the PHWA highlights that achieving the vision of healthy and vibrant BC First Nations children, families, and communities requires strong foundations of self-determination, culture, language, and connection to land. The development of the PHWA itself is an act of self-determination: First Nations are controlling their own data and telling their own story in a way that reflects their strengths and resilience, and what is important to them.

Though several frameworks have been developed worldwide to illustrate the importance of the determinants of health, measuring the health of populations has continued to focus on downstream factors, such as health behaviours and health outcomes. Population health reports are also often constrained to biomedical paradigms that fail to recognize the physical, emotional, mental, and spiritual dimensions central to First Nations understandings of health and wellness.

The PHWA aims to disrupt these patterns by reinforcing the centrality of the determinants of health and demonstrating that when the roots or systems (social, cultural, economic, and environmental) are nourished, they result in environments where children, youth, adults, and Elders can reclaim and own their health and wellness journeys. This all leads to physical, spiritual, emotional, and mental balance—and ultimately to good health outcomes.

Figure 20.3: First Nations Population Health and Wellness Agenda
© FNHA. Reprinted with permission.

Given that self-determination is the foundation for achieving the FNHA's vision, it was identified as one of the key indicators for the PHWA. Because the concept of self-determination is so complex, there have been many challenges to defining a single or set of measurable, quantifiable variable(s) to reflect it; therefore, efforts are ongoing, and an agreed-upon measure will be included in the next PHWA report.

While a measure is not currently in place for self-determination, there are many concrete, measurable ways to see this indicator in action in BC. As this chapter described, the creation of the FNHA has enabled health programs for First Nations across BC to be planned, designed, managed, and delivered by a First Nations-led organization. The FNHA is committed to self-determination at individual and Nation levels by being a partner to BC First Nations children, families, and communities on their own health and wellness journeys. It also supports sustainable and effective processes that enable First Nations to make their own decisions about their health and well-being.

CONCLUSION

In BC, First Nations are reclaiming their inherent right to self-determination in a multitude of ways and across all sectors, including the health sector. Self-determination has been supported in BC by hardwiring First Nations decision making alongside federal and provincial governments, through a new First Nations health governance structure. The FNHA as an institution by and for BC First Nations is championing the BC First Nations perspective on health and wellness across strategies, policies, and programs. It is also advancing cultural safety and humility as a way to empower First Nations individuals to lead their own health and wellness decision making. A new set of indicators firmly positions self-determination as a key "root of wellness" along with other indicators that reflect First Nations worldviews and seek to dismantle colonial narratives about First Nations health and wellness. BC First Nations and their allies and partners have laid the foundation, with further work ahead to shift the paradigm from sickness to wellness, rooted in the self-determination of First Nations peoples.

CRITICAL THINKING QUESTIONS

1. How might the paradigm shifts described in this chapter (e.g., "moving from sickness to wellness") also reflect the goals and aspirations of the non-Indigenous population?
2. Describe a time when you personally experienced bias, racism, or inequities that affected your health and well-being and/or left you with feelings of disempowerment, lack of control, hopelessness.

3. Given that interpersonal and structural bias underlies all social, political, and economic systems, making racism one of the most profound determinants of health for Indigenous peoples, how can individual processes of cultural humility support and promote Indigenous self-determination at individual, community, and Nation levels?

NOTE

1. Importantly, this data was provisioned, interpreted, analyzed, reported, and published under the leadership of BC First Nations while upholding First Nations data governance principles.

REFERENCES

Allan, B., & Smylie, J. (2015). *First peoples, second class treatment: The role of racism in the health and well-being of Indigenous people in Canada*. https://www.wellesleyinstitute.com/wp-content/uploads/2015/02/Summary-First-Peoples-Second-Class-Treatment-Final.pdf

Canada. (1996). *Report of the Royal Commission on Aboriginal Peoples*. https://www.bac-lac.gc.ca/eng/discover/aboriginal-heritage/royal-commission-aboriginal-peoples/Pages/final-report.aspx

Castellano, M. B., & Neil, R. (2000). Education and renewal in Aboriginal nations: Highlights of the report of the Royal Commission on Aboriginal Peoples. *Voice of the Drum*, 261–276.

Chandler, M. J., & Lalonde, C. (1998). Cultural continuity as a hedge against suicide in Canada's First Nations. *Transcult Psychiatry*, *35*(2), 191–219.

Davis, J. E. (2016). To fix or to heal. In J. E. Davis & A. M. González, (Eds.), *To fix or to heal: Patient care, public health, and the limits of biomedicine* (pp. 1–29). NYU Press.

First Nations Health Authority (FNHA). (2013). *Our story: A made-in-B.C. tripartite health transformation journey*. http://www.fnha.ca/Documents/FNHA_Our_Story.pdf

First Nations Health Authority (FNHA). (2019). *FNHA summary service plan: An operational plan for the fiscal year 2019/20*. https://www.fnha.ca/Documents/FNHA-Summary-Service-Plan-2019-2020.pdf

First Nations Health Authority (FNHA). (n.d.a). *First Nations perspective on health and wellness*. Retrieved December 30, 2019, from https://www.fnha.ca/wellness/wellness-and-the-first-nations-health-authority/first-nations-perspective-on-wellness

First Nations Health Authority (FNHA). (n.d.b). *Vision, mission and values*. Retrieved December 30, 2019, from https://www.fnha.ca/about/fnha-overview/vision-mission-and-values

First Nations Health Authority (FNHA), British Columbia Ministry of Health, & Indigenous Services Canada. (2019). *Evaluation of the British Columbia tripartite framework agreement on First Nation health governance*. https://www.fnha.ca/Documents/Evaluation-of-the-BC-Tripartite-Framework-Agreement-on-First-Nations-Health-Governance.pdf

First Nations Health Authority, & Provincial Health Officer of B.C. (2020). *The First Nations population health and wellness agenda baseline report.* https://www.fnha.ca/Documents/Vancouver-Island-Regional-Caucus-November-2018-Presentation-First-Nations-Population-Health-and-Wellness-Agenda.pdf

First Nations Information Governance Committee. (2020). *The First Nations principles of OCAP®.* Retrieved January 9, 2020, from https://fnigc.ca/ocap-training/

Gallagher, J. (2016, June 20). First Nations Health Authority calls for cultural safety in B.C. *Globe & Mail.* Retrieved January 9, 2020 from https://www.theglobeandmail.com/news/british-columbia/first-nations-health-authority-calls-for-cultural-safety-in-bc/article30516735/

Gallagher, J. (2019). Indigenous approaches to health and wellness leadership: A B.C. First Nations perspective. *Healthcare Management Forum 32*(1), 5–10.

Gallagher, J., Mendez, J. K., & Kehoe, T. (2015). The First Nations Health Authority: A transformation in healthcare for B.C. First Nations. *Healthcare Management Forum, 28*(6), 255–261.

Goss Gilroy, Inc. (GGI). (2020a). *Evaluation of First Nations Health Authority: Final evaluation report.* https://www.fnha.ca/Documents/FNHA-Evaluation-Report.pdf

Goss Gilroy, Inc. (GGI). (2020b). *Evaluation of First Nations Health Authority: Technical case study report.* https://www.fnha.ca/Documents/FNHA-Evaluation-Case-Study-Technical-Report.pdf

Harding, R. (2006). Historical representations of Aboriginal people in the Canadian news media. *Discourse & Society, 17*(2), 205–235.

Harris, C. (2002). *Making Native space: Colonialism, resistance, and reserves in British Columbia.* UBC Press.

Johnson, H., Ulrich, C., Cross, N., & Greenwood, M. (2016). A journey of partnership: Transforming health care service delivery with First Nations in Northern B.C. *International Journal of Health Governance, 21*(2), 76–88.

National Aboriginal Health Organization. (2006). *Resources for First Nations on injury prevention: Annotated bibliography.* https://ruor.uottawa.ca/handle/10393/30534

O'Neil, J., Gallagher, J., Wylie, L., Bingham, B., Lavoie, J., Alcock, D., & Johnson, H. (2016). Transforming First Nations' health governance in British Columbia. *International Journal of Health Governance, 21*(4), 229–244.

Provincial Health Services Authority. (2017). Introduction to Indigenous health in Canada: Impacts of colonization and racism [PowerPoint]. Vancouver: Provincial Health Services Authority.

Reading, C., & Wien, F. (2009). *Health inequalities and social determinants of Aboriginal Peoples' health. National Collaborating Centre for Aboriginal Health.* https://www.ccnsa-nccah.ca/docs/determinants/RPT-HealthInequalities-Reading-Wien-EN.pdf

UN General Assembly. (2007). *United Nations Declaration on the Rights of Indigenous Peoples: Resolution / adopted by the General Assembly,* 2 October 2007, A/RES/61/295. Retrieved December 30, 2019, from: https://www.refworld.org/docid/471355a82.html

PART IV CREATIVE CONTRIBUTION

ᐃᑦᑧᑐᖅ (to sit down for a long time)

Norma Dunning

what's the point to write and write and write and think that no one will ever read it. we sit in front of computers and put together words hoping it will have some impact but instead it is read by a few who shrug and move on to the next bit of writing – what the hell, what's the point, what the fuck?

meeting other Inuit and realizing that they don't give a shit about who you are or who they are.

they say not to speak of the past because it's painful and talking of pain is not respected in our culture. laughing stops the bad spirits from sitting next to you. don't disturb the north or the south by bringing up the truth of what life really is.

Ipummiq (mouth shut, say little)

suicide runs through communities, hides in the
shadows and laughs when it invites someone to come out and play.

Qanuiliviqanngituq (no way of talking about it)

some say it's the bad spirits, that the Inuit who talk to themselves in public places are plagued with, the bad spirits who munch on their brains and spit out their souls like white people do at
baseball games with sunflower seeds.

Uqummiapuq (keeps in his mouth, on his tongue)

26 teenagers kill themselves in 2010 in Nunavut. don't talk about alcohol or drug abuse, put into the nunatsiaq news at Christmas time that alcohol will not be shipped into communities because the children are going to see one alcohol-free day in a year. parents for one day will remember family and what life was like before chemicals began to seep into their brains and take over their souls like white missionaries who taught us to genuflect and memorize prayers. don't talk about the return of tuberculosis and how the north is not healthy. family upon family stacked up in shacks and people who return home and never leave that chair in the living room because if they do they'll have nowhere to sit or sleep for the rest of the night. holding in their piss and shit and not daring to move.

Qaangani (on top of)

houses crowded with each other.

Don't talk the truth about anything because people want us to be these beings with fur-trim hooded parkas and a harpoon in our side pocket, it sells, it brings white people north and for a season a bit of money is made. Like all good southern people they walk around putting Prada and Gucci footprints on the tundra and return home.

Michaelle Jean bites into a seal heart, it headlines the CBC National News and her face is splashed all over the Globe and Mail.

GLOSSARY

Aboriginal Peoples: In Canada, a collective name for the original peoples of North America and their descendants. Section 35 of the *Constitution Act of 1982* categorizes Aboriginal Peoples into three distinct groups: First Nations (historically referred to as Indian), Inuit, and Métis (FNIM). This term fails to acknowledge distinctions between FNIM peoples' histories, languages, cultural practices, and spiritual beliefs. It is being used less often because of its association with the destruction of Indigenous identities, loss of land and language, and other colonial acts. In Canada, it is frequently replaced with Indigenous Peoples.

Band: Under the *Indian Act* (1876), a "body of Indians" who are ruled by the federal government. Many First Nations communities are now self-determining.

Child neglect: The terms "neglect" and "serious risk of neglect" emerge primarily from a Western perspective, appearing for the first time in the *Youth Protection Act* in the 1970s.

Clan: Several family groupings that trace their origins to a common male or female ancestor.

Colonialism: Leading to colonization, the theory that one race, culture, and/or nation has an inherent right to claim dominion over and exploit lands and peoples it perceives to be unclaimed and inferior.

Coloniality: A legacy of colonialism in present-day societies, including Canada. Appears as social discrimination that has extended beyond the formal period of colonialism and includes hierarchical racial, political, and social orders executed by European colonialism. Assigns and defines the value of certain peoples and societies while marginalizing and excluding others.

Colonization: Rooted in politics, religion, and economics, the acts of various European nations exploring, subjugating, settling, and abusing vast regions and diverse peoples.

Cultural competency: Having the knowledge and ability to effectively communicate with, as well as adapt and deliver services to, culturally diverse peoples.

Cultural humility: A process of self-reflection in order to understand personal and systemic biases and to develop and maintain respectful processes and relationships based on mutual trust. Involves humbly acknowledging oneself as a learner when striving to understand another's experience.

Cultural safety: An outcome based on respectful engagement that recognizes the contemporary conditions of Indigenous Peoples and strives to address power imbalances inherent in the health care system by prioritizing the perspective of the Indigenous client over the service provider. It results in an environment free from racism and discrimination, where people feel safe when receiving health care.

Decolonization: The practice of divesting authorities and individuals of colonial power. In the context of First Nations, Inuit, and Métis Peoples, this means the process of relinquishing control of bureaucracy, culture, languages, health, education, etc. to Indigenous Peoples.

Distinctions-based: Refers to, and supports the recognition of, First Nations, Inuit, and Métis as unique cultural groups with distinct rights rather than as a homogeneous group (e.g., Aboriginal, Indigenous).

Ecological knowledge: The sacred and vast knowledge developed over millennia from First Nations, Inuit, and Métis Peoples' intimate and deep relationships with local environments.

Eco-philosophy: Knowledge held by First Nations, Inuit, and Métis Peoples that developed from sacred relationships with the plants, animals, lands, and waters.

Enfranchisement: The legal process for replacing a person's Indian status with Canadian citizenship. Voluntary enfranchisement was instituted in 1857 and became mandatory under the *Indian Act* (1876), until 1961.

Eugenics: The practice or promotion of controlled, selective breeding of human populations (such as through sterilization). Based on the belief that an evolved society is one where its citizens have a specific set of biological, physical, and moral qualities.

First-line social services: Culturally adapted, affordable, accessible primary care services (e.g., clinical and assistance services, promotion and prevention initiatives) offered to address immediate health concerns of a large number of individuals within, and with full participation of, First Nations communities.

First Nations health data governance: A framework for ensuring that First Nations have sovereignty over their health data. Data collection must adhere to appropriate Indigenous data stewardship agreements, and Indigenous Peoples must be principal players in decision making about how to collect and use these data.

Food insecurity: Not having the ability to obtain or consume a sufficient quality or quantity of food, or feeling unsettled about being able to do so.

Foodways: The customary cultural practices and traditions associated with gathering, harvesting, processing, and consuming foods.

Hegemony: When one group dominates and influences another socially, culturally, ideologically, or economically.

Highway of Tears: A 724-kilometre stretch of highway between Prince George and Prince Rupert, British Columbia, also known as Highway 16. Name was created in the late 1990s to recognize the disproportionate and alarming number of missing and murdered Indigenous women who have not returned or have been stolen after travelling this road since 1960. For more information, visit: http://www.highwayoftearsfilm.com/watch (if the link is broken, Google "Highway of Tears film" to help you navigate to the site).

Indigenous Peoples: Refers to the population of a country/geographical area prior to the arrival of people of different cultures or ethnicities, the latter of whom became dominant through violent resettlement. They possess unique languages, knowledge systems, and beliefs and maintain a special relationship with their traditional land. Though diverse, they nevertheless share challenges respecting the protection of their rights to political, economic, social, cultural, spiritual, and environmental self-determination. In Canada, used in reference to First Nations, Inuit, and Métis collectively and frequently replacing *Aboriginal Peoples*.

Indigenous women: In Canada, self-identifying women who are First Nations, Inuit, or Métis. Not a homogeneous term or identity. Often used as a pan-Indigenous term while acknowledging unique cultural expressions of womanhood.

Intergenerational trauma: In the context of Indigenous Peoples, past and ongoing traumatic events inform how survivors pass their thoughts, behaviours, and coping mechanisms to subsequent generations. Examples of such events are disruptions to families and communities through Indian Residential Schools, Sixties Scoop, and child welfare.

Inuk: Singular form of Inuit.

Inuktitut: *see Inuktut.*

Inuktut: Inuit language, encompassing all the different dialects, including Inuktitut and Inuinnaqtun.

Kelowna Accord: A 2005 agreement created in consultation with and collaboration between federal, provincial, and Indigenous governments. Aimed to improve health, education, and employment in Indigenous communities through government funding. Never implemented because of a change in federal governments in 2006.

Knowledge Keeper: A trusted, respected, and valued person by the communities they serve. Recognized for their many experiences, the knowledge they have received from others, and their willingness to share these with others.

Land: In an Indigenous context, refers to earth *and* water. A physical and spiritual place and space. Connected to and in relationship with all living and non-living things.

Land-based healing: Healing that occurs when individuals are empowered to return to or reconnect with the land and recover their traditional healing practices.

Midwife: A medical professional trained to assist a woman in labour with childbirth.

Millennium Scoop: Refers to the current child welfare system in Canada, in which Indigenous children continue to be taken into care at devastating rates.

Nanabozho: A hero and great teacher of humanity in a variety of Indigenous oral traditions. Part human, part powerful spirit.

Nationhood: The status of having a separate identity and independence as a Nation, with a group of people united by a shared language, culture, and/or economy.

Paradigm shift: A fundamental change in underlying assumptions or beliefs.

Perinatal: The period immediately before and after birth.

Population health: The health of a group of individuals. Takes interactions and relationships within the group into consideration.

Potlatch: A tradition of the Northwest Indigenous Peoples involving the ceremonial distribution of food and gifts. A public event to acknowledge individual and clan rights.

Reappropriation: To take back ownership of something. Indicates that a people, group, or individual has suffered a loss they wish to regain. In the context of Indigenous Peoples, refers to actions taken to reaffirm the inherent right of First Nations, Inuit, and Métis to self-govern and recover the different methods for exercising this right, of which colonialism deprived them.

Reciprocity: Refers to the sacred relationships, mutual duties, and responsibilities between Indigenous Peoples, plants, and animals.

Resilience: The capacity to recover from difficulty, challenges, and trauma. In the context of Indigenous Peoples, related to ongoing colonial violence.

Resource extraction: The removal of what are often called "natural resources" from the earth and water. Frequently involves heavy machinery and extensive critical infrastructure (e.g., roads) to access, harvest, refine, and transport raw materials. Common forms of resource extraction are forestry, mining, and oil and gas.

Royal Commission on Aboriginal Peoples (RCAP): Established by Prime Minister Mulroney after the 78-day armed standoff between the Mohawk community of Kanesatake, the Sûreté du Québec, and the Canadian army in 1990 ("the Oka Crisis"). RCAP's mandate was to examine and recommend solutions to the challenges affecting the relationship between Indigenous Peoples, the federal government, and Canadian society more generally.

Self-determination: The right to act with autonomy, freely determine political status, and freely pursue economic, social, and cultural development in matters relating to internal and local affairs. With respect to Indigenous Peoples in Canada, to no longer be governed by the *Indian Act*.

Seven generations: Based on an ancient Iroquois philosophy but part of a way of life for many Indigenous Nations. Decisions made now should support stewardship of land and family for seven generations.

Sixties Scoop: A period from the 1960s to the mid-1980s in which tens of thousands of Indigenous children became wards (property) of the Canadian government and were forcibly removed from their families, homes, and communities and placed in primarily non-Indigenous environments, in Canada and internationally. Often happened without the family's consent and without their knowledge about where their children went. Children lost their families and languages, and they suffered multiple types of abuse, neglect, racism, and discrimination.

Smudging: A practice in many Indigenous cultures, though each culture may hold different beliefs/related customs. Generally carried out to purify/cleanse a person or place. Involves sacred plants, fire, and smoke. The smoke resulting from the burning of the sacred plants is wafted around the person/place being cleansed.

Status Indian: A term used to designate the legal status of a person registered as an "Indian" under the *Indian Act*. Status Indians, also known as Registered Indians, are eligible for certain federal, provincial, and territorial benefits and rights.

Steward: A caretaker that has a relationship with what or whom they care for.

Subsistence: Traditional modes of working on and with the land to generate food and medicine.

Survivance: Goes beyond survival to encompass lifeways that resist colonialism and foster Indigenous knowledges.

Sweat lodge ceremony: A purification ceremony in which individuals enter a sacred lodge and sweat out the toxins/negative energy that create imbalance. The heat in the lodge is usually generated by pouring hot water on heated rocks. Ceremonies differ among individuals and communities.

Systemic racism: A form of racism engrained in education, health care, law enforcement, justice, and other systems within a society. It creates and perpetuates inequality for First Nations, Inuit, and Métis populations, and people of colour.

Treaty: A constitutionally recognized agreement between First Nations and the Canadian government. Many were signed between 1701 and 1923, primarily centring on the Crown's obligations to Indigenous Peoples in return for use of their ancestral lands. The Canadian government has historically failed to uphold Treaties. Some modern Treaties were signed beginning in 1975.

Truth and Reconciliation Calls to Action: The Truth and Reconciliation Commission of Canada (TRC) (2008–2015) was one of the elements of the Indian Residential Schools Settlement Agreement, implemented to facilitate reconciliation among former students, their families and communities, and all Canadians. The TRC issued 94 Calls to Action to be taken by all levels of government to rectify the wrongs perpetuated by the residential schools and promote reconciliation between Indigenous and non-Indigenous peoples in Canada.

Turtle Island: Another name for North America or the Earth. Originated in the oral histories of First Nations Peoples who inhabit the lands now known as northeastern Canada. In these stories, a turtle held the world on its back.

Two-Eyed Seeing: Refers to learning to strengthen understanding by seeing from one eye with Indigenous ways of knowing and from the other eye with Western ways of knowing.

Two Spirit people: A term capturing diverse gender and sexual orientations, and cultures of First Nations, Inuit, and Métis people who do not fall within heteronormative binary gender- and sexually oriented categories. Many Indigenous Nations had and have distinct terms and roles for people who fall outside of these binaries. Indigenous Peoples chose the term in 1994 at the Annual Native American Gay and Lesbian Gathering in Winnipeg, Manitoba, as a pan-Indigenous reference to the range of Indigenous 2SLGBTQQIA (Two Spirit, lesbian, gay, bisexual, transgender, queer, questioning, intersex, asexual) identities and non-binary gender identities specific to Indigenous Peoples.

Unceded: The unrelinquished authority of First Nations over their traditional and ancestral territories. Many First Nations emphasize that even those who have signed Treaties have not ceded or surrendered their territories and continue to exercise self-determination and decision making over their lands.

United Nations Declaration on the Rights of Indigenous Peoples (UNDRIP): Adopted by the General Assembly in 2007 and eventually adopted by 148 states (11 abstentions in the original vote). The UNDRIP outlines the minimum standards necessary to ensure the survival, dignity, and well-being of Indigenous Peoples worldwide.

Watershed: A relationship between an area of land and the water that journeys through it, which collects from rainfall and snowmelt as it flows to an outlet, such as streams, rivers, or oceans.

Well-being: A state of being that considers health holistically. In an Indigenous context, often includes considerations of physical, spiritual, emotional, and intellectual well-being, with the aim of maintaining balance and harmony between these elements.

Western: White European values from the Global North, i.e., countries or societies that are generally considered wealthy, democratic, politically stable, and dominant.

CONTRIBUTOR BIOGRAPHIES

Christine Añonuevo's ancestors are from the Philippine provinces of Batangas, Pangasinan, and Quezon. She was born and raised in the Okanagan Valley on Syilx territory. She has been involved with anti-oppressive informal and formal learning spaces that intersect youth, health, arts, and land for the past 20 years. She is a PhD student in Health Sciences and a contributor to the Health Arts Research Centre at the University of Northern BC. She continues to explore the connections between lived experience, cultural identity, and mental, physical, and spiritual well-being with her partner and family on Gitxsan territory.

Rachel Bach is Ktunaxa from ʔakisq̓nuk First Nation. Her heart is in Manitoba, where she completed her bachelor's degree at the University of Manitoba and master's degree in Development Practice in Indigenous Development at the University of Winnipeg. Bach has extensive experience working with Indigenous women and youth. Her work and research demonstrate a long commitment to reproductive safety and culturally based services for Indigenous people. She recently completed the Midwifery Education Program at Toronto Metropolitan University (formerly Ryerson University) and currently serves Indigenous pregnant people in Winnipeg.

Lindsay Beck was born and raised in Yellowknife, Northwest Territories, and is a third-generation Canadian settler with English and Norwegian ancestry. Since 2015, Beck has worked in the Office of the Chief Medical Officer at the First Nations Health Authority (FNHA). In this role, she is one of the project leads on the First Nations Population Health and Wellness Agenda. Prior to joining the FNHA, Beck worked as a consultant, serving First Nations communities across BC. She also project managed several community-based research initiatives in rural and remote Indigenous communities. Beck obtained an MSc in Community Health from the University of Northern British Columbia in 2013.

Danièle Behn Smith is Eh Cho Dene of Fort Nelson First Nation and French Canadian/Métis of the Red River Valley. Her paternal grandparents are George Behn and the late Mary Behn (Adin). Her maternal grandparents are the late Gédèon Dumaine and Lucienne Dumaine (Phaneuf). Dr. Behn Smith is grateful to live, work, and play on the unceded territories of the Lekwungen and SENĆOŦEN speaking peoples of the Songhees, Esquimalt, and W̱SÁNEĆ nations. Her experience in Indigenous health spans 20+ years of work with diverse Indigenous communities and Elders. She is grateful for their teachings and works to honour them. She is a family and public health physician and currently works as the Indigenous Health Physician Advisor to BC's Provincial Health Officer.

Leila Ben Messaoud is a Child and Family Services Advisor at the First Nations of Quebec and Labrador Health and Social Services Commission (FNQLHSSC). She has been a lawyer since 2018, specializing in youth protection. She holds a bachelor's degree in law from the Université Laval, with an international profile, as well as a certificate in economics. After completing her bar admission course, she did an internship at the Quebec Bar, with the youth protection branch in Trois Rivières. In her current role, she contributes to the advancement and defence of the interests of the First Nations in Quebec in terms of youth protection and prevention.

Lisa Boivin is a member of the Deninu Kue First Nation. She is an interdisciplinary artist and a doctoral candidate at the Rehabilitation Sciences Institute at University of Toronto Faculty of Medicine. Boivin uses images as a pedagogical strategy to bridge gaps between medical ethics and aspects of Indigenous cultures and worldviews. She is working on an arts-based thesis which confronts the colonial barriers Indigenous patients navigate in the current healthcare system. Boivin strives to humanize clinical medicine as she situates her art in the Indigenous continuum of passing knowledge through images.

Yvonne Boyer is a member of the Métis Nation of Ontario with ancestral roots in the Métis Nation—Saskatchewan, Manitoba, and the Red River. With a background in nursing, including in the operating room, Dr. Boyer has over 22 years of experience practising law and publishing extensively on how Aboriginal rights and treaty law intersect with the health of First Nations, Métis, and Inuit. She is a member of the Law Society of Ontario and the Law Society of Saskatchewan and received her Bachelor of Laws from the University of Saskatchewan, and her Master of Laws and Doctor of Laws from the University of Ottawa. In 2013, she completed a Post-Doctoral Fellowship with the Indigenous Peoples' Health Research Centre at the University of Regina. She was a full professor and former Canada Research Chair in Aboriginal Health and Wellness at Brandon University.

Jaime Cidro is a Professor in the Department of Anthropology, the Director of the Master of Arts in Development Practice Program, a Canadian Institutes of Health Research-funded Canada Research Chair in Health and Culture, and the Co-Director of the Kishaadigeh Collaborative Research Centre at the University of Winnipeg. Dr. Cidro takes a collaborative approach to her research on Indigenous maternal and child health, partnering with many Indigenous organizations and communities for her projects. Her current project, "She Walks With Me," examines how an Indigenous doula program can address health, social, and cultural outcomes for urban Indigenous women in Winnipeg, Manitoba.

Charlotte Coté is associate professor in the Department of American Indian Studies at the University of Washington (UW). Dr. Coté is from the Nuu-chah-nulth community of Tseshaht on Vancouver Island. Her personal and academic life is dedicated to creating awareness about Indigenous health and wellness, and she actively works with Indigenous peoples and communities to address health disparities through the revitalization of traditional foodways and ancestral ecological knowledge. Coté's many publications include *Spirits of Our Whaling Ancestors: Revitalizing Makah and Nuu-chah-nulth Traditions*, which considers Indigenous self-determination, eco-colonialism, and food sovereignty, and *hišukʔiš ćawaak, Everything is Interconnected: Food Sovereignty, Health, and haʔum (food) in Northwest Coast Indigenous Communities*, which examines the revitalization of Northwest Coast Indigenous food traditions. Coté is the founder and chair of the Living Breath of wəɬəbʔaltxʷ Indigenous Foods Symposium, held annually at UW.

Sarah de Leeuw is an award-winning creative writer (poetry and literary non-fiction) and Canada Research Chair (Humanities and Health Inequities) with the University of Northern BC's Northern Medical Program, the Faculty of Medicine, UBC. Dr. de Leeuw's activism, writing, scholarship, and teaching all focus on unsettling geographies of power and on the role of humanities in making health and medicine more socially accountable.

Michel Deschênes worked as a consultant and trainer in the field of public safety for many years. He is Program and Policy Analyst at the First Nations of Quebec and Labrador Health and Social Services Commission (FNQLHSSC), a position he has held for 12 years. Deschênes holds a bachelor's degree in political science from the University of Montréal as well as a Master of Laws degree and a Doctor of Laws from Laval University. His functions include dealing with various legal issues on a regular basis and working with attorneys of FNQLHSSC. Deschênes has published a number of articles, including "La Loi sur la sécurité civile et la prévention des catastrophes en aménagement du territoire" (with Jacques Tremblay), "Communication des risques, secrets industriels et droit à l'information, un équilibre, à établir," and "Les pouvoirs d'urgence et le partage des compétences au Canada."

Thomsen D'Hont is a Métis, born and raised in Yellowknife, Northwest Territories (NWT). D'Hont grew up hunting, fishing, and camping with his family and continues to spend as much time as possible out in the bush. In 2017, D'Hont completed a public policy project with the Jane Glassco Northern Fellowship about training and retaining Indigenous medical doctors in the NWT. One of his policy recommendations was fulfilled after years of groundwork by local physicians: the creation of a new family medicine residency program in Yellowknife in 2020. D'Hont is currently training at this site as a resident physician in the program's first cohort of trainees. He plans to pursue a career as a family physician in the NWT, where he hopes to improve the healthcare system for Indigenous people.

Madeleine Kétéskwew Dion Stout, a Cree speaker, was born and raised on the Kehewin First Nation in Alberta. After graduating from the Edmonton General Hospital as a Registered Nurse, she earned degrees from the University of Lethbridge (BSN) and Carleton University (MA). She has served on several Indigenous and non-Indigenous boards and committees, including the National Collaborating Centre for Indigenous Health and the First Nations Health Authority. Currently self-employed as the President of Dion Stout Reflections Inc., Dion Stout adopts a Cree lens in her research, writing, and lectures on First Nations health. She was appointed as a Member of the Order of Canada in 2015.

Miyawata Dion Stout has revelled in hearing "old-time" stories from her *kohkom*, Madeleine Kétéskwew Dion Stout, since she was a small child. Through this lifelong listening, she has also developed a joy of storytelling and was invited to be the youth participant in the "Power of Story" sessions and the "human book" delegate at the "Everybody has the Right," both held at the Museum for Human Rights. Dion Stout is a vocal advocate for Indigenous rights and climate action. She is an avid fancy shawl dancer and is currently writing her first novel. Miyawata's preferred pronouns are she/her.

Norma Dunning is an Inuit writer, scholar, researcher, and grandmother. Dr. Dunning's debut collection of short stories, *Annie Muktuk and Other Stories*, received several literary awards. Her first poetry collection, *Eskimo Pie: A Poetics of Inuit Identity*, was released in 2020. Her second collection of short stories, *Tainna: The Unseen Ones*, was published in 2021. Her first book of non-fiction, *Tukitaaqtuq (speak to one another) and the Eskimo Identification Canada System*, which is focused on assimilative practices used on Inuit Canadians, releases in 2022.

Cassandra Felske-Durksen: I am Otipemisiwak: "the free people; the people who own themselves; the people that rule themselves." My family is, and is from, the Northern Prairies of Turtle Island. My roles and responsibilities continue to evolve. Currently, I feel my responsibility as an Indigenous person and physician is to act as observer, witness, and facilitator. My role is to make space and hold it for others. I stand on the shoulders of giants. I am humbled by the knowledge, skills, and ways of my colleagues and communities. I learn every day. I am humbled by my mistakes and missteps, every day.

Garry Gottfriedson is from Kamloops, BC. He is strongly rooted in his Secwepemc (Shuswap) cultural teachings. He holds a Master of Arts Education degree from Simon Fraser University. In 1987, the Naropa Institute in Boulder, Colorado, awarded Gottfriedson with a Creative Writing Scholarship. There, he studied under Allen Ginsberg, Marianne Faithful, and others. Gottfriedson has 10 published books. He has read from his work across Canada, the United States, South America, New Zealand, Europe, and Asia. His work has been anthologized and published nationally and internationally. He works at Thompson Rivers University.

Richard Gray is the Social Services Manager at the First Nations of Quebec and Labrador Health and Social Services Commission. He has held this position for over 10 years, and his main mandate is to support First Nations communities in achieving their health, wellness, culture, and self-determination goals. Gray is a Listuguj Mi'gmaq who holds a bachelor's degree in social work. He was the Director of Social Services for the Listuguj Mi'gmaq Government for seven years, and he was also an elected Band Councillor for several years, working as the community's chief negotiator for many files.

Margo Greenwood, Academic Leader of the National Collaborating Centre for Indigenous Health, is an Indigenous scholar of Cree ancestry. Dr. Greenwood is also Vice-President of Indigenous Health for the Northern Health Authority in British Columbia and Professor in both the First Nations Studies and Education programs at the University of Northern British Columbia. Her academic work crosses disciplines and sectors, focusing on the health and well-being of Indigenous children and families and public health. Greenwood has undertaken work with UNICEF, the United Nations, the CCSDH, PHN of Canada, and the CIHR, specifically, the Institute of Population and Public Health.

We'es Tes, Sandra Martin Harris is from the Wet'suwet'en Nation of the Laksilyu, Little Frog Clan and is a member of the Witset First Nation. Since 1997, Harris has worked as an Indigenous community developer at the Wet'suwet'en Hereditary Chiefs Office and at the Gitksan Government Commission. She loves community development work and watershed planning. Harris is also an Indigenous Focusing Complex Trauma (IFOT) practitioner for frontline workers in health and social justice. This work helps her share teachings about intergenerational trauma, grief, loss, and wellness using a body-centred and land-based approach.

Ashley Hayward is a PhD student in Peace and Conflict Studies at the University of Manitoba and a 2020 Canadian Institutes of Health Research (CIHR)-funded Vanier Canada Graduate Scholar. Hayward is currently a doctoral trainee on the "She Walks with Me" urban Indigenous doula project and works as the Research Coordinator for *Kishaadigeh*, the CIHR Network Environments for Indigenous Health Research project housed at the University of Winnipeg. She has won numerous awards, including the Indigenous Award of Excellence: Trailblazer from the University of Manitoba for visionary thinking that has resulted in advancing Indigenous engagement, leadership by example, and mentorship.

Jaimie Isaac is the Curator of Indigenous and Contemporary Arts at the Winnipeg Art Gallery, interdisciplinary artist, and member of Sagkeeng First Nation in Treaty 1 Territory. Isaac holds a Master of Arts degree from the University of British Columbia, with a thesis on decolonizing curatorial practice. Isaac co-founded of The Ephemerals Collective, which was long-listed for the 2017 and 2019 Sobey Art Award. Isaac has contributed articles and features to *Art + Wonder*, *C Magazine*, and *Bordercrossings*, and essays to numerous exhibition catalogues. Isaac is on the Advisory Committee for the Winnipeg Art Gallery and Manitoba Museum and the Board of Directors for *Bordercrossings*.

Harmony Johnson is of the Tla'amin Nation, descended from her grandmother, Elsie Paul, and grandfather, William Dave Paul. She is the co-author of a book honouring her community and grandmother, *Written as I Remember it: Teachings from the life of a Sliammon Elder*. For the past 20 years, Johnson has served in a number of policy and executive roles in BC First Nations organizations and her home community. She has a master's degree in Health Administration from the University of British Columbia and is the co-author of many publications on First Nations health and wellness, and health governance.

Aluki Kotierk is the President of Nunavut Tunngavik Incorporated (NTI). Kotierk has a passion to improve the living conditions of Inuit and to ensure Inuit culture and language are better incorporated into programs and services. She focuses on priority issues identified by NTI membership: Inuit employment, Inuit language, and education. Kotierk recognizes that equitable investments are needed for Nunavut Inuit to take their rightful place within Canada while maintaining and asserting a strong Inuit identity. After attaining bachelor's and master's degrees from Trent University, Kotierk worked for various Inuit organizations, including Pauktuutit Inuit Women of Canada, Inuit Tapirisat of Canada (now Inuit Tapiriit

Kanatami), and Nunavut Sivuniksavut. Kotierk returned to Nunavut where she has held senior management positions in the Government of Nunavut and the Office of the Languages Commissioner. Fluent in Inuktut, English, and Spanish, Kotierk is originally from Igloolik and lives in Iqaluit with her family.

Donna Kurtz is a nurse educator and qualitative researcher of European and Métis descent. She is the Faculty of Health and Social Development Aboriginal Faculty Liaison at the University of British Columbia. She also has the honour of serving her people as an Elder in Training. Kurtz is a mother, grandmother, sister, and auntie who continues to learn from Indigenous People and allies from around the world. Her Indigenous-led, community-based, culturally relevant, and gender-appropriate research is in health promotion, including policy and practice change, and Indigenous wellness. She has led multi-sector university–Indigenous community education and research teams in the development and delivery of university level health science cultural safety curriculum, among other topics. She strives to learn from people and communities and share knowledge to develop sustainable solutions for respectful, non-racist, non-discriminatory health care and education provision.

Roseann Larstone is Research and Community Engagement Lead with the Indigenous Health team at the Northern Health Authority (NH) in north-central British Columbia. She is a proud member of the Manitoba Métis Federation with ancestral and family roots in the communities of St. Laurent and Duck Bay. Before coming to NH, Dr. Larstone was a Research Associate with the National Collaborating Centre for Indigenous Health and the Northern Medical Program at the University of Northern British Columbia. Her research currently focuses on Indigenous people's health, medical education, and public health.

Jennifer Leason. *Boozhoo, Aniin Keesis Sagay Egette Kwe nindiznikaaz (greetings, my name is First Shining Rays of Sunlight Woman)*. Dr. Leason is Anishinaabek and a member of Pine Creek Indian Band in Manitoba, and the proud mother of Lucas and Lucy. She is a Canadian Institutes of Health Research, Canada Research Chair, Tier II, Indigenous Maternal Child Wellness and an Assistant Professor at the University of Calgary. Her research aims to address perinatal health disparities and inequities by examining maternity experiences, healthcare utilization, and social-cultural contexts of Indigenous maternal child wellness.

Rod Leggett has master's degrees in Religious Studies from McMaster University and Political Studies from Carleton University. He taught political science in Quebec's collegial system, was a public servant with an Agent of Parliament, and currently advises as a Parliamentary Affairs Advisor. He has published in the fields of political philosophy and Canadian politics and has translated, from French to English, works by André Burelle and Gary Caldwell.

Noni MacDonald is a Professor of Paediatrics (Infectious Diseases) at Dalhousie University and the IWK Health Centre in Halifax. Dr. MacDonald's two current major areas of interest involve global health. The first is vaccines, including vaccine safety, hesitancy, demand, pain mitigation, education, and policy. The second is MicroResearch, building capacity in community focused research in developing countries. She has published over 450 papers, was the founding Editor-in-Chief of *Paediatrics & Child Health*, and was former Editor-in-Chief of *Canadian Medical Association Journal*. MacDonald has long been recognized in Canada and internationally as an advocate for children and youth health and as a leader in paediatric infectious disease and global health. She is an Officer of the Order of Canada and a recipient of the Order of Nova Scotia.

Lee Maracle is a member of the Sto:lo Nation. She authored several critically acclaimed and award-winning books, including *I Am Woman, My Conversations with Canadians*, and *Ravensong*.

Laura McNab-Coombs is a Métis woman studying Biomedical Studies at the University of Northern British Columbia (UNBC). She is the Research Manager at the Health Arts Research Centre in the Northern Medical Program at UNBC and is passionate about rural and Indigenous health.

Patricia Montambault has been a Research Agent at the First Nations of Quebec and Labrador Health and Social Services Commission for over 10 years. She participated in the update of the 2014 First Nations in Quebec and Labrador's Research Protocol. She also produced and collaborated on various evaluation projects and situational portraits, such as the Portrait of the First Nations Social Economy in Quebec. She is currently involved in a research project on child neglect being conducted in collaboration with several First Nations communities, the Université de Montréal, the Université du Québec à Trois-Rivières, and McGill University.

Jessie Nyberg's traditional name is Busy Ant, given to her by her Grandmother when she was an infant. She was an Elder of the Shuswap Nation, registered to the Canoe Creek Band, and a mother, grandmother, daughter, and aunty to many. Her lifework as an Indigenous nurse, researcher, activist, and visionary for social justice and equity—for the health and education of all Peoples—spanned over fifty years. Until her passing in 2021, she was an advocate for her People—especially those living in urban areas. She was a passionate supporter of cultural safety as a way of being for all. Though the years, Elder Jessie carved new pathways respectful of Indigenous and Western Knowledges, and honouring Traditional ways of knowing and doing. She received acknowledgement for her work, including receiving the Queen's Diamond Jubilee Medal for work done for and with her People.

Ryan O'Toole is Gisbutwada (Killer Whale Clan) from Gitxaala Nation. She is an Indigenous Planner studying First Nations Planning at the University of Northern British Columbia. O'Toole's research considers how Indigenous peoples' knowledges around the world support Indigenous self-determination in light of settler colonialism. She focuses on resistance and generative refusal globally, including Indigenous community planning in Canada, Central America, and Aotearoa New Zealand.

Marie-Pier Paul is a Pekuakamiulnu (Ilnu from Mashteuiatsh) and a psychoeducator, with a bachelor's degree in psychoeducation from the Université de Trois-Rivières as well as a master's degree in psychoeducation from the Université Laval. She is a Child and Family Services Advisor at the First Nations of Quebec and Labrador Health and Social Services Commission. She supports First Nations communities and organizations in development, implementation, and take-over monitoring related to first-line services and youth protection services. Paul contributes to the advancement and defence of the interests of the First Nations in Quebec in terms of youth protection and prevention, with a view to fostering wellness among First Nations children and families.

Lisa Richardson is a clinician-educator in the University of Toronto's Division of General Internal Medicine. Dr. Richardson practices at the University Health Network where she is also an Education Researcher at the Wilson Centre. Her academic interest lies in the integration of critical, Indigenous, and feminist perspectives into medical education. She currently holds the role of Indigenous Health Strategy Lead for Women's College Hospital and co-leads a new portfolio for the Department of Medicine called Person-Centered Care Education. She chairs several provincial and national committees to advance Indigenous medical education.

Tabitha Robin is a mixed ancestry Cree researcher, educator, and writer with a PhD in Indigenous Food Sovereignty from the University of Manitoba's Faculty of Social Work and the Department of Native Studies. She spends much of her time on the land, working with her people, and learning traditional Cree food practices.

Armand Garnet Ruffo was born and raised in Chapleau, northern Ontario, and is a member of the Chapleau Fox Lake Cree First Nation. His publications include

Norval Morrisseau: Man Changing Into Thunderbird (2014) and *Treaty#* (2019), both finalists for Governor General's Literary Awards. Other projects include "Sounding Thunder: The Song of Francis Pegahmagabow," a musical based on the life of the renowned WWI sniper and political activist, and a collaborative video-poem, "On The Day The World Begins Again," (https://vimeo.com/336947329) concerning the incarceration of Indigenous people. Ruffo teaches at Queen's University in Kingston.

Stephanie Sinclair (Anishnawbe) has been a First Nations Health and Social Secretariat of Manitoba researcher for over 12 years and has worked on the iPHIT (Innovation Supporting Transformation in Community-Based Primary Healthcare Research) project. She is the current lead on the CIHR-funded Indigenous Healthy Life Trajectories Interventions Development (iHelTI) project with First Nations communities. Sinclair is a PhD student and a clinical psychologist. She is the Research Manager on the Northern Manitoba Indigenous Doulas project with Dr. Cidro. Sinclair is a former Board Member of the First Nations Information Governance Centre.

Marjolaine Sioui is Wendat, and she is currently Executive Director of the First Nations of Quebec and Labrador Health and Social Services Commission (FNQLHSSC). Previously, Sioui was Manager of Operations, Manager of the Early Childhood Sector, and Communications Officer for this same organization and held various positions within federal departments. Following her college studies in administration, she began a degree in preschool and elementary teaching, followed by various professional courses in alternative medicine, as massage therapist-kinesitherapist, and in communications. In 1993, she founded her own business and in 2013, she completed a 2nd cycle short program in Public Management. At FNQLHSSC, Sioui is involved in the development of priorities in health, social services, social development, early childhood, informational resources, and research, thereby contributing to the advancement and defence of the interests of First Nations in Quebec.

Onyx Sloan Morgan is an Assistant Professor of Political Ecology and Critical Geography at the University of British Columbia, Okanagan. A queer White settler of primarily Irish and Scottish ancestry who grew up on unceded Coast Salish territories on Vancouver Island, Dr. Sloan Morgan works with communities and youth to support self-determined relationships to environments and one another.

Roberta Stout is a member of the Kehewin First Nation (Alberta). She holds an undergraduate degree in Interdisciplinary Studies (Carleton University), a graduate degree in Latin American Studies (Simon Fraser University), and a Cree

Language Immersion Certificate (Blue Quills University). Since 1998, Stout has led community-focused research projects on the determinants of health with Pauktuutit Inuit Women's Association, the National Aboriginal Health Organization, Prairie Women's Health Centre of Excellence, the University of Winnipeg, and the National Collaborating Centre for Indigenous Health. She is currently a Senior Policy Advisor in the Health Sector at the Assembly of First Nations.

Julie Sutherland is a Research Associate with the National Collaborating Centre for Indigenous Health. Dr. Sutherland holds an MA and PhD in English Studies and 17th-Century Studies from the University of Durham (UK) and has published in the areas of Indigenous health, English literature and theatre, and applied humanities. Among other publications, Sutherland is the author of an illustrated book, *Bright Poems for Dark Days: An Anthology for Hope* (2021), which is rooted in the belief that literature and the arts contribute to mental wellness.

Mary Teegee is Gitk'san and Carrier from Takla Lake First Nation; she is a proud member of the Luxgaboo Wolf Clan and holds the Hereditary Chiefs name Maaxswxw Gibuu (White Wolf). She was raised to live her culture, customs, laws, and traditions. Teegee is the Executive Director of Child and Family Services at Carrier Sekani Family Services (CSFS), where she oversees provincially delegated programs, youth services, family preservation, maternal child health, the Highway of Tears Initiative, and violence prevention programs. She also develops and implements Community Health programs for CSFS nations and was part of the development of the CSFS Family Justice Facilitation Program, in partnership with the University of Northern British Columbia, the Justice Institute, and the BC Mediators Roster Society.

Shannon Waters is Coast Salish and a member of Stz'uminus First Nation on Vancouver Island. Dr. Waters completed the First Nations Family Practice program at the University of British Columbia and worked as a family doctor in Duncan, BC. While honoured to work close to home, Waters became frustrated with seeing people mostly when they were unwell and wanted to focus on keeping people healthy, so she returned to school and completed her specialty training in Public Health and Preventive Medicine. Waters worked as the Director of Health Surveillance at First Nations and Inuit Health Branch and, at First Nations Health Authority, as the Acting Senior Medical Officer for Vancouver Island Region. She has worked with Vancouver Island Health Authority as a Medical Director and with the Ministry of Health as the Aboriginal Physician Advisor. She is honoured to have come full circle, now working in her home territory as the local Medical Health Officer with Vancouver Island Health Authority.

INDEX

Aboriginal Healing Foundation (AHF), 45–46
abuse
    child, 96
    cycles of, 46
    in schools, 53–54, 55, 59
    sexual, 46
    spousal, 93, 95–96
    substance, 83, 87, 93
Adams, Evan Tlesla II, 208
Adams, K. C., 156–157
agriculture, 30, 149, 164
alcohol abuse, 83, 87
Alianait Inuit Mental Wellness Action Plan, 19
"all my relations", 28, 124n2
An Act Respecting First Nations, Inuit and Métis Children, Youth and Families, 189–190
An Action Plan for Safe Drinking Water (BC), 117, 119
Ancient Ones, 82, 84–86, 88
Angry Inuk (film), 151–152
Anguhadluq, Luke, 151
Anishinaabemowiin, 51, 163, 201
anti-racism, 204
Arnaquq-Baril, Alethea, 151–152
Assembly of First Nations (AFN), 117, 120
Assembly of First Nations Quebec-Labrador (AFNQL), 182
assimilation, 7, 39, 172, 206, 253
Atikamekw Nation, 187
Atleo, Richard (Chief Umeek), 233
Aware 360 app, 108

bannock, 157
BC Coroners Service, 257–258
BC First Nations health governance structure, 254–259
biodiversity, 123, 148
Birth Evacuation Policy, 61–62
birth workers, 238, 242, 244, 245
birthing. *See* childbirth
bison, decimation of, 153–154, 155
Black, Jaime, 108
Blackstock, Cindy, 91
Bolivia, 121
Breathing Hole (Gruben), 150

British Columbia, Government of, 10, 117–120
Buffalo Bone China (Claxton), 153–155

Canada, Government of
    and AHF, 45, 46
    banning of Potlatch, 7
    and child services, 96
    commitment to distinctions-based approach with Indigenous, 120
    and Nunavut Agreement, 133
    passes *Act Respecting Indigenous Families*, 189, 190
    and sterilization investigations, 43
    and underfunding of child services for First Nations, 185, 186
    and water safety, 117
Canadian Human Rights Tribunal (CHRT), 185, 186
Canadian Medical Association (CMA), xviii
Canadian National Railway (CNR), 108
CanMEDs, 203
Caron, Nadine, 167, 170
Carpenter, Noah, 170
Catholic Church, 51–52, 54, 158–159
Cedano, Maria Ysabel, 42
ceremony, 28. *See also* spirituality
Charter of Rights and Freedoms, 44–45
Chartrand, Eva Cecile, 51
child abuse, 96
child neglect, 182–183, 183–184
child removal, 92, 93, 95
child services, 96, 185, 186, 188–190
childbirth
    and birth workers, 238
    Indigenous retaking control of, 239–240, 244–245
    Indigenous traditions of, 237, 241–243
    infant mortality rate, 241
    and maternal evacuation, 240–241
    taken over by Western biomedicine, 238–239, 243–244
Chippewa, 244
Clarke, Bernice, 129
Claxton, Dana, 153–155
clerk interpreters, 135

climate change, 88
Coastal GasLink, 10, 105, 106
collective trauma, 227
colonialism/colonization
    and acquisition of lands, 103
    and bans on seal hunting, 153
    of Canadian government policy, 39–40, 154–155
    committing to fight against, xvii–xviii, xx
    effect on determinants of health, xvii, 213
    effect on First Nations, 181, 253
    effect on Indigenous childbirth, 237–238
    effect on Indigenous institutions, 37
    effect on Indigenous women, 37, 39, 40, 45, 47, 55–56
    effect on Inuit, xix
    effect on traditional approaches to mental wellness, 16–18, 19
    and food choices, 148–149
    and food security, 26
    and forced medical procedures on Indigenous peoples, 145–146
    and gendered violence, 100, 103–104
    and Indigenous health, xviii, 213, 226–227
    and Indigenous reproductive practices, 238–239
    and Indigenous self-determination, 4
    and M. Teegee's account of violence on Indigenous peoples, 91–95
    need to restructure institutions of, 21
    and policies meant to destroy First Nations connection to land, 149, 190
    and processed food, 157, 158
    and racism in med school, 170–172, 204
    and reaction of non-Indigenous to, xix
    of resource extraction, xix, 102–103
    and spread of epidemics, 161
    tie to church of, 159, 160
    and view of natural resources, xix, 102
    of water, 117
consent
    in Declaration on the Rights of Indigenous Peoples Act, 10
    and Inuit healthcare, 128
    and Makara's story, 258
    and medical experimentation, 206
    in Quebec legislation, 188
    and resource extraction, 105
    and sterilization, 43, 46, 62
Constitution, Canadian, 44
COVID-19 vaccine hesitancy, 145, 146
Cowichan Watershed Board, 123

creative contributions, 138–141, 195–196, 264
Cree, 81–89
criminal justice system, 94
cross-cultural care, 201
cultural appropriation, 161
cultural awareness, 205–206
cultural competency training, 200, 214
cultural disconnection, 172–173
cultural humility, 200, 216, 256–257, 258
cultural immersion, 208
cultural reclamation, 149, 161, 163, 164, 228
cultural safety
    actions of physician practicing, 203
    and childbirth, 244
    explained, 215–216
    in healthcare, 200–201
    as part of BC First Nations health governance structure, 256–257
    and reflexivity, 205–206
    as a right, 221
    UBC School of Nursing program in, 217–220
    vision for education in, 220–221
    what an education in provides, 217

data and information, self-determination of, 258–259
Death of a Virgin (Monkman), 161–162
Declaration on the Rights of Indigenous Peoples Act (DRIPA) "Bill 41," 10, 119–120, 122–123
decolonization
    and food sovereignty, 31, 225–226, 230–231, 233–234
    of healthcare, 61–62
    of medical education, 202–203
    of Nuu-chah-nulth, 233
    and self-determination, 227
    and traditional food, 233–234
defund the police movement, 97
Delgamuukw case, 9
diabetes, 26, 155, 156–158
disconnection/disharmony
    from culture, 170–173
    and grief, 11, 33
    from the land, 81, 89
    from nature, 87
    policies which aid, 149, 190
    of Wet'suwet'en, 5
distinctions-based approaches, xx, 20, 119–120, 251
diversity, 82, 181, 233
Doctrine of Discovery, 103, 116–117
doulas, 238, 244, 245

Drinking Water Protection Act (BC), 117–118, 122–123
drug addiction, 93

Echaquan, Joyce, xviii, 145, 199
Ecuador, 121
education, 59
Elders, 214–215, 217–218, 219, 221, 254
emotional trigger warning, xv
environmental dispossession, 33
environmental health, 107–110
environmental personhood, 120–122
environmental violence, 104–106
epidemics, spread of, 161
eugenics movement, 40–41
European contact, 30, 103, 116–117, 161
European cultures, 38
experiential learning (EL), 208

fetal alcohol syndrome (FAS), 40, 161
First Nations
    and BC First Nations health governance structure, 254–259
    and BC's Bill 41, 120
    and child neglect, 182–183
    and childbirth, 243
    and control of data and information, 258–259
    effect of colonialism on, 181, 253
    effect of Western bio-medicine on, 253
    efforts towards self-determination of, 253–254
    and first-line social services in Quebec, 185–186
    and food security, 60
    influence on *Youth Protection Act*, 186–188
    and PHWA, 259–261
    policies meant to destroy their connection to land, 149, 190
    in Quebec, 180–181
    and self-determination of child services in Quebec, 188–189
    and social determinants of health, 183
    view of mental wellness, 19
    view of wellness, 251–252
    and water safety, 117
First Nations Health Authority (FNHA), 254, 255, 257, 258, 259–261
First Nations Mental Wellness Continuum Framework, 19
First Nations of Quebec and Labrador Health and Social Services Commission (FNQLHSSC), 182, 185–186, 188–189
First Nations Population Health and Wellness Agenda (PHWA), 259–261
first-line social services, 185–186
food health, 60
food industry, 149, 156
food security, 17, 25–27, 60
food sovereignty. *See* Indigenous food sovereignty (IFS)
food systems, 27–28, 30, 33–34, 155–159
foodways, 148, 149, 157, 225–226, 233
fur trade, 39

gender-based violence
    M. Teegee's views on, 92, 93
    and Man Camps, 106
    and REDress Campaign, 108
    from resource extraction, 99–100
    against women and Two Spirit people, 93, 103–104, 106
generative medicines, 85
generative refusal, 76n2
genocide
    in artwork, 159
    and Highway of Tears, 94
    and MMIWG, 40
    and residential schools, 39, 55
    and sterilization, 41, 47
    trauma as result of, 206
The Gifts (Adams), 156–157
Gitk'san Nation, 8, 92
glyphosate, 106
Greenpeace, 152
grief and loss, 11, 33
Gruben, Maureen, 150
Guardian and Ward Theory, 42, 48n2

Happynook, Tom Mexsis, 233
healthcare
    and anti-racism, 204
    and CanMEDs framework, 203
    and case study of emergency room experience, 216
    and Constitution, 44
    and cultural competency training, 200–201
    and effect of social determinants of health on Indigenous, 212–213, 221
    how to deal with trauma, 206–207
    and Inuit unable to receive in own language, 128–132
    in Nunavut, 127–128
    power dynamics of, 200

healthcare (*continued*)
    and racism, 61–62, 146, 199, 200
    and reproductive violence against Indigenous women, 62
    ways of improving in Nunavut, 134–135
    ways to improve for Indigenous, 214. *See also* wellness
Highway of Tears, 100, 101, 102, 105, 108
Highway of Tears Symposium, 94
holism, 20
homophobic/transphobic violence, 106
Hope for Wellness Help Line, xv
housing, 61, 86–87, 161
human trafficking, 40
hunting, 93, 150–153, 170–171, 173
Huson, Freda, 9, 10, 107

Igloliorte, Mark, 151–152
In Plain Sight: Addressing Indigenous-Specific Racism and Discrimination in B.C. Health Care (Turpel-Lafond), xviii
Indian Act, xix, 39
Indigenous food sovereignty (IFS)
    in artwork, 155–156
    built on reciprocity with non-humans, 229–230
    and decolonization, 31, 225–226, 230–231, 233–234
    described, 25–26
    four principles of, 228–229
    history of, 29–31
    as Indigenous right, 148
    initiatives in, 30, 31–32, 228–229
    origins of, 227–228
    and wellness, 34, 230–231
Indigenous knowledge
    of Anishinaabe, 163
    and childbirth, 239
    and food system, 27–28
    incorporated into medical education, 201–203
    M. Teegee's background in, 91
    and mental wellness intervention, 21
    of Nuu-chah-nulth, 233
    and PHWA, 259
    and reciprocal relationships with non-humans, 229–230
    through example setting, 87
Indigenous peoples
    age of population, 21n2
    birthing traditions of, 241–243
    and COVID-19 vaccine hesitancy, 145, 146
    and distinctions-based terminology, xx
    and environmental personhood, 121–122
    importance of land to, 33
    and lack of food security, 26–27
    perspectives on water, 115–117, 118, 119
    and poor health of, 204
    role in reform of BC water management, 122–123
    and self-determination of child services, 189–190
    and social determinants of health, 183, 184, 190
    and spirituality of children, 18
    successes of, xviii. *See also* colonialism/colonization; First Nations; Indigenous women; Inuit; Métis; self-determination; Wet'suwet'en
Indigenous physicians
    barriers to, 168–169, 170–172, 175
    and cultural disconnection, 172–173
    policies for increasing, 169, 175–176
    and racism, 170–172
    story of being accepted into med school, 166–167
    underrepresentation of, 168, 200
    and use of mentors, 169–170, 173–175
Indigenous Reference Group (IRG), 202
Indigenous women
    and Aware 360 app, 108
    and *Charter* rights, 44–45
    and contributors to poor perinatal health, 56–61
    and discrimination from healthcare, 61–62
    effect of colonialism on, 37, 39, 40, 45, 47, 55–56
    effect of resource extraction on health of, 106
    how statistics obscure the truth about, 110
    leadership of, 109
    and REDress Campaign, 108
    reproductive and obstetric violence against, 62
    resilience of, 64
    role in traditional Indigenous society, 38–39, 47
    sterilization of, 41–43
    suppression and marginalization of, 55–56
    violence toward, 29, 93, 95–96, 103, 104, 106. *See also* childbirth; gender-based violence; Missing and Murdered Indigenous Women and Girls (MMIWG)
Indigenous-Focused Oriented complex therapy, 11
industrial development, 104, 106
infant mortality rate, 241
intergenerational trauma
    and collective trauma, 227
    depicted in artwork, 160

and drug addiction, 93
effects on Indigenous children, 16–18
of Indigenous men, 94
of Inuit, 131, 132
and mental health, 15
and residential schools, 17, 55
of Wet'suwet'en, 5
Inuit
and BC's Bill 41, 120
character of, 136
and childbirth, 242, 243
effect of colonialism on, xix
encompassing lands of, 22n4
expectations of Nunavut Agreement, 127
and intergenerational trauma, 131, 132
lack of health data on, 19
and midwifery, 239–240
and prose narrative, 264
and Qikiqtani Truth Commission, 133
Quebec government consultation with, 187
and reconciliation, 134, 135
and seal hunting, 150–153
and systemic racism, 153
unable to receive healthcare in Inuktut, 128–132
view of mental wellness, 19–20
ways of improving healthcare for, 134–135
and whaling, 231
Inuktut, 127, 128–131, 133, 135

Joseph, Alfred, 5, 9

Kamloops Indian Residential School, xvii
Kanesatakeronnon, Kanatiio (Allen Gabriel), xx
Kayak is Inuktitut for Seal Hunting Boat (Igloliorte), 151–152
Kehewin First Nation, 82, 88
Kimmerer, Robin Wall, 102, 103
kinship ties, 86, 89
Knowledge Keepers, 237, 244, 254
Kooneeliusie, Geela, 129
Kootoo, Annie, 128–129, 131

La Via Campesina, 29
LaDuke, Winona, 31, 164, 234
Lafontaine, Alika, xviii
Lamoureux, Catherine Beaulieu B., 167
land claim agreements, 191n2
land-based healing, 6, 84
land/territory theft, xix, 32, 92, 160, 226
Last Supper (Stevens), 157–159
Leason, Patricia V. M., 51–54, 57–58, 63, 64
Lombard, Alisa, 43, 62

Makara's story, 257–258
malnutrition, 26, 27
Man Camps, 106
Mandamin, Josephine, 116
Marshall, Albert, 115, 201
mass graves of Indigenous children, xvii
maternal evacuation, 239, 240–241
McEachern, Allan, 9
medical education
and anti-racism, 204
and being informed about trauma, 206–207
contribution of Elders to, 214–215
and cultural competency training, 200–201
incorporating Indigenous knowledge in, 201–203
and increase of Indigenous faculty, 207
and promoting reflexivity, 204–206
and ways to promote Indigenous client care, 207–208
The Men Hunting Caribou in Kayaks (Anguhadluq), 151
mental wellness
described, 15
effect of colonization on, 16–18, 19
how Western views pathologize Indigenous, 18–19
Indigenous view of, 15, 16, 19–20
interventions for, 20–21
and sterilization, 43
Western view of, 15–16
WHO definition, 18
mentoring programs for doctors and nurses, 169–170, 173–175
meritocracy, 41
Métis, 19, 20, 120
Meuse, Frank, 33
Michell, Brenda, 10
midwifery, 238, 239–243, 245
Mi'kmaq, 33
Millennium Scoop, 17
Miner, Dylan, 162–163
Missing and Murdered Indigenous Women and Girls (MMIWG)
and evidence of gendered violence, 103, 104
as form of genocide, 40
M. Teegee's view of, 94
people detained during a ceremony for, 10
recommendations regarding resource extraction, 107
and REDress Campaign, 108–109
success in revealing women's plight, 47
and Two Spirit People, 110n3
Monkman, Kent, 160–161

Muldoe, Earl, 9
Muldoe, Ken, 9

National Aboriginal Health Organization (NAHO), 174, 243
Nativity Scene (Monkman), 160–161
nature, 84–85, 87–88, 121–122, 123
New Zealand, 121–122
non-Indigenous people, xix. *See also* settlers
Northern Lights, 89
Nunavut, 126–132, 134–135
Nunavut Agreement, 126, 127, 133
nursing, 174, 217–220
Nuu-chah-nulth Nation, 232, 233

Obed, Natan, 153
OCAP® principles, 259
Ojibwe, 121
Oshutsiaq, Omalluq, 155–156
owls, 87–88

paternalism, 7
Peltier, Autumn, 107, 116
People for the Ethical Treatment of Animals (PETA), 152
perinatal health, 56–61, 106
Peru, 42
poetry, 138–141, 195–196
pollution, 88–89
population health, 12, 114, 120, 212–213, 256, 259–261
Potlatch, 7, 232–233
poverty, 26–27, 40, 59–60, 226
prenatal stress, 56
present and self-aware, 6
processed foods, 155–159, 161, 227, 231

Qikiqtani Truth Commission, 133
Quebec, Government of, 186–190
Qumaluk, Akinisie, 242

racism
    and Canada's healthcare system, 146
    forms of, 203–204
    of government systems, 94
    in health care, 61–62, 146, 199, 200
    in med school, 170–172, 204
    and *In Plain Sight*, xviii
    systemic, 17, 105, 153, 256–257
    and underfunding of First Nations child services, 185. *See also* colonialism/colonization
radical resistance, 76n1

RCAP (Royal Commission on Aboriginal Peoples), xx, 44–45, 168, 214, 242
RCMP (Royal Canadian Mounted Police), 10, 96–97, 132
reciprocal relationships, 12, 27–28, 229–230
reconciliation, xx, 46, 89, 122, 134, 135. *See also* Truth and Reconciliation Commission of Canada (TRC)
REDress Campaign, 108–109
reflexivity, 204–206
relationship building, 19
reserve system, 30, 61, 84, 86–87, 154, 253
residential schools
    creation of under *Indian Act*, 39–40
    and health, 226–227
    and intergenerational trauma, 17, 55
    and Inuit, 133
    and mass graves, xvii
    method of sitting in, 53–54
    in Quebec, 181
    and storytelling, 51–53
resilience, 16, 21, 64, 163, 244, 253
Resistance Comes from the Four Directions (Miner), 162–163
resistance movements, 163–164
resource extraction
    and art piece, 154
    colonialism of, xix, 102–103
    effect on women's health, 106
    and gender-based violence, 99–100
    health impacts of, 104
    and Highway of Tears, 100
    and ignoring Indigenous complaints, 104–105
    and Indigenous food sovereignty, 31
    and MMIWG report, 107
    and water quality, 118
Roundup®, 106
Royal Canadian Mounted Police (RCMP), 10, 96–97, 132
Royal Commission on Aboriginal Peoples (RCAP), xx, 44–45, 168, 214, 242

Safe Drinking Water for First Nations Act, 117
Safe Food for Canadians Act, 31
seal hunting, 150–153
self harming, 97
self-care trigger warning, xv
self-determination
    and BC First Nations health governance structure, 254–259
    of child services federally, 189–190
    of child services in Quebec, 188–189, 190

of childbirth, 238, 245
colonialism's intention to eliminate, 253
and control of bodies, minds and spirits, 99
and control of data and information, 258–259
and COVID-19 vaccines, 146
and decolonization, 227
and determinants of health, 4
First Nations' efforts toward, 12, 253–254
and First Nations Population Health and Wellness Agenda, 259–261
importance of land to, 8, 95
of Nuu-chah-nulth, 233
in relation to water in BC, 119–120
and *Resistance Comes from the Four Directions*, 162–163
and resource extraction, 105
undermined by racism, 256
and UNDRIP, 4, 251
settlers, 8, 132, 226, 238
Sewid-Smith, Daisy, 156
sexual and reproductive health, 68–75
sharing, 27
Sinclair, Brian, xviii, 146, 199
Sinclair, Murray, 39
Sixties Scoop, 17
Sleydo' (Molly Wickham), 10
smudging, 56, 161
social determinants of health
  affecting perinatal health, 59–61
  as cause of low numbers of Indigenous doctors, 168
  effect on Indigenous health, 212–213, 221
  and framing of illness, 12
  global report on, 16
  impact on Indigenous child care, 183–184
  and PHWA, 260
  three levels for Indigenous peoples, 183, 184, 190
social media, 97, 163
spirituality
  and childbirth, 242, 243, 245
  and children, 18
  in Cree stories, 81–82
  of food, 157, 230, 231
  and food shortages, 30
  and stress, 56
  and water, 116
stars, 88–89
sterilization, 40–43, 45–47, 62
Stevens, CMaxx, 157–158
Store Items I remember in 1950s (Oshutsiaq), 155–156

stories/storytelling
  and childbirth, 243
  of Cree grandmother, 81–89
  of Elders, 215
  and experience of residential school, 51–53
  and Highway of Tears, 101
  as medicinal practice, 162
  and wellness, 12
subsist (art exhibit), 149–157
subsistence lifestyle, 149, 154–159, 164, 229
substance use, 83, 87, 93
substantive equality, 186
suicide, 97, 254–255
survivance, 149
sweat lodge ceremonies, 56
systemic racism, 17, 105, 153, 256–257

Tait, Albert, 9
Tait, Karla, 10
Talking Circle, 219–220
Teegee, Mary, 91–92, 95–97
terra nullius, 103, 104
traditional foods, 27, 34, 208, 226, 231–234
traditional medicine, 173, 174, 208
trauma, 206–207. *See also* intergenerational trauma
treaty negotiations, 9, 77–78
treaty rights, 44, 116
trees and health, 6
Truth and Reconciliation Commission of Canada (TRC)
  Canadians' awareness of, 37
  on improvements to healthcare, 214
  and Indigenous health, 149, 245
  lack of action on, xix
  and lack of Indigenous doctors, 168
  and racism in healthcare, 200
T'Seleie, James, 173
Tseshaht, 225, 232
Turpel-Lafond, Mary Ellen, xviii
Two Spirit people
  and gendered violence, 93, 103–104, 106
  how statistics obscure the truth about, 110
  lack of services for, 106–107
  leadership of, 109
  and MMIWG inquiry, 110n3
  role in Indigenous communities, 104
Two-Eyed Seeing, 115, 122–123, 201–203

Unistot'en, 9–10
United Nations Committee on Torture (UNCT), 43

United Nations Declaration on the Rights of Indigenous People (UNDRIP)
    BC government adopts legislation of, 119–120
    and food sovereignty, 229
    as guide for suggested sterilization legislation, 46
    and Indigenous right to land, 95
    lack of action on, xix
    and peoples' right to subsistence, 149
    recognizes Indigenous right to self-determination, 4, 251
University of British Columbia School of Nursing, 217–220
University of Toronto Mississauga, 202

vaccine hesitancy, 145, 146
Via Campesina, 29, 227–228
violence
    environmental, 104–106
    M. Teegee's account of, 91–95
    reproductive, 62
    toward women, 29, 93, 95–96, 103, 104, 106. *See also* gender-based violence

wagon trail, Cree, 86
water rights and legislation, 115–120, 122–123
wellness
    Anishinaabe view of, 201
    and BC First Nations health governance structure, 254–259
    BC First Nations' view of, 251–252
    in Cree stories, 82
    and cultural disconnection, 172–173
    and environmental health, 107–108
    and environmental personhood, 120–122
    and First Nations Population Health and Wellness Agenda, 259–261
    and food sovereignty, 34, 230–231
    methods of reaching, 11–12
    and storytelling, 12
    and traditional foods, 231–232. *See also* mental wellness
Western agriculture, 30
Western biomedicine, 238–239, 240–241, 243–244, 253
Western diet, 226
Western worldviews, 15–16, 18–19, 117–119
Wet'suwet'en Nation
    background, 4
    and Coastal Gaslink, 105, 106
    and court case for Indigenous title, 8–9
    and federal government paternalism, 7
    and fishing, 8
    health of, 5
    importance of land to, 4–5, 8, 10, 107
    and industry blockades, 9–10
    laws of, 7–8
    and self-determination, 12
    teachings of, 5, 6
whale products, 32
whaling, 231
women. *See* Indigenous women
Working Group on Indigenous Food Sovereignty (WGIFS), 30, 228–229
World Health Organization (WHO), 18

youth, 12, 169–170, 181, 182–183, 186–190
Youth Protection Act (Quebec), 181, 186–188
Yurok Tribe, 121